A GLOSSARY
OF
GOSPEL TERMS

RESTORATION EDITION

ISBN 978-1-951168-25-4

FOREWORD

There is much to be accomplished before the Restoration can be completed. In a very real sense, the Restoration Joseph attempted was aimed to renew an ancient religion, complete with ordinances, principles, terms, and definitions. He was unable to fully complete the Restoration. Much of what he did restore has been neglected, pushed aside, and forgotten. Before the Restoration can advance, we must first remember all of what began through Joseph Smith.

A Glossary of Gospel Terms is an attempt to restore ideas that have been neglected, pushed aside, and forgotten. Its objective is to confirm truth, and establish a vocabulary for discussing the Restoration Edition scriptures.

The terms in the *Glossary* are by no means exhaustive terms or complete definitions; it doesn't pretend to be an unabridged dictionary. The *Glossary* is not an answer book. Its purpose is to provide direction when you are seeking clarification, or answers to basic questions. It will aid you in making a connection with Heaven, from where you can receive answers from the only source that matters.

Real answers to sincere questions are found in the revealed word. Joseph Smith instructed "the immediate will of heaven is found in the scriptures" (*TPJS*, 54).

This *Glossary* may not be for everyone. It's not for those who have a profound indifference to what is happening in our day—those who remain uninterested in the signs of the times or what the Lord is revealing. It is not for the impatient, the demanding, and the immature. And it's not a substitute for authentic searching of scripture and revelation from heaven. "The things of God are of deep import; and time, and experience, and careful and ponderous and solemn thoughts can only find them out" (*TPJS*, 157).

It is hoped this will be a worthy contribution to understanding God's word. Even if this *Glossary* does nothing more than point you to the scriptures, it has accomplished its objective.

This *Glossary* is also available in the Appendix of the Teachings and Commandments, the third volume of the Restoration Edition scriptures.

— Denver C. Snuffer, Jr.

INTRODUCTION

THIS WORK is intended as a helpful, inspired commentary that offers explanations and insights into words or phrases found within the Restoration Edition Scriptures. It should not be viewed with the traditional definition of a glossary. It is not a dictionary that includes specific definitions for each entry, limiting other possible meanings of the term or phrase. Its intent is to provide the reader with insights that will propel him or her to seek for further light and knowledge from the Lord. All of the material herein comes from the works of Denver Snuffer and Joseph Smith, the Scriptures, sources pointed to by Denver, or explanations made by Denver during the editing process. Except when noted, all scriptural references are from the Restoration Edition.

> *I have inserted a possible new context into the words for you to consider. I would remind you, however, that scripture is not something for "private interpretation," but can only be unlocked through the Holy Ghost (see 2 Peter 1:5; see also JSH 14:4). The meaning belongs to and is controlled by God.[1] Please keep Everything in mind together. Do not think one isolated statement or paragraph explains Everything. Further, do not think everything has yet been revealed that needs to be revealed. Thus far I am only taking the things already before us in scripture and weaving them together to persuade some few to believe the Restoration can continue. When the time comes, a great deal more can be taught if the Restoration does continue.[2]*

This glossary establishes a correct foundational vocabulary for a discussion about the Restoration Edition scriptures, which include the following three volumes:

- **The Old Covenants** teaches mankind about the first Fathers and the covenants that God established with them. It prophesies of the time when Christ would live upon the earth and the yet future time of Zion and the New Jerusalem, when the Lord would establish his people and dwell among them in glory.

- **The New Covenants**
  - The New Testament is a record of the mortal life of Christ and recounts the covenants that He established while living at Jerusalem.
  - The Book of Mormon is the covenant of the last days and teaches one how to enter into God's presence while yet in this life. It teaches one how to connect back into God's family and foretells the coming of the Kingdom of God on the earth.
  - **The Teachings and Commandments** lays the groundwork for the establishment of Zion, a necessary step for the return of Christ to this earth in the last days.

Certain entries or topics have been excluded or avoided so as to inspire readers to pursue those subjects on their own. The Lord encourages all to *seek learning, even by study and also by faith* (T&C 123:2). There is a distinction between what is learned from (or confirmed by) study and what is revealed directly through the spirit by faith. The greater blessing lies in the latter. The Book of Mormon teaches that the Lord will impart a portion of His word, according to the heed and diligence which is given (*see* Alma 9:3). The holy ghost imparts significantly more than what we are able to accomplish or understand on our own. It is hoped that this effort will assist your learning, *by study and also by faith*.

ABBREVIATIONS

CHL Church History Library, The Church of Jesus Christ of Latter-day Saints.

D&C Doctrine and Covenants, The Church of Jesus Christ of Latter-day Saints (Salt Lake City, UT: Church of Jesus Christ of Latter-Day Saints, 1989).

DHC *History of the Church of Jesus Christ of Latter-day Saints*, 7 vols., ed. B. H. Roberts, 2nd ed. Rev. (Salt Lake City: Deseret Book, 1957), also referred to as *Documentary History of the Church*.

JSH Joseph Smith History, Parts 1–20 (1805–1830), comprising Section 1 of Teachings and Commandments, Restoration Edition.

JSP *Joseph Smith Papers* (Salt Lake City: The Church Historian's Press, 2008–ongoing).

KJV King James translation of the Bible.

LOF Lectures on Faith, comprising Section 110 of Teaching and Commandments, Restoration Edition. The Lectures on Faith were once a part of the Doctrine & Covenants, prepared for the School of the Prophets and approved by Joseph Smith. Their presence in the scriptures was the reason for the change in the title from the earlier Book of Commandments to Doctrine and Covenants in 1835. The "Doctrine" portion of the book was comprised of these lectures and they were subsequently removed from the D&C by a committee in 1921.

T&C Teachings and Commandments, Restoration Edition, comp. Restoration Scriptures Foundation (Salt Lake City: Restoration Scriptures Foundation, 2018).

TPJS *Teachings of the Prophet Joseph Smith*, comp. Joseph Fielding Smith (Salt Lake City: Deseret Book, 1976).

WJS *The Words of Joseph Smith*, comp. Andrew F. Ehat and Lyndon W. Cook (Provo, UT: Religious Studies Center, Brigham Young University, 1980).

WWJ *Wilford Woodruff's Journal, 1833–1898: Typescript*, 10 vols., ed. Scott G. Kenney (Midvale, UT: Signature Books, 1983).

SOURCES

All references are attributed to Denver Snuffer, unless noted. Published books, talks, recordings, etc., are available at www.denversnuffer.com and www.restorationarchives.com.

Aaronic Priesthood Priestly authority that is believed by Mormons to automatically descend by lineage from Aaron to his descendants, but which can also be conferred by the laying on of hands upon gentiles who would otherwise not possess such authority. It has the right to perform outward ordinances, including baptism. This priesthood was conferred on Joseph Smith and Oliver Cowdery on May 15, 1829 by the resurrected John the Baptist.[3] The Aaronic or Levitical priesthood is an association with angels.[4] This lesser priesthood holds some connection with Heaven, with an opportunity to associate with the Powers of Heaven.[5] "The law was given under Aaron for the purposes of pouring out judgments and destructions."[6] T&C 54:2 is a description of the authority of this lower priesthood. It has the authority to seal up unto destruction. These who go forth with this power condemn and are, in a word, Aaronic. Notwithstanding the condemnatory role, the Aaronic priesthood is not without hope, having the power to baptize, which is an ordinance of hope.[7] The Aaronic priesthood holds the keys of the ministering of angels. Angels were the source from which priesthood was restored. Angels can lead people to the Son of God. The Son of God can take a person to the throne of the Father. Every bit of what is to be accomplished through priesthood is possible to achieve so long as one gets Aaronic priesthood into the hands of someone. Looking at the lay of the land today, there are not many who can say that they have been in fellowship with angels or realized the blessings of Aaronic priesthood. There are fewer still who can say that they have been in fellowship with Christ, and there are only a small handful who have been in fellowship with the Father. Everything that is necessary to start down the pathway comes as a consequence of receiving some portion of priesthood.[8] The elected offices associated with Aaronic priesthood in the church organized by Joseph Smith were Priest, Teacher, Deacon, as well as Bishop, and were no different than any other office in that church. These offices still continue in many of the various religious groups claiming Joseph Smith as their founder. *See also* ELDER.

Abomination The use of religion to suppress truth or impose a false form of truth.[9] It involves the religious justification of wrongdoing. That is, something becomes abominable when it is motivated out of a false form of religious observance or is justified because of religious error.[10]

Accountability All are accountable before God for their own sins (*see* T&C 101:17). No one can escape responsibility based on their willful ignorance. If one has the scriptures, he knows he cannot be *even if he* saved in ignorance.[11] All have been warned that the scriptures have *doesn't rea* information that is able to teach them about salvation (*see* 2 Timothy 9). There also is the Lord's warning to search into the scriptures if one expects eternal life (*see* John 5:7). When this is before one, it is impossible to sin ignorantly, even if that ignorance is a result of one's own neglect (*see* 3 Nephi 3:3).[12] King Benjamin's testimony was that the atonement would allow everyone to repent, and even those who sin "ignorantly" would be forgiven of their sins (*see* Mosiah 1:15). To king Benjamin's thinking, the great error was willfully doing what one knows was against God's will. However, even then, king Benjamin invited his listeners to repent and reclaim the mercy God offered (*see* Mosiah 1:15). His sermon presumes that his audience were sinners and suffered from myriad shortcomings. As King Benjamin explained, *the natural man is an enemy to God, and has been from the fall of Adam, and will be for ever and ever but if he yields to the enticings of the holy spirit, and putteth off the natural man, and becometh a saint through the atonement of Christ the Lord, and becometh as a child: submissive, meek, humble, patient, full of love, willing to submit to all things which the Lord seeth fit to inflict upon him, even as a child doth submit to his father* (Mosiah 1:16).[13] This doctrine is astonishing because it: makes each person individually accountable to follow the holy spirit; presumes that the holy spirit will entice you directly; puts each person in a position to be submissive to God; accepts the fact that life will always "inflict" even the best of us; makes God the one who is responsible for life's challenges; and bids us to accept these afflictions, because they come from a wise Eternal Parent. King Benjamin is remarkably democratic in his view of God and His involvement in men's and women's lives. God is direct, immediate, and involved with everyone.[14] "The Book of Mormon is a record that will be used as evidence we have been warned. In plain language and with sufficient truth to hold us all accountable, this is the standard by which we are to find our way back to the Lord in this last dispensation before His return."[15]

Accountability, Age of Children should be taught to understand the Doctrine of Christ and may be baptized when eight years old (*see* T&C 55:5; Genesis 7:30; 1 Peter 1:14). In Moroni 8 (a letter from Mormon to his son, Moroni), Mormon quotes the Savior as having said, in relation to infant baptism, the following: *I came into the world not to call the righteous, but sinners to repentance. The whole need no physician, but they that are sick. Wherefore, little children are whole, for they are not capable of committing sin. Wherefore, the curse of Adam is taken from them in me, that it hath no power over them. And the law of circumcision is done away in me* (Moroni 8:2). Little children are exempt from these requirements, as they are fulfilled in every respect by Christ's atonement. Therefore, they needn't be baptized, needn't be confirmed, needn't have circumcision, and they needn't comply with any of the requirements for salvation because Christ atoned for all sin arising from the Fall of Adam. Little children are not sick, and therefore, do not need a physician. Christ removed all accountability for any law in the atonement for all infants, through the age of eight, who are not accountable before Him.[16] The Lord has given instructions in two other modern revelations: *But behold, I say unto you that little children are redeemed from the foundation of the world through my Only Begotten. Wherefore, they cannot sin, for power is not given to Satan to tempt little children, until they begin to become accountable before me. For it is given unto them, even as I will, according to my own pleasure, that great things may be required at the hand of their fathers. And again, I say unto you, who, having knowledge, have not I commanded to repent? And he that has no understanding, it remains in me to do according as it is written. And now behold, I declare no more unto you at this time. Amen* (T&C 9:14). *And again, inasmuch as parents have children in Zion, that teach them not to understand the doctrine of repentance, faith in Christ, the Son of the Living God, and of baptism, and the gift of the holy spirit by the laying on of the hands, when eight years old, the sin be upon the head of the parents. For this shall be a law unto the inhabitants of Zion, and their children shall be baptized for the remission of their sins when eight years old, and receive the laying on of the hands. And they also shall teach their children to pray and to walk uprightly before the Lord* (T&C 55:5).

Accuse Joseph Smith taught in DHC 4:445: "If you do not accuse each other, God will not accuse you. If you have no accuser you will enter heaven, and if you will follow the revelations and instructions which God gives you through me, I will take you into heaven as my back load. If you will not accuse me, I will not accuse you. If you will throw a cloak of charity over my sins, I will over yours — for charity covereth a multitude of sins." This notion of accusing one another is an important principle. Joseph is explaining something directly relating to obtaining salvation. Accusing someone is Satanic. One of the titles for Satan is "the accuser of the brethren." Satan's accusations are not said to be unwarranted or unsupported. He is not necessarily accusing his victims unjustly. It is probable some, if not all, of the accusations were, or are, just. If all were measured by an absolute standard of obedience, faithfulness, or virtue, all would necessarily fail. Satan does not need to use an unfair standard to accuse and condemn: …*all have sinned and come short of the glory of God* (Romans 1:16). "So if you want to condemn any of us, you need only look at our actual deeds and you will find sufficient reason to accuse us. Yet the negative and condemned role of accusing belongs to Satan. Those who take it upon themselves to do the condemning are acting the part of Satan. What Christ has asked us to do is forgive each other. Or, as Joseph put it, we are asked not to accuse each other."[17] *See also* SATAN; LUCIFER.

Adam   *Adam, who was the first man, who is spoken of in Daniel as being the Ancient of Days, or in other words, the first and oldest of all, the great grand progenitor, of whom it is said in another place he is Michael, because he was the first and father of all, not only by progeny, but he was the first to hold the spiritual blessings, to whom was made known the plan of ordinances for the salvation of his posterity unto the end, and to whom Christ was first revealed, and through whom Christ has been revealed from Heaven and will continue to be revealed from henceforth. Adam holds the keys of the dispensation of the fullness of times; i.e., the dispensation of all the times have been and will be revealed through him, from the beginning to Christ, and from Christ to the end of all the dispensations that are to be revealed* (T&C 140:3).[18] The creation of the man Adam was primarily and specifically "in the image of my Only Begotten" — meaning Jesus Christ — and secondarily in the image of God the Father. God the Father was the Father of Jesus Christ in the spirit, as well as the biological Father of Jesus Christ in the flesh. God the Father was also the Father of the spirit of the man

Adam, but the biological Father of Adam in the garden was "in the image of my Only Begotten." Christ and His companion were the physical Parents of the man Adam.[19] Adam, *the son of God* (*see* Genesis 3:23; Luke 3:38 KJV), possessed the Holy Order after the Order of the Son of God, which was given to him in the beginning, before the world began (*see* Abraham 1:1,3).[20] Included within this order is the right to preside over all of the human family and the right to minister to Adam's posterity. Adam continues to hold this presiding position and will do so until the end of time.[21] "The keys [of the Holy Order] have to be brought from Heaven whenever the Gospel is sent. When they are revealed from Heaven, it is by Adam's authority.... He (Adam) is the father of the human family, and presides over the spirits of all men, and all that have had the keys must stand before him in this grand council. This may take place before some of us leave this stage of action. The Son of Man stands before him (Adam), and there is given Him glory and dominion. Adam delivers up his stewardship to Christ, that which was delivered to him as holding the keys of the universe, but retains his standing as the head of the human family."[22] *See also* EVE.

Adam-Ondi-Ahman The phrase means "Adam in the presence of Son Ahman." The first occurrence of Adam-Ondi-Ahman happened near the place now known as Spring Hill in Missouri. Since it was an event — in which the location acquired significance because of what happened there — the term describes a *future event*, rather than just a fixed location. Latter-day Saints think the future event will take place at the same location as the first event, but — like the location of the New Jerusalem — it may happen elsewhere.[23] At that meeting the posterity of Father Adam will give an accounting to Christ, preliminary to Christ's return as the One whose right it is to preside over all things.[24]

Adoption Joseph Smith first mentioned "adoption" in a discussion about the Kingdom of God in October 1843, eight months before his death. He began the actual practice of adopting men, but it did not get well enough defined for the rite to continue following his death.[25] Joseph's original instruction connected the living faithful to the "fathers" Abraham, Isaac, and Jacob. This connection was through Priesthood, not genealogy. Joseph was connected by his Priesthood, becoming a "father" to all who would live after him. Families would be organized under Joseph, as the father of the righteous in this dispensation. Accordingly, men were sealed to Joseph Smith as their father, with they as his sons. This was referred to as "adoption" because the family organization was priestly, according to the law of God, not biological. As soon as Joseph died, the doctrine began to erode, ultimately being replaced by the substitute practice of sealing genealogical lines together. In between the time of original adoptive sealing to Joseph Smith and the current practice of tracking genealogical/biological lines, there was an intermediate step when families were tracked back as far as research permitted, then the line was sealed to Joseph Smith. That practice is now forgotten and certainly no longer practiced. The growing uncertainty, redefinition, and abandonment of the practice of "adoption" has been traced in an article which appears in the *Journal of Mormon History*.[26] It demonstrates how quickly the topic became confused.[27] When Joseph died, all understanding of the practice of "adoption" was quickly lost. Joseph Smith regarded adoption to be important for salvation. It was lost when he died. Before the Lord's return, this will need to be clarified by the Lord returning to a place on the earth in which He can *come and restore again that which was lost…even the fullness of the Priesthood* (T&C 141:10) and its attendant rites. This is an orderly process that was ordained in Heaven before the creation and implemented at the time of Adam, and it must be followed in every generation. Until mankind receives the "kingdom" (or Family of God) and the Fathers in Heaven, in strict order, they will remain unprepared for the Lord's return. The hearts of the Fathers and hearts of the children must be sealed together. Pretenders cannot accomplish it, because they will neither know how nor have the authority.[28]

Adultery To *look on a woman to lust after her…or…commit adultery in their hearts* (T&C 50:4; *see also* Matthew 3:21; T&C 26:8; 3 Nephi 5:27) means the actual scheming or mental planning to engage or seduce. It is not just a passing biological attraction that is subdued by one's will to obey God, nor is it a whispered temptation from a mischievous spirit. Subduing and rejecting that temptation is part of living righteously.[29] Divorce also leads to adultery. When forced away by the man she loves, a woman is then adulterated by the act of the man. He is accountable for the treachery involved in dissolving the marriage that the woman wanted and forcing her into the relation with either no one or with another man. In either case, it is adulterating the marriage which she had with him. He is accountable for that uncharitable, unkind, and unjustified treatment of the woman. On the other hand, when she has lost affection for him and the union has become hollow and without love, then the marriage is dead, and continuation of the relation is a farce. It is not a marriage. In fact, it is a pretense and an abomination unworthy of preservation. It will not endure.[30] "We reject adultery by any name or description. It is morally wrong, even if you call it plural wives, polygamy, 'celestial marriage,' or any other misnomer. Adultery is prohibited in the Ten Commandments and remains an important prohibition for any moral society."[31] There is a reason why such a serious sin as adultery ought to be altogether avoided; even if it is only as a foolish temptation contemplating the possibility of a plural wife. All need greater light and knowledge. The only way it can be acquired is by heed and diligence to the commandments of God. Any other path is a diversion, intended to waylay a person and prevent him or her from developing as God intends. Those who think they can follow God and yet commit adultery are deceived and giving heed to a false spirit. It is impossible to be both on the path to greater light and also engaged in such a serious sin.[32] In addition to referring to a physical act involving sexual union with another, the term adultery is often used with the connotation of unfaithfulness, as in Israel becoming unfaithful and playing the part of an adulteress, worshiping other gods (*see* Jeremiah 2:1).[33]

Agency Freedom or agency really means "accountability." That is its chief, if not only, meaning. Men are free; therefore, they are accountable before God for all their acts. The atonement affords men and women relief from that accountability for their sins when they repent. Taking advantage of the atonement for that purpose, however, does require them to obey Christ's conditions.[34]

Ancient of Days This name means the oldest man, our Father Adam; Michael.[35]

Angel *For he that receives my servants receives me* (T&C 82:17). The word "servants" in this context means "angels." Angel is derived from the Greek word *ággelos* [ἄγγελος] which means "messenger." The messenger must bring a message from the Lord. It does not matter if the messenger is mortal.[36] The word describes a category of messenger that includes not only pre-mortal and post-mortal spirits, but also living men. When anyone, man or angel, is entrusted with a message from God, the message is God's. God makes no distinction between the messenger and Himself.[37] *And now I have spoken the words which the Lord God hath commanded me* (Mosiah 1:18). The angel added nothing. He hid nothing. He delivered what the Lord told him to deliver. These are not merely the words of an angel. Because the angel certifies they originated from God, they are the words of God (*see* T&C 54:7).[38] Joseph explained that all angels either have or do belong to this earth: *But there are no angels who minister to this earth but those who do belong or have belonged to it*.[39] Their status as angel comes from the fact they have met with God, received their assignment and authority from Him, and deliver only the message He instructs should be delivered. They are in His service, and the message is confined to what He has told them to do.[40] Angels minister to mankind and confer power, light, and truth. They prepare one to receive the Lord.[41] *Neither have angels ceased to minister unto the children of men. For behold, they are subject unto him, to minister according to the word of his command, shewing themselves unto them of strong faith and a firm mind in every form of godliness. And the office of their ministry is to call men unto repentance, and to fulfill and to do the work of the covenants of the Father which he hath made unto the children of men, to prepare the way among the children of men* by declaring the word of Christ unto the chosen vessels of the Lord, that they may bear testimony of him; and by so doing, the Lord God prepareth the way that the residue of men may have faith in Christ, *that the holy ghost may have place in their hearts, according to the power thereof; and after this manner bringeth to pass the Father the covenants which he hath made unto the children of men* (Moroni 7:6). Angels minister to "chosen vessels" or mortal messengers, as the Three Nephites did with Mormon and Moroni (*see* Mormon 4:2). Then these vessels testify and bear testimony so that the way is prepared *that the residue of men may have faith in Christ*. These three visited with Mormon, but the people to whom Mormon ministered didn't see them. They ministered to Moroni, and those to whom Moroni ministered didn't see them. The chosen vessels also become as ministering angels. Many people have received ministering angels. Men, women, and children have, can, and do receive angelic ministers. Angels minister to those with faith, then they are supposed to preach salvation to others. Appearances of angels, like the post-resurrection ministry of Christ, happen with the faithful. Christ appeared as a resurrected minister only to the faithful in Jerusalem. Likewise, He showed Himself to "the more righteous" who had been spared among the Nephites.[42]

Angel of Light A servant or messenger of God whose presence or appearance is characterized not only by his or her light, but by the content and intelligence of the message, as well as the absence of darkness. To avoid deception, we must have light. Light comes to all by keeping God's commandments (*see* T&C 93:9).[43] The defect Moses perceived in Lucifer when Lucifer came tempting him (as stated in Genesis 1:3) was not merely his appearance. Satan was (and is) an angel. T&C 69:6 describes him as *an angel of God who was in authority in the presence of God* and was cast down. Such a being does not look vile. Visually, he may appear to have light and glory. Because he is a liar, he uses his appearance as a pretense to be an angel of light. Moses was able to discern between Satan and an actual messenger from God, but that had nothing to do with the appearance of Satan. It was because of the content of the message. Moses distinguished between his message and the Lord's. The Lord's was a message of glory, which is intelligence, or in other words, light and truth. Satan's message takes one into a dark and dreary waste.[44]

Anger Those who become angry at the truth have "the spirit of the devil" in them. That is, they are under the devil's influence and are deceived. Nephi understood this principle because of his older brothers' reactions (*see* 1 Nephi 5:1). When someone becomes angry at the truth, they are in darkness. Christ gave this as one of the signs of the deceived. They argue against the truth and become angry (*see* 3 Nephi 5:8). Those who are Christ's, however, join with Nephi in glorying in plainness, even if it cuts or requires repentance. They appreciate the plain direction which allows them to follow in the true path. They appreciate truth, even when it condemns their acts and requires them to change. They glory in Christ, preferring Him over unbelief, traditions of men, or the arm of flesh.[45]

Anti-Christ Those who invite people to follow them and deliberately seek devotees. Those who put themselves up for adoration and worship are mistaken, are practicing priestcraft, are anti-Christ, and are in the employ of the enemy to mankind's souls.[46] Anti-Christs are also all those who practice a religion that rejects Jesus Christ as the Son of God and Redeemer of mankind.[47] "Any teaching or person who draws us to them and does not point us to the Lord is unable to help us. If they try to supplant Christ as the object of admiration, then they are anti-Christ and a false prophet."[48]

Apostasy A deliberate, intentional, or willful rejection or refusal to accept what God offers to man; a rebellion. When mankind limits what they will permit God to reveal, setting boundaries to His teachings, they rebel. But that rebellion only limits themselves.[49] Mankind, whether as a group or a single person, is either gaining (restoring) light and truth or losing (apostatizing) from light and truth. This world is a world of change. Nothing remains the same. Either growth or decay are at work everywhere. They are also at work within every person. One either searches out new truth — finds it, lives it, and thereby becomes restored to truth — or one backs away from it. If one is backing away, losing it, neglecting it, and discarding it, one is in the process of apostasy.[50] With respect to God's people, apostasy is always marked by a change of ordinances and breaking of the covenant.[51] "In ancient times, apostasy never came by renouncing the gospel, but always by corrupting it…. The great apostasy in the time of the apostles was not a renouncing of faith but its corruption and manipulation."[52]

Apostle The word apostle (from the Greek *apóstolos*, ἀπόστολος) literally means "someone sent away," implying that someone with this title is sent to deliver a message. An English equivalent would be "messenger." There is no such thing as priesthood called "apostle." It is also an office in the LDS church institution, like that of relief society president, primary president, or scout leader. It is only an office in that church.[53] Before 1835, the term apostle did not mean 12 men belonging to a quorum. It meant men who were ordained to the High Priesthood who had seen Christ. The June 1, 1833 revelation (*see* T&C 94:4) referred to the School of the Prophets as *the school of my apostles*. The school was *to prepare mine apostles* (par. 1). However, the identity of the apostles was expansive, including *the officers, or in other words, those who are called to the ministry in the church, beginning at the high priests, even down to the deacon* (T&C 87:1), describing those for whom the school of the prophets was to be built. After an appearance of Christ to members of the school of the prophets, Joseph declared: *Brethren now you are prepared to be the Apostles of Jesus Christ, for you have seen both the Father and the Son, and know that They exist, and that They are two separate Personages.*[54] It was not membership in a "quorum," but knowledge that originally defined the meaning of apostle when used in all notes, minutes, revelations, and preaching before 1835.[55] The church originally organized in 1830, like the Book of Mormon church, had offices of elders, priests and teachers. Then the term "apostle" began to be used. But the term "apostle" did not mean the same thing in institutions then that it does today. A quorum of twelve apostles did not exist in Mormonism until February 1835. Prior to that, many individuals were identified as "apostles." The term meant someone sent with a message from God.[56] The term was originally used to identify all the missionaries sent to preach the Book of Mormon and restoration. The revelations given through Joseph Smith specifically identified a number of men as "apostles" before the organization of a quorum of twelve apostles in 1835: Oliver Cowdery and David Whitmer in 1829; Joseph Smith and Oliver Cowdery in 1830; Sidney Rigdon, Parley Pratt and Leman Copley in 1831. A series of revelations likewise referred to "apostles" and included admonitions, instructions, and commandments to different audiences composed of "apostles" before the organization of a quorum of twelve in 1835. The Seventy were also regarded as "apostles.[57] The New Testament account of what qualifies an apostle included the necessary credential of witnessing Christ's resurrection (*see* Acts 1:6).[58] *See also* TWELVE APOSTLES.

Archangels, the Four There are four great angels who hold *power over the four parts of the earth, to save life and to destroy. These are they who have the everlasting gospel to commit to every nation, kindred, tongue, and people, having power to shut up the heavens, to seal up unto life, or to cast down to the regions of darkness* (T&C 74:8). They are real. They are known as Michael (Adam), Gabriel (Noah), Raphael (Enoch), and Uriel (John); they hold control over air, water, fire, and earth, respectively — the four parts of the earth. In spite of their ministry, mankind should not worship them, nor pray to them. Egypt may have identified and understood them better, acknowledging them as the "four sons of Horus," but Egypt erred by exalting them to worship and prayer (along with other heavenly beings the Egyptians called *neteru* and the Hebrews called angels — these comprise the host of heaven led by Jehovah). The first error God corrected for Moses was this idolatry of angels, who are not to be worshipped but are to be recognized and respected as God's messengers and servants (*see* Exodus 20:3–5).[59] *Michael* means "who is like God"; *Gabriel* means "the strength of God"; *Raphael* means "the healing of God"; and *Uriel* means "the light or fire of the Lord."[60]

Ascension   There is a relationship between ascension in this life and the right to ascend in the afterlife which is mentioned, but not well explained, in scripture. There are two ascents. One is temporary and happens when men are "caught up" but then return to this world. It represents overcoming the world and returning the individual back to the presence of God. It is called *redemption from the fall* (Ether 1:13) because it brings the individual back into God's presence. This form of temporary ascent is designed to establish a covenant or promise related to the other, more gradual ascent through development of the individual. The temporary mortal ascent secures a promise for the individual that they will be permitted to make the eternal ascent to where God and Christ dwell in the afterlife. The second form is the actual ascent, involving redemption, and securing eternal life. It is a methodical process over eons of time to bring those who ascend to reside where God and Christ dwell (*see* T&C 69:14,28). In the "King Follett Discourse," Joseph Smith said this: "Thus you learn some of the first principles of the gospel about which so much has been said. When you climb a ladder, you must begin at the bottom and go on until you learn the last principle; it will be a great while before you have learned the last. It is not all to be comprehended in this world; it is a great thing to learn salvation beyond the grave."[61] This is the growth, by degrees, which results in exaltation. "Here, then, is eternal life — to know the only wise and true God. And you have got to learn how to be Gods yourselves — to be kings and priests to God, the same as all Gods have done — by going from a small degree to another, from grace to grace, from exaltation to exaltation, until you are able to sit in glory as do those who sit enthroned in everlasting power."[62]

The second form of ascent cannot happen in mortality but is accomplished over time. It requires attaining to the resurrection, meaning that death has no claim on this person because he or she merits eternal life. This is what Christ gained in His life and through His sacrifice here. Men are dependent upon His merits to overcome death. But all will have to attain the same thing before they finish the second form of ascent. Christ is the *prototype of the saved man* and all must *be precisely what he is and nothing else* or not be saved, according to the Lectures on Faith (LOF 7:9).

The first form of ascent is possible for all mortals. The scriptures, in particular the Book of Mormon, contain accounts of those who have ascended to God's presence and overcome the fall of mankind. Many Old Testament prophets did likewise, but their accounts were redacted by the Deuteronomists because of hostility to the doctrine. The reality is that most people — even very good, believing people whose lives are filled with Christian charity and love for their fellow man — are not going to ascend, even temporarily, while they live in this fallen world. The first ascent is covenant-filled. God brings one before Him to establish a covenant, assuring the Eternal ascent. Most people will ascend over eons of time, because the process is based on the determination and commitment people have to follow God and His Christ.[63]

Ask The principle of asking and receiving, on the one hand, and the spirit of prophecy and revelation, on the other, are directly related. Without an inquiry, one is not able to receive,[64] for those who *are* willing to receive always ask. Asking is the way those who are ready identify themselves for Heaven.[65] "[In First Nephi 3:6 we] have Nephi telling us he *desired* to know things. He believed God could make them known. And he was *pondering* the things he was seeking. Then in response to this process, the Lord sent an angel who inquired of Nephi…. What ought to stick out most in this passage is that Nephi is now granted an audience with an angel, and the angel is inquiring of him: *What desirest thou?* He is in the presence of an angel, but before he can learn anything, the angel first asks him: What do you

(handwritten margin note: "What if he answered 'everything'?")

want? That should tell you something of great significance. Heaven responds to inquiries! This is one of those eternal principles. Heaven is controlled by ordained limits or governing principles. Just as we must abide the conditions for obtaining blessings, Heaven's help comes in response to ordained limitations, principles, laws and ordinances. This is why the angel does not launch into a lecture right away. Instead, the angel asks Nephi what he wants to know so the balance and limits are maintained. If you aren't asking, you are sealing the Heavens. You disqualify yourself from further knowledge. God did not come in response to Joseph Smith's silent desire to know more. The First Vision came as a result of a specific vocal and private prayer in which he asked to know more. When the Father and Son appeared, the first words spoken were: *Joseph: This is my beloved Son. Hear Him!* Then nothing further happens until Joseph *asked the Personages who stood above [him] in the light, which of all the sects was right.* God did not force an answer upon Joseph, nor comment further until Joseph had first asked a question. It is not Heaven's responsibility to force upon us answers to questions which we do not ask. Unless we are willing to ask, we will not (in fact cannot) receive. This is why teaching we should not ask to know more of God's mysteries is so pernicious. It is not only false, it limits Heaven's ability to provide light and truth to us. We seal the Heavens when we comply with such instruction. Nephi asks, *I desire to behold the things which my father saw* (1 Nephi 3:6). Then the angel asks Nephi whether he believed the things his father had been teaching him. Nephi says he did believe. Indeed, Nephi said he believed *all the words of my father.* Having now secured from Nephi both a question to answer and a confession of faith in the Lord's spokesman (Nephi's prophet-father), the angel reacts with overwhelming joy: *And when I had spoken these words, the Spirit cried with a loud voice, saying, Hosanna to the Lord, the Most High God, for he is God over all the earth, yea, even above all! And blessed art thou, Nephi, because thou believest in the Son of the Most High God; wherefore, thou shalt behold the things which thou hast desired* (1 Nephi 3:6). An angel shouting for joy! Here we have a clear indication of just how much it pleases God and His holy angels when a person finally shows their willingness to receive further light and truth by conversing with the Lord through the veil. It is a rare thing.

Heaven rejoices over someone who comes with a question, and with faith, and with a desire to know these things, believing the Lord can make them known. This particular alignment of things is so rare an event Heaven cannot contain the joy, exultation, and wonder when it occurs.... The Heavens long for communion with mankind. The silence which prevails is due to our wickedness, and not Heaven's unwillingness to open to us. If silence prevails, it is mankind who stopped the dialogue."⁶⁶ If asking must precede receiving, and if Joseph Smith was also required to ask before the great revelations of this dispensation were unfolded to him, then all must ask. Failing to ask causes the way to be hedged up and prevents Heaven from answering.⁶⁷

Ask, Seek, Knock *Ask and it shall be given unto you, seek and ye shall find, knock and it shall be opened unto you; for everyone that asketh, receiveth, and he that seeketh, findeth, and to him that knocketh, it shall be opened* (3 Nephi 6:3). "Just after the caution to not give holy things to the unworthy, Christ reminds all of their obligation to ask, seek, and knock. If you will ask, it will be given to you. If you seek, you will find it. If you knock, things will be opened to you. <u>But be careful not to give what is holy to the unworthy</u>. These ideas are related in two ways: First, if you want what is holy, then stop being a *dog* or a *swine*. Ask, seek, and knock. Second, if you are one who is qualified and will receive holy things by your willingness to be repentant, then press forward by asking, seeking, and knocking. If you do, the things which are most holy will be given. *For everyone that asketh, receiveth.* Really? Everyone? Even you? That is what Christ is saying. However, the manner in which you will receive is illustrated by 'The Missing Virtue' in *Ten Parables*.⁶⁸ <u>Meaning that the effort to receive what you have asked the Lord could take nearly two decades, and a great deal of internal changing before you acquire what you lack.</u> Receiving may include not only what you've asked to receive, but also everything you do not have in order to finally qualify to receive what you seek. What do you associate with *findeth?* Does it suggest to you active effort, or passive receipt? To *find* something you are missing (even a small thing) what must you do? If searching is required to locate, then what do you suppose the Lord is implying by the word *findeth?* What does it mean that *it shall be opened?* Does *opening* imply merely a view? Does it suggest also *entering in*? If it opens to view, and you then fail to *enter in*, has *opening* been worthwhile? Has anything been accomplished? Does it suggest that there is activity required of someone who has something *opened* unto them? It is my view that the words chosen all imply a burden upon the one who asks, seeks, and knocks. They are not entitled to anything just by speaking the words. They must make the effort to search into and contemplate the things they seek. Then they must change and repent of everything amiss in their lives that is revealed to them. This is to be done before they can see what is to be shown to them. If, for example, a person wants to see the other side of the mountain, they can ask daily for a view to be opened to them without ever seeing the other side. But if the Lord prompts them to take the path to the top, the Lord has given them the means to *find* and *have opened* to them the very thing they seek. Provided, of course, they are willing to walk in the path to the top of the mountain. When they remain on the valley floor, asking or demanding more, they are not really asking, seeking, and knocking. They are irritating and ungrateful. The Lord's small means are capable of taking the one who seeks to the very thing they desire (Alma 17:8). But without cooperation with Him they can receive nothing. The Lord's small means are how great things are brought to pass (1 Nephi 5:8). But for some people the Lord's answers are never enough. However, when the humble who ask, seek, and knock follow Him in these small means, they will eventually stand in His presence and partake of eternal life. But not until they have done as all others have done before them."[69]

Mankind is impatient, wanting quickly what can sometimes only be obtained in patience. Human nature is to rush, but development requires patience. Some things require time and persistence to prepare one for the blessings they seek. Joseph remarked: *The things of God are of deep import, and time, and experience, and careful and ponderous and solemn thoughts can only find them out* (T&C 138:18). This is the way of God. It is adapted to give all what they lack, even if they are unaware of what they lack. The Father always intends to give to those who ask, seek, and knock, just as Christ explained; the Father knows *much more* how to *give good things to them that ask* (3 Nephi 6:3). He will not merely give the thing requested. He will add to it such things as are needed to prepare them to be received. "This, then, is the process: We ask. Without a request, the laws governing things prevent bestowal. We can't be given until first we ask. When we have asked, the Father will give. He will give *every good gift* needed, and not just what has been asked (3 Nephi 6:3). If there is (as is almost always the case) a gulf between what you have asked of Him and your capacity to receive it, then He will set about giving you every needful thing to enable you to receive. If you ask for strength, He will provide you with that experience necessary to develop the strength you seek. If you seek for patience you will be given Divinely ordained experiences by Him that are calculated to develop in you what you have sought. He knows you and knows what you need. Whatever is asked of Him, He will set about to ordain. It will come in a perfectly natural progression. It will occur in accordance with both natural and eternal law. If you fight against it, you prolong the time when you will receive what you have asked of Him. If you cooperate, it will flow unto you without compulsory means in a natural progression (T&C 139:6). If you do not ask, it will not be given. If you do not seek, you cannot possibly find. If you are unwilling to knock, the door will remain shut to you. But if you do these things, then you must cooperate with Him as He prepares you to receive what He will bestow. After asking, seeking, and knocking, then a process is invoked in which the Father prepares you to receive. You will receive as soon as He can prepare you by experience, by careful, thoughtful, ponderous thought through time and experiences adapted to give you what is asked. When, at last, you have been adequately prepared, you will have gone through exactly what every other soul before you has experienced to prepare them. There are no shortcuts. There are no exceptions. It is in accordance with laws ordained before the foundation of the world. Everyone who has obtained what you seek will have done so in conformity with the very same laws. The Father will work with you to prepare you to receive what you seek. This is a reaffirmation by Christ of the process and the Father's role in bringing it to pass. If you trust Him, trust also His Father's deliverance of you. You will be delivered. You will receive from Him who knows how to bestow every good gift what you have asked of Him."[70]

Atonement Atonement is a 16th century English contraction of the words *at* and *one,* attributed to William Tyndale's biblical translations; it signifies the state of being *at-one*, *at-oneness,* or *at-one-ment* and the process of reaching that state—unity with God. The word appears over a hundred times in the Old Covenants from the root *kaphar* (כָּפַר), meaning to cover, [71] and appears in the New Testament only once in Romans 1:22 as *katallagē,* (καταλλαγή), meaning reconciliation, exchange, esp. money.[72] "From all the meanings of *kaphar* and *kippurim*, we [conclude] that the literal meaning…is a close and intimate embrace, which took place at the *kapporeth* or the front cover or flap of the tabernacle or tent. The Book of Mormon instances are quite clear: *Behold, he sendeth an invitation unto all men; for the arms of mercy are extended towards them, and he saith, Repent and I will receive you* (Alma 3:6). *But behold, the Lord hath redeemed my soul from hell—I have beheld his glory, and I am encircled about eternally in the arms of his love* (2 Nephi 1:3). To be redeemed is to be atoned…. [This] kind of oneness is meant by the atonement—it is being received in close embrace of the prodigal son, expressing not only forgiveness but oneness of heart and mind that amounts to identity."[73] "The standard guide to the atonement is the Gospel of John. Four solid chapters, 14–17 [in the KJV], are devoted to showing that the atonement is literal; it is real"[74] (*see* John 9 and The Testimony of St. John, chapters 8–10). Mankind is placed in a situation on this earth where, without a Redeemer and an atoning sacrifice, progression—as well as any hope of escape from the grave and the justice of the Lawgiver—would be impossible. Without the atonement, the possibility of ascension and return to the presence of God could not take place.

The Father's doctrine is that *all men everywhere [must] repent and believe in [Christ]* (3 Nephi 5:9). This is what the whole of creation hangs on: the atonement of the Son. It is through the Son's sacrifice that the Father's plan became operational. Now, in order to return to the Father, all must do so in reliance upon the merits of the Son (John 2:2).[75]

It is impossible to become altogether clean in this fallen world. Despite mankind's best efforts, in the end they're going to find they are lacking. The scriptures admit this. All are in need of redemption from an outside power – someone with greater virtue and power who can lift mankind from the fallen condition into something higher, cleaner, and more godly. This is the role of Christ. His atoning sacrifice equipped Him to accomplish this. The atonement, however, is not magic. Through it, Christ accomplished some very specific things and has the power to lead all back to the presence of God, the Father. The process was difficult for Him and is necessarily difficult for each person seeking it.

Christ participated in the ordinance of the atonement to acquire two things, the first of which is knowledge (*see* Isaiah 19:2). It is through His knowledge that He is able to *justify many*. This knowledge was acquired through His suffering the pains of all mankind, which allowed Him to know exactly what weaknesses afflict mankind and how to overcome them. This allows Him to succor, relieve, and teach mankind how to overcome every form of guilt, affliction, and weakness (*see* Alma 5:3). This knowledge was gained by suffering guilt and remorse for sins He had not committed, exactly as if He were the one who perpetrated them. He performed this great burden in the presence of His Father, who would never leave Him, even in His hour of temptation, despite the fact that all His followers would abandon Him (*see* John 9:18). When He suffered the guilt of all mankind, it was necessary for His Father to draw near to Him (*see* Luke 13:9), because it was impossible for Christ to know how to redeem mankind from the guilt and shame of sin unless He experienced the pain of uncleanliness before God the Father, just as mankind will do if they are unclean in the day of judgment (*see* Mormon 4:6). Unlike all of mankind, however, Christ knows how to overcome this shame, because He has done so. Secondly, Christ acquired the keys of death and hell by suffering, reconciling, dying, rising, and reuniting with the Father (*see* Revelation 1:6). Because the keys of death and hell belong to Him, He has the power of forgiveness. He can forgive all men all offenses, but He requires them to forgive others (*see* T&C 51:3). If they fail to forgive others, they cannot be forgiven (*see* Matthew 3:30).

Mankind does not move from a state of evil to redemption by Christ's sacrifice alone. It is required for them to follow Him (*see* John 6:29). They follow Him when they allow Him to succor them, to impart knowledge to them, and when they forgive others through His knowledge gained from the atonement. Through the keys of death and hell, Christ's atonement cleanses them from errors, from failings, and from deliberate wrong choices. He provides cleansing from those failings. But His atonement does not change their character unless they follow Him. The atonement, if properly acted upon, frees them to develop character like His, unencumbered by the guilt of what they've failed to do. He removes guilt. But developing character like His is mankind's responsibility. They cannot be passive and obtain what He offers. They are required to actively pursue the redemption they seek from Him. When the sin is removed from them, they are free to pursue virtue without the crippling effects of remorse which He removed (*see* Alma 14:7). When freed from the guilt of sin, the past mistakes no longer haunt them. Their sins are no longer remembered by the Lord, and they are free to confess and forsake them (*see* T&C 45:9). The reason they can publicly confess their sins is because they are no longer a part of them. The sin does not define them. They have chosen to follow Him into a new life.

The development of a godly character happens in stages, gradually, but forgiveness comes in an instant, suddenly (*see* Alma 17:4). The forgiven one necessarily turns to a new life, in which sharing the joy of forgiveness and the joy of redemption through Christ is the abiding desire (*see* Alma 17:5). The mind changes in proportion to the joy found in the new life (*see* Romans 1:33). Such new people are no longer the sons of men, but they become the sons of God (*see* Romans 1:34). They know the joy of having the voice of the Father declare to them that they have been begotten by the Father and are the sons of God (*see* Psalms 2:2). The fullness of the atonement is the fullness of knowledge, which comes by following Him and abiding the conditions. No one can receive what He offers unless they conform to the conditions He has established for redemption (*see* T&C 93:9). This is the Gospel of Christ. This is the news which comes from the Lord, the Messenger of Salvation. Those who know Him will declare these things in unmistakable words to allow others to come and partake of the same fruit of the tree of life. (See *Come, Let Us Adore Him*, chapter 12.)[76] Christ described what He went through, saying, *I...finished my preparations* (T&C 4:5). The atonement is not really a singular event, apart from the completion of the preparation. The atonement process is Christ reasoning with, persuading, and forgiving each repentant sinner on an ongoing basis to redeem them. The atonement (not capitalized) is His great work, while the Atonement (capitalized) is when it is done, finished, and over.[77] *See also* REDEMPTION.

Attain to the Resurrection of the Dead More than merely coming forth from the grave (although that is termed "resurrection," also); Joseph Smith more accurately referred to this as an achievement following exaltation: "[Y]ou have got to learn how to be Gods yourselves, and to be kings and priests to God, the same as all Gods have done before you, namely by going from one small degree to another, and from a small capacity to a great one; from grace to grace, from exaltation to exaltation, until you attain to the resurrection of the dead, and are able to dwell in everlasting burnings, and to sit in glory, as do those who sit enthroned in everlasting power (*TPJS*, 346–347)."[78] Arising from the grave does not mean one has "attained to the resurrection of the dead," nor holds the keys of resurrection. No one will attain this until they, like Christ, have gone from exaltation to exaltation, until they can obtain the power to resurrect all that depends upon them. To "attain to the resurrection of the dead" requires one to have the power to resurrect not only themselves, but also those who are dependent on them. "This is what the prototype of the saved man did. This is Who we worship. This is who and what we must precisely and exactly become."[79]

Authoritative Approved by God and binding upon man.[80]

Awake and Arise There are two things that generally stir one up to repentance: first, to awaken to one's awful situation (*see* 2 Nephi 1:3; 2 Nephi 3:8); and second, to arise and connect with the source that will cure what is wrong with one (*see* Moroni 10:6). "We are not self-curing. We are filled with that same shame that came in the beginning as a consequence of doing what we were not supposed to be doing. The greatest way the adversary keeps us in a state of slumber is to prevent us from looking about and awakening to the awful situation we find ourselves in."[81]

Babylon The counterpart to Zion is Babylon, identified in the scriptures as *the world*.[82] "It is described just as fully, clearly and vividly in the scriptures as Zion is, and usually in direct relationship to it.... Just as surely as Zion is to be established, Babylon is to be destroyed.... Babylon is not to be converted, she's to be destroyed.... Today's world is the *substance...of an idol which waxes old and shall perish in Babylon, even Babylon the great which shall fall* (T&C 54:3). *For after today comes the burning...and I will not spare any that remain in Babylon* (T&C 51:7). Babylon is nothing but the inverse image of Zion. Babylon is a state of mind, as Zion is, with its appropriate environment.... Babylon is described fully in Revelation chapter 7: She is rich, luxurious, immoral, full of fornications, merchants, riches, delicacies, sins, merchandise, gold, silver, precious stones, pearls, fine linens, purples, silks, scarlets, thyine wood, all manner of vessels, ivory, precious wood, brass, iron, marble, and so on. She is a giant delicatessen, full of wine, oil, fine flour, wheat; a perfume counter with cinnamon, odors, ointments, and frankincense; a market with beasts and sheep. It reads like...a guide to a modern supermarket or department store...and it is all for sale. In her power and affluence she is unchallenged.... Babylon is number one. She dominates the world. Her king is equated to Lucifer, who says, *I will be like the Most High* (Isaiah 6:6).... And when Babylon falls, all the world is involved."[83]

Nephi used similar typology when he described the two churches — Babylon is a type. It is the world and worldly power, where everyone and everything has a price. The Lord has called his people to *go out from Babylon* (T&C 58:1), and *go out from among the nations, even from Babylon, from the midst of wickedness, which is spiritual Babylon* (T&C 58:2). Out of Zion and out of Jerusalem will go the law and the teachings that will constitute the effort, the government, the society, and the culture that's going to finally free itself from the toxic influences and the corrupt traditions that have been passed down from generation to generation, being influenced all the way back to Babylon. "That's why the prophecies of John talk about the fall of Babylon the great. Because the head of gold is still with us. The Babylonian influence remains with us still in our banking, in our profit motives, in our culture, in our education, in our false ideas about what's important and what's not, in our desire for power, and wealth, and influence. All of those things remain with us still today. And they corrupt everything. They corrupt business; they corrupt governments; they corrupt churches. They corrupt society. Everyone is vying with one another to gain influence, power, and in turn, wealth and the acclamation of this world. And it all goes back to Babylon. Which is why John prophesies the fall, not of every one of these components of the great image that Nebuchadnezzar saw, but he goes right to the head. Because as soon as you destroy the head, everything else is going to unravel. And he prophesies about the destruction of Babylon, the head of gold that holds sway over all else."[84]

Baptism An ordinance that is intended to communicate light and truth into the mind of the individual, not merely to fulfill an initiation rite. It is meant to enlighten. The ordinance is performed by following the instructions taught by Christ in 3 Nephi 5:8. One must be put under the water and then *come forth again out of the water.* The purpose of baptism is to follow Christ's example (*see* John 6:29; 9:8). It symbolizes the death of the old man of sin and the resurrection into a new life in Christ (*see* Romans 1:25). This symbol cannot be mirrored by sprinkling. It must involve immersion. One is placed below the surface of the water, in the same way the dead are buried below ground. The breath of life is cut off while under the water and restored anew when *[coming] forth again out of the water.* The officiator, having obtained power and authority from God (see *Preserving the Restoration*, 512; T&C 175:26–32) is the one who immerses and then brings the recipient up out of the water. Performing this ordinance puts the officiator in the role of the Lord, who holds the keys of death (*see* Revelation 1:6) and resurrection (*see* 2 Nephi 1:6). [85]

Christ prescribes the exact words to be used in the ordinance. Authorization comes from Jesus Christ, but the ordinance is performed *in the name of the Father, and of the Son, and of the holy ghost.* The power to do the ordinance comes from the Son, but the ordinance is in the name of each member of the Godhead. Though they are one, they occupy different roles and hold different responsibilities. In this fallen world, God communicates with man primarily through the holy ghost. However, when a person rises up through the merits of Jesus Christ to receive Him as a minister, they are living in a Terrestrial law and inherit Terrestrial blessings. When He has finished His preparations with the person and can bring them to the Father, the person is brought to a point where the Father can accept and acknowledge them as a son. They are then begotten of the Father (*see* T&C 86:3–4).[86]

The ordinance of baptism symbolizes some eternal truths regarding the plan of salvation. In the very moment the ordinance is performed, there is a renewal in the symbols of life, innocence, forgiveness, and resurrection. The earth itself is blessed by baptism, as well as other ordinances. The earth itself is defiled when the ordinances are not kept exactly as prescribed (*see* Isaiah 7:1; Genesis 5:12). The earth knows that God ordained the ordinances of Heaven and earth. As regular and reliable as the movements of the sun and moon are, so too should the ordinances of the Lord be kept in their appointed ways (*see* Jeremiah 13:10). The Heavens and earth rejoice when the ordinances are kept. They symbolize eternal hope, man's acceptance of God's plan, and a presence of righteousness in a fallen world. Mankind's participation in ordinances is vital to his or her own renewal and the renewal of all creation through redemption of each individual soul. The baptism ordinance, like all those that follow after, is intended not merely to fulfill an initiation rite. It is intended to communicate light and truth into the mind of the individual who is performing and receiving the ordinance. It is meant to enlighten. In the same way that Christ restored life to Lazarus and commanded him to *come forth* (John 7:6), baptism allows all to rise from the tomb of sin, which imprisons them, into the new life awaiting them in Christ.[87] *See also* REBAPTISM.

Baptism of Fire and the Holy Ghost A sign of redemption, purification, and holiness that is included in the "gate" for entering into God's presence. The baptism of fire and the holy ghost, as taught by Christ in the Doctrine of Christ (*see* 2 Nephi 13:3), is given without man's involvement, comes from heaven, and is promised by both the Father and the Son. God is a "consuming fire," and those who enter into His presence must be able to endure that fire (*see* Hebrews 1:57; Deuteronomy 2:5). Without the capacity to do so, a person would be consumed by the flames (*see* Leviticus 2:25). The fire and the holy ghost are given as a sign to the recipient that they may know it is safe for them to enter into God's presence and not be consumed.[88] The baptism of fire purges and removes sin, and its effect is to permit one to speak with the *tongue of angels* (2 Nephi 13:2). Nephi cautions that once this gift has been conferred, if one *should deny me [Christ], it would have been better for you that ye had not known me* (2 Nephi 13:3). This process comes after repentance and baptism; it comes to *show all things* and to *teach the peaceable things of the kingdom* (T&C 23:2). "To *speak with the tongue of angels* means you are elevated — your knowledge and your inspiration reckons from heaven itself. You have been elevated by fire, which purges sins and purifies. In effect, you receive holiness through the sanctifying power of the Holy Spirit. This in turn makes *your own* spirit holy. Your spirit or your ghost is within you, connected to heaven to such a degree through this process that you are in possession of a holy spirit or a holy ghost within you."[89] Recipients of the baptism of fire and the holy ghost receive the Father's testimony of the Son. "*And thus will the Father bear record of me* (3 Nephi 5:9). You cannot receive this baptism and not have a testimony given to you by the Father of the Son."[90]

Beast "The Prophets do *not* declare that [they] saw a beast or beasts, but that [they] saw the *image* or *figure* of a beast. They did not see an actual bear or lion but the images or figures of those beasts. The translation should have been rendered *image* instead of *beast* in every instance where beasts are mentioned by the Prophets. But John saw the actual beast in heaven, to show to John that that being did actually exist there. When the Prophets speak of seeing beasts in their visions, they saw the images, the types to represent certain things and at the same time they received the interpretation as to what those images or types were designed to represent."[91]

Become as a Little Child *Except you are converted and become as little children, you shall not enter into the kingdom of Heaven* (Matthew 9:10). According to Christ's words, returning to the mind of a child is necessary as a precondition for all to be able to enter His kingdom.[92] The chief characteristic of childhood is inquisitiveness and the search for greater understanding (*see* Mosiah 1:17).[93] Repentance is not likely unless a person is willing to undergo a change to become more "childlike" in perspective and attitude. This is more than just an analogy or good advice. It is a prerequisite. It is the only way you can "inherit the kingdom of God." Children are open to change and willing to learn. They welcome new ideas, for all ideas are new to them. The world is new to them. They feel their ignorance and are anxious to fill it with information and understanding. They know they are unable to cope with the world they live in unless they obtain more understanding than they have. They relentlessly search to know more. On the other hand, adults believe they already know something and are unwilling to receive more.

"Adults learn disciplines of study and then think the Gospel should be viewed by the tools of the scholar. To the economist, all of the Gospel appears to be financial. To the philosopher, all of the Gospel appears to be dialectic. To the lawyer it is a legal system. But the Gospel is separate from the understanding of men. It requires us to surrender our arrogance and foolishness and come as a child to learn anew everything about life and truth. This is why the Gospel always begins with creation, informs of the Fall, and preaches the atonement. We must *repent* because the foundation of accepting new truth begins with the realization that we're not getting anywhere by what we've already done. We need to abandon old ways and begin anew. Until we are open to the new truths offered through the Gospel,we can't even start the journey. We're headed in the wrong direction and don't even know it. First, we need to realize our direction is wrong. Then, stop going that way. When we turn to the new direction, we've begun repenting. From repentance comes light and truth. At first, just turning to face the new direction is a great revelation. But you've not seen anything until you walk in that direction for a while. As you move toward the light and receive more, the world itself changes meaning and nothing you used to think important remains important.

"Becoming as a little child, or repenting,must precede baptism if you are to be saved. Otherwise, you cannot *receive these things* or, in other words, you cannot accept the new truths and perspectives the Gospel will require you to know and accept. Unless these steps are taken you cannot *inherit the kingdom of God* because only such people will be able to enter. Teachable. Open. Willing to receive more. Able to endure difficulties as a result of the changes that come to them.

Patient. Submissive to God. And eager to learn more. Not arrogant. Not trying to fit the new truths into your existing framework of false notions. Not resisting truth and arguing against it. Not proud or boastful, secure in your own salvation. Not holding a testimony that you will be saved while others around you will be lost because they do not believe as you do. How few there will be who find it. Most people are simply unwilling to repent. They have such truth as they are willing to receive already, and want nothing more."[94] *See* DOCTRINE OF CHRIST.

Becoming One All are to become "one" with the Father, the Son, and the holy ghost. It is a distant goal, to be accomplished after being "added upon" for a long time. To become "one" will be to reach the end of a long journey. All can be given promises of that end; all can receive covenants that will bring them there. But arrival will "be a great while after [they] have passed through the veil" for "it is not all to be comprehended in this world" (*TPJS*, 348). One may be initiated, but to enter in will be "a great work to learn our salvation and exaltation even beyond the grave."[95] The ideal of being "one" with the Father, Son, and holy ghost is, for mankind, something that is distant, to be sought after, to be kept before them, but not to be obtained until some time later. But to be "one" with *each other* is another matter. Being "one" is required for Zion to return. Zion is required for the Lord to dwell among His people again. He is going to return to a Zion, no matter how few may be involved. He will come even if only two or three gather in His name (*see* Matthew 9:14). Zion may be small, but it will, nonetheless, be Zion before He can visit with her.[96] *Do not watch for iniquity in each other. If you do, you will not get an endowment, for God will not bestow it on such* (T&C 117:4). Belief in Christ necessarily means belief in the Father. To believe Christ is to accept His message of the Father's primacy and authority. One sees in these three members of the Godhead a full establishment of interconnected roles and responsibilities. The Father ordains the plan; it is He who presides. The Son implements the plan; it is He who makes the required sacrifice to save us. The holy ghost activates the plan; it is the "fire" of the holy ghost which makes new, cleanses, and perfects the man's understanding. These three are "one" and united. They provide mankind with the possibility for salvation and exaltation.[97]

Belief Understanding and accepting true doctrine (*see* 3 Nephi 7:4).[98] Belief comes after mere hope (meaning "desire") and is based upon the conviction a proposition is true. There is a difference between belief and faith and between faith and knowledge. It is a spectrum. At one end there is desire, and it is then followed by belief. By degrees this belief grows into faith, and faith can progress by degrees into knowledge. Knowledge is at the other end of the spectrum. Belief is a step toward faith. Belief can come from study and from trusting others. Belief can be very weak, or it can be a strongly held conviction.[99] In the Book of Mormon, Jacob makes a startling promise for those who live when the destruction begins preliminary to the cleansing of the world before the Lord returns. He says, *none will he destroy that believeth in him. And they that believe not in him shall be destroyed, both by fire, and by tempest, and by earthquakes, and by bloodsheds, and by pestilence, and by famine* (2 Nephi 5:5). This amazing promise is predicated on "believing in Him." This requires us to understand what the word "believe" means in the parlance of the Book of Mormon. Those who believe in Him know and accept correct doctrine — or the truth — about Him. Those who do not know and will not accept correct doctrine or the truth have dwindled in unbelief. They do not believe in Him. They may have religion, may belong to churches, may be active in all their observances, but they are not in possession of belief in Him. Instead they accept for doctrines the commandments of men and their hearts are far from Him. They teach false and vain things. As a result, they neither enter into the kingdom nor suffer those who are entering to go in. This includes those who, though they are humble followers of Christ, are nevertheless led that in many instances they do err in doctrine (*see* 2 Nephi 12:2). There will be many who are destroyed who will be quite surprised by it. They will complain that they have prophesied in Christ's name, have cast out devils in His name, and done many wonderful works, but they do not know Christ, and therefore, never did believe in Him (*see* Matthew 3:47–48). "If you are one of those who believe in Him, and who will not dwindle in unbelief, will not accept the commandments of men as doctrine, but will take the spirit for your guide, then Jacob promises that Christ will not destroy you. The rest He will destroy."[100] To believe in Him is to accept, study, contemplate, and ponder His teachings. It is not to just go along with the group, but to rise up from one's position and awaken from one's slumber. It is to grow into knowledge about Him. Belief leads to faith and faith to knowledge. But the process is initiated by one's belief and correct understanding of His teachings (see the Lectures on Faith).[101]

Bishop   From the Greek *episkopos* (ἐπίσκοπος), meaning an "overseer" (one who sees "over"); literally "looking on intently"; "one who keeps an eye on" others, the flock, the fellowship.[102] In the church organized by Joseph Smith, "the historical development of this office has been the most complex and the least understood.... Smith first appointed 'general' bishops with broad geographical jurisdiction. Only later did he introduce the possibility of local bishops for smaller geographical units [such as wards and branches] and a Presiding Bishop for the entire church. Again retrospective interpretations and changes in the historical record have muddied the story of this development."[103] Joseph Smith was church president, and Hyrum Smith was in the church presidency and also patriarch to the church, but choosing the bishop was left for the members' vote.[104] Even the duties of a bishop were decided by common consent in the beginning of the restoration.[105] The office of bishop still continues in many of the various religious groups claiming Joseph Smith as their founder.

Blessed   Enos tells us the Lord promised him, *thou shalt be blessed* (Enos 1:1). Words matter, and this statement can be read in the future tense. Enos is not promised that he *is* blessed but that in some future event or events he "shalt" be blessed.[106] If Blessed is another name given to Enos by the Lord, then here is another wonderful revelation about Enos' relationship with God. These words could be punctuated: "...thou shalt be Blessed," meaning the Lord gave to Enos the new name "Blessed" at the time of their first meeting. If so, then in the concluding verse of his record, Enos is telling us of the future time when the Lord will call him by the new name "Blessed," while assuring him of the mansion which belongs to him in the Father's kingdom.[107]

Enoch was 25 years old when he was ordained by the hand of Adam, and forty years later (when he was 65), Adam "blessed" him. Once the power came (from the "blessing"), *he saw the Lord, and he walked with him, and was before his face continually; and he walked with God three hundred sixty-five years, making him four hundred thirty years old when he was translated* (T&C 154:15). So, he is ordained (the first requirement), then he is "blessed" (the second part), which has the effect of him becoming "continually before the Lord" (the intended result of ordination). *And Enoch lived sixty-five years and begot Methuselah* (Genesis 3:25). Enoch had been ordained to the priesthood but was not a father until he was "blessed" and entered the Lord's presence.[108]

Blessings Joseph Smith linked blessings with knowledge. He linked knowledge with obedience to laws. "And if a person gains more knowledge and intelligence in this life through his diligence and obedience than another, he will have so much the advantage in the world to come. There is a law, irrevocably decreed in Heaven before the foundations of this world, upon which all blessings are predicated — and *when we obtain any blessing from God, it is by obedience to that law upon which it is predicated.*"[109] "If we want a blessing, we must find the law upon which the blessing is predicated, and then follow that law. If we do, we get the blessing. There is a majestic simplicity to this orderly procedure. It is from such an understanding Joseph authoritatively declared God was no respecter of persons. Joseph's declaration made profoundly more sense than what other religionists were teaching. Joseph made this whole process of gaining blessings through knowledge a natural one that grew out of conformity with natural law. Of course, God ordained that natural law."[110] This whole process is a gift from God. He set the bounds and terms by His grace. So if mankind elects to abide those conditions, they are entitled to receive the grace or blessing He promises. But it still remains a gift. King Benjamin explained this process of keeping commandments, receiving blessings, and remaining in God's debt in Mosiah 1:8–9. (The term "entitled" is used here to make the point that once man has done his part, God will do His. Man will not go down the road only to find it closed at the end. God keeps His promises.)[111]

Blessings of the Fathers Abraham wrote, *Finding there was greater happiness and peace and rest for me, I sought for the blessings of the fathers*

(Abraham 1:1). The blessings of the fathers he wanted to obtain was the original Holy Order. He wanted to be like the first fathers.[112]

Blood Crying for Vengeance Blood "crying from the ground" is not the same thing as a person crying out for vengeance. Keep the context in mind. It is the blood that was shed upon the earth which cries out for vengeance, fairness, or retribution. Something unfair has occurred, and the cry of the blood "upon the ground" is a reminder of the injustice of it all. The ground is a reference to the earth, which has a spirit, intelligence, and is able to communicate (if a person were capable of listening). The earth is a female spirit, and she regards herself as "the mother of men." This earth is offended when the men who are upon her kill one another or engage in any form of wickedness upon her surface. As she beheld the disorder and murder caused by that generation upon whom the flood was unleashed, she lamented: *Woe, woe is me, the mother of men. I am pained; I am weary because of the wickedness of my children. When shall I rest and be cleansed from the filthiness which is gone forth out of me? When will my Creator sanctify me, that I may rest, and righteousness for a season abide upon my face?* (Genesis 4:20). Even if the person whose blood was shed departed this earth forgiving those who made offense against him, yet would "the ground" cry out for vengeance because the earth has become filthy by reason of the killing that took place upon her. She, as the "mother of men," regards the killing of men upon her as an abomination. She cries out. She is offended. She wants righteousness to appear on her, as has happened before. She longs that it be brought about again. When, instead of Zion, she has the murder of men upon her face, it is so great a lamentation by her spirit that "the ground cries out for vengeance" because of the atrocity.[113]

Book of Mormon as Covenant Nephi's power to "seal" his writings at the command of the Lord (and his obedience to that command) make his words binding on all. They become covenantal. Hence the reference to remembering *the new covenant, even the Book of Mormon* (T&C 82:20). It is not merely interesting doctrine, nor even prophecy, but has reached covenantal status by virtue of the priestly seal placed upon it by Nephi. Mankind ignores it at their peril. It is a great loss when it is defined as just another volume of scripture. It was intended to be studied and followed as the means to reassert a covenant between man and God. By following its precepts, all can return to God's presence where they are endowed with light and truth and can receive intelligence and understanding. All are invited to make that return. Nephi lived it and, as a result, was able to teach it. All should follow his example and live it to be able to understand and then teach it. It is the doing that leads to the understanding.[114]

"If I had to say one thing will do more to bring a person into harmony with the Lord than any other thing it would be this: Take the Book of Mormon seriously. I have assumed it is an authentic and ancient text written by prophetic messengers whose words ought to be studied for how they can change any person's life. Though all the world may treat it lightly, I have tried to not do so. For that I believe the Lord's approval has been given to an otherwise foolish, vain, error-prone and weak man. Take the Book of Mormon seriously. Apply it to yourself. Not as a means to judge others, but as a means to test your own life. It is one thing to evaluate our circumstances, which the book compels us to do, but we needn't go further than to realize our terrible plight. From that moment the warning should work inside ourselves to help us improve within, see more clearly our day, think more correctly about what is going on, and act more consistent with the Lord's purposes."[115] The Book of Mormon is not merely a book of scripture. It is the preeminent volume of scripture for this day. All other volumes of scripture are vastly inferior to it. It is the covenant that mankind has been condemned for neglecting.

"It is the reason I have found Him. For above all else, I have used the Book of Mormon to direct my thoughts, actions, teachings and understanding. He is inviting us, using the text of the Book of Mormon to find Him, individually, for ourselves. This Book is the restoration of the Gospel. Unfortunately, most people have missed that. Nevertheless, it is true."[116]

Book of the Lamb of God   The New Testament.[117]

Bowels   (Greek: *splagchnon*, σπλάγχνα) Bowels or intestines (the heart, lungs, liver, etc.) and refers to the inward parts, the internal organs, viscera; the heart, affections, and the seat of the feelings, as regarded by the Hebrews as the place of the tenderer affections, i.e., kindness, benevolence, and compassion. Often translated as "tender mercies."[118] Our bowels must become like Christ's, *moved* *with compassion* (Matthew 8:3; Mark 4:2) for others. This may only be imitative at first, but after it is informed by the experience, when one has acted consistent with His laws, what begins as imitation grows within to become genuine compassion for others.[119] *See also* HARDNESS OF HEART.

Branch When the word branch is used in scripture, it should remind one of Christ's description of Himself in John 9:10. Christ compared Himself to a "true vine" to which all must connect if they are going to bear fruit. Christ inspired prophecies about a coming servant. All should be His servants. For any of His servants to produce "fruit" they must connect with Him, "the true vine." Life comes from that connection. All are preserved by Christ, nourished by His word, and the sacrament prayers ask that we *always have His spirit to be with us*. The "vine" and "fruit" refer to the "family of God." The context is about becoming a "son of God."[120]

Broken Heart - Contrite Spirit Repentance is accompanied by a broken heart and contrite spirit. "When you turn to Him and see clearly for the first time how dark your ways have been, it should break your heart. You should realize how desperately you stand in need of His grace to cover you, lift you, and heal you. You can then appreciate the great gulf between you and Him (Genesis 1:2). If you had to bear your sins into His presence it would make you burn with regret and fear (Mormon 4:6). Your own heart must break. When you behold how little you have to offer Him, your spirit becomes contrite. He offers everything. And we can contribute nothing but our cooperation. And we still reluctantly give that, or if we give a little of our own cooperation, we think we have given something significant. We have not. Indeed, we cannot (Mosiah 1:8). He honors us if He permits us to assist. We should proceed with alacrity when given the chance to serve. How patiently He has proceeded with teaching us all. We have the law, we have the commandments. Still we hesitate. Still He invites and reminds us: Repent. Come to Him. Do what was commanded. The law is fulfilled, and He is its fulfillment. Look to Him and be saved. The heart that will not break does not understand the predicament we live in. The proud spirit is foolish and blind. Our perilous state is such that we can forfeit all that we have ever been by refusing Christ's invitation to repent and turn again to Him."[121] If man will finally surrender his pride and come forward with a broken heart and real intent, returning to his Father, He will joyfully receive him (*see* Luke 9:13–14). There is joy in Heaven over everyone who awakens. Weakness is nothing, for all are weak. It is a gift, given to break one's heart. A broken heart qualifies man for His company. Whether a leper, an adulteress, a tax collector, or a blind man, He can heal it all. But what He cannot do — and man must alone bring to Him — is that broken heart required for salvation.[122] The purpose of putting a man in such a dependent state before God is not to find out whether God can take care of him. God already knows what a man needs before he should even ask. But the man will, by becoming so dependent upon God, acquire a broken heart and a contrite spirit, always quick to ask, quick to listen, quick to do. Vulnerability makes a man strong in spirit. Security and wealth make a man incorrectly believe in his independence from God. He wants His disciples to be dependent upon Him. He wants them praying and grateful to Him for what He provides. He wants them, in a word, to become holy.[123] The Book of Mormon gives account after account of encounters between mankind and God where the only qualification was a broken heart and a contrite spirit. Those who do not have the required broken heart and contrite spirit come away saying, *the Lord maketh no such thing known unto us* (1 Nephi 4:2).[124] "In the quiet service for others, when our minds finally come to rest on the only one who can save us, we can find that peace where the Lord comes to us and speaks words of comfort. He is real. He exists, and He comforts those who come to Him offering a broken heart and contrite spirit, and to none other."[125] *See also* HARDNESS OF HEART.

Call/ed/ing Service to others, which precedes being "chosen" by God.[126] In 3 Nephi 5, Christ calls Nephi by name. Being called by name by the Son of God is important! When God calls someone by name, they are not merely being addressed. In the instant the Lord calls out their name, they are "called." That is, the Lord will never speak one's name to them unless He calls them to a work. When the Lord spoke to Nephi, the Lord both called Nephi's name and called the bearer of that name to do a work. Nephi knew it. The crowd knew it. All present would have understood that Nephi just became the chief prophet of those present. Nephi knew what he had to do — for the servant who had been called to stand above his peers needed to descend below them. Pride is unthinkable when in the presence of such a meek and humble figure as our Lord. It is required that the balance be restored. Nephi, who had been made to rise, had to choose, on his own, to descend and abase himself.[127] Note that a person cannot receive an ordinance without also having their name stated. "Why do you suppose it is necessary to first call out the name of the person before they receive an ordinance? Why would the Lord's instruction require a person to be 'called' first? Though they are submitting to the ordinance voluntarily, why call their name? Does it matter if the full legal name is used? That is done in some churches, of course. But does it matter? If the Lord called Joseph by name at the time of the First Vision (and He did, *see* JSH 2:4), what name do you suppose was called? Was it 'Joseph Smith, Jr.?' Or was it 'Joseph?' Or was it that name used by his most intimate friend at the time? Whenever a name is given by an angel in an appearance to parents, the name is always the first name, or the name their friends would call them. (*See*, e.g., Luke 1:3; Luke 1:5.) Similarly, when the Lord calls a man's name, He uses his first, given name. (*See* 1 Samuel 3:8; Exodus 2:3.) The Lord does not use formal names, but uses intimate names when addressing His servants."[128]

Call upon God An invitation for God to come; not just prayer. One *calls Him* by being devoted, in humility, to living every principle He has taught through His messengers and in His scriptures. It's not a laundry list of "to-dos." It is meekness and prayerful watching, humbling oneself and accepting what His spirit will advise you to do. When He testifies that a principle is true, one should accept it, no matter the effect it may have upon one's life.[129] Look for God alone to provide guidance and understanding. "Change your life, but never abandon His truths. Call, listen, and obey what you are told. Never close that line of communication. Don't trust a message that does not come from Him."[130] *See* CRY UNTO THE LORD.

Calling and Election "After a person has faith in Christ, repents of his sins, is baptized for the remission of his sins, and receives the Holy Ghost (by the laying on of hands), which is the first Comforter, then let him continue to humble himself before God, hungering and thirsting after righteousness and living by every word of God.

The Lord will soon say unto him, 'Son, thou shalt be exalted.' When the Lord has thoroughly proved him and finds that the man is determined to serve him at all hazards, then the man will find his calling and election made sure, then it will be his privilege to receive the other Comforter, which the Lord hath promised the Saints, as is recorded in the testimony of St. John [KJV], in the 14th chapter, from the 12th to the 27th verses" (*TPJS*, 150; *WJS*, 5; *see* John 9:7–9). "I've not said much about Calling and Election. I think focusing on that topic is a mistake. It will take care of itself if you can get the Second Comforter."[131] Joseph Smith said: "1st key: Knowledge is the power of salvation. 2nd key: Make your calling and election sure. 3rd key: It is one thing to be on the mount and hear the excellent voice, etc., and another to hear the voice declare to you, *You have a part and lot in that kingdom*."[132] Nephi speaks again with the Father's words: *Wherefore, if ye shall press forward, feasting upon the word of Christ, and endure to the end, behold, thus saith the Father: Ye shall have eternal life* (2 Nephi 13:4). This is the purpose of receiving the Second Comforter. Christ's objective, as a tutor, is to bring His followers to the Father. It is the voice of the Father which finally declares to His children they are assured Eternal life.[133] When the Lord promises a blessing, it is always tied to faithfulness and obedience.[134] Even when promises are unconditional, such as in having one's calling and election made sure, years of faithfulness precede the promise. The promise is premised on the continuation of faithfulness. And no one is relieved of the necessity of enduring to the end, even when their calling and election is made sure.[135] The highest form of acceptance and redemption is to have one's calling and election made sure, to be washed and cleansed from sin every whit.[136]

Cast Out   Even if you know someone has violated the commandment, *ye shall not cast him out from among you* (3 Nephi 8:9). Instead, the Lord places on His disciples the burden of making intercession for him, praying *unto the Father in [Christ's] name* for such a man. For the Lord reminds us that, *if it so be that he repenteth and is baptized in [His] name* then the man's repentance will take care of his failure. Notice the burden on His disciples. What does it mean to *minister unto him* who has transgressed? What does it mean to *pray for him unto the Father*? This again testifies of how serious the Lord is about how kind and patient His followers are with others. "How long are you to bear with the offender, hoping for his repentance? When do you decide that he is determined to *repent not*? What does it mean, after you have determined the man will not repent that *he shall not be numbered among my people*? Now, even if you think you have a basis for deciding all this against the man, *nevertheless, ye shall not cast him out of your synagogues, or your places of worship.* Did you see that? We are not to forbid even the man who is intent upon destroying the Lord's people from our places of worship. What selfless behavior is this? Enduring persecution! It is as if the Lord expects His followers to bless those who curse them, to do good to them who despitefully use them. Why such patience? Because *ye know not but what they will return and repent and come unto me with full purpose of heart, and I shall heal them, and ye shall be the means of bringing salvation unto them.* If there is a chance for repentance, the Lord wants us to bear with, succor and uplift the non-repentant soul who drinks damnation."[137]

The question then arises about "what a fellowship should do when a predator or threatening individual comes among them. Apparently some people think that you must allow anyone to participate, no matter how argumentative or threatening they behave. The adulterous and predatory almost always cannot be reformed, and must be excluded. They will victimize and destroy. We are commanded to cast out those who steal, love and make a lie, commit adultery and refuse to repent. We have been instructed: *You shall not kill; he that kills shall die. You shall not steal, and he that steals and will not repent **shall be cast out**. You shall not lie; he that lies and will not repent **shall be cast out**. You shall love your wife with all your heart and shall cleave unto her and none else, and he that looks upon a woman to lust after her shall deny the faith, and shall not have the Spirit, and if he repent not he **shall be cast out**. You shall not commit adultery, and he that commits adultery and repents not **shall be cast out**; and he that commits adultery and repents with all his heart, and forsakes and does it no more, you shall forgive him; but if he does it again, he shall not be forgiven, but **shall be cast out**. You shall not speak evil of your neighbor or do him any harm. You know my laws, they are given in my scriptures. He that sins and repents not **shall be cast out**. If you love me, you shall serve me and keep **all my commandments*** (T&C 26:8, emphasis added). This is still binding. If your fellowship includes those who ought to be 'cast out' you have the obligation to do so rather than encouraging evil by tolerating it. Be patient, but be firm. If a person refuses to repent and forsake sins, end fellowship with them and invite penitent others who are interested in practicing obedience and love. Christ's gospel is not impractical. It is designed to give those who seek righteousness to be able to achieve it. Tolerance and compassion are needed. But tolerance and compassion do not include acceptance of sin. Particularly the sins listed in the above revelation. One should not go out of his or her way to uncover the sins of others. But if they wear their sins openly, you have an obligation to 'cast them out'"("Predators," March 6, 2019, blog post).

Casting Pearls Before Swine The improper disclosure of sacred knowledge; profaning sacred knowledge by disclosing it to the unprepared or unworthy. One gains the Lord's confidence by showing the Lord he is willing to keep the things which are sacred as holy things before Him.[138] "And so it is with [sacred] things. They can be learned, but they cannot be taught. Those who are willing to receive them, however, will receive them. But only when they are prepared to respect the limits which should always separate the sacred from the profane. Putting jewelry on pigs is no more appropriate today than it was when Christ advised against it. When entrusted with sacred things, you must respect them. If you cannot respect their sacred nature, you are not a candidate to receive them.... Honor the type, and you prove you will honor the reality. Dishonor the type, and you prove you are not worthy of the reality. God will not be mocked in large measure by keeping the mockers away from His presence. The nature of their forfeiture is far greater, and takes place far earlier than they suspect. They forfeit here and now the chance to receive the Second Comforter. If you fail to respect a covenant made with God to keep...knowledge sacred and apart from the world, then you cannot hope to receive sacred knowledge from God through revelation and visitations."[139] Joseph Smith said: "The reason we do not have the secrets of the Lord revealed unto us, is because we do not keep them but reveal them; we do not keep our own secrets, but reveal our difficulties to the world, even to our enemies, then how would we keep the secrets of the Lord?" (*DHC* 4:479; *TPJS*, 195; *WJS*, 81). Elsewhere Joseph admonished: "If

God gives you a manifestation; keep it to yourselves" (DHC 2:309; TPJS, 91). The Second Comforter is for one's individual comfort and instruction. Not for public display or to gratify one's pride or serve one's vain ambition. Sacred things tend to lose their luster as they are profaned by being made common. Just as the white snow tends to stain the longer it is trodden underfoot by men, so also does the purity of revelation become denigrated by being revealed without regard to the audience's preparation and worthiness to learn of sacred things. This is a binding limitation and an essential part of the process. To be qualified, one must be someone who can be trusted to keep sacred things sacred.[140] "Of course, when required to testify of something by the Lord, the Lord's insistence upon that testimony always takes precedence. The general rule is you keep them to yourself. The exception is when the Lord constrains you to do otherwise."[141]

Cephas A name which is, by interpretation, a seer or a stone.[142] When Christ gave Simon a new name, it was the Aramaic *kēpā* which, when translated into the Greek Πέτρος (*Petros*), is also defined as rock or stone.

Ceremony of Recognition In 3 Nephi 5:5–6, the Nephites were asked to perform a ceremony of recognition and witnessing. They first felt His side. To do this they embraced the Lord, for they could not feel His side without embracing Him. Embracing Him is an essential part of the ceremony of recognition. Ceremony and holiness are connected with each other. All encounters with God are, in one way or another, a ceremony. Having embraced the Lord and felt His side, the witnesses were asked to take a step back and feel His hands. Feeling the Lord's hands is also a part of this ceremonial process. At an arm's length, holding His hands, they felt the marks of the nails. Then, having touched these sacred emblems of the atonement, they were permitted to kneel and feel the prints in His feet. This part of the ceremony is the easiest for men to observe. For kneeling at His feet is the natural position for anyone who has witnessed for themselves the price He paid on their behalf and feels the love within Him. This is ceremony, and this is ritual, but it employs such rich witnesses in the body of the Lord as to be convincing beyond all doubt that He is the Christ, the Anointed One, the Deliverer, and the Holy One of Israel![143] *See also* SACRED EMBRACE.

Chains of Hell *And they that will harden their hearts, to them is given the lesser portion of the word until they know nothing concerning his mysteries; and then they are taken captive by the Devil and led by his will down to destruction. Now this is what is meant by the chains of hell* (Alma 9:3).[144] *See also* TAKEN CAPTIVE BY THE DEVIL.

Charity The *pure love of Christ* (Moroni 7:9). The Apostle Paul elevated charity (the pure love of Christ) to such high importance that salvation itself depends upon a person's charity (*see* 1 Corinthians 1:51).[145] It is through grace that one obtains charity. It is through charity that one can bless others. One cannot bless anyone or hold priesthood designed to bless, not curse, unless they have charity. This is never given unless the recipient is willing to do things he would rather not, thereby offering himself as a sacrifice to God. No one is trusted by God to hold this honor unless he will subordinate his will to the will of the Father.[146] Charity cannot be manufactured, but only bestowed, and Moroni directs us to *pray unto the Father with all the energy of heart that ye may be filled with this love, which he hath bestowed upon all who are true followers of his Son Jesus Christ* (Moroni 7:9).

Charity is sometimes viewed as an emotional or deeply-felt connection that seems unattainable with a stranger but something that is capable to be done for your wife, husband, children, or your parents—someone with whom you are intimately connected. But it doesn't appear, from the example of Christ, that His willingness to die on behalf of others meant that He had to feel emotionally connected with them in order to do so. He forgave the Romans that were nailing Him to the cross—this was not the traditional definition of love. Instead, it was a commitment—a determination—to do good despite the opposition or hindrance of anyone else. The very people He went into the temple and provoked with His *Woe unto you, scribes and Pharisees* (Matthew 10) discourse (deliberately controlling the timing of their outrage so that He would be sacrificed at the appropriate time during the Passover), were the same people on whose behalf He also died. He was committed to giving His life to others as an act of charity, as an act of service, and as an act of kindness in a way that demonstrates what charity really is. Charity is a fixed determination to do something on the behalf of others. Whether they appreciate it, whether they love you in return or not, charity is simply doing what needs to be done. The mistreatment that Nephi received at the hands of his older brothers did not change whether or not he had charity towards his older brothers, even though he knew that (for the safety of his own wife, children, offspring, and compadres) he needed to separate from his brothers. Nephi only ever had charity for them.

Charity is a determination to live a certain way and to not allow oneself to be overcome by the jealousies, envies, and all the negative things that make it so easy to excuse giving kindness to others. In a very real sense, charity is trying to see others in the same way that the Father sees them — even if that generosity is not reciprocated; even if they despise and abuse; even if they speak all manner of evil against one falsely. Living the kind of life that has charity, the pure love of Christ — in it is a determination; a vigor; a resolution; a firm, fixed determination to abide a certain standard, being committed to the wellbeing of one's fellow man — even if one's fellow man is not committed at all in a reciprocal way. Do it for the sake of righteousness. Don't do it for the sake of recognition. Recognition rarely comes, except maybe posthumously, to the truly charitable. It's an approach and a value that one assigns to the lives of others that allows one to do good to them even if they refuse to do good back. It's the only way that one can ever eradicate the kind of jealousies, envies, and strife that produce war, conflict, and injured feelings. The world is plagued by the absence of charity, and the best evidence of that is the presence of conflict, fighting, and hurt feelings.

"If I have charity towards someone who despises and abuses me, then their attitude towards me is irrelevant. Even if they want to spend time berating me, I don't waste any time either considering or being motivated by that. I'm motivated by something else. Blessed are the peacemakers. Well, why are they peacemakers? Because they are willing to charitably proceed in a world that is riddled with conflict. There's no room for envy in the charitable approach. It's not puffed up; it's not seeking its own. It's really trying to please God and serve Him. And not to serve himself. It is the greatest, because if we had charity, we could live in peace with one another. Even if we have any number of unresolved issues that exist between one another, we can still live in peace with one another. Even if we absolutely disagree on a number of issues we think are fundamental, we could still live in peace with one another, if we had charity.

"Joseph Smith once remarked that the problem with councils and conferences is that we wouldn't agree to hold our disagreements long enough in order to reach a proper resolution. We have to be willing to allow for differences as we search for the solution. Sometimes the solution requires years of differing opinions, differing viewpoints, differing ways of approaching things. That's not evil. It's only evil when we allow that to crowd our hearts in such a way that we begin to envy and be jealous and be resentful and be hateful and to have our pride injured. If we are charitable, then we look upon the things we think are the shortcomings of someone else in a way that is tolerant and kindly. We think Zion is going to be the great, peaceful community, and it surely will be. But that doesn't mean that the residents aren't going to have differing opinions.

"Art, literature, great thought, very often...music, all the creative impulses very often are stimulated by a conflict that the person who is doing the creating is grappling with. Zion may not be a place in which there is the absence of potential for conflict, but it will be a place where the potential for conflict is resisted because of the charitable impulse to abide peaceably with one another while we work on the things that separate us, that make us different. Our differences aren't evil. Our differences are something to be considered, thought about, to be explored, to be understood. Because charity is the peaceful means of dealing with these diverse ways of understanding life, of understanding why we're here, what we're trying to do, of understanding how we can be kindly towards one another. Sometimes, the kindest thing is a rebuke. Sometimes the kindest thing, in turn, is to carefully consider the rebuke, to not open your mouth in return, to think deeply about what was said and why it was said and to allow the possibility that the person who expressed the rebuke did so out of love, out of kindness, out of their concern for you. Sometimes that rebuke is based on a wealth of misinformation and misunderstanding. So, instead of returning with another rebuke, telling the rebuker how stupid they are because they don't understand things, think about why they have their understanding and what can be done to overcome the gap between you and someone else. Zion is going to be, above all other things, a place that necessarily demands that people be charitable towards one another and kindly disposed to dealing with the misunderstandings, the differences of opinion, the different educational backgrounds, the different life experience backgrounds that make for different opinions and different viewpoints. All of them are valuable, assuming you will charitably allow people to be where they are and to help you understand them in their context, while they are kind enough to try and understand you in your context."[147] *See also* LOVE.

Cherubim One of the fixed classes of the Powers of Heaven.[148] In the Bible, a cherub is described as a winged Heavenly being or angel that is placed by God to guard the way of the tree of life. *So I drove out the man and I placed at the east of the Garden of Eden cherubim and a flaming sword which turned every way to keep the way of the tree of life* (Genesis 2:19). The image of a flaming sword and the cherubim go together (*kherev* or *chereb* means sword). The Hebrew word *kərūv* (כְּרוּב, pl. *kərūvîm* כְּרוּבִים) is said to be borrowed from the Assyrian *kirubu*, "to be near" or "to bless" or "to be great or mighty," hence the possibility to describe these as mighty, near ones, who surround and bless God.[149] In the holy of holies of Solomon's temple, symbolic cherubim, comprising huge creatures, were placed over the ark of the covenant and spread their wings, which formed the golden throne where the Lord was enthroned: *You that dwell between the cherubim, shine forth* (Psalms 80:1).

Children of God For the redeemed are the children of God, and He dwells in them (*see* 1 John 1:18).[150] Christ taught and lived this: *And blessed are all the peacemakers, for they shall be called the children of God* (Matthew 3:12).[151]

Children of the Prophets When one has accepted, believed, and followed the Lord's true messengers, they become the children of Abraham and receive priestly authority sealing them into the family of God; joining the "fathers." From the time of Abraham until today, all who are redeemed have become a part of Abraham's household.[152] *See also* SEED OF ABRAHAM.

Chosen/Chosen People When God begins to work with a people, the group becomes "chosen" and, therefore, the focus of His continuing efforts to save mankind. Although "chosen people" do not always remain faithful to Him, they do remain the center of His work.[153] When a people are "chosen" by the Lord, He generally endows them with specific gifts or blessings. Whether they are ancient or modern, in the Old World or New, they are almost always given a specific set of gifts as part of a covenant. These covenant-based gifts generally include the following, in no particular order: a promised land, self-government, sacred space with sacred artifacts, angelic visitors, "signs" of His presence, sacred records which expand through a growing body of revelation, and ordinances.[154]

What about the question of *chosenness* of the Gods' special people? Israel was, after all, at one point chosen by the Gods as Their special people. But that does not mean what most people think it means. Being chosen means someone/some people are put on display as either the faithful servant (elevating others) or the unwise steward (who is condemned, beaten with a rod, and made the display of Divine ire).[155] "Chosenness does not mean what we oftentimes think chosenness means. We tend to view that as something laudable, and it means that we're better than someone else because God's focused attention on us, and therefore, since we get his attention, there is something great about us.... If you go through and read the scriptures about the concept of chosenness, almost always you run into words about forging in a fire the product that God regards as His people, which means that God has a fairly realistic assessment of what people are like, and choosing them doesn't mean He's found a finished product. Choosing them means He's found something with which He's determined to work. High carbon steel requires iron, and it requires a matrix of that carbon to be within the element. Life—all life—is based on carbon. We breathe oxygen. We are carbon based, all of us. In a very real sense, every breath we take, we take and burn it in our furnace. The way that we convey that oxygen throughout the body is by oxidizing iron in our blood. That's why our blood cells turn red when exposed to oxygen, because the iron element fused with the oxygen oxidizes, or rusts, and so it looks red. And then, when it drops the oxygen off where it's going to be consumed in the limbs, it loses that element, and it returns, and it's blue. Forging us in the fire of affliction, breathing into us the breath of life, talking about being chosen, the example of what it takes in order to fashion something that will withstand and hold an edge, all of these things are types and shadows of what it means to be chosen. Chosenness puts you on display in order for the Lord to either prove what foolishness is in the person chosen, or if they succeed, to put them through an ordeal that demonstrates faithfulness and commitment, desire, and earnestness, so that everyone stands back and says: This people represented God, either by the shabby performance and the persecution and the failure and the folly; or it represents God by the diligence and the effort and the faithfulness.... Within every group of chosen people there are always those who are resilient and faithful enough to pass the test, to hold the edge, to survive when the difficulties come. And when the Lord puts us through the furnace of affliction, our burdens are designed to get us to be able to qualify. Our burdens are designed to make us a little more realistic about our own limitations."[156] When the Lord came to Bountiful, why were the twenty-five hundred witnesses of Christ chosen (*see* 3 Nephi 5)? The answer is they were where they should be (in Bountiful, near a surviving temple), doing what they should be doing (preparing to celebrate the year-end festivals). They chose themselves by doing what they should be doing, where they should be doing it. It is not the Lord who makes arbitrary choices. It is His children who elect to be and do what they are asked and thereby, qualify themselves. All are alike to God. But some abide the conditions, and the rest do not. Anyone could abide the conditions. Only a few decide to do so. Those who do are self-selecting themselves to receive the things being offered to all.[157] *See also* COVENANT.

Chosen Vessel Anyone and everyone to whom Christ ministers as the Second Comforter, as well as anyone who has received a visit from an angelic messenger.[158] Angels minister to "chosen vessels" or mortal messengers, as the Three Nephites did with Mormon and Moroni. These vessels then testify and bear testimony so that the way is prepared *that the residue of men may have faith in Christ* (Moroni 7:6).[159]

Christian *And if ye do always remember me, ye shall have my Spirit to be with you* (3 Nephi 8:6). The prayer pronounced upon the sacrament reflects these same aspirations. However, this is not a petition in prayer, but a promise from the Lord. He affirms that for those who have "repented" of their sins and "are baptized" in His name, He promises a result. When, having done as He has asked, a person remembers His blood through this ordinance, bearing in mind that it was shed *for you*, then one can properly *witness unto the Father*. The witness one makes to the Father by this remembrance is that *ye do always remember Christ*. This memorial before the Father, when done correctly, results in the promise of Christ that *ye shall always have His spirit to be with you*. This is a covenant. This is the Lord promising. His word cannot fail. He is establishing the means by which one can have, as his guide and companion, His spirit. His light. His presence in one's life. This is more intimate than touching His side, hands, and feet. This is to have His spirit within one's touch at all times. The believer becomes an extension of Him, properly taking His name upon him. For he is then, indeed, a Christian. He will christen or anoint him, not with the symbol of oil, but with the reality of His spirit. This anointing is the real thing, of which the oil was meant only to testify. The Greek word *chrió* (χρίω) means to anoint and is from where the title Christ and the appellation "Christian" originates (*Christos*), meaning "the anointed one." The holy ghost was intended to become a companion at the time of baptism. The spirit of Christ is intended to become a companion in the believer's very person, as well. When there are two members of the Godhead represented in a living person, then it is the Father who receives this testimony of him, about him, by him, and for him. He becomes His, for these three are one. There is more going on here than an ordinance and a testimony. This is the means by which a link is formed that can and will result in the Father taking that which is corruptible and changing it into that which is incorruptible. Though, like Christ, a man or woman may be required to lay down their life, they shall have power given them to take it up again. For that which has been touched by the incorruptible power of His spirit cannot be left without hope in the grave. All such people die firm in the knowledge they are promised a glorious resurrection. This, then, is eternal life.[160]

Church The Lord defines His church as: *whosoever is…baptized unto repentance* (Mosiah 11:21). More clearly, in this day He has said, *Behold,* *this is my doctrine — whosoever repenteth and cometh unto me, the same is my church* (JSH 10:21).[161] The Lord's church means those who repent and are baptized in His name.[162] The word "church" comes from the Greek word *ekklēsia* (ἐκκλησία), meaning an "assembly" or a "calling out or forth," used throughout the Old and New Covenants. It is a group of people gathered together, not necessarily as a formal institution or organization.[163] The modern word is derived from "the Old English *cirice, circe,* 'place of assemblage set aside for Christian worship; the body of Christian believers, Christians collectively; ecclesiastical authority or power,' from the Proto-Germanic *kirika* (Dutch *kerk*, German *Kirche*), which is probably borrowed via an unrecorded Gothic word from Greek *kyriake (oikia), kyriakon doma* 'the Lord's (house),' from *kyrios* 'ruler, lord.' The Greek *kyriakon* (adj.) 'of the Lord' was used of houses of Christian worship since c. 300, especially in the East, though it was less common in this sense than *ekklesia* or *basilike*."[164]

The original development under Joseph Smith was something quite distinct from all existing faiths. It was not just a new religion. It was a wholesale resurrection of an ancient concept of "Peoplehood." It was radical. Its purpose was to change diverse assortments of people, from every culture and faith, with every kind of ethnic and racial composition, into a new kind of People. They were to be united under the banner of a New and Everlasting Covenant, resurrecting the ancient Hebraic notion of nationhood and Peoplehood. No matter what their former culture was, they were adopted inside a new family, a covenant family. Status was defined not by virtue of what one believed or confessed, but instead by what covenants they had assumed. What returned through Joseph Smith was not a religion, nor an institution, nor merely a faith. It was, instead, the radical notion that an ancient covenant family was being regathered into a separate People. This return to ancient roots brought with it, as the hallmark of its source of power, the idea of renewed covenants that brought each individual into a direct contract with God. It did not matter what they believed. It only mattered that they accepted and took upon them the covenant. Reconciliation between what Joseph Smith restored and other religions should never have been a goal. Joseph's restoration was not a church. It was not a religion.

It was not a bundle of beliefs. The original Restoration could never be like any other mainstream Christian faith. They were churches. Joseph restored Peoplehood. "To go from what Joseph restored to a common footing with other contemporary Christian faiths requires us to first abandon the concept that we are neither a new form of Christianity nor a return to Jewish antecedents. We are something quite different from either. We are a Hebraic resurrection of God's People, clothed with a covenant, and engaged in a direct relationship with God that makes us distinct from all other people."[165] *See also* SYNAGOGUE; GREAT and ABOMINABLE CHURCH.

Church of the Firstborn Those who have been adopted into the Family of God and are part of the hosts of heaven. This requires a sealing ordinance and covenant.[166]

Church of the Lamb Those who are Christ's and for whom His blood covers their sins and transgressions. They are like those who were spared by the destroying angel during the Passover because of the lamb's blood on the doorposts and lintel. They are spared from condemnation.[167] *See also* "Lamb of God" under NAMES OF GOD IN SCRIPTURE.

Coat of Many Colors "The idea of a garment of many colors is an invention. It's not a garment of many colors at all. A garment of certain marks is the term that should be used. This garment had belonged to Abraham, and it already had a long history. Its history was lengthy because it went back to the Garden of Eden. That's the garment; it's the only one. Just as we treat the story of Cain and Abel, we trivialize this. We say, 'Joseph was the youngest kid, so his father favored him and gave him a pretty garment of many colors.' There is no mention in any ancient source of a garment of many colors. That's an invention of modern editors trying to explain it. But here it was the garment he gave him. It was the garment of the priesthood. No wonder they were jealous of him, they being the elder brothers and he the younger in the patriarchal line coming down from Abraham. This garment had belonged to Abraham and had come down to Joseph instead of to the other brethren."[168] They stripped him of his sacred garment — not of many colors, but of sacred markings. Having stripped him of the garment that belonged to the heir and assured him of his exaltation, they cast him into a pit without water.[169]

Comforter, The There are two Comforters. The first is the holy ghost. Christ promised His followers He would send a "Comforter" to them. He said, *If you love me, keep my commandments. And I will ask the Father, and he shall give you another Comforter, that he may be with you for ever – even the Spirit of Truth, whom the world cannot receive because it sees him not, neither knows him. But you know him, for he dwells with you, and shall be in you* (John 9:8). The promise about the Comforter is preceded and followed by two important conditions. It is preceded with the statement: *If you love me, keep my commandments*. There is a direct and unavoidable connection between the Comforter and the scriptural requirements to both love the Lord and keep His commandments. One cannot love Him and reject His commandments. More importantly, He cannot send this Comforter if one disregards, disobeys, or neglects His commandments. It is through obedience to the commandments that the Comforter (holy ghost) is obtained. If one is not prepared to obey His commandments, it is not possible to receive these two Comforters.[170] *See also* COMFORTER, THE SECOND.

Comforter, The Second The return to Christ's presence. The term comes from Christ's reference to "another Comforter" in John 9:8. The concept involves Christ appearing to His disciples, as well as His ministry. The holy ghost has a ministry to bring a believer to receive angels and then to Christ. Christ, in turn, has a ministry to take the faithful servant and bring him to the Father.[171] "Now what is this other Comforter? It is no more nor less than the Lord Jesus Christ himself.... When any man obtains this last Comforter he will have the personage of Jesus Christ to attend him or appear unto him from time to time" (*TPJS*, 150–151; *WJS*, 5). *John 14:23 [KJV; see also John 9:8]—The appearing of the Father and the Son, in that verse, is a personal appearance; and the idea that the Father and the Son dwell in a man's heart is an old sectarian notion, and is false.*[172] The ministry of the Second Comforter is to bring those to whom He ministers to the Father and have them accepted by Him. This means that the Father accepts them as a member of the Heavenly Family, or in other words, promises them exaltation. The end of the Lord's ministry is to have the person accepted by the Father as a son or daughter of God.[173]

"Receiving the Second Comforter means you will meet Christ. You will know, without a doubt, He exists. You will know, through Him, the atonement has been provided and the scriptures that testify of Him are true. You will no longer have faith in the existence of God nor in your standing before Him but will have knowledge."[174] Receiving an audience with the Second Comforter is the fullness of the Gospel of Jesus Christ.[175]

"The question was asked as to whether receiving the Second Comforter is necessary before you die, or if the afterlife supplies an adequate substitute. This requires the evaluation of two separate concepts. First, the Second Comforter means a visit or personal appearance to someone by Christ. However, the appearance is not as important as the ministry of the Lord. He 'comforts' those to whom He appears. He will *not leave you comfortless, [he] will come to you* (John 9:8). Christ and His Father will *make [their] abode with [you]* (John 9:8), meaning that the Son will bring you to the Father, and the Father will receive you as His son. This appearance is not merely 'in the heart,' but is an actual appearance or visit."[176] However, the purpose of the ministry, the reason for the "abode," the "comfort" that is promised by the Lord, involves the promise of eternal life. The promise of eternal life has been made an equivalency by the Lord in a revelation given in modern times. That is, the end or result of the ministry of Christ as the Second Comforter is to have the promise of eternal life. In a modern revelation the word of the Lord was given to a group of Latter-day Saints in which the promise of their exaltation was extended to them, and the Lord made this the equivalent to "another Comforter." Here is what was said: *Wherefore, I now send upon you another Comforter, even upon you my friends, that it may abide in your hearts, even the Holy Spirit of Promise, which other Comforter is the same that I promised unto my disciples, as is recorded in the testimony of John. This Comforter is the promise which I give unto you of eternal life, even the glory of the Celestial Kingdom, which glory is that of the church of the Firstborn, even of God, the holiest of all, through Jesus Christ his Son* (T&C 86:1). "Therefore, as a singular appearance, should the Lord appear to you, you have received the Second Comforter. However, His ministry is to bring you to the point at which you can receive the promise of eternal life, membership in the Church of the Firstborn, and the promise of the Celestial Kingdom as your eternal inheritance. In the fullest sense, therefore, the final promise of exaltation in the Celestial Kingdom can also be called the Second Comforter, since that is the result of His taking up His abode with you. The second concept is really a question: Would it be preferable to have the promise of eternal life now than to die uncertain as to your eternal state? If so, then why would you waste your life now in hopes that some other opportunity may exist at some other stage? If the answer to these questions are 'yes,' then the original question is simply unimportant. Why wait? The opportunity given to you now should not be forfeited, nor should the work be delayed. Don't dismiss the Lord's offered assistance for what you can achieve in mortality for the possibility of something in the after-life."[177] The reason Christ calls Himself the "Comforter" is because when He comes, the recipient will need comfort. He or she will pass through distresses, sorrows, and difficulties at first, and then He will provide comfort.[178] *See also* COMFORTER, THE.

Commandment Usually defined in the Bible from *mitzvâh* (מִצְוָה) in the Old Covenants[179] and *entolé* (ἐντολή) in the New Covenants as "an order, command(ment), charge, precept, injunction."[180] The Lord, in the Gospel of John, says, *If you love me, keep my commandments* (John 9:8). Modern revelation clarifies that a *commandment* is a *communication* that is sent by God. *If you love me, stand ready, watching for every communication I will send to you.... He that treasures my teaching, and stands ready, watching for every communication I send him, is he who shows love for me.... If a man loves me, he will stand ready, watching for every communication I will send him* (Testimony of St. John 10:11–12). As in the case of Adam and Eve who partook of the fruit "out of season," mankind is commanded *not* to partake of some things out of season. Then they *are* commanded to partake within season. "That which is wrong under one circumstance, may be, and often is, right under another. God said, *Thou shalt not kill;* at another time He said, *Thou shalt utterly destroy.* This is the principle on which the government of Heaven is conducted — by revelation adapted to the circumstances in which the children of the kingdom are placed. Whatever God requires is right, no matter what it is, although we may not see the reason thereof till long after the events transpire" (*TPJS*, 256).

When man gets the timing wrong, he winds up with difficulties and problems he should not have encountered.[181] "You can gain a command of many skills in this life by study and formal education. You can acquire wealth by effort and care. Skills in sport come from practice and good coaching. But an increase in light and truth is acquired through keeping the commandments and in no other way. Light and truth do not come by study alone, nor by effort, practice, coaching, or tutoring. Light and truth come to you from above, as you keep the commandments in your life. You must obey to obtain. The commandments are a revelation to you of God's nature. By keeping them, you obtain from God light and truth as a by-product of obedience to them. They reveal to you, in a very personal way, what the mind of God is for your life. It is intensely personal because it is all internal. You cannot measure, count, or tally it. You must become something new through this process."[182] Christ defined Himself as the fulfillment of God's commandments. When introducing Himself to the Nephites He explained, *Behold, I am the light and the life of the world; and I have drank out of that bitter cup which the Father hath given me, and have glorified the Father in taking upon me the sins of the world, in the which I have suffered the will of the Father in all things from the beginning* (3 Nephi 5:4). He is glorious and worthy of worship, possessing Powers, Principalities, Dominions, Kingdoms, and Thrones because He did what the Father commanded Him to do. The effect of obeying the Father was to fill Him with light and truth. By doing what the Father commands, anyone can qualify to receive the same things. Christ was unique in that He alone has done it perfectly. Because of Him, however, anyone can do it imperfectly and be forgiven of their sins and errors. His perfection in this undertaking allows all to become a perfect similarity, through His atonement. There is no magic, though. There is nothing given without effort. Christ paid the price to allow us to repent. But it is up to each person to choose for themselves the amount of truth and light they are willing to receive. The light and truth one is willing to receive is dependent upon his obedience. "How much light and truth are you willing to receive?"[183] Christ says: *I give unto you these sayings that you may understand and know how to worship, and know what you worship, that you may come unto the Father in my name, and in due time receive of his fullness* (T&C 93:7). So Christ gives men these sayings to teach them "how to worship." This is no idle statement. In this is the essence of what everyone must do to worship the Father. Worship Him by keeping His commandments. Keep His commandments to follow the example of His Son. That example allows men to go from grace to grace. Eventually, having grown from grace to grace by keeping His commandments, everyone can receive a fullness. *For if you keep my commandments you shall receive of his fullness and be glorified in me as I am glorified in the Father. Therefore, I say unto you, you shall receive grace for grace* (T&C 93:7). Keeping commandments is not keeping statistics. Nor is it to attract notice from others. It is not to finish some checklist of questions in an interview. It has a deeper meaning and serves a much higher purpose. "Would you like to proceed from a lesser to a greater degree of grace? Would you like to receive a fullness of what God offers to mankind in mortality? Then you must worship the Father in this way. He wants you to worship Him by keeping the commandments and growing thereby in light and truth and grace. *And no man receives a fullness unless he keeps his commandments. He that keeps his commandments receives truth and light until he is glorified in truth and knows all things* (T&C 93:9)."[184]

"There is an opposition to getting there. All must face an adversary who is committed to keeping them from receiving light and truth. He knows very well how this process works. Unlike you, he has no doubts about this process. So the adversary directs his efforts to keep men from closing the distance between themselves and God. Interestingly, his role in this process is described with perfect clarity in the scriptures as well: *And that wicked one comes and takes away light and truth, through disobedience, from the children of men, and because of the tradition of their fathers* (T&C 93:11). The Adversary is trying to keep you from gaining light and truth. He understands how to do that: Get you to disobey the commandments. You think you are just struggling with a problem or weakness. You think you are having some temptation that drives you to distraction. The criticism, complaint, or weakness you have that challenges your faith is not that at all. It is your enemy working on taking light and truth away from you. This is the balance in which you find yourself. Choose the light."[185]

Mortal men desire a list of "commandments" to keep; many people are sincerely trying to keep the commandments but lack a comprehensive list of them. It is not possible to list all commandments. In one sense, there are only two: Love God. Love your fellow man. All others are extensions of those. "If you love God you will do what He asks of you. Whenever something comes to your attention He would have you do, you do it. For example, Christ was baptized and said to 'Follow Him.' So because of your love of God, you follow Him. But Christ also showed, repeatedly, that the second commandment was greater than the rules. Keeping the Sabbath day holy, for example, was subordinate to loving and freeing His fellow man. He freed men from sin on the Sabbath by forgiving sins. He freed them from physical injury or disease by healing on the Sabbath. Both were considered work and, therefore, an offense to the commandment to keep the Sabbath day holy. At some point you will find that individual service and obedience to God's will for you will create disharmony between you and others. It can't be avoided. If you're following Christ, you will find the same things He found. Helping someone in need will take you away from church meetings on occasion. You can't make a list and keep it, because as soon as you do, the list will interfere with loving God and loving your fellow man. So the whole matter can be reduced to this: Follow Christ, receive the ordinances, accept the holy ghost, who will teach you all things you must do. Any list beyond that will inevitably result in conflicts and contradictions."[186] Commandments are given to teach men and women how they can continue to receive and renew a continuing conversion to Christ's way of life. Commandments are not a burden to bear, but a roadmap to follow. They are not a measuring stick to judge and then abuse others. It is a light for man to follow.[187] Commandments are often the things that produce condemnation. Encouragement and invitation are almost always the things that produce blessing. [188]

Common Consent A principle of decision-making where all participants in a particular group (e.g., a fellowship or conference) are eligible to either affirm or reject an action or proposal; such action can be sought after with either a majority or a unanimous vote. The word consent is used "in cases where power, rights, and claims are concerned. We give *consent* when we yield that which we have a right to withhold; but we do not give *consent* to a mere opinion, or abstract proposition."[189] The early church (established in 1830) governed themselves by common consent, with no man dictating to them. Equality prevailed, and authority was disbursed into equal and independent groups that prevented autocratic rule and guarded against apostasy of the whole body.[190] They conducted all of their business in conferences. Someone would be elected (by common consent) to preside at the conference and to conduct the business. If Joseph Smith was present, it was common for the saints to elect him, but they could have elected anyone. Business could be introduced by anyone, which could include complaints, suggestions, and discipline. The purpose of conferences was to take care of the business and to make sure that the community was cohesive and that issues were dealt with.[191] Although both Joseph Smith and Oliver Cowdery had the priesthood conferred on them by the voice of God, they only obtained an office in the church by common consent from the body of the church.[192] Even when the founding prophet was in direct communication with the Lord, the church body still retained the final control through common consent: *And all things shall be done by common consent in the church, by much prayer and faith, for all things you shall receive by faith* (T&C 6:1).[193]

Today, the right of internal governance within fellowships belongs to the members through their common consent. Because the right to govern arises from this common consent, with no internal hierarchy, the decisions of fellowships can be varied. Their decisions may change from time to time, based on experiences. But each fellowship has the right to decide, as well as the right to decide to change.[194] Believers are allowed to "organize themselves" in any manner they choose. The right to organize stems from "common consent" given by both men and women. This right is so fundamental that it holds greater right than a first presidency, a twelve, a seventy, or a high council. All authorities derive their institutional right to preside solely from the consent of the governed. It is through "common consent" that any right to government is established in the church (*see* T&C 6:1; 10:4).[195] *See also* SUSTAIN.

Condemnation, To Remove "I seek constantly to use the Book of Mormon as a tool to move my understanding upward. I would like to have my meditation informed by passages from that book and to exhaust its contents of meaning. To the extent I succeed in taking the Book of Mormon seriously, I believe it incumbent upon the Lord to remove from me any condemnation resting upon mankind because of disrespect of the Book of Mormon (*see* T&C 82:20), and provide further light and knowledge by revelation, as promised in Alma 9:3."[196]

Consecration Consecrate (from the root *qâdâsh*, שׁדָק)[196] means "to set something or someone apart as sacred or holy; to pronounce clean; to purify or sanctify" (*see* T&C 82:16; T&C 123:5). The antonym is *desecrate*. Do not "perform anything" for the Lord until you have "in the first place" prayed to consecrate your performance. "In 2 Nephi 14:3 Nephi teaches you how to live the law of consecration. You don't need others to join you. You don't need a city to live where all things are held in common. You only need your own pure intent, acting no hypocrisy, consecrating your performance to the Lord for the welfare of your soul."[198] Speaking in January 1841 of a new location for Zion, "the Lord required a temple to be built in Nauvoo and once again offered to establish a protected place for the saints to gather. The Lord offered: *And you shall build it on the place where you have contemplated building it, for that is the spot which I have chosen for you to build it. If you labor with all your mights I will consecrate that spot that it shall be made holy* (T&C 141:13). Essentially the Lord said, 'Are you going to build the temple in Nauvoo? I will command you to do it. And if you do it, I will consecrate that spot. I will make that spot holy for you. I will make it so your enemies cannot move you out. I will come there and I will restore to you what has been lost: the fullness.'"[199]

Contention The more one contends with others the more he is taken captive by the spirit of contention. Everyone becomes subject to the spirit they submit to follow. Those who are prone to contention become more contentious as they listen to that spirit. Eventually they are overcome by that spirit, and it is a great work involving great effort to subdue and dismiss that spirit from the heart and mind of the victim.[200] There are many who dispute the inspiration others have received. There are two concerns with the decision a good person makes to dispute with others: First, the Lord's example is to refrain from disputing, as He did. When confronted, He would respond, but He did not go about picking a fight with others. He responded. The only exception was when He went up to Jerusalem to be slain. Then He went into the seat of Jewish power and authority to throw it down and provoke their decision to finally judge, reject, and crucify Him. He, and not they, controlled that timing. His provocation at that time was a deliberate act on His part because His "time had come," and His sacrifice needed to be made. Second, the Lord has given the Doctrine of Christ in scripture. Just before the Doctrine of Christ, He says what His doctrine is not: *Neither shall there be disputations among you concerning the points of my doctrine, as there hath hitherto been. For verily, verily I say unto you, he that hath the spirit of contention is not of me, but is of the Devil, who is the father of contention; and he stirreth up the hearts of men to contend with anger, one with another. Behold, this is not my doctrine, to stir up the hearts of men with anger, one against another, but this is my doctrine, that such things should be done away* (3 Nephi 5:8). And then He proceeds to declare His doctrine of Christ. The more contention and disputation there is with one another, the better the people become at contention. Rhetorical skills are polished. That spirit of contention can take possession, and when it does, one is hard-pressed to be a peacemaker with others. Christ said: *And blessed are the merciful, for they shall obtain mercy. And blessed are all the pure in heart, for they shall see God. And blessed are all the peacemakers, for they shall be called the children of God* (Matthew 3:10–12). But peace should not be made at the cost of truth. Truth must be the only goal. Truth, however, belongs to God. Desires, appetites, and passions are prone to make people stray well beyond the bounds set by God. Therefore, when pride is gratified, one should question if truth is being advanced. When one's ambition is served, he should question if he is in the Lord's employ or his own. When someone insists upon control, one should question if he is like the Lord or, instead, like His adversary. When one uses any means for compelling others, one should wonder if he is mocking the God who makes the sun to shine and rain to fall on all His fallen children without compulsion. When one displays unrighteous dominion, he should question whether he is worthy of any dominion at all. Our tools must be limited to persuasion, gentleness, meekness, love unfeigned, and pure knowledge, with all of them marshaled "without compulsory means" to persuade others to accept the truth. And if we fail to make the persuasive case, then the problem is not others, the problem is that we've yet to figure out how to be sufficiently knowledgeable so as to bring them aboard.[201] *See also* MUTUAL AGREEMENT.

Continuation of Seed Man and woman together, as the image of God, are potentially infinite through their descendants. In a very real sense, through their posterity, Adam and Eve are still here. Although all will die, all will also endure throughout ages of mortality, like God, by multiplying to replenish the earth. Adam and Eve became in the image of God. This is at the core of redemption, the core of the work of God. This is what it means for God to complete His work and to have the continuation of the seeds.[202] *Therefore the marriage covenant is needed for all those who would likewise seek to obtain from me the right to continue their seed into eternity, for only through marriage can Thrones and Kingdoms be established* (T&C 157–43).[203]

Covenant Man does not make covenants with God. God offers a covenant, and people either accept or reject God's offer. But until God offers, mankind can do nothing to create a covenant with or for God.[204] The Book of Mormon *is* intended by God to be a covenant. In it there are examples of covenant making provided so man can understand the process. The covenant offered through the Book of Mormon has never been received by any people until the Boise Conference in 2017. When the 1835 conference adopted scriptures, they adopted only the Doctrine & Covenants and not the Book of Mormon. The Book of Mormon, as an offered covenant to the gentiles, is an essential step required for the gentiles to become numbered with the remnant and obtain the right to inherit the promised land. If it is not received as a covenant by the gentiles, they have no right to be here on this land or on any other land of promise.[205] Paragraph 9 of Lecture Sixth says, *And in the last days, before the Lord comes, he is to gather together his saints who have made a covenant with him by sacrifice.* This event will be in the "last days" but still "before" His Second Coming. The wording is important. A covenant will be made "by" sacrifice; not a covenant "to" sacrifice. Only through actually sacrificing is it possible to obtain a covenant with the Lord.[206] To know the Lord is to have a covenant with Him.[207] The way in which one accepts the covenants is set out by Joseph Smith: "There is a law, irrevocably decreed in Heaven before the foundations of this world, upon which all blessings are predicated — And when we obtain any blessing from God, it is by obedience to that law upon which it is predicated."[208] Therefore, it is important to understand and learn what the relevant law requires. The way in which man accepts the covenant offered to him is by learning the principle or the law upon which the blessing he seeks is predicated. Then having learned what the law ordains, he follows through by obeying it.[209] "God can offer you something, but it's up to you to accept it. You accept it by what you do. It's not enough to say, Yea, Lord, I'll go out and do as I'm bidden. Instead you must actually do it. Because it is only through doing that the covenant is kept by you. It is only through doing the covenant is able to be empowered sufficiently to give you the blessing which a law has been established to allow you to lay ahold. You can't get there without God offering you the covenant and you accepting God's invitation."[210] "God only works to bring people into His good graces by covenants. They have to be made. Without covenants you cannot participate in what the Lord sets out."[211]

Covenant, Everlasting The covenant established by the Lord with Adam; it was renewed with each of the Fathers and reintroduced to Abraham for his posterity after an apostasy. It has again been renewed in the last days as an integral part of the latter-day Restoration that began with Joseph Smith. Joseph's work was intended to bring back the very religion of the first man. This was to be more than merely a church; *this is a new and an everlasting covenant, even that which was from the beginning* (JSH 18:10).[212] "The new and everlasting covenant in our day is 'new' only as a consequence of it having been restored to our attention recently. What is going to happen in our day was predicted and promised as a consequence of Adam."[213] Modern revelation tells us: *And for this cause — that men might be made partakers of the glories which were to be revealed — the Lord sent forth the fullness of his gospel and his everlasting covenant, reasoning in plainness and simplicity to prepare the weak for those things which are coming upon the earth* (T&C 58:7). *Blessed are you for receiving my everlasting covenant, even the fullness of my gospel sent forth unto the children of men, that they might have life and be* *made partakers of the glories which are to be revealed in the last days as it was written by the prophets and apostles in days of old* (T&C 52:1).

The Lord affirms that the everlasting covenant is the means by which His people are gathered. *The fullness of my gospel which I have sent forth in these last days, [is] the covenant which I have sent forth to recover my people which are of the House of Israel* (T&C 23:3). *And even so, I have sent my everlasting covenant unto the world, to be a light to the world and to be a standard for my people, and for the gentiles to seek to it, and to be a messenger before my face to prepare the way before me* (T&C 31:3). Joseph Smith also referred to the sealing authority in connection with the Second Coming of Christ and the everlasting covenant: "Four destroying angels holding power over the four quarters of the earth until the servants of God are sealed in their foreheads, which signifies sealing the blessing upon their heads, meaning the everlasting covenant, thereby making their calling and election sure" (TPJS, 321). The everlasting covenant to bring Zion that was originally promised to Adam and later to Enoch was made again by God with Noah. The covenant requires some generation at the end to rise up and vindicate it.[214] *And the bow shall be in the cloud. And I will look upon it that I may remember the everlasting covenant which I made unto your father Enoch: that when men should keep all my commandments, Zion should again come on the earth, the city of Enoch which I have caught up unto myself. And this is my everlasting covenant that I establish with you: that when your posterity shall embrace the truth and look upward, then shall Zion look downward, and all the heavens shall shake with gladness and the earth shall tremble with joy. And the general assembly of the church of the Firstborn shall come down out of Heaven and possess the earth, and shall have place until the end come. And this is my everlasting covenant which I made with your father Enoch* (Genesis 5:22). As of September 3, 2017, a covenant to reconnect again as a people with the Lord and the Fathers has been offered again to mankind (*see* T&C 156, 157, 158). Eventually a temple will be built in which the remaining steps to fully recover the original religion will occur.

Cry Unto the Lord   There is a difference between *praying* and *crying* to God. A petitioner who cries comprehends his desperate and lowly position. It is used eleven times in the Ether chapters to describe the brother of Jared.[215] Amulek's sermon to the Zoramites advises them eight times to cry unto God (*see* Alma 16:35).[216] In these examples the petitions to God are not called "prayer," but are called "crying" to Him.[217] *Yea, and when you do not cry unto the Lord, let your hearts be full, drawn out in prayer unto him continually for your welfare, and also for the welfare of those who are around you* (Alma 16:35). *For I pray continually for them by day, and mine eyes water my pillow by night because of them. And I cry unto my God in faith, and I know that he will hear my cry* (2 Nephi 15:1).

Curse/ing Condemnation by God.[218]

Damned To cease progressing or to regress.[219] Damnation merely means the end of progress.[220] So when one fails to progress in understanding, he voluntarily damns himself.[221] "When God offers a blessing or knowledge to a man, and he refuses to receive it, he will be damned."[222] If mankind is to be saved, it will be through their acquisition of knowledge. Put otherwise, it is stupidity that damns them; it is knowledge which saves man.[223] Damnation means hedging up the way so that one cannot progress.[224]

Day A varying increment of time used to specify the completion of a distinct work. The work of the creation is generally referred to as a *day*. "There is no reason to believe that calling it a day in the language that gets employed in scripture has reference to anything other than a discrete event. It would be more accurate to say that there were labors that were performed during the incremental progression of the creation which took however long, and when the labor was completed then that labor was called 'a day.' There is nothing to suggest that the labor of the first day was exactly the same amount of time as the labor of the second day, nor is there anything to suggest that the labor of the third day was equal in time to either the first or the second, and so on. How many eons of time were required in order for God (through the process that we see in nature) to form the earth — [that] was the first day. However long it took (through seismic, volcanic, and other activities to cause the dry land to appear) was labor that took however long it took."[225]

Deacon In its earliest form (meeting informally for worship), small groups were led by both men and women called *diákonos* (διάκονος), a word that is translated into English as either "deacon" or "deaconess." That Greek word means "servant."[226] It was in these home meetings where original Christians worshipped and learned of Christ and Christianity.[227]

Deny the Holy Ghost "If your spirit has become sanctified, and you have received the presence of both the Father and the Son such that you (as Joseph described it) stand in the 'noon-day sun' in your understanding, then you have received the Holy Spirit of Promise. This means that your own spirit reflects the promise of Eternal life. You are then a Spirit of Promise, assured of Eternal life. Then denying the Holy Ghost, as Joseph described it, involves taking what has become sacred within you and polluting it with deliberate rejection of the God you have received and who now dwells within you."[228]

Destroy In the vernacular of the Book of Mormon, to destroy did not mean annihilation. It merely meant to end the organized existence of a people or to terminate their government, deprive them of a land, and end their cultural dominance.[229] In the Book of Mormon, a people were destroyed when they lost control over their government and land. Their ability to preserve their own values and choose the way they were governed was taken over by others. Most often it was from a different ethnic group, though not always. Once people were destroyed, they were oppressed and suffered. Often they were oppressed with grievous taxes and had religious liberties removed. Then they faced a choice: either repent, in which case they came through the period of oppression with another chance; or if they were angry and rebellious, they would then be "swept away." Being destroyed is not at all the same as being "swept away." It is possible for people to have been destroyed and not even realize it. But when they are "swept away," they face extinction and cannot help but notice it.[230]

Disciple The word "disciple" is derived from discipline. A disciple follows the Master.[231]

Dispensation The beginning and ending of a gospel epoch or order.[232] Dispensations have their bounds. Beforehand, the prophets give, through prophecy, a limit on the things that are to come. When the prophesied events have unfolded and the measure has been met, then one Dispensation comes to an end while another opens.[233] "It is in the order of heavenly things that God should always send a new Dispensation into the world when men have apostatized from the truth and lost the priesthood...."[234] Every Dispensation of the Gospel is the "last Dispensation" — until it fails. Then another is sent, and it is the "last" — until it fails. This will continue for so long as man continues to fail.[235] When a dispensation of the Gospel is conferred on mankind through a dispensation head (like Enoch, Moses, Joseph Smith), then those who live in that Dispensation are obligated to honor the ordinances laid down through the Dispensation head by the Lord. For so long as the ordinances remain unchanged, the ordinances are effective. When, however, the ordinances are changed without the Lord's approval (*the* critical question), they are broken. At that point, the cure is for the Lord to bestow a new Dispensation in which a new covenant is made available.[236] The Lord sends ministers with a commission to transition from one Dispensation of the Gospel to another.[237] A new Dispensation occurs when some lost (or never completed) components of the work need to be dispensed to mankind, either anew or for the first time.[238] "In Abraham we have an example of...an isolated, faithful individual who honored the Fathers and was doing everything that he could in his day but for whom there was no existing possibility for having it occur. God was able to fix that problem for that individual, not in order to establish a new Dispensation in which salvation proceeds with the gathering of a people, and a making of a people. But it was a dispensation to that individual for purposes of trying to call others to repentance."[239] When God gives a man a Dispensation from heaven, there is a labor to be done in His vineyard. The authority to complete the labor is implicit with the assignment given by God. When someone receives a Dispensation and discharges the assignment with honor, he holds the keys, owns the rights, enjoys the honors, and possesses the Dispensation of that assignment to all eternity. A new Dispensation is founded on knowledge from those who went before who *all [declare] their dispensations, their rights, their keys, their honors, their majesty and glory, and the Powers of their Priesthood; giving line upon line, precept upon precept; endowing them with knowledge, even here a little and there a little* (T&C 157:31) to the new Dispensation.[240] Though this could be interpreted to suggest that every assignment from the Lord could be a "dispensation," the broader statement clarifies that there is one dispensation supported, in turn, by many assignments.

Man may have received power and authority to complete the labor assigned, and the inspiration from God to complete the assignment may have been provided to them, but that alone does not constitute a dispensation. For example, Nephi was sent to retrieve the plates of brass, but that was not a dispensation; it was an assignment, a request from the Lord. Many assignments are needed to fulfill a dispensation. All who complete an assignment with honor hold the keys of that work. But a dispensation is better understood as "restoring and making overall progression of the covenants, promises, and prophecies to advance and vindicate God's work to reclaim the world from apostasy."[241]

Dispensation of the Fullness of Time The current time is called the Dispensation of the Fullness of Time because this time is leading to that return to fullness. However, in one sense, Joseph Smith was much like the Protestant Fathers who laid groundwork for a greater, further return of light. They did not see the full return. This generation might.[242]

Disputation The Lord's elaboration on "disputations" and "contentions" in 3 Nephi 5:8-9 is important and consistent enough that it should all be considered together. First, He clarifies that baptism must be done as He "commanded you." Deviations are not permitted and should not be asked for or entertained. That is the thing about ordinances. When given, they are to be kept in exactly the manner they come from Him. When man changes them, they risk breaking the covenant between Him and themselves (see Isaiah 7:1). The Book of Mormon is silent about the "disputations" which existed among them over baptism. However, when Christ says there has "hitherto been" disputes, it is evident they existed. It becomes apparent from later passages that one practice which caused some of the argument was the issue of baptizing infants. There were likely others, as well. The Lord wants that to end. Perform the ordinances as He sets them out, and stop arguing about the manner. The reason arguments arise is because men stop gathering light by righteous behavior. When they lose light, they cease to understand the truth. They stray from the correct practice of the ordinance because they are unable to understand its importance. They see no reason to continue the ordinance in one form when another seems to work just as well. The result is a change to the ordinance. It is ever the same. By the time the change is made, the ones making it are unaware of any importance associated with the ordinance they changed. They discard what they view is meaningless. It would require a good deal more light and truth for them to understand the importance of what was given them. But that light and truth has passed away from them because of their conduct.

Into the darkness the devil enters with arguments over the ordinances: *Why do it that way? It really doesn't mean anything. It is arcane and outdated. It doesn't really matter as long as you still have faith in Christ.* (That particular lie is very effective because it allows the person to presume they have faith, when in fact they haven't the faith sufficient to obey Christ.) *People will get more out of the changes if we make them. People will have greater peace of mind if we baptize their infants. We'll save more souls, because by baptizing them when they're infants, we include everyone who would die before getting baptized. Our numbers will increase. We'll look more successful by getting more followers by adding their numbers into the group. What we change isn't important, anyway. If it were important, we would know that, and since it doesn't seem important to us, it must, in fact, not be important. Those who rebel at change are not really faithful. This shows inspiration; it's faith affirming. Change is proof that God is still leading us....* And other such arguments and persuasions from our adversary.

On the other hand, Christ is saying to keep the ordinances unchanged. And further, don't even begin to dispute them. They are off limits for argument, dispute, and discussion. "When you open the opportunity to dispute over the ordinances, you are allowing the devil an opportunity to influence the discussion and change the ordinances. Disputes lead to contention, contention leads to anger, and anger is the devil's tool. So don't start down that road. Accept and understand the ordinances. If you are perplexed by them, then let those who understand speak, exhort, expound, and teach concerning them. As they do, you will come into the unity of faith and become one. Perplexity cannot exist when there is light and truth. Light and truth comes from understanding the ordinances, not changing them. So do not begin the process through dispute. The purpose of discussion is not to dispute, which leads to contention, which leads to anger. When the Gospel and its ordinances turn into something angry and contentious, then the spirit has fled, and souls are lost. It is the devil's objective to prevent you from practicing the ordinances in the correct manner. But, more importantly, it is his objective to prevent you from becoming one. When he uses arguments over ordinances to cause disunity, he is playing with two tools at the same time. First, changing the ordinances brings about cursings, and second, encouraging contention and anger grieves the spirit, and prevents the saints from becoming one. The devil knows this, even if men do not. Men are urged to take steps they presume have little effect, all the while being lied to by the enemy of their souls. When men arrive at the point they are angry in their hearts with one another, they are not united by love as they are intended to be. These are the end results of the two paths. One leading to love and joy (Helaman 2:25), and the other to anger and wrath (T&C 69:7)."[243] *See also* CONTENTION.

Dives *Therefore, if any man shall take of the abundance which I have made and impart not his portion, according to the law of my gospel, unto the poor and the needy, he shall with Dives lift up his eyes in Hell, being in torment* (T&C 105:5). The parable of the rich man and Lazarus (also called "the Dives and Lazarus" or "Lazarus and Dives") is a well-known parable of Jesus, appearing in Luke 9:20. Traditionally used as a personal name, "Dives" is not actually a proper name, but a description meaning "rich or wealthy man," from the Latin *dives*.[244] The parable begins in the Latin Vulgate as "*Homo quidam erat dives*," meaning "There was a certain rich man." Its English origin dates back to the 14th century, and reference to *dives* in literature has been made by Shakespeare, Chaucer, and Melville, among others. The word *dives* was changed from the earliest revelation manuscripts to the word *wicked* in the printed 1835 Doctrine and Covenants.

Doctrine of Christ Christ explained His Doctrine immediately following His instruction on baptism: *Behold, verily, verily I say unto you, I will declare unto you my doctrine. And this is my doctrine, and it is the doctrine which the Father hath given unto me — and I bear record of the Father, and the Father beareth record of me, and the holy ghost beareth record of the Father and me — and I bear record that the Father commandeth all men everywhere to repent and believe in me. And whoso believeth in me,* *and is baptized, the same shall be saved, and they are they who shall inherit the kingdom of God. And whoso believeth not in me, and is not baptized, shall be damned. Verily, verily I say unto you that this is my doctrine, and I bear record of it from the Father. And whoso believeth in me believeth in the Father also, and unto him will the Father bear record of me, for he will visit him with fire and with the holy ghost* (3 Nephi 5:9). The Doctrine of Christ is connected to the ordinance of baptism. Once baptized, all can receive the Father's testimony of His Son by the power of the holy ghost. It comes as a result of baptism. If Christ lays hands on someone, then that person can also confer the holy ghost by the laying on of hands. Even in the absence of such an ordained man, the holy ghost is given according to the Doctrine of Christ to any who repent and are baptized following His direction. *And again I say unto you, ye must repent, and become as a little child, and be baptized in my name, or ye can in nowise receive these things. And again I say unto you, ye must repent, and be baptized in my name, and become as a little child, or ye can in nowise inherit the kingdom of God. Verily, verily I say unto you that this is my doctrine. And whoso buildeth upon this buildeth upon my rock, and the gates of hell shall not prevail against them. And whoso shall declare more or less than this, and establisheth it for my doctrine, the same cometh of evil and is not built upon my rock, but he buildeth upon a sandy foundation, and the gates of hell standeth open to receive such when the floods come and the winds beat upon them. Therefore, go forth unto this people and declare the words which I have spoken unto the ends of the earth* (3 Nephi 5:9). This is Christ's doctrine, nothing more and certainly nothing less. This is His doctrine. This is the power of redemption. This is the way the holy ghost is obtained. This is not all of Christ's teachings, tenets, precepts, covenants, commandments, or principles, but it is all of His doctrine. There is no more doctrine than this, according to Christ. The word "doctrine" is used very liberally among mankind. This was also the case when Joseph was alive, but Christ used the word very specifically and confined His doctrine to only a few statements. He accompanied it with the warning: *Whoso shall declare more or less than this, and establisheth it for my doctrine, the same cometh of evil and is not built upon my rock* (3 Nephi 5:9). Sometimes the word "doctrine" is used when what is really meant is a "tenet," "teaching," "precept," "principal," or "covenant." Christ has narrowly defined His doctrine and did so in order to avoid the "coming of evil."[245] "This doctrine of Christ will bring you in contact with God. You were meant to return to the Family you came from. It is the homecoming you have always felt was needed. You do not belong here. There is something higher, something more holy calling to you. It is not found in an institution, or program, or a ward, or office. It is only found in God, who is your home. The Doctrine of Christ is the doctrine of God's return to be with you and abide with you. It is Him coming to sup with you. He has been knocking at the door all these years seeking entry into your life (Revelation 1:20). If you let Him come in, He will prepare a throne for you (Revelation 1:20). Only those who have descended will be permitted to rise. Only those who humble themselves can be exalted (Matthew 10:26)."[246] The reason for this doctrine is that it will allow those who accept and follow it to endure against all enemies. It will allow them to prevail. Even the "gates of hell shall not prevail against them," meaning that death and hell can have no claim upon them. They will not be taken captive, either in this world or when they leave this world.[247] *See also* GOSPEL OF JESUS CHRIST.

Doctrine of the Two Ways This ancient doctrine describes the direction that Israel, the church, or an individual may follow. It makes no difference whether it is an individual or a community; all are on a single path that goes two ways — forward or backward. Man is either gaining, or he is losing. He cannot stand still. Whether a group or a person, everyone is either gaining (restoring) light and truth, or they are losing (apostatizing from) light and truth. This world is a world of change. Nothing remains the same. Everywhere, one sees either growth or decay. These forces are at work everywhere. They are also at work within each individual. "You either search out new truth, find it, live it, and thereby become restored to truth, or you back away from it. If you are backing away, losing it, neglecting it, and discarding it, you are in the process of apostasy. In a restoration process, there are moments along the way that are marked and notable. Having the inspiration of the spirit, or feeling the remission of your sins, or receiving revelation, or having a visit of an angel are notable. The culmination of the restoration would be to return to God's presence. Should that happen, through the Second Comforter's ministry, then you have been restored in full. There are two ways — forward or backward. It is not required that you finish the course in a day; but times are coming in which the environment will require of you a greater commitment as 'wheat' on the one hand, or leave you to descend into becoming a 'tare' on the other. So the direction you are on now is quite important. Either you are restoring truth or you are discarding it."[248] "It is easy to imagine absolutes, and to think and argue in terms of absolutes...good and evil, light and darkness, hot and cold, black and white — we know exactly what they are; but in the real world we have rarely experienced the pure thing — our own experience lies between. Yet standing on that middle ground, we *are* faced with absolute decisions. It is not where we stand, says Ezekiel, that makes us good or evil in God's eyes — no one has reached the top or bottom in this short life — but the direction in which we are facing. There we have only two choices. The road up and the road down are the same. It all depends on the way *you* are facing.... You are either repenting or not repenting, and that is, according to the scriptures, the whole difference between being righteous or being wicked."[249] *There are only two ways: the way I lead, that goes upward in light and truth unto Eternal lives — and if you turn from it, you follow the way of darkness and the deaths. Those who want to come where I am must be able to abide the conditions established for my Father's Kingdom. I have given to you the means to understand the conditions you must abide. I came and lived in the world to be the light of the world. I have sent others who have testified of me and taught you. I have sent my light into the world. Let not your hearts remain divided from one another and divided from me* (T&C 157:52).[250]

Dominion The word "dominion" in the understanding of the gentile can convey the impression of a prison warden exercising control over captives. "Dominion" should be understood, instead, to convey the idea of a gardener who is responsible for making the garden thrive, grow, and bear fruit. To be clear, the three greatest examples of wielding "dominion" in the correct manner as mankind should understand it are, first: Christ, who is probably without any peer, unquestionably the greatest example of one holding the greatest dominion, and who also, likewise, showed the greatest example of how to wield dominion. He beseeched people to believe. He pled with them for their own good. He knelt to serve them. He denied that He had a kingdom of this world (*see* John 10:7). He tried to prepare people for a better one. But He was more intelligent than they all, and He was the greatest of them all (*see* Abraham 5:4). Unquestionably, He held the greatest dominion, and He wore it as a light thing. His yoke was easy (*see* Matthew 6:8). In this world, Adam, after Christ, held the greatest dominion (*see* Genesis 2:8). Adam taught and pled and instructed (*see* Genesis 3:4), but he did not abridge the agency of his children, even when one of his sons killed another of his sons. Adam did not execute Cain. Cain was sent away. Adam held dominion, but he exercised it like our Lord, pleading for the best interest of others. Adam invited and solicited all to obey God, hoping for their best interests. The third great example of holding dominion in a godly way was Moses. He is called in scripture, *meek above all men which were upon the face of the earth* (Numbers 7:22), and yet gentiles depict him as a bully and a strongman. Moses saw no reason to be jealous when others were out prophesying: *Would that all the Lord's people were prophets, and that the Lord would put his spirit upon them* (Numbers 7:19). Moses, like Adam and Christ, is an example of how the word "dominion" should be understood. All three were gardeners, responsible for trying to make their garden thrive, grow, and bear fruit. In reality, those who have held the greatest dominion given by God have invariably lived lives of meekness and service. They were the opposite of what gentiles regard as a strongman. They were the opposite of a dictator or boss. They were more like loving grandfathers, gentle gardeners, and encouraging friends — trying to get the best from those who would allow them to teach.[251]

Dominions *See* POWERS OF HEAVEN.

Dragon The Greek word for dragon is *draco* (*drákōn*, δράκων), which means "serpent" and occurs in the New Covenants 13 times (*see* Revelation 4:2, 3, 5,7,9; 6:8; 8:4).[252] The word can specifically refer to *the great dragon who was cast out, that old serpent called the Devil, and also called Satan, who deceives the whole world* (Revelation 4:3).

Dreams Dreams are the will o' the wisp, so insubstantial that modern, sophisticated society dismisses them without thought. Yet they are the stuff from which great messages have come from God throughout the scriptures. Dreams are the stuff of prophetic inspiration and the voice of God. The scriptures define God's dealings with men in these terms: *And he said, Hear now my words: If there is a prophet among you, I the*

Lord will make myself known unto him in a vision and will speak unto him in a dream (Numbers 7:22). In Job one reads this about God speaking with man: *Behold, in this you are not just. I will answer you that God is greater than man. Why do you quarrel against him? For he gives not account of all of his matters. For God speaks once — yea twice — yet man perceives it not. In a dream, in a vision of the night, when deep sleep falls upon men in slumberings upon the bed* (Job 11:7). "If, therefore, this is one of God's historic and well-established ways of speaking to mankind, then you should expect it will be one of the means He will speak with you. If He elects to make Himself known to you in this manner, you have the high privilege and honor of having spoken with God. Do not expect Him to physically appear to anyone who has insufficient faith to accept His messages in dreams. If you will not accept the whisperings of His spirit through the feelings He sends to you, then why should He send more? If you are given a dream from Him but cannot accept it in faith, then why should He give more? If you are not willing to accept His proofs in faith, which come exactly as He promises they will come, then why should He send more? He has told us what to expect. When we do not expect them, or refuse to have faith in them, or refuse to accept them as proofs, then we are not following His path. But, if we accept them in faith as ... His mind, His will, and His voice, then our faith is sufficient. Signs follow faith. They do not produce it."[253]

Dwindle in Unbelief When one prizes his or her errors and holds them as true (when they are not), one dwindles in unbelief.[254] Unbelief is often used in connection with losing truth, forsaking doctrine, and therefore, "dwindling." The phrase "dwindling in unbelief" is the Book of Mormon's way to describe moving from a state of belief, with true and complete doctrine, to a state of unbelief, where the truth has been discarded. Miracles end because men dwindle in unbelief.[255]

Elder An office in the church that Joseph Smith organized on April 6, 1830. This office had the right to preside, preach, teach, exhort, and expound scripture. Originally, Elders were elected to this position by the body of members, but the practice has since changed in the LDS Church to become a "calling" by a presiding authority and a sustaining (vote of approval) by a congregation, preliminary to ordination to the office. Joseph Smith was the First Elder in the church; Oliver Cowdery was the Second Elder.[256] Joseph Smith recorded: "The authority of the Melchizedek priesthood was manifested and conferred, for the first time, upon several of the elders" at the June 1831 conference.[257] This clarifies that "elder" is a church office that is not related to the High Priesthood, because these men were already serving in their church office of "elder" before the High Priesthood was restored.[258] The office of "elder," like other offices (priests, deacons, teachers), were offices in the church. They were not coincidental to having priesthood. They were offices in the *Church of Christ* (T&C 59:1,6–10,12). These offices were elected, approved by common consent, and then filled by those elected (*see* T&C 6:1; JSH 16:17). It was some time later, after D&C 3 (1835 Edition), that this church office and priesthood were conflated to mean the same thing. The office of elder belongs to the church, and whether there is priesthood present or not, the right to preach, teach, expound, exhort, baptize, lay on hands for the holy ghost, and bless and pass the sacrament are all things which the Lord commissioned the church to perform. This is also why, at the time Joseph and Oliver received only the Aaronic Priesthood, they began to call one another the First and Second *elder of the church* (JSH 14:2).[259] The Lord often spoke to "the elders of my church" as one category, in contrast to "priesthood," which is another category. Mormons conflate the two. An elder is invited to become an actual priesthood holder, but that is dependent upon Heaven alone. It may be conferred on men, but Heaven must ratify (*see* T&C 139:5). Therefore, there are a lot of elders in the church who have no priesthood. Yet they have an authoritative invitation to connect with Heaven and rise up and receive it.[260] The office of elder still continues in many of the various religious groups claiming Joseph Smith as their founder. The term is derived from respecting the holy wisdom of experience most often gained from living a long life. The term "elder," in that sense, means "wise" or "experienced" — meaning someone who can provide answers because of their experience. It is used in this sense in 1 Peter 1:20: *Likewise, you younger, submit yourselves unto the elder*. Peter was not referring to offices, since there is no office of "younger." He was referring to those who were to be respected because of their wisdom born from experience.[261]

Elect *And you are called to bring to pass the gathering of my elect, for my elect hear my voice and harden not their hearts* (T&C 9:3). *For whoever is faithful unto the obtaining these two priesthoods of which I have spoken, and the magnifying their calling, are sanctified by the spirit unto the renewing of their bodies, that they become the sons of Moses and of Aaron and the seed of Abraham, and the church, and kingdom, and the elect of God* (T&C 82:16). *For in those days there shall also arise false christs and false prophets, and shall show great signs and wonders, insomuch that if possible, they shall deceive the very elect, who are the elect according to the covenant. Behold, I speak these things unto you for the elect's sake* (Matthew 11:6). "And all those who will obey his commandment are his elect, and he will soon gather them from the four winds of heaven, from one quarter of the earth to the other, to whithersoever he will and be numbered with the House of Israel."[262] Christ's parables about the latter-day church at His return are another disturbing reminder that even the very elect will be deceived.[263] Joseph's addition about the "elect according to the covenant" makes clear this passage is not about Historic Christianity.[264] There are, and always have been, two churches only. One is true. Its members belong to the Lamb of God — the Lamb, who is their Father. One either belongs to the elect family of Christ, the Church of the Firstborn, or he doesn't. All other religions and philosophies are false.[265] When a man or woman elects to receive Him, He elects, at that moment, to receive them. They determine whether they are elect by their election to receive Him.[266]

Elias A title (not a name) that is applied to all those whose keys were returned in this Dispensation. Those included, as Joseph wrote, *divers angels from Michael or Adam down to the present time,* or anyone holding any key from any Dispensation from the past (T&C 151:15–17).[267]

Elias, Elijah, Messiah Joseph Smith tells us "there is a difference between the spirit and office of Elias and Elijah…. The spirit of Elias is to prepare the way for a greater revelation of God."[268] "The spirit, power, and calling of Elijah is, that ye have power to hold the key of the revelations, ordinances, oracles, powers and endowments of the fullness of the Melchizedek Priesthood and of the kingdom of God on the earth; and to receive, obtain, and perform all the ordinances belonging to the kingdom of God, even unto the turning of the hearts of the Fathers unto the children, and the hearts of the children unto the Fathers, even those who are in Heaven."[269] "Messiah is above the spirit and power of Elijah, for he made the world.... Elijah was to come and prepare the way and build up the kingdom before the coming of the great day of the Lord, although the spirit of Elias might begin it.... The spirit of Elias is first, Elijah second, and Messiah last. Elias is a forerunner to prepare the way, and the spirit and power of Elijah is to come after, holding the keys of power, building the temple to the capstone, placing the seals of the Melchizedek Priesthood upon the house of Israel, and making all things ready; then Messiah comes to His temple, which is last of all."[270]

There is the Spirit of Elias, the Spirit of Elijah, and the Spirit of Messiah. These three great spirits unfolded in the work of God, in the generations of man, in a steady descent. Like a chiasm, they will again unfold, inverted, and return in an ascent, so that at the end, it will be as it was in the beginning. Father Adam prophesied, *Now this same Priesthood which was in the beginning shall be in the end of the world also* (Genesis 3:14). This scripture shows Moses quoting Enoch, who was, in turn, quoting Adam.

The spirit at the beginning was the Spirit of Messiah. Adam dwelt in the presence of God. Adam represents that original fullness. Adam was the first man. Adam received instructions and spoke to God face to face. He dwelt in a temple setting called Eden, from which he was cast out, but he dwelt in a temple. Therefore, Adam represents the Spirit of Messiah.

Secondly, the Spirit of Elijah is represented by Enoch who, when the Earth was threatened with violence and men were to be destroyed because of the wickedness upon the face of the earth, was able to gather people into a city of peace and to have the Lord come to their city of peace and remove them from the coming violence and destruction. Enoch is a type of the Spirit of Elijah, because it is the Spirit of Elijah that ascends into Heaven to prefigure the return of the Spirit of Messiah in the last day. The Spirit of Elijah is needed to gather a people to a place that God will acknowledge, will visit, and will shield from the coming violence at the destruction of the world. And so Enoch becomes the great type of the Spirit of Elijah, although the name of Elijah is associated with a man who lived later. (Elijah would likewise ascend in the fiery chariot into Heaven. He duplicated, among a hardened people in a fallen world, the same achievement as Enoch accomplished; albeit, Enoch did so with a city, and Elijah did it as a solitary figure.) It will be Elijah and his spirit that, in the last days, will likewise prepare a city for salvation and preservation.

Lastly, there is the Spirit of Elias, represented by Noah, wherein everything that had gone on before was lost. Things began anew, and Noah had a ministry to preach repentance, to preserve what had been taught before and was lost. Noah — as the messenger or the Elias — bears testimony of what once was.

Before the Lord's return, these same three spirits need to come again into the world. These will complete the plan Adam described in prophecy. It has always been in the heart of the Lord, from before the foundation of the world, for the Fall of man to be reversed. Man will return through the same stages as man fell. The Spirit of Elias, declaring the gospel, will come again into the world and has returned in the person of Joseph Smith — in the message he delivered, in the scriptures that he restored, and in the message and practices he taught. No matter how short-lived his message was, he laid a foundation in the Spirit of Elias. Without Joseph's ministry, we could not now move forward. Elias — and the Spirit of Elias — came through Joseph Smith into the world.

Man has yet to take the Spirit of Elias seriously enough to move on to receive something further. There are only two processes. The instant one process ends, the other begins. The first process is "restoration," and the second is "apostasy." There is no pause between them. Either there is an active restoration underway, with greater things revealed constantly; or there is apostasy, and light is lost. It is impossible to preserve light. Without an active connection to the Living Vine, there is only death (see John 9:10). Joseph was a restorer, and when he died, restoration ended. The moment Joseph and Hyrum were killed, the world began to lose light. The pace at which light is now being lost among the various Mormon sects has accelerated. But a new restoration has begun, and a new dispensation of the gospel has opened. Whether the light now offered will achieve anything more than came in Joseph's time remains an unanswered question. The Lord cannot force anyone to receive Him; He can only offer. We must accept. This generation is now facing a crossroads in which it is possible to continue the work and move forward. Moving forward successfully, however, will require an acceptance of the Spirit of Elijah. This time, the Spirit of Elijah is not coming to prepare a people to ascend *into* Heaven, but instead to prepare a people so that *those who come will not utterly destroy them*. There must be a people prepared to endure the burning that will come. Just as Enoch's people were prepared, shielded, and then worthy to ascend (so as to avoid destruction by the flood), the Spirit of Elijah must prepare people to endure the day that *shall burn the wicked as stubble*. The Spirit of Elijah will gather people to a place of peace, to be the only people who are not at war one with another (*see* T&C 31:15). They must be people willing to accept the Lord's teachings and allow those teachings to govern their daily walk — with each other and with God. Being eager to receive *commandments, not a few*, and also *revelations* from the Lord is what the people of Zion must necessarily be willing to do.[271]

"*Elias* for our day is, I believe, Joseph Smith. I expect *Elijah* to return the same way he departed. That's one of the great assignments to him. He must return because he will reopen the way through which others will follow. It will be, I believe, the same person as departed and not someone who self-proclaims or self-identifies as being *Elijah*. It will be him. Not another. Anyone making that claim would (to me at least) be someone who does not understand the scriptures and is not to be taken seriously."[272] Elias is the spirit and assignment of a "forerunner" who goes before to prepare the way. He lays a foundation for what comes next and is the one who commences to restore what has been lost; a recoverer. Elijah is the spirit and assignment to reconnect Heaven and earth; he who unites realms and initiates man's access to ministering angels and the church of the Firstborn by opening the stairway of ascent [an *axis mundi* or *columna lucis*] into Heaven.[273] Messiah is the presence of the Lord.[274]

End, The A name for Christ. As He said, *I am Alpha and Omega, Christ the Lord, yea, even I am he, the beginning and the end* (JSH 17:2). *See also* NAMES OF GOD IN SCRIPTURE.

Endowment A ritual instituted by Joseph Smith in Nauvoo, Illinois that was later finalized by Brigham Young. It presents a symbolic account of the creation of the world, including Adam and Eve. The ritual uses Adam and Eve to portray the mortal experience of every man and woman. The ritual takes initiates to converse with the Lord through a veil, preliminary to entering into His presence. The Lord questions the initiates to determine if they obeyed, sacrificed, were chaste, and consecrated their lives. After appropriate answers are given to the Lord, they are permitted to enter into His presence. A reduced version of the ceremony is still presented in LDS temples.[275] The ceremonial ritual was to be housed in a temple still under construction at the time Joseph Smith was killed. The temple rites he restored in Nauvoo, Illinois reaffirmed that God is accessible. The rites claimed that by obedience to God's commandments, every man and woman could receive further light and knowledge by conversing directly with the Lord through the veil. Joseph wanted God to be at the center of every Christian's faith. The temple ceremony explained that man could approach God directly and, thereby, avoid being "darkened in their minds by depending" on another man.[276]

Endure to the End *And now my beloved brethren, I know by this that unless a man shall endure to the end in following the example of the Son of the living God, he cannot be saved* (2 Nephi 13:3). "Enduring to the end — or the fixed purpose to always serve God so that you may always have His spirit to be with you — is essential to salvation. You claim this is your determination every time you take the sacrament. Whether you take this commitment seriously or not determines whether you are destined for salvation or not. It also determines if you are qualified to receive His personal ministry and comfort. The Lord also knows whether it is in you to endure to the end. Whether the end has come is irrelevant to Him. He beholds all things, past, present, and future (2 Nephi 6:7). Therefore, He knows if you are willing to endure to the end before your life is complete."[277] Endure to the end — meaning both here and in the hereafter. It will be a great while beyond this life before any will reach the "end" He desires all to attain. Therefore, enduring requires one to fight against all that opposes truth, for so long as he is allowed to participate in the battle — not passively, taking in what is wrong and showing tolerance for it, but instead actively standing for truth as long as he exists, here and hereafter.[278] How long must the enduring last, if it is to result in "Eternal life?" It will be a great deal after this life before you have learned enough to be saved. "You need to endure then, as now, for Eternal life to be yours."[279] Nephi tells us that his words persuade men *to endure to the end, which is life eternal* (2 Nephi 15:1). *See also* END, THE.

Eternal Life The definition of Eternal life was given by the Savior and recorded by John, who wrote: *Jesus spoke these words, and lifted up his eyes to Heaven and said, Father, the hour has come. Glorify your Son, that your Son also may glorify you, as you have given him power over all flesh, that he should give eternal life to as many as you have given him. And this is life eternal: that they might know you, the only true God, and Jesus Christ whom you have sent* (John 9:19). To know God is Eternal life. To know God, in the fullest of the sense in this life, is to receive the Second Comforter.[280] Of course, it is possible to have knowledge of Him through faith and without the Second Comforter, as well.[281]

Eternity "That which is without beginning or end."[282]

Eve The parable of the creation of the woman differs from the creation of the man. She was not formed from the dust of the ground. She was formed from a "rib" — from an already existing part of the man. She was born from something equal to him and able to stand beside him in all things. But the parable about the woman, Eve, means a great deal more. She was at Adam's side before the creation of this world. They were united as "one" in a prior estate when they progressed to become living "souls" with both bodies and spirits. They were sealed before this world by the Holy Spirit of Promise and proved true and faithful. They once sat upon a throne in God the Father's Kingdom. In that state, they were equal and joined eternally together. She sat beside him and was a necessary part of his enthronement. Her introduction into this world to join her companion was needed to complete Adam. It was not good for him to be alone. They were "one," and therefore, Adam without Eve was not complete — or in the words of the parable, *not good to be alone.* Like the man Adam, the woman Eve was the spirit offspring of Heavenly Father and Heavenly

Mother. But unlike the man Adam, who was the physical offspring of Christ, the woman Eve needed to be the physical offspring of God the Father and God the Mother. Eve was Adam's sister in spirit. Eve was also his physical aunt. She needed to be a direct descendant of the Heavenly Mother in order to be endowed with her Mother's creative abilities. That power belongs to the Mother. The fertility of Eve, and thereafter of all the daughters of Eve, came because of the power given from direct descent from the Heavenly Mother. Women descend from mother Eve, who was born the biological daughter of Heavenly Mother. Women descend from Heavenly Mother to endow them with Her creative power of fertility to bear the souls of men.

Eve was not beneath Adam, nor subject to his rule, when first created. Eve was put beside him to complete him and be his helpmeet. There was another condition required to enable Christ to lawfully redeem the daughters of Eve, as well as the sons of Adam. The parable of the creation includes this step to put Eve under Adam's responsibility. The account explains that Eve (and by extension her daughters) was put under Adam's rule. Adam was handed responsibility and accountability for Eve. These are the words in the parable: *Thy desire shall be to thy husband, and he shall rule over thee.* Adam was made accountable to "rule" in the fallen world. All the mistakes, mismanagements, failings, wars, and difficulties of mortality are the responsibility of the appointed "ruler." Adam would not have been accountable for Eve unless she was made subject to his "rule." Once under Adam's rule, the redemption of Adam became also the redemption of Eve. Therefore, Adam and the sons of Adam, and Eve and the daughters of Eve, were all rescued through Christ's atonement for mankind. The parable continues with another allusion to Heavenly Mother: *And Adam called his wife's name Eve because she was the mother of all living, for thus have I, the Lord God, called the first of all women, which are many* (Genesis 2:18). One of the names of Heavenly Mother is "Eve." She was the "mother of all living" because She was the one who mothered the spirits of Adam and Eve and was, therefore, parent of them both. Out of respect for Her, Adam called his companion by the same name as the Heavenly Mother. Redemption of all mankind, male and female, required Adam to descend from Jesus Christ. It also required Adam to "rule," or be responsible to teach, all those in his dominion. That role, assigned to Adam, was in order to extend the legal effect of Christ's redemption to Adam, Eve, and their posterity. However, for women to bear the souls of men, Eve had to be a direct descendant of Heavenly Mother.[283] *See also* ADAM.

Exaltation To become like God and inherit Celestial glory.[284] Elevation to the highest degree in which all powers are increased.[285]

Excess Wealth (an explanation in T&C 46:4).[286]

Extortion To compel the poor (an explanation in T&C 46:4).[287]

Eye of Faith First one sees with an "eye of faith" and then by the eyes themselves. The faith to see precedes seeing.[288] This is set out in the following passage: *And there were many whose faith was so exceeding strong, even before Christ came, who could not be kept from within the veil, but truly saw with their eyes the things which they had beheld with an eye of faith; and they were glad* (Ether 5:3). Development of the faith to see within the veil comes after having first seen "with an eye of faith."[289] Unless a person sees these things through the eyes of faith as a necessary first step, he cannot behold the real thing. The one qualifies for the other. The one is a necessary precondition for the other. God has created mortals in such a way that they must progress in these things, from grace to grace, before they can receive the fullness. If they cannot first see the "type" in faith, nothing doubting, then there is no reason for the Lord to send the real thing. That would be sending a "sign" to produce faith, rather than having the sign follow faith. When someone accepts the "type" as the real thing, and drains from it all of its symbolic meaning, then there is no reason to withhold the real thing any longer. Then come the signs that follow faith. That is the process irrevocably decreed before the foundation of the world. If a man or woman conforms to it and receives the types in faith, then he or she will grow from grace to grace.[290]

Faith More than belief; a principle of action that requires one to act on belief in order to produce faith. The Lectures on Faith are a study on the topic. Joseph Smith defined faith as a principle of power through action, in which one puts those beliefs into action and thereby acquires power. Joseph related faith to having power.[291]One can spend a lifetime as a "believer" without ever developing faith. Before belief can turn into faith, action is required. Without some action consistent with belief, a disciple cannot move along from mere belief to developing faith. It is action, obedience, and living in conformity to God's will that yields faith. The commandments give us a chance to develop faith, which begins in very small ways. Emotional, sympathetic feelings are the beginnings of this seed sprouting. After that, the mind begins to "get" or to "see" the truthfulness of the system. Faith covers a broad spectrum. It begins embryonic and weak but can develop into an "unshakable faith" in the truthfulness of a principle. Jacob described this kind of faith; it results in actual power (*see* Jacob 3:2).[292] In the Book of Mormon, the word "faith" is used when an angel has ministered to someone.[293] Moroni 7:7 says, *Behold, I say unto you…it is by faith that angels appear and minister unto men. Wherefore, if these things have ceased, woe be unto the children of men, for it is because of unbelief, and all is vain.*[294]

The development of faith will save one, but faith is not the end, and much more is offered if one is willing to receive it. Belief becomes faith, and faith becomes knowledge. Knowledge is what one gets when they are "redeemed from the fall" as Christ explained to the Brother of Jared.[295] "Faith in Him comes by hearing the word of God, delivered as He authorizes, by whomever He chooses to deliver it. If we receive God's word preached by someone He sends, then we can have faith in the Son of God. We can receive Him. But if we harden our heart, blind our mind and refuse to receive what He offers today, then we do not and cannot have faith in Him. We fall short of the faith required by His sons and daughters. This has always been the test. This will always be the test. I have been sent, and God is proving you. Joseph Smith testified to these things, and I am now a second witness. Therefore, two proclaim the same doctrine."[296]

Faith, Hope, and Charity There is a direct relationship between faith, hope, and charity. Faith comes from obedience and sacrifice. Hope comes when one's faith secures a promise directly from God. And charity comes when those holding faith and receiving hope seek to have all others share in the same promises (*see* 1 Corinthians 1:53; Ether 5:5; Moroni 7:1; Moroni 10:4; and JSH 15:35).[297] Fear, anger, and selfishness are Satan's counter to faith, hope, and charity.[298]

Fall of Man God's withdrawal from Adam, causing man's "spiritual death." T&C 82:13 states *this Moses plainly taught to the children of Israel* *in the wilderness, and sought diligently to sanctify his people that they might behold the face of God, but they hardened their hearts and could not endure his presence.* These next words are important: *Therefore, the Lord in his wrath (for his anger was kindled against them) swore that they should not enter into his rest — which rest is the fullness of his glory — while in the wilderness.* He did this in "His wrath." Mankind thinks God is very loving and benign because of the sacrifice of Christ. These words seem "Old Testament-like" and not "New Testament-like." But consider how God's wrath is manifested. He withdraws. When one wants Him present and He withdraws, that disapproval can feel terrible.[299] *All mankind were in a lost and in a fallen state, and ever would be save they should rely on this Redeemer* (1 Nephi 3:2). *Yea, behold, this death bringeth to pass the resurrection and redeemeth all mankind from the first death (that spiritual death); for all mankind, by the Fall of Adam, being cut off from the presence of the Lord, are considered as dead, both as to things temporal and to things spiritual* (Helaman 5:12). *See also* WRATH.

False Christ Those who claim "leadership" and want people to "follow" them put themselves in the place of Christ. They are, in effect, a false Christ. It was prophesied they would come in the last days to deceive the "very elect" as false Messiahs (*see* Matthew 11:3,6).[300]

False Prophet The idea of a *wolf* concealing itself in *sheep's clothing* (Matthew 3:46) comes from men with the pretense of piety whose hearts are actually set on the things of this world. *Wolves* are still trusted with the treasury, given honor, and smothered with adoration. Joseph Smith had little confidence in mankind's ability to discern between the real and the imitation. He explained it this way: *The world always mistook false prophets for true ones, and those that were sent of God they considered to be false prophets, and hence they killed, stoned, punished, and imprisoned the true prophets, and they had to hide themselves "in deserts, and in mountains, and dens and caves of the earth" [Hebrews 1:49], and though the most honorable men of the earth, they banished them from their society as vagabonds, while they cherished, honored, and supported knaves, vagabonds, hypocrites, impostors, and the basest of men* (T&C 147:11). Anything claiming to be truth should conform with the truths already given in scripture. Everyone's motives should be questioned until it is determined by sufficient observation that they are *sheep*. "Any teaching or person who draws us to them and does not point us to the Lord, is unable to help us. If they try to supplant Christ as the object of admiration, then they are anti-Christ and a false prophet."[301]

False Spirit A spirit that misleads and confuses; not limited to the idea of a devil, imp, or mischievous personage but it includes the much broader attitude, outlook, or cultural assumptions that people superimpose atop religion. False spirits take the form of ignorant, incomplete, or incorrect ideas that are easily conveyed from one person to another. People convey false spirits when they teach a false idea that the student accepts. False spirits infect every religious tradition on earth. This is not limited to Eastern religions that deny Christ but includes Christianity and Mormonism. So long as anything false is being taught, any error, a false spirit prevails. Different religious structures can be overtaken by false spirits through different means. If there is a religious hierarchy, only the top needs to be taken captive by a false spirit for the entire religion to be misled. If there is a diffused religion, then only the theological seminaries need to be taken captive in order to spread the false spirit. But if the religion is individual and each person is standing on his own — accountable for his relation to God; accountable to learn, to pray, to reach upward, and to have God connect with him or her individually — then the only way to corrupt such an individual religion is to corrupt every single believer, every single practitioner. Joseph Smith tied the discerning of false spirits to priesthood, meaning a fellowship or association (*see also* PRIESTHOOD). When a person has an association with Heavenly angels, they are not apt to be misled by fallen, false spirits (*see* T&C 147:6,9,11). "False spirits are actively involved whenever God begins a work. And there are many false spirits vying for your acceptance, now at work among us."[302] A false spirit is not difficult to identify. It stirs up fear, anger, resentment, envy, jealousy, and false accusation. It makes a man spread false rumors and make accusations that are untrue and unwarranted. Too many of those who should be lending their strength to the restoration effort, currently underway, are now laboring to undermine it, claiming to have a better path to offer. They want to divide the Lord's sheep, encouraging each individual to "find Jesus" alone and apart—a plan which would prevent Zion and please the adversary, who knows that if he can prevent Zion, he can continue to falsely claim to be the god of this world.[303]

False Traditions False traditions are as destructive for man as outright disobedience. The result is the same. The difference is that when one knows he disobeys, he feels guilt. But false traditions fool man into thinking he's obedient when he is actually misled. Thus, Satan leads many to destruction as mankind mistakenly follows darkness rather than Christ's light.[304]

Fasting *And blessed are all they who do hunger and thirst after righteousness, for they shall be filled with the holy ghost* (3 Nephi 5:15). This scripture is not about hunger or poverty. It is about fasting and seeking after righteousness. All qualify for this blessing by "hungering after righteousness." All qualify by "thirsting after righteousness." In other words, one receives the holy ghost in proportion to the hunger and thirst he or she displays. Fasting is a promised means for increasing the holy ghost in one's life. When Alma served as High Priest over the church, he said: *And this is not all; do ye not suppose that I know of these things myself? Behold, I testify unto you that I do know that these things whereof I have spoken are true. And how do ye suppose that I know of their surety? Behold, I say unto you, they are made known unto me by the holy spirit of God. Behold, I have fasted and prayed many days that I might know these things of myself* (Alma 3:8). Fasting and praying opens the spirit. It allows man to know a matter through the power of the holy ghost. The sons of Mosiah, as they were completing their service as missionaries, reunited with Alma, and *Alma did rejoice exceedingly to see his brethren; and what added more to his joy — they were still his brethren in the Lord. Yea, and they had waxed strong in the knowledge of the truth, for they were men of a sound understanding, and they had searched the scriptures diligently that they might know the word of God. But this is not all. They had given themselves to much prayer and fasting, therefore they had the spirit of prophecy and the spirit of revelation; and when they taught, they taught with power and authority, even as with the power and authority of God* (Alma 12:1). They not only searched the scriptures, but they also spent time praying and fasting that they might show God their earnest commitment to know the truth. The result was the *spirit of prophecy and the spirit of revelation,* or in other words, they were filled with the holy ghost. The Lord speaks in simple formulas; they work. When tried in sincerity, acting no hypocrisy, with real intent, they work. Half-hearted efforts are not so effective. But when a soul, any soul, hungers and thirsts after righteousness, they are filled with the holy ghost.[305]

"Fasting is the most effective way to slacken the grasp of this telestial world on the mind and to move toward another ambience. To fast is to do without some normal necessities; your everyday considerations must be put aside because you will be doing other things that require a totally different mind-set. To fast is to disengage from the temporal and wasteful activities of the 'real world.'"[306] Underlying the idea of the fast are two things: first, submission to God; and second, aiding the poor. One can accomplish these purposes even if the "fast" chosen has nothing to do with food. However, man's appetite for food is one of the most direct ways to discipline the will of the body. It is in one's thoughts, not his belly, where the real battle is fought. For someone who is unable to fast, but who can surrender some part of their diet — abstaining from all sweets, for example — it can serve the same purpose. For others, refraining from food and drink is possible without any danger to their health, but if they choose to do so for more than a day, then eating once in the evening allows the fast to continue the next day.[307] One may not be able to hunger and fast for many consecutive days. But by reducing one's caloric intake and "living with fasting," while still eating enough to subsist, one can subordinate the flesh to the spirit while still eating and maintaining health. Sometimes it takes days to receive an answer. Do not abandon the powerful tool of fasting. Instead, "fast" while eating enough for subsistence, and one's purposes can be accomplished without jeopardy to health.[308]

Father of Many Nations The role that is occupied by the head of the human family; a priesthood line in which only one in each generation stands at the head as the Father. "Upon the death of one of these Fathers (speaking about the rights belonging to the Fathers), the family knew who stood next in line in order to be *the father of all, the father of many nations*. [The] Priesthood appoints one who stands as *the father of all*, and this is the reason for Abraham's desire to become *a father of many nations*. This is why he is called *father Abraham*

(Luke 9:20; John 6:16; Acts 4:3; Romans 1:19; Joshua 5:3) — because if Abraham stepped into the line, he necessarily stepped into the role of providing the government of God by assuming the duty of *father*. Christ is the one to whom all generations belong. He is the Redeemer of all mankind, and as the Savior of mankind He becomes the Father of all (1 Corinthians 1:63; Mosiah 8:5; Alma 8:15; Ether 1:13)."[309]

Fathers, The The Fathers in heaven, among whom are Abraham, Isaac, and Jacob, and (because of this Dispensation being what it is) Peter, James, and John. Elijah made a promise (*see* JSH 3:4) about reconnecting mankind to the Fathers. Joseph called them the Fathers in heaven. "These are not our kindred dead, because our kindred dead are required to be redeemed by us."[310] *See also* RIGHTS BELONGING TO THE FATHERS; HEARTS TURNED TO THE FATHERS.

Fear The opposite of faith and hope.[311] Fear is not only the opposite of faith, but it contains within it the bitterness of hell (*see* Genesis 1:4). Man has become too fearful.[312] Closing down because of fear hinders the process of bringing one to the Lord, as the devil knows (*see* T&C 22:8).[313] The path to God can only be found when one refuses to share in the confederacy of fear held by his fellow man. For those controlled by their fears, they will view Christ's way as a stumbling block and an offense (*see* Isaiah 3:7; 2 Nephi 9:8).[314] No one should let borrowed fears become the barrier to one's faith. One cannot respect men too much without respecting God too little.[315] In contrast to fear, Moroni affirms that angels appear only to those with "a firm mind" (*see* Moroni 7:6).[316] The happiest of people are those who live without fear.[317]

Fellowship An individual, a couple, a family, or a group of families where there is no hierarchy; a group of equals who come together to learn, worship, fast, pray, and assist each other who *are desirous to come into the fold of God and to be called His people, and are willing to bear one another's burdens* (Mosiah 9:7). "We own no buildings and, like the early Christians, meet in homes. Our numbers are small. We do not compensate ministers. Fellowships are informal, based on the Doctrine of Christ…. Every denomination in the world can be represented in these fellowships. One may join with other like-minded people for worship, fellowship and growth."[318]

First Presidency Joseph Smith said, "The [Holy Order] was first given to Adam; he obtained the first presidency." When Joseph taught this in 1839, there was a church position called the "First Presidency." The church position was a proper noun. When the *Teachings of the Prophet Joseph Smith* was published — the publisher was the LDS church — the phrase "First Presidency" was treated as if it referred to the church position. However, the position Adam occupied was the first presiding father, or first presidency, of the family of God; this was not a church position. The family of God is not the same thing as an institutional church. The institutional church will never comprise the family of God, although it was intended as a tool to bring about the recovery of the family of God. Unfortunately, the institution grew to hinder the restoration of the family of God. God must now use a different means to fulfill His promises.[319] "[The Holy Order] was first given to Adam; he obtained the [first presiding position on the earth], and held the keys of it from generation to generation. He obtained it in the Creation, before the world was formed, as in [Genesis 2:8]."[320]

First Principles of the Gospel In early Mormonism, the "first principles" were conceptualized as "faith, repentance, and baptism" — largely as a result of the Restoration Movement influence from which both Sidney Rigdon and Parley P. Pratt came, being formerly Campbellite ministers. Joseph Smith's 1842 Wentworth Letter included the "first principles [ordinances] of the gospel" among Latter-day Saint beliefs. He accepted his converts' characterization and used their terminology (*see* T&C 146). On June 27, 1839, Joseph Smith added that "the doctrines of the resurrection of the dead and the eternal judgement are necessary to preach among the first principles of the Gospel of Jesus Christ."[321] "In this statement [he] emphasized that [these] doctrines…should be taught as part of the fundamental articles of faith by the missionaries. He repeatedly referred to and amplified this theme in discourses during the Nauvoo period."[322] In his final church conference in April 1844, Joseph Smith redefined the term "first principles of the gospel," tying it to the progression of men into gods. When he redefined the "first principles about which so much hath been said," he addressed members, not the unconverted and untaught. He wanted them to comprehend much more about the gospel and learn a new, higher ideal. Christ's gospel includes attaining to the resurrection from the dead, becoming gods, and walking the same path as the Lord walked.[323] These are the real first principles.[324]

Follow Christ *Ye shall follow the Son with full purpose of heart, acting no hypocrisy and no deception before God, but with real intent, repenting of your sins, witnessing unto the Father that ye are willing to take upon you the name of Christ* (2 Nephi 13:2).[325] To "follow Christ" is not merely an action; it requires the underlying intent of the action to include full purpose of heart, acting without hypocrisy or deception before God, having real intent, seeking to repent of one's sins, and witnessing unto the Father that one is willing to take upon him or her the name of Christ.[326]

The Father declares: *Yea, the words of my Beloved are true and faithful* (2 Nephi 13:3). The reason Christ is the Father's "Beloved" is directly related to His words being "true and faithful." That is, Christ only does and says what He knows represents the Father's will. He has done this *from the beginning* (3 Nephi 5:4). He represents the "Word" of the Father because one can find in Christ's words and deeds the very word of the Father (*see* T&C 93:2). It is this that qualified Christ to be the Redeemer. His words are faithful and true. So are Nephi's words — his words are the Lord's, though they were delivered by a man. Nephi, having been true and faithful in all things, was able to converse with the Father and the Son through the veil and receive from them further instruction, counsel, warning, and comfort because of the things he learned. This is the pattern for all. This is the culminating message of the Gospel of Christ.[327] "What does the idea of *following Christ* imply, if it were taken to its fullest extent? Why would that require someone to go *from one small degree to another*? What would be involved for someone to pass *from exaltation to exaltation* as Joseph mentions in his discourse in April, 1844?[328] How fully must we follow Christ?"[329]

For Ever This has typically been made the compound word *forever*, but the meaning of that word doesn't align with the old languages' statements. *Forever* means "ongoing in infinite perpetuity." But then how does one add "ever" to that, as in *forever and ever*? You cannot add more to infinite perpetuity. The old Hebrew phrase translated into

this phrase meant "to the horizon, and again" (l'olam va'ed לְעוֹלָם וָעֶד).
It maintained finite limitations, but of great degrees. By keeping *for
ever* as two words, *ever* may be understood as some finite portion to
which additional *ever* can be added.

The term connotes cycles or returning patterns, as in Christ's
statement *in my Father's house are many mansions* (T&C 98:3). When
the term "mansion" was used in King James-ian English, it meant
"a temporary stop" or what modern language would term a "motel."
For ever and ever implies moving from place to place — or going from
estate to estate — in cycles that continue endlessly.[330] *See also* WORLDS
WITHOUT END; MANSION.

Forgetting Ignoring Joseph Smith; refusing the gift God offered.
Man's first obligation now is to remember. Until man remembers
what was given before, there is no reason for God to give more.
Forgetting includes re-interpreting the language by divorcing it
from context, supplying new meaning not originally intended, and
improperly using Joseph to vindicate later improper innovations.[331]
"How much study should be given to the history of the restoration?
How carefully should Joseph's teachings be preserved, studied, and
followed? When the Lord commanded us to *give heed to all his [meaning
Joseph Smith's] words and commandments* to what extent are we justified
in forgetting his words and teachings? (JSH 18:4–5)."[332]

Forgiveness God is no respecter of persons. All are alike to Him.
Qualifications are based upon the behavior and faith of the person,
not on their status or past mistakes. Most people think their errors
are too serious an impediment for them to find acceptance from
God. He doesn't want to judge His children; He wants to heal them.
He wants to give them what they lack, teach them to be better, and
to bless them. He doesn't want to belittle, demean, or punish them.
When they ask Him to forgive, He forgives. Even very serious sins.
He does not want them burdened with sin. He wants them to leave
it behind. His willingness to leave those errors in the past and
remember them no more is greater than any can imagine. It is a
guiding principle for the atonement. Asking for forgiveness is
almost all that is required to be forgiven. What alienates mankind
from Him is not their sins — He will forgive those. What men lack
is the confidence to ask in faith, nothing doubting, for His help. He

can and will help when asked.[333] In most cases, it is man's disrespect for themselves that impedes them from coming to Him. They tend to think they are not good enough. However, because He is quick to forgive sins, it really doesn't matter if they aren't good enough. One of the first things He does when man enters His presence is to forgive all sins. He cannot look upon sin with the least degree of allowance, but He has the capacity to forgive sin. Therefore, "although your sins may be as scarlet, He can, He will, and He does make you white as snow, no longer accountable for your limitations. Therefore you need not fear, but you can approach boldly."[334] Christ taught His followers to forgive so that they may, in turn, merit forgiveness. He said: *For if you forgive men their trespasses who trespass against you, your Heavenly Father will also forgive you. But if you forgive not men their trespasses, neither will your Heavenly Father forgive you your trespasses* (Matthew 3:30). Christ taught that there is atoning power in forgiving others. As a result of the things He suffered, He understood that men must forgive others in order to be able to obtain forgiveness. There are many things men do in which they lack the capacity to make amends. The price they must pay for their own transgressions is paid by forgiving all others of their offenses.[335]

Form of Godliness The opposite of godliness; having the pretense of godliness or a form that mimics it. The Lord condemned the doctrines of men being taught for commandments when He said, *They draw near to me with their lips, but their hearts are far from me.... They teach for doctrines the commandments of men, having a form of godliness, but they deny the power thereof* (JSH 2:5). What does *having a form of godliness, but [denying] the power thereof* mean? Godliness means to be godly or close to God. It is possible to pretend to godliness (i.e., have a "form" that mimics it) without actually being close to God.[336] The Lord lamented in the First Vision to Joseph Smith that men have merely a form of godliness — insubstantial, unredeeming, incapable of saving.[337]

Froward The Hebrew פָּתַל (*pâthal*), from the primitive meaning to twine or twist, is translated in the KJV as froward, wrestled, or twisted.[338] Froward is a 12th century English word meaning moving or facing away from something or someone, as opposed to *toward* which means moving or facing in the direction of something or someone. Frowardness means stubbornness or contrariness. "If we are froward, we are stubborn or contrary with one another. We dispute. We find it difficult to agree. Much debate and anger is produced by frowardness."[339] It requires strength to refrain from contention and disputes with froward and arrogant people. When one feels strongly that he is right or is firmly convinced someone else is wrong, it is difficult to bridle one's tongue and meekly persuade without contention.[340] The Heavenly Mother, as "Wisdom," mentions her opposition to the froward. She declares She hates the froward mouth. We repel Her by being argumentative and contrary with one another. The Mother must possess great strength because She hates the froward — the contentious. She does not welcome that spirit in Herself or any of Her offspring (*see* Proverbs 1:34).[341]

Fruit A genealogical term, in many instances; family. Adam and Eve were commanded to *be fruitful and multiply* (Genesis 2:9). Christ's gospel involves perpetuating a "family of Gods." Marriage mirrors the infinite. The "fruit" to be saved refers to an eternal family, with God at the head.[342] "In John 9:10 Christ compared Himself to a *true vine* to which we all must connect if we are going to bear fruit. Christ inspired prophecies about a coming servant. We should all be His servants. For any of His servants to produce *fruit* they must connect to Him, the *true vine*. Life comes from that connection. We are preserved by Christ, nourished through His word, and we pray in our sacrament prayers to always have His spirit to be with us. The *vine* and *fruit* refer to the *family of God*. The context is about becoming a *son of God*. He intends to make many sons of God, to bring many sons unto glory."[343] Throughout Zenos' allegory of the olive tree, fruit means "salvation," in a covenantal sense. It requires the promises made to the fathers (*see* Abraham 1:1) to be the same covenant given to you.[344]

"The Savior provided a test whereby one can easily distinguish between true and false prophets. *You shall know them by their fruits* (Matthew 3:46). The question was, 'Well, if there is a test to apply, in order to determine whether or not he [Joseph Smith] was a prophet, the presence of the test suggests the possibility of a prophet.' I thought that an interesting point. Why would you have a test if there is not going to be another prophet? So, *you shall know them by their fruits* suggests the possibility that there will, in fact, be someone you better apply that test to, someone for whom the test will become both relevant and important. So I couldn't categorically dismiss Joseph Smith as a prophet for the reason there absolutely could never be more. Therefore, I needed to ask the next question: What are Joseph's fruits?"[345] In Matthew 6:14, Christ explained how to measure "fruit." *Either make the tree good and his fruit good, or else make the tree corrupt and his fruit corrupt, for the tree is known by the fruit. And Jesus said, O you generation of vipers. How can you, being evil, speak good things? For out of the abundance of the heart the mouth speaks. A good man, out of the good treasure of the heart, brings forth good things; and an evil man, out of the evil treasure, brings forth evil things. And again I say unto you that every idle word men shall speak, they shall give account thereof in the day of judgment; for by your words you shall be justified, and by your words you shall be condemned.* Christ determined that the test for "fruit" is the words one speaks. But how should "words" be measured? Anger, conflict, violence, war, and division amongst families were just some of the results of the words Christ spoke. If Christ's words were measured by how people were affected by them, then Christ produced bad fruit. Therefore, the reaction people have to words cannot be an accurate measure of "fruit." It must be the substance, the truth, or the independent value of the words — separate from how people respond to a man's words. Prophets and righteous individuals have been arousing anger, provoking violent reactions, and being called anything from foolish to vile because of their words, and that does nothing to diminish the goodness of their fruit.[346]

Full of Love Charity; the *pure love of Christ*. Mosiah 1:16 speaks of being *full of love*. This is what 1 Corinthians 1:51–53 is all about. Charity is the *pure love of Christ*. This childlike attribute comes from a natural disposition to share love that children enjoy by their native status. As mortals progress into adulthood and experience the disappointments of others' failings, they become less willing to love others. They suspect others' motives. Adults distrust others' worthiness to be loved. They guard against others' potential for causing them mischief. These are learned fears. Little children are "too trusting," because they find it easier to love than to fear. All men and women found it easier to love when they were children.[347] *See also* CHARITY and LOVE.

Fullness Completion of development. Each stage of experience has its own definition of what it means to gain a fullness. Fullness in the preexistence is not the same thing as a fullness in mortality. In turn, the fullness of mortality is not the same thing as the fullness that comes next. Each stage of development has conditions, limitations, and an agenda. Right now one is only accountable for seeking a fullness of what pertains to mortality.[348] "We are not here to 'get exalted.' We are here to continue progression which began a long time before our current birth. At the moment, you are being 'added upon' by what you experience here (*see* Abraham 6:2). At some point, you will have received what you need in this sphere, and can move on to the next stage of development. When you have gained everything you need from this life, you will have received the 'fullness' from God. It is called the 'fullness' because it is all that can be obtained here. It is not possible, however, to inherit everything God ultimately offers while here."[349] *Jesus lived as the example, proving the pattern for redemption from the Fall as he progressed from grace to grace, until he received a fullness, or in other words, grew in light and truth until he was filled with truth and stands as the light of the world.*[350] *And in this way He qualified to be called to become the Son of God, because He received not of the fullness at the first. And I, John, bear record that He received a fullness of the glory of the Father. And He received all power, both in heaven and on earth, and the glory of the Father was with Him, for he dwelt in Him.*[351] The Lord explained in the "Answer to Prayer for Covenant" that *the fullness is to receive the truth of all things, and this too from me, in power, by my word and in very deed* (T&C 157:53).

Fullness of the Gospel This is used a number of ways in scripture: First, it is an explanation of what the Book of Mormon contains (*see,* e.g., JSH 3:3; T&C 26:7). In that sense, the term refers to a collection of prophetic testimonies about Jesus Christ as their Redeemer and guide to salvation and, in turn, Christ's role as universal Savior and Redeemer of mankind. Second, it is a way to identify Christ revealing Himself to mankind, thereby redeeming mortals from the fall. It is in this sense that the term is used in T&C 69:3: The ascent to God *is the fullness of the gospel of Jesus Christ.* It shows up very early in the first chapter by Lehi. Then it is repeated by Nephi, Jacob, Enos, Mosiah, and Alma, describing their ascent experiences. It continues throughout.[352] Third, the Lord has used it to describe an everlasting covenant: "...*the fullness of my gospel which I have sent forth in these last days, the covenant which I have sent forth to recover my people which are of the house of Israel* (T&C 23:3; 31:3; 52:1; 1 Nephi 3:4). Joseph Smith used the term in his writings and teachings at different times with different meanings. "Learning these 'mysteries [of God]' is the fullness of Christ's Gospel."[353] The fullness of the Gospel consists of asking God, receiving answers, revelations, knowledge, and finally, in the Second Comforter.[354]

Fullness of the Priesthood A term that was used by Joseph Smith at different times with different meanings. It always conveyed that the recipient had accepted all that had been given to a point in time. The willing readiness to accept all that had been offered by the time of the dedication of the Kirtland Temple meant the believer had been ordained to the Aaronic and Melchizedek priesthoods, had been baptized, and as the then-current practice involved, had been re-baptized and passed through an initiatory washing and anointing. The term used later during the late-Nauvoo period of Joseph Smith's life involved all of the foregoing and, in addition, an endowment and sealing, second anointing, and finally an adoption process tying the individual into a family relationship that would endure after death. Because the fullness of the priesthood was used dynamically and not statically by Joseph Smith, various revelations making use of the term should not be read as having a single meaning. In a final sense, fullness of priesthood will be post-resurrection and will come to those who have continually manifested a willingness to accept the dynamic and progressive fullness of the priesthood offered by God to man in the development and restoration of all things.[355]

Fullness of the Scriptures Joseph Smith restored the Book of Mormon as his first assignment. But he was also required to revise the Bible. Joseph referred to the revision of the Bible as "the fullness of the scriptures." He referred to the Book of Mormon as only "the Book of Mormon." Joseph's reference to "the fullness of the scriptures" was exclusively to the Bible. In the minutes of an October 1831 conference, Joseph made this statement, "God had often sealed up the Heavens because of covetousness in the church. Said the Lord would cut his work short in righteousness and except the church receive the fullness of the scriptures they would yet fall."[356] After that warning on July 17, 1840, two men were assigned to go on a mission for the purpose of raising money to publish scriptures. This included a new edition of the Book of Mormon and the Joseph Smith Translation of the Bible. (It is called a "translation" but is more correctly understood as the prophet's inspired revision clarifying the text.) In October 1840, a letter to all the saints was published in the *Times and Seasons* asking for their full support in the effort to publish "the new translation of the Scriptures." That effort failed to put the Joseph Smith Translation in print, and Joseph died without it ever being published. Excerpts with edits done by others were published by the Reorganized Church of Jesus Christ of Latter Day Saints, but it failed to include Joseph's entire work.[357] The fullness of the scriptures, or Joseph Smith's inspired revision of the Bible, has never been available in full, in print, until now. They are published for the first time in the new set of Restoration Edition scriptures. They can be found in the Old Testament (now called The Old Covenants) and in half the volume called The New Covenants. The fullness of the scriptures, without which the church would fall, is being made available for the first time.[358]

Garments Washed White   *Their garments were washed white through the blood of the Lamb* (Alma 10:1). "To have white garments is to have the blood and sins of your generation removed from you; to be purified; to be sanctified by the Lamb – removing from you, and taking upon Himself, the responsibility to answer for whatever failings you have. This is not ritual purity. This is purity in fact."[359]

Gathering of Israel   An event that is foretold to happen at the end of the times, when Christ returns. In one sense, any time there has been a restoration since the time of Israel (Father Jacob), the goal has been to gather Israel from their lost and ignorant state. But the final Gathering of Israel is to happen preliminary to the return of Christ in glory, when the dispersed remnants are grafted in through authoritative sealings using the power of heaven to accomplish, through temple rites, their return to full covenantal status. It is a re-creation of the Family of God on earth.[360]

Generation The time in which the teaching/religion/movement remains in an unaltered state. Almost invariably, however, the way a new revelation from heaven works is that God will reveal himself in a generation, and then when the prophet/prophets of that time — the mortals living, the messengers — die, what survives cannot be kept intact. It simply cannot be kept in an unaltered, fully-preserved condition. You need another Peter or another Paul or another Moses; you need another one with that standing, or it falls into immediate disrepair. While there are living oracles that are in communication with God, that is the best definition of a generation. Uninspired men cannot add to the work of a prophet.[361]

Gentiles The word is used in Nephi's writings to include literal descendants of Israel — particularly the Northern Tribes — once they have intermarried and lost their identities, thereby becoming gentiles. However, as they convert and remake restored covenants with the Lord through baptism, the same people who were gentiles at one point become "Israel" at another, after their conversion.[362] The church restored through Joseph Smith is referred to throughout the Book of Mormon as the gentiles. Joseph knew this, and the Kirtland Temple dedicatory prayer, which came to him as a revelation, explained how the church was regarded by the Lord (*see* T&C 123:18).[363] All the prophecies of the Book of Mormon upon the gentiles are references to what the latter-day gentile church will accomplish (or fail to accomplish).[364] Christ's prophecy (*see* 3 Nephi 7:5) does not anticipate gentile success. The gentiles will reject the fullness offered to them. *At that day when the gentiles shall sin against my gospel* does not raise the possibility of *if*, but only *when*. According to Christ, the gentiles *shall reject the fullness of my gospel*. Taking these words at their plain meaning, it leaves no room for gentiles to obtain and perpetuate the fullness of the priesthood. They will, instead, reject it when it is offered them. But despite having rejected it, gentiles are allowed to repent and join the remnant of the Book of Mormon people and be saved.[365]

Therefore, woe be unto the gentiles if it so be that they harden their hearts against the Lamb of God (1 Nephi 3:26). Notice that the relationship is between the *Lamb of God* and the gentiles. It is not between the gentiles and leaders or prophets or administrators or general authorities or even messengers. It is between the gentiles and *the Lamb of God*. It's no wonder that after making great promises to the gentiles, *if they will but repent*, the angel cries out, *Woe be unto the gentiles!* They won't receive: 1) the Gospel, nor 2) the testimony of Jesus, nor 3) the prophets sent to warn them or the message given to them, nor 4) the everlasting covenant offered to them.[366] The church restored through Joseph may be referred to as "latter-day Israel" or similar terms, but the Book of Mormon vocabulary applies the term "gentiles" to all members of the latter-day churches.[367] The Book of Mormon prophecies still do not refer to the latter-day gentiles as anything other than "gentiles," even when they are *numbered among the seed of Lehi*. In prophecy, their identification remains "gentiles," even though they are adopted as Lehi's seed. Hence Joseph Smith's reference in the Kirtland Temple dedicatory prayer to the Latter-day Saints as "gentiles" by identity (*see* T&C 123:18). Whenever a gentile manages to acquire this adoption, they do not become identified as the "remnant" as a result. Instead, they become heirs to share in the promised blessings, but they do so as "gentiles." They will get to assist the "remnant," but they do so as "gentiles," not as the "remnant." Still, those who are adopted as Lehi's seed do inherit, with the "remnant," the Lord's promises. But they are nevertheless called "gentiles" throughout prophecy.[368]

Some of the prophecies outlined for the gentiles in our day include: *The Lord God will proceed to do a marvelous work among the gentiles...unto the making known of the covenants of the Father of Heaven unto Abraham* (1 Nephi 7:3). *And blessed are the gentiles...if it so be that they shall repent, and fight not against Zion, and do not unite themselves to that great and abominable church, they shall be saved* (2 Nephi 5:5). *And the gentiles are lifted up in the pride of their eyes, and have stumbled because of the greatness of their stumbling block, that they have built up many churches; nevertheless, they put down the power and the miracles of God, and preach up unto themselves their own wisdom and their own learning, that they may get gain and grind upon the face of the poor* (2 Nephi 11:15). *Woe be unto the gentiles, saith the Lord God of Hosts, for notwithstanding I shall lengthen out mine arm unto them from day to day, they will deny me. Nevertheless, I will be merciful unto them, saith the Lord God, if they will repent and come unto me* (2 Nephi 12:7). *As many of the gentiles as will repent are the covenant people of the Lord* (2 Nephi 12:11). *In the latter day shall the truth come unto the gentiles, that the fullness of these things shall be made known unto them* (3 Nephi 7:4). *And, thus commandeth the Father that I should say unto you: At that day when the gentiles shall sin against my gospel, and shall reject the fullness of my gospel, and shall be lifted up in the pride of their hearts above all nations and above all the people of the whole earth, and shall be filled with all manner of lyings, and of deceits, and of mischiefs, and all manner of hypocrisy, and murders, and priestcrafts, and whoredoms, and of secret abominations, and if they shall do all these things, and shall reject the fullness of my gospel, Behold, saith the Father, I will bring the fullness of my gospel from among them* (3 Nephi 7:5). This is to be done after the gentiles — the European Latter-day Saints who descend from the bloodlines that overran and dispossessed the native people in North America — have rejected the fullness of the Gospel.[369] *But if the gentiles will repent and return unto me, saith the Father, behold, they shall be numbered among my people, O house of Israel* (3 Nephi 7:5). *Therefore, when these works and the works which shall be wrought among you hereafter shall come forth from the gentiles unto your seed which shall dwindle in unbelief because of iniquity — for thus it behooveth the Father that it should come forth from the gentiles* [not the "book" which was brought forth in 1830, but the "works" of preaching the gospel of Christ; someone must preach repentance, declare Christ's doctrine, and baptize by the authority of Christ, allowing the remnant of the Nephites to be baptized by fire and the Holy Ghost],[370] *that he may shew forth his power unto the gentiles for this cause, that the gentiles, if they will not harden their hearts, that they may repent, and come unto me, and be baptized in my name, and know of the true points of my doctrine, that they may be numbered among my people, O house of Israel — and when these things come to pass, that thy seed shall begin to know these things, it shall be a sign unto them that they may know that the work of the Father hath already commenced unto the fulfilling of the covenant which he hath made unto the people who are of the house of Israel* (3 Nephi 9:11). All of Israel should recognize this witness. But it does require them to recognize or accept this sign. To be fulfilled, God need only give the sign.[371] *But if they [the gentiles] will repent, and hearken unto my words, and harden not their hearts, I will establish my church among them, and they shall come in unto the covenant and be numbered among this the remnant of Jacob, unto whom I have given this land for their*

*inheritance. And they shall assist my people, the remnant of Jacob, and also
as many of the house of Israel as shall come, that they may build a city which
shall be called the New Jerusalem. And then shall they assist my people, that
they may be gathered in, who are scattered upon all the face of the land, in
unto the New Jerusalem* (3 Nephi 10:1).

Gift of the Holy Ghost Alma recounts the many blessings the
Nephites had received in their generations: *Having been visited by
the spirit of God, having conversed with angels, and having been spoken
unto by the voice of the Lord; and having the spirit of prophecy and the spirit
of revelation; and also many gifts: the gift of speaking with tongues, and the
gift of preaching, and the gift of the holy ghost, and the gift of translation*
(Alma 7:4). According to Alma, these many blessings come from *the
spirit of God* and include *the gift of the holy ghost*.[372] "If God sustains
everything through His holy spirit, which is also sometimes called
the Light of Christ, then is it not already within you? If it is already
within you, then you can decide to 'receive' it by opening yourself
up to its influence. If you decide to 'receive' it by opening yourself
up to its influence, then you may be able to take it into yourself as a
gift from God[.] If that gift becomes a permanent source of influence
within you, then have you received the *gift of the holy ghost*? If this is
within you, then is it your own? If your own, then do you have the
holy ghost as your constant companion?"[373] The holy ghost can come
and visit with a person but not tarry with them.[374] If it comes and
visits with them, then it is said the person has "received" the holy
ghost. This kind of visit is conditional. It is dependent upon the
worthiness and desire of the recipient. If they "grieve" the spirit by
misbehavior, it will depart from them. For the holy ghost to become
a constant companion which tarries, it is said to be *the gift of the holy
ghost,* because the one with this endowment has received a gift from
God, and it is given to them by God to be theirs.[375]

Baptism and the holy ghost have always been linked together, but
laying on hands has not always been included. Baptism and the holy
ghost are linked whether or not there is someone who can lay on
hands to give the gift. Baptism precedes the holy ghost, and the holy
ghost always follows, if the baptism was proper. The only condition
for receiving the holy ghost is sincere repentance before baptism. If a
person is sincere, then the gift follows automatically. Nephi relayed

some truth about baptism and the holy ghost: *And [Christ] said unto the children of men, Follow thou me. Wherefore, my beloved brethren, can we follow Jesus save we shall be willing to keep the commandments of the Father? And the Father said, Repent ye, repent ye, and be baptized in the name of my beloved Son. And also the voice of the Son came unto me, saying, He that is baptized in my name, to him will the Father give the holy ghost like unto me. Wherefore, follow me and do the things which ye have seen me do. Wherefore, my beloved brethren, I know that if ye shall follow the Son with full purpose of heart, acting no hypocrisy and no deception before God, but with real intent, repenting of your sins, witnessing unto the Father that ye are willing to take upon you the name of Christ by baptism – yea, by following your Lord and Savior down into the water according to his word – behold, then shall ye receive the holy ghost. Yea, then cometh the baptism of fire and of the holy ghost, and then can ye speak with the tongue of angels and shout praises unto the Holy One of Israel. But behold, my beloved brethren, thus came the voice of the Son unto me, saying, After ye have repented of your sins, and witnessed unto the Father that ye are willing to keep my commandments by the baptism of water, and have received the baptism of fire and of the holy ghost, and can speak with a new tongue – yea, even with the tongue of angels – and after this should deny me, it would have been better for you that ye had not known me. And I heard a voice from the Father saying, Yea, the words of my beloved are true and faithful. He that endureth to the end, the same shall be saved* (2 Nephi 13:2–3). "Therefore, according to Christ and the Father, as reported by Nephi, the steps are: one, repent; two, be willing to take upon you the name of Christ; three, be baptized; and four, … the holy ghost will come upon you." There is no mention of laying on of hands, because the process and promise given by Christ and the Father does not require laying on hands. It only requires exactly what Nephi reported from conversing with Christ and the Father. Likewise, in modern revelation the Lord explained His Gospel while omitting any requirement for laying on hands for the holy ghost: *And verily, verily I say unto you, he that receives my gospel receives me. And he that receives not my gospel receives not me. And this is my gospel: repentance, and baptism by water, and then comes the baptism of fire and the holy ghost, yea, even the Comforter, which shows all things and teaches the peaceable things of the kingdom* (T&C 23:2). Similar to Nephi's explanation, Christ makes no mention of laying on of hands in this revelation to Joseph, because it is not required. Christ set the example. He was baptized and immediately received the holy ghost. No one laid hands on Him. The gift was given because of His qualification for baptism. But there have been those who were given conditional authority to bestow the gift. They could only do so by consulting with the Father and Christ beforehand to ensure it was God's decision, not man's, to give the gift.[376] Christ, however, can give the permanent gift of the holy ghost by His touch (*see* 3 Nephi 8:10; Moroni 2:2).[377] *See also* HOLY GHOST.

Gift of Tongues "*The gift of tongues…even cloven tongues as of fire* (T&C 123:10). This is a strange figure. To cleave means both to stick together, glue, *kleben*, etc., and also to split or separate. A cloven tongue is a loosened and articulate tongue. The image here employed recalls both the two-edged sword which is the word or tongue of God, which *is quick and powerful, sharper than a two-edged sword, to the dividing asunder of the joints and marrow, soul and spirit* (T&C 16:1) and the fiery sword of the cherubim (*kherev* means sword). The next [sentence] confirms the use of metaphors, where 'tongues *as* of fire' is matched by the filling of the house '*as* with a rushing mighty wind.' Was there real fire or a real wind? No, but there was something real that can best be described in those terms. We know that things really happened in the Kirtland Temple, where we read also of a sound *as* of rushing waters and hair *as* white wool."[378] The Lord can give the Gift of Tongues, which constitutes the ability to speak "foreign" or non-native languages (*see* Acts 1:7–8; T&C 32:5), and He is also able to endow men and women with a loosened and articulate tongue, which speaks the words of God. To speak with a new tongue is to speak worthily of sacred things. It is to correctly weigh the truth of a matter, know by the power of the spirit that what is said is true and in conformity with God's will, and then to speak it.[379] *See also* SPEAK WITH THE TONGUE OF ANGELS.

Gifts of the Spirit Gifts are given to bless all of God's children and are a means to avoid deception. Men and women are commanded to not only seek gifts, but to seek earnestly the best gifts (*see* T&C 32:4–5). Gifts of the spirit are *not* coincident with, nor dependent upon, priesthood. Anyone — man or woman, young or old, with or without priesthood — can have gifts of the Spirit (*see* T&C 32:4–7). Paul's instruction to the saints at Corinth suggested they all (men, women, and children) should seek for the best gifts (*see* 1 Corinthians 1:54–60). The great high priest for whom the Holy Priesthood after the Order of the Son of God was renamed did not perform miracles through his priesthood. Like every other person, he performed miracles through his faith. [380] His faith to perform miracles preceded his ordination to the priesthood (*see* Genesis 7:18). Because he exhibited great faith, he was subsequently ordained (*see* Genesis 7:18). Before his ordination, he worked miracles. This means, just as T&C 32:4–7 confirms, that gifts of the spirit are not limited to men who hold the priesthood. Any person of any age or sex can work miracles through faith. The result of this, of course, is that women, as well as men, can prophesy, heal the sick, speak in tongues, have visions and inspired dreams, and other remarkable works through the spirit. [381] These great gifts of the spirit are always acquired in exactly the same way in every generation when they appear, by everyone who acquires them. It is always through the exercise of the person's faith. The way people exercise their faith is always by conforming their outward actions to their innermost true beliefs, even when the actions taken are difficult — "even when the Lord asks of you something you are very reluctant to place upon the altar; even when everyone will hate you for what it is you do." [382] There are "gifts" given (or acquired) by people which are based on real sensitivities or talents. They exist as part of the talents brought into this life. Some people have the talent to sing, compose music, or create art. There are those who have developed spiritual gifts. There are many kinds of gifts, but they all come from God (*see* Moroni 10:3). Possession of a gift, however, does not mean a person will use that gift in conformity with God's will or plan. If a person does not seek to follow the Lord's will, they can be misled and use gifts for improper ends. People who fail to remain obedient (who begin to use their gifts to gratify their pride or to achieve their ambitions) can drift away from the light and take others with them. Just because a person possesses a gift does not mean they live their lives in conformity to truth. Nor does it mean they will not mislead. Proper use of a gift should show gratitude to — and promote faith in — God. There are aids to faith that can help someone who is weak to still act in faith — modalities that focus thought, bolster confidence, and assist in believing the Lord can heal and can aid in the process. In the end, it is the authority of God and faith in Him that allows good things to follow. It comes from Him. If an act helps focus thought and confidence in Him, then the act is worthwhile. The problems creep in when the modality — a particular mode of treatment or handling, e.g., a holistic healing or gift — is regarded as an independent authority apart from God. As soon as a person begins to view God as uninvolved or that they can control the outcome independent of God's will, there is an opening for evil or deception. Gifts were not intended to produce a monetary profit and should not be practiced for money (see Acts 5:4). Gifts belong to the body of believers and should be used to promote faith in God.[383]

"Many things can be faked, but you cannot fake spiritual power. People pretend to espouse beliefs and/or traits all the time which do not belong to them. But power in the spirit cannot be a mere pretense. Gifts of the spirit cannot be feigned. New and inventive ways to describe what is passed off as gifts of the spirit cannot substitute for the absence of the traditional gifts named in scripture. Some talents are commonly possessed by mankind, whether they have ever been converted or not. Calling such common talents a 'gift of the spirit' may be a humble acknowledgment of the fact all things come from God, but such things are not the *gifts of the spirit* which are identified in scripture. The scriptures are unequivocal in telling us healing, prophecy, ministering angels, speaking in tongues, etc., are the hallmark gifts of the spirit. If you have had such a witness and such an experience, you do not need to pretend something is a proof of the power of godliness when it is not. You will experience the real thing. And when you do, there will be no need for pretending something else is the power of godliness which Christ promised He was returning to the earth. The seventh Article of Faith says: *We believe in the gift of tongues, prophecy, revelation, visions, healing, interpretation of tongues, and so forth.* This specific statement of belief, composed by the founding Prophet of the Dispensation, does not say we believe in administration, patience, love, listening, tolerating, or other merely human virtues possessed in common with all mankind, are going to be called the gifts of the spirit. The gifts of the spirit have something unusual about them and are based upon power from God. There is no need, if you have received a witness from the spirit, to pretend any longer a mere human virtue is evidence of God's power in your life. You can and will actually find God bestowing upon you the power of prophecy, revelation, visions, healing, tongues, and interpretation of tongues, etc."[384]

Glory   *The glory of God is intelligence, or in other words, light and truth* (T&C 93:11), and is obtained by obedience to law.[385] The word glory refers to intelligence — or knowledge and understanding.[386] "God says this is His *work and [His] glory: to bring to pass the immortality and eternal life of man* (Genesis 1:7) — that mankind returns to His presence and with Him partakes of eternal life and exaltation. Since His glory is intelligence, He shares it with us. Glory is shared intelligence."[387]

God of Abraham, God of Isaac, God of Jacob   Abraham, Isaac, and Jacob each separately held a covenant with God; therefore, He was their God, and they were His son (*see* 1 Chronicles 8:21; 2 Kings 4:47). It is not the "God of Abraham, Isaac, and Jacob;" it's the "God of Abraham, the God of Isaac, and the God of Jacob" (*see* Exodus 2:3,6; Matthew 10:22; Mark 5:43; 1 Nephi 2:1; 3 Nephi 2:14; Mormon 4:7). The scriptures refer to it in this way to acknowledge the covenantal sonship that they *each* had. *See* SEED OF ABRAHAM.[388]

Godliness   "To be godly" or "close to God." It is possible to pretend to godliness (i.e., have a "form" that mimics it) without actually being close to God. In the truest sense, to be close to God is to be in His presence.[389]

Gospel of Jesus Christ   "You need to know what [this] term really means. If you do not, then you have not received it. You have claimed, like others, to be 'of Christ' without ever comprehending what His Gospel includes and does not include."[390] The word gospel comes from the Old English *godspel* (good spell); literally from *god* (good) and *spel* (story, message, spell, narrative, or form of words; often defined as glad or good tidings). When a story or spell is cast that is good, it is a "gospel." It has the same origin as "to spell," meaning to read letter by letter or speak. The original had a long "o," and later became associated as "God," as in "God-story." The word is a translation of the Greek *euangelion* (εὐαγγελίου) meaning "good message" and translated in the KJV as "gospel."[391]

Jesus Christ defines His gospel in the Book of Mormon: *Behold, I have given unto you my gospel, and this is the gospel which I have given unto you: that I came into the world to do the will of my Father because my Father sent me. And my Father sent me that I might be lifted up upon the cross. And after that I had been lifted up upon the cross, I might draw all men unto me — that as I have been lifted up by men, even so should men be lifted up by the Father to stand before me, to be judged of their works, whether they be good or whether they be evil. And for this cause have I been lifted up. Therefore, according to the power of the Father, I will draw all men unto me, that they may be judged according to their works. And it shall come to pass that whoso repenteth and is baptized in my name shall be filled, and if he endureth to the end, behold, him will I hold guiltless before my Father at that day when I shall stand to judge the world. And he that endureth not unto the end, the same is he that is also hewn down and cast into the fire from whence they can no more return, because of the justice of the Father. And this is the word which he hath given unto the children of men, and for this cause he fulfilleth the words which he hath given; and he lieth not, but fulfilleth all his words. And no unclean thing can enter into his kingdom, therefore nothing entereth into his rest save it be those who have washed their garments in my blood because of their faith, and the repentance of all their sins, and their faithfulness unto the end. Now this is the commandment: Repent all ye ends of the earth, and come unto me, and be baptized in my name that ye may be sanctified by the reception of the holy ghost, that ye may stand spotless before me at the last day. Verily, verily I say unto you, this is my gospel* (3 Nephi 12:5). He defines it in modern times as: *And verily, verily I say unto you, He that receives my gospel receives me. And he that receives not my gospel receives not me. And this is my gospel: repentance, and baptism by water, and then comes the baptism of fire and the holy ghost, yea, even the Comforter, which shows all things and teaches the peaceable things of the kingdom* (T&C 23:2).

"The terrible problem of mortality is that we are all prone to drift and fail. It is only by constant renewal of faith that we can hope to succeed. No matter how far we have come, what great things we have obtained, we are still subject to failure. This is why the *first* principles and ordinances of the Gospel are: faith, repentance, baptism, and laying on of hands for the gift of the holy ghost. We never outgrow these *first* principles. I believe them to be *first* in the sense of primacy, not a singular event which happens and then you can take them off the list of stuff to do. They are primary. They are foundational. They are required to be used constantly. Therefore, they are *first*. So, we always go forward in faith. No matter how much we already know, we must use faith to go forward. We live within the limitation of linear time. We experience things in a flow that happens without our control. Life unfolds as an unknown to us, and we must cope with all it hands us from day to day. That requires faith to confront this uncontrolled, unfolding stream of time in which we are presently confined. Repentance is required because even if we are doing what we should be doing, we are always going to learn more. It is the nature of the Gospel that our light should increase. Whenever we learn more, we must change to reflect what we have just gained. Change is the heart of repentance. Baptism is to have sins washed away. The holy ghost should be a regular participant in our lives. Its renewed companionship is also primary. Its witness to us that we are on the right path is the only way to wage the necessary war against entropy which seeks to take you into darkness. It is the source of renewed light that always enlightens when it comes. These are the only means by which we can avoid the same dismal fate as all others of all prior dispensations. "[392]

Almost everything about the Gospel plan is a process and not an event. Most people most of the time are only working through the process. A great deal of the scriptures has been written by those who have been through the process and who are trying to give mankind instructions of how to repeat it in their own lives. There are events which occur in the scriptures, as well, but man will never arrive at the events unless he first realizes there is a process, and he begins to participate actively in that process.[393] In the April 1844 conference talk, Joseph Smith redefined the term "first principles." Joseph wanted the saints to comprehend much more about the gospel and learn a new, higher ideal. Christ's gospel includes: attaining to the resurrection from the dead, becoming gods, and walking the same path as our Lord walked. These are the real first principles of the gospel. That is why he wished he had the trumpet of an archangel with which to declare it. His words were worthy of an archangel: "You thus learn some of the first principles of the Gospel, about which so much hath been said. When you climb up a ladder, you must begin at the bottom, and ascend step by step, until you arrive at the top; and so it is with the principles of the Gospel — you must begin with the first, and go on until you learn all the principles of exaltation. But it will be a great while after you have passed through the veil before you will have learned them. It is not all to be comprehended in this world; it will be a great work to learn our salvation and exaltation even beyond the grave" (*TPJS*, 348; *WJS*, 358). "We have such a long way to go even after this life that we hardly comprehend how great a work remains. We will not learn everything needed 'in this world.' These are the basics of the gospel of Christ. This is the foundation upon which salvation itself rests. This is the climb we must make to be like Him. We can go from exaltation to exaltation, and from grace to grace, but we will only arrive at the end when we have learned all we will need to know to be like Christ. To understand Christ is to understand salvation. He is the prototype, and therefore we must be exactly like that prototype to be saved."[394]

Ether 1:13 confirms: *And when he had said these words, behold, the Lord shewed himself unto him and said, Because thou knowest these things, ye are redeemed from the Fall. Therefore, ye are brought back into my presence; therefore I shew myself unto you.* This is the gospel of Christ. Eternal life requires each person to know Him. Ether affirms the brother of Jared was redeemed when Christ came to him. Christ redeemed him from the Fall: *Because thou knowest these things, ye are redeemed from the Fall* (ibid.). Christ defines redemption. Reconciliation comes through Christ, with Christ, and by Christ. He has the power to redeem all.[395] The unchanging Gospel of Jesus Christ is always the same, and its blessings are always available.[396] There are a few important ideas that define an understanding of the Gospel of Jesus Christ as restored by the Lord through the Prophet Joseph Smith. These are the ideas that make the Gospel whole and not just a group of disconnected thoughts. First and foremost is that no one should follow any man or men. No man is worthy of discipleship. There is only One who is worth following. He is the way, the truth, and the life (*see* John 9:7). There is no other person who can save (*see* Mosiah 1:16). Second (and equally important), it is not the depth of one's study that matters, but it's the quality of one's connection with Heaven. Expounding doctrine is not only insufficient, it is oftentimes a distraction from what matters. Man goes from unbelief to belief when he learns truth. Not every source, including institutional sources, can be trusted to tell one the truth. Only the light of Christ, followed by the holy ghost, is a reliable guide to distinguish between unbelief and belief. Man goes from belief to faith as he takes action consistent with belief in truth. Faith is a principle of power. It will lead one to receive angels who still minister to those of a sound mind, not given to flights of fantasy or unstable behavior (*see* Moroni 7:6). Man is brought from faith to knowledge as angels prepare him through their ministry (*see* Moroni 7:4,6; Alma 16:26). Knowledge comes from contact with Jesus Christ (*see* Ether 1:14). This is the knowledge that saves and nothing else (*see* John 9:18). "The idea that knowledge of Christ through His personal appearance to you is now unavailable is an old sectarian notion and is false (John 9:8)."[397] Third, there is no written record, including the scriptures, which are able to tell man all he must know. One can only know the truth by having it revealed to him from Heaven itself (*see* T&C 69:29). This is the reason Joseph said, "If you could gaze into Heaven for five minutes you would know more than you would by reading everything that has ever been written on the subject" (*TPJS,* 324).[398] Either one does, as Jacob (formerly known as James) says, and asks of God, or he will for ever remain ignorant of the only knowledge which can save a man (*see* JSH 2:3 referring to Epistle of Jacob 1:2). Fourth, the truth is intended to save all. "We should welcome corrections. Too often, however, we are offended and think the truth is a hard thing to endure (1 Nephi 5:1). That is a product of pride and arrogance. It is impossible to learn what must be learned unless we are willing to be corrected (Mosiah 1:16). Therefore, only the qualified will arrive at the gates, because the rest are unwilling to take the trip required of them." Fifth, this is a personal journey which each must take for themselves. It cannot be shared. One must approach the Throne alone. "Joseph was alone when he met the Father and Son. Moses was alone when he ascended the Mount to meet the Lord. Enoch was alone when he was caught up to Heaven. Elijah was alone on the mountain when the whirlwind, lightning, and earthquake preceded the Lord's own voice. Daniel alone saw the vision of the Lord. Paul alone saw the light. Nephi alone saw his father's vision. Enos was alone in the wilderness in his encounter with God. Abraham was alone when the Lord spoke to him. Jacob slept alone when the ladder to Heaven descended for him. You will also be alone should the Lord come to visit you. This cannot be borrowed from another. These are the core. This core is what faith, repentance, baptism, and the gift of the holy ghost are meant to bring about. The religion of Heaven always involves Heaven. It does not involve men, and administration, and popularity. It is solitary, between you and God. The proud, however, are content to proclaim their righteousness and sit in judgment of others. They live without God in the world (Mormon 2:6), and their end will be destruction. They think their own imagination is revelation, and they foolishly value only their conceit (Proverbs 4:34–35)."[399] The point at which the person's journey is completed and he may enter into the rest of the Lord is when the Lord declares, by His own voice, that the man's offering has been accepted, and he is sealed up to eternal life. The Gospel is the same now, as always before. Therefore, no matter how one receives blessings of the Lord in the afterlife, it will be through the Gospel of Jesus Christ and by the ordinances instituted for claiming blessings. These were established as law to govern man's conduct here even before the world was.[400] *See also* DOCTRINE OF CHRIST.

Government of God The family of God; the practice of "sealing to the Fathers" is to put together a family. The mother of John requested of Christ, *Grant that these my two sons may sit, the one on your right hand and the other on your left, in your kingdom*. And Christ replied, *To sit on my right hand, and on my left, is for whom it is prepared of my Father, but not mine to give* (Matthew 10:2). The purpose of organizing the family on earth, through the sealing process, is to make sure that one gets into the kingdom. Once one gets into the kingdom, then how the kingdom gets organized is entirely up to the Father. And that organization at the end is relevant to what will come thereafter.[401] The government of God is not and never has been limited to an organizational structure. Instead it hails back to things that were committed, by God, in promises made to the fathers that have yet to be fulfilled.[402] It is not an organization of stakes, wards, districts, missions, or areas.[403]

Grace The free, unmerited love and favor of God.[404] Grace is a gift, but the gift must be received. Only those willing to "receive" it merit grace (*see* T&C 86:4–5). It is "received" in the way the Lord ordained and in no other way. There is no space between faith in Christ and behavior evidencing that faith. There is no dichotomy between "grace" and "works" because it is by one's conduct that he or she merits grace. Christ received grace by the things He did. The manner by which each person receives grace is through keeping His commandments (*see* T&C 93:7). Grace — or power to move closer to God — is also an increase of light. Light grows only as one moves closer to it. But man has choice, and he must elect to move closer to the light.[405] If man receives the light from Him, he receives grace, and he becomes more like Him. He will be more gracious and patient with others.[406] How was the Lord able to accomplish all He did? In Abraham 5:4 the Lord explains, *I am the Lord thy God, I am more intelligent than they all.* He was more intelligent because He grew from grace to grace until He understood all things — because He had been through all things, He had descended below all things, and He had risen above all things — therefore He comprehends all things.[407] Comprehension of the "doctrine of Christ" is not based on the command of a vocabulary or mastery of an argument. It is based on gathering light. Light is gathered by heed (obedience) and diligence alone. "We consider that God has created man with a mind capable of instruction, and a faculty which may be enlarged in proportion to the heed and diligence given to the light communicated from heaven to the intellect...."[408] By following the light one has received already, one grows in light (*see* T&C 36:4). This process leads to the "perfect day" where the light has chased away all darkness. This is how all, like Christ, can grow from grace to grace until they also receive a fullness (*see* T&C 93:7).[409] As man keeps the commandments, he gains light and truth. Experience will be his guide. It works. If anyone finds this odd or difficult to grasp, he just needs to keep the commandments, and he will find it becoming increasingly easy to understand. Man will get light and truth as he follows the process. Do it, and see it unfold. This is the way in which Christ grew from grace to grace. This is how He received the fullness. It is also the way man can get greater grace, greater light and truth. It is the way man will obtain the fullness of light and truth.[410] Moroni first asked Christ to give the gentiles grace (*see* Ether 5:7), but Christ could not promise it. Therefore, Moroni asked that the gentiles seek for it; Moroni pled for the latter-day gentiles to seek grace. It is through grace one can obtain charity. It is through charity one can bless others.[411]

Great and Abominable Church Mankind is commanded to not unite with the great and abominable church. This is not a single congregation; it is the world itself. The entire world is divided into two — one is the church of the Lamb of God; the other is everything else (*see* 1 Nephi 3:27). This is a bigger problem than it may first appear. Inasmuch as there are endless ways to belong to the great and abominable church, but only a single way to avoid it, the odds are gentiles will not find Zion. Instead, they will fight against her — Zion — and join the worldly minions who are opposed to her.[412] The abominable church is always ready to preach false, vain, and foolish doctrines to man. It will offer anything to distract people and keep them from seeing the Lord "bring again Zion." It will even use the words of Zion to preach a false faith. It is abominable because its false teachings are clothed in the vocabulary of truth.[413]

Using a typological description, the prophet Nephi prophesied that the world, in the last days, will be separated into two divisions. There will be only two "churches" (or "assemblages" or "cultures"); namely, *the one is the church of the Lamb of God, and the other is the church of the Devil. Wherefore, whoso belongeth not to the church of the Lamb of God belongeth to that great church which is the mother of abominations, and she is the whore of all the earth* (1 Nephi 3:27). Therefore, based on what Nephi says, unless one is part of that body of believers whose Father is Christ and who possess a covenant from Him that they will be His, he belongs to the whore of all the earth, a church of abominations. Those who are believers are they whom He has declared to His Father as *having been true and faithful in all things*. The other, all-inclusive, great church is comprised of all philosophies, all belief systems, all unbelief systems, all rationalizations, all theories, and all vanities that distract people from repenting and following Christ. These vary from very good things that are uplifting (and possess even great portions of truth) to the degrading and perverse. This all-inclusive church is a "whore" because she is completely indiscriminate and open for all to have her acceptance and affection. She welcomes all, the only requirement being that one have false beliefs. "The great illusion of a whore is to imagine she likes you. To imagine she cares for you. To imagine she desires what you desire and is cooperating with you because she finds you attractive, appealing, and that you fulfill her longing. It is a lie, an illusion, and a fraud. Her bodily diseases are less virulent than her contamination of the soul. Empty, false, vain, and foolish thoughts occupy the imagination of those who have intercourse with the great whore. She prefers the lie, relies on it. You would not be her customer if not for the lies."[414] This contrast is drawn for Nephi because these are two extremes. Both of them are religious. One is founded on a true religion; the other is a false religion. One follows the Father's covenants and will result in God's promised results. The other follows the commandments of men who have mingled their own philosophies with scripture so that their doctrines are all corrupt. They share a vocabulary but nothing else.[415] *See also* CHURCH; BABYLON.

Great Knowledge and Greater Knowledge The man and woman who entered into the Holy Order were taught truths about the creation, heaven, and man's relationship to the universe. When Abraham was seeking to obtain what was given to Father Adam, he studied records that came down from "the fathers." This included not just a chronology back to Adam, but also *to the beginning of the creation, for the records have come into my hands* (Abraham 2:3). This is the knowledge that is conveyed to those who belong to the Holy Order. When the return of the original Holy Order is contemplated, it will involve restoring great knowledge that is hidden from the world. The fathers knew it would be restored in the last days. Joseph Smith also prophesied of its return and explained the forefathers of mankind anxiously anticipated its return.[416] Abraham *sought for the blessings of the fathers and the right whereunto I should be ordained to administer the same, having been myself a follower of righteousness, desiring also to be one who possessed great knowledge and to be a greater follower of righteousness, and to possess a greater knowledge* (Abraham 1:1). Knowledge is a critical component of the Holy Order. Rather than worldly status or rank, the Holy Order involves "great knowledge" from God. The greater knowledge of the Holy Order is the reason a man cannot be saved in ignorance. The "knowledge" Joseph Smith refers to is that same "knowledge" Abraham sought after. Its purpose is to allow the one who possesses it to become a greater follower of righteousness. Godly knowledge must be implemented to save one's soul. There is no salvation without obedience to the principles of righteousness learned. It is the same for everyone as it was for Abraham: *to possess a greater knowledge and to be a father of many nations, a prince of peace, and desiring to receive instructions, and to keep the commandments of God.*[417] In Abraham's case, he had both "great knowledge" and "greater knowledge." Those are important words and were important parts of "this Gospel" to which God made reference. If men are to be taught enough to have "great knowledge," as Abraham had, then the information must be revealed from heaven.[418] These words are like Abraham's words. Joseph Smith affirms he had "great knowledge" and sought for and obtained "greater knowledge."[419] The purpose of the coming last days' temple in Zion is to allow the communication of great knowledge and greater knowledge and to restore what has been lost since the time of Adam. Important knowledge is required for those who receive the Holy Order. Man does not get saved in ignorance.[420]

Hades *Hades*, the Greek, or *Sheol*, the Hebrew, these two significations mean a world of spirits. *Hades*, *Sheol*, paradise, spirits in prison, are all one: it is a world of spirits.[421]

Handmaid When Mary was visited by the angel Gabriel and told of Her ministry to bear the Messiah, She responded, *Behold the handmaid of the Lord; be it unto me according to your word* (Luke 1:6). The term "handmaid" includes the possible meanings: wife, female partner, or consort. Mary was all of these to God the Father.[422] When Mary said the words, *He has regarded the low estate of his handmaiden* (Luke 1:8), the "condescension of God" seems to apply particularly for Her. She laid aside glory to be here, and the Father still held "regard" for His "handmaiden" in this "low estate." What a great work our Heavenly Parents have undertaken for their children![423]

Hardness of Heart Nephi gives a clear description: *For [Lehi] truly spake many great things unto them which were hard to be understood save a man should inquire of the Lord. And they being hard in their hearts, therefore they did not look unto the Lord as they ought. And now I, Nephi, was grieved* *because of the hardness of their hearts* (1 Nephi 4:1). *And I said unto them, Have ye inquired of the Lord? And they said unto me, We have not, for the Lord maketh no such thing known unto us. Behold, I said unto them, How is it that ye do not keep the commandments of the Lord? How is it that ye will perish because of the hardness of your hearts? Do ye not remember the thing which the Lord hath said, If ye will not harden your hearts, and ask me in faith, believing that ye shall receive, with diligence in keeping my commandments, surely these things shall be made known unto you?* (1 Nephi 4:2). Hardness of heart is usually accompanied by a hardness of head; that is, people tend to not be willing to live in accordance with principles, even though they want to know about them. They are often more curious than they are obedient, becoming voyeurs rather than visionaries. Oddly enough, one's curiosity gets satisfied as he obeys — but man is usually unwilling to make that exchange (cf. Alma 9:3,10; 1 Nephi 3:26).[424] Man determines whether he has a hard heart or an open heart. Anciently, the "heart" was considered the seat of understanding rather than emotion; therefore, an "open heart" belonged to the seeker, the asker, the knocker on the door (*see* Matthew 3:42,44).[425] *See also* BOWELS; BROKEN HEART – CONTRITE SPIRIT; REINS.

Hearts Turned to the Fathers The phrase *turning the hearts of the children to the fathers* is a reference to the restoration of sealing authority, allowing a connection between man living on the earth and the fathers (Abraham, Isaac, and Jacob). In this Dispensation, that restoration occurred when Joseph Smith was given the sealing authority and priesthood whereby he could ask and receive answers.[426] *For behold, the day cometh that shall burn as an oven, and all the proud, yea, and all that do wickedly shall burn as stubble; for they that come shall burn them, said the Lord of Hosts, that it shall leave them neither root nor branch. And again, he quoted the fifth verse thus: Behold, I will reveal unto you the Priesthood, by the hand of Elijah the prophet, before the coming of the great and dreadful day of the Lord. He also quoted the next verse differently: And he shall plant in the hearts of the children the promises made to the fathers, and the hearts of the children shall turn to their fathers. If it were not so, the whole earth would be utterly wasted at his coming* (JSH 3:4). "Everything about this prophecy differs from present LDS teaching. The prophecy mentions Elijah and priesthood. Children get *plant[ed] in [their] hearts* because the children are living. But what is to be planted are the *promises made to the fathers*. Who are the referenced fathers? What promises were made? When were they made? Then Nephi speaks of children's hearts *turn[ed] to their fathers*. These prophecies lay at the very foundation of Zion, but traditions have taken away our understanding. The foundation of Zion requires reestablishing a connection between living children and those fathers to whom God made promises. There must be a welding link connecting the two. Contrary to the traditions, it does not involve connecting us to dead ancestors imprisoned in the Spirit World. Our dead and imprisoned ancestors are in desperate need of our connection to the fathers in heaven. That connection is the only way our ministrations will help them. If all we do is to connect ourselves to our imprisoned dead, then we are tied to the damned, the dead, and the disembodied, who look for a way to escape their fate. The fathers who are in heaven are the ones with whom we instead must form the link. Our salvation and the salvation of our kindred dead depend on it. The purpose behind these promises given the fathers, and this prophecy given to Joseph by Nephi, was to fix this problem. Because if it were not so, the whole world would be utterly wasted at His (and *their*) coming."[427] The gulf which must be bridged through the work of Elijah — "to form a bond or connection," in the words of Joseph Smith — is not completed unless some group of people has been sealed to "the fathers in heaven." Those there include Enoch's City and Melchizedek's City and extend further to Abraham, Isaac, and Jacob.[428] (*See also* "The Mission of Elijah Reconsidered," in *Essays: Three Degrees*.) *See also* THE FATHERS.

Heavenly Gift An offer made directly from the Lord, often through a new gospel dispensation, with Heaven's intent to bestow the fullness of the gospel and priesthood upon a generation. This fullness includes an expanding scriptural canon, revelation, Heavenly visitors, and prophetic power, as well as all blessings and sealing power necessary for fullness of salvation and exaltation.[429] It has been offered by the Lord more often than it has been welcomed and accepted by mankind. This is reflected in the Lord's lament, *O ye people…of the house of Israel, how oft have I gathered you as a hen gathereth her chickens under her wings and have nourished you. And again, how oft* would I have gathered you as a hen gathereth her chickens under her wings, yea, O ye people of the house of Israel who have fallen. Yea, O ye people of the house of Israel, ye that dwell at Jerusalem as ye that have fallen, yea, how oft would I have gathered you as a hen gathereth her chickens and ye would not. O ye house of Israel whom I have spared, how oft will I gather you as a hen gathereth her chickens under her wings if ye will repent and return unto me with full purpose of heart. But if not, O house of Israel, the places of your dwellings shall become desolate until the time of the fulfilling of the covenant to your fathers* (3 Nephi 4:9). The Lord's offer can only be accepted on the condition of obedience and faith. When the fullness is accepted, people live in peace and happiness: *And they had all things common among them; therefore, there were not rich and poor, bond and free, but they were all made free and partakers of the Heavenly gift* (4 Nephi 1:1). *He has shewn himself unto the world, and glorified the name of the Father, and prepared a way that thereby others might be partakers of the Heavenly gift* (Ether 5:2). When the fullness is refused (by mankind not complying with the conditions of the covenant), the opportunity to establish a Heavenly order and Zion is lost. [430]

Heavenly Host Men and women may see Christ in vision or in an appearance as a solitary personage, but no person has ever seen God the Father without also seeing a host of others. They are referred to in scriptures as a *Heavenly host* or *numerous angels* or *concourses of angels*. "There is a reason that a company is always shown at the appearance of the Father. You should look into the matter. Within the answer lies a great truth about God the Father."[431] Throughout scripture, the Father is described as the God of Hosts. Seeing Him includes an accompanying *host* or *concourses of angels* or *train* or a similar reference to others with Him. He appears with the Heavenly Host because God has a family, including a spouse.[432] *See also* NAMES OF GOD IN SCRIPTURE, JEHOVAH SABAOTH.

Heed and Diligence "We consider that god has created man with a mind capable of instruction, and a faculty which may be enlarged in proportion to the heed and diligence given to the light communicated from Heaven to the intellect."[433] One of the great and succinct declarations about coming to know God is found in Alma 9:3. Men and women come to God by giving "heed and diligence" to what God asks of them. "I cannot do that for you, nor can you do it for me. It is the sojourn of every individual. The mysteries of God are His hidden but simple truths. They set a man's bones on fire. To pay heed to God requires that we not harden our hearts. When we have hard hearts we know less. Even what we once knew can be lost."[434]

Hell The Prophet Joseph Smith described the true nature of hell: "A man is his own [tormentor] and his own [condemnor]. Hence the saying, They shall go into the lake that burns with fire and brimstone. The torment of disappointment in the mind of man is as exquisite as a lake burning with fire and brimstone."[435] It is a misnomer to speak of the "kingdom of the devil," because the description presumes something more organized than is the case. It is difficult to organize when fear, hatred, and anger are the primary motivations. Love is a far more cohesive, creative, and loyalty-producing motivation. All that Satan does is designed to destroy itself, as well as all those who follow him.[436] An endless "Hell" is an invention of the historic Christian faith.[437] How can the gates of hell be opened? It requires someone upon whom death and hell could have no claim to go there. When justice itself requires Him to be released, then death and hell are conquered. This is what He would do. He would suffer the wrath of the guilty and vile, fully assume their punishment and abuse, and bear their penalty of death itself. When the fury relented and the wrath ended, He could reclaim life. His captivity ended the captivity for all. Having then returned to life, because it was just for Him to do so, He acquired the keys of death and hell. Now He can open those gates for any and all because it was unjust for Him to have been put through either. He can now advocate for others by virtue of what He suffered and the injustice of that suffering.[438] Death and hell are the devil's domain. He's the god of that world, and since we have death and suffering here, he calls himself the god of this world. Those who come here are subject to his buffeting and his will. They are tormented, tempted, troubled, and then they die. While captive here, they endure the insults of the flesh and the difficulties of trying to find their way back to God.[439] The references to the "hell that hath no end" is that same play on words that is defined in T&C 4:1–4. It is a place of torment, where people suffer as in the telestial kingdom (or the world in which you presently reside, to paraphrase the LDS Endowment). How long will people endure such an experience?

Until they repent (*see* T&C 69:26). What if they do not repent? They will suffer, worlds without end (*see* T&C 69:28).[440]

Holiness Purity of heart.[441] *See also* SANCTIFICATION.

Holy Ghost The holy ghost is most correctly understood as the individual spirit within each man or woman — it is the heavenly record from each one's prior experiences, although now veiled. In that sense it is a *he* (or, if one is female, a *she*). The holy ghost is the light of truth. In that sense, it is an *it*. The holy ghost is also the received communication, inspiration, or light from above, and the source of that light can be any number of *holy beings* sent to shed that light upon mankind. In that sense, it is a *they*. But mankind wants it to be singular, because that makes it easier to grasp.[442] The holy ghost is a personage. It is an individual. It is a spirit that will dwell inside man. The holy ghost, which resides inside of each person, receives intelligence from Christ. The holy ghost is the *record of heaven* that man has lost contact with because of the veil. It is a personage of spirit who resides inside each man or woman, and one must "receive" it after baptism by finally listening to that inner *truth of all things* or *record of the Father and the Son* (Genesis 4:9–10). The holy ghost bears record of the Father and the Son (*see* Genesis 3:4). When the Son speaks to individuals through the holy ghost, they hear the words in the first person — hence, the holy ghost speaking that it *is the Son* in Genesis 3:4.[443] "Your spirit or your ghost is within you, connected to heaven to such a degree through this process that you are in possession of a 'holy spirit' or a holy ghost within you."[444] From Adam until Christ, the holy ghost was the primary voice by which revelation was delivered from God to mankind. It is active and has been active in delivering the words of prophecy to "holy men" throughout history.[445] The scriptures have explained that the holy ghost which dwells in man — this personage of spirit — has the following other descriptions or attributes: *the Record of Heaven, the Comforter, the keys of the kingdom of Heaven, the truth of all things, that which quickens all things — which makes alive all things, that which knows all things, and has all power according to Wisdom, mercy, truth, justice and judgment* (Genesis 4:9). This is a description of the personage of spirit that dwells inside each person. This is the holy ghost. This is something that can be in contact with the holy spirit, or the *mind of the Father and Son*.[446]

There are many times when the term "ghost" and the term "spirit" are used interchangeably. The distinction is not appreciated by some translators. Therefore, if there is a difference between these two, one will need to be careful about trusting different translator's use of the terms. They may not have any distinction in mind.[447] "No man can receive the holy ghost without receiving revelations. The holy ghost is a revelator."[448] God is no respecter of persons and makes the holy ghost available and accessible to all (*see* Acts 6:3–6; Epistle of Jacob 1:2,5). The holy ghost, which is the *mind of the Father and the Son*, can be communicated by pure intelligence, light poured into the mind of a man, a ministering angel sent with a message, a ministering spirit sent with a message, an open vision, a voice from heaven, or any other means designed to convey into the mind of the man receiving it the truth of things from God.[449] "This first comforter, or holy ghost, has no other effect than pure intelligence."[450]

"By doing as the Father and Son have asked, you *receive the holy ghost*. Did you notice the Father and Son promise the holy ghost, and when you receive it, the holy ghost bears witness of the Father and Son? *Ye have done according to the commandments of the Father and the Son, and ye have received the holy ghost, which witness of the Father and the Son unto the fulfilling of the promise which he hath made* (2 Nephi 13:3). The first promises to you the last, and the last bears witness of the first. In one eternal round, the Doctrine of Christ includes all members of the Godhead combined into a witness that will come to you, take up residence within you, and make you a vessel of the promises fulfilled. You are to return home and take your abode again. Or, more correctly, permit Them to take up Their abode with you (John 9:8). You become the record of God's dealings with mankind. You become the promise of God's presence, for you fulfill *the promise which He hath made*. You receive the *record of Heaven* or, more correctly, the Record of Heaven, for it is a proper name and title (Genesis 4:9). When it has come to you, then this Record of Heaven will abide with you.... You will know *the truth of all things* for it will reside within you (Genesis 4:9). You will understand Wisdom, for she will be with you. You will know mercy, possess truth, and be capable of performing judgment, for the judgment you judge will not be yours, but will be given to you (3 Nephi 13:1). God will dwell within you. When He appears to you, you will see Him as He is, for you will be at last like Him (1 John 1:13). If you can understand this, then you will purify yourself to receive it (1 John 1:13). For the baptism of fire and the holy ghost will purge and purify, refining you with that holy fire (Malachi 1:6)."[451] The purpose of the holy ghost is to allow you to see things in their true light with the underlying intent behind them and to allow you to do that without distortion and without confusion.[452] "The holy ghost bears record. And record, *recordare*, means 'to put back into the heart.' It means 'to intensify in the heart, to have knowledge and remembrance of what you had before.' This has to do with your previous existence. See, your heart is your core. To record is to stir up again in the heart. And [Christ] says this is why the Father will bear record of [Christ], and the holy ghost will bear record (3 Nephi 5:9). That will recall things to you. That's what a record is."[453] The holy ghost allows one to resonate with the same frequency as the writer and to "hear" what he is writing about. The process is far more abstract than logic, reason, rhetoric, and historic precedent will uncover. Capturing the thought of the inspired fisherman requires an inspired reader. The holy ghost is a guide to speak to man as he studies the scriptures. It will lead each person to understanding, harmony, clarity, and truth. If one has not experienced this kind of awareness while studying the scriptures, then it needs to be attempted[454] *See also* GIFT OF THE HOLY GHOST.

Holy Order "The Holy Order is the channel through which all knowledge, doctrine, the plan of salvation, and every important matter is revealed from Heaven."[455] Among other things, the purpose of the Holy Order is to put in place a mechanism by which God can reveal from heaven what is necessary for the salvation of man on Earth. In every generation, when God has provided salvation for mankind, it is the Holy Order that is used by God to fix what is broken, restore what has been lost, repair, heal, forgive, and reconnect those who are willing to give heed to the message sent from Heaven to enable mankind to become sons of God.[456] It conveys blessings and information that are withheld from the world.[457]

The Holy Order commenced before the world with Adam. He obtained the Holy Order in the beginning and before the world. Included with it is the right to preside over all of the human family and the right to minister to Adam's posterity. Adam continues to hold that presiding position and will do so until the end of time.[458] The Holy Order was much greater in scope than later priesthoods. Later priesthood functions should not be used to define the original. Something as narrow and limited as a man (or angel) laying hands on another man did not and could not convey the original Holy Order.[459] After the time of Eden, conveying the original Holy Order required either a temple or an ascent into heaven.[460] The other fathers were holders of the order, but it is the role of the oldest living holder of it to ordain others into the line.[461]

Many think that the renaming of the Holy Order to the Melchizedek Priesthood (in order to avoid the too frequent repetition of the name of the Son of God), was done out of respect for the Messiah, Jesus Christ — and that is true enough. But the Holy Order after the Order of the Son of God includes the first man, Adam, who is also identified as a "son of God." There are other "sons of God."[462] The Holy Order after the Order of the Son of God makes those who inherit it, by definition, the sons of God. Therefore, in a way, calling it the Holy Order after the Order of the Son of God is a way of identifying the recipient as someone who has become one of God's sons.[463]

The Holy Order, in its truest sense, is much more comprehensive and far reaching than just laying on hands to convey permission to perform ordinances.[464] When the return of the original Holy Order is contemplated, it will involve restoring great knowledge that is hidden from the world. The fathers knew it would be restored in the last days. Joseph Smith also prophesied of its return and explained the forefathers of mankind anxiously anticipated its return.[465] Priesthood, in its most meaningful sense, involves the Holy Order after the Order of the Son of God. The restoration at the end of creation must return to the beginning. Before the return of Christ, everything — including the original Holy Order with all its components — must be restored. That has not yet been revealed to the world.[466] It will return before the Lord comes again in glory. It will be necessary before the return of the Lord for the original Holy Order to exist in all of its ramifications. It must be established on the earth and include all of the rights that originally belonged to Adam. It must be accounted for and returned back to Adam and then to Christ.[467]

It will include men and women, as husband and wife. They will be given understanding of things which the world cannot know.[468] Initiation into the Holy Order provides greater knowledge and fortifies the soul for one's ministry.[469] It includes the right of dominion over all creation — the same right originally given to Adam that belonged to God. The right of dominion over this creation is why God is God. In essence, the Holy Order is to create of flesh and blood a living, mortal surrogate for the Father and Mother. [470] It is the nature of this Holy Order that it is conferred upon the man and woman jointly (*see* 1 Corinthians 1:44).[471] The Holy Order is familial. It does not involve establishing a church but, instead, connecting together the Family of God, or in other words, the Government of God. This can only be done in a temple prepared for that purpose.[472] Because there is still a great conspiracy to destroy the souls of men and to capture this creation, the Holy Order is guarded by carefully qualifying those who receive it and is under God's control and supervised by Adam and Eve.[473]

Holy Spirit The power of God which fills the immensity of space (*see* T&C 86:1). Sometimes the Holy Spirit is called the "Light of Christ" rather than the Holy Spirit (*see* T&C 86:1). The relationship between the Holy Spirit or Light of Christ and every living thing, whether a planet, plant, animal, human, or ecosystem is direct, immediate, and continual. They are all borrowing power from the Holy Spirit to live, move, breath, remain organized, and do according to their own wills (*see* Mosiah 1:9–10).[474]

Holy Spirit of Promise The sealing word of God; it must confirm or ratify a sealing for it to become eternal, as described in T&C 158:35–39. All mankind's ordinances contemplate a further ratification from heaven.[475] If one does not obtain this promise sealed by God, through His word — sealed by the Holy Spirit of Promise — then there is no promise as pertaining to the ordinance. The only thing that will endure is that which is established by God or, more completely, through His word, which is then sealed by the Holy Spirit of Promise.[476] The sealing of things through the Holy Spirit of Promise must come in mortality. This hope is to be gained in mortality as a gift of faith to empower the recipient to be able to claim it in the next life. Mortality is the time and place for obtaining faith and hope. When out of this life, the season for faith has passed, and the opportunity for hope has ended. It cannot be developed there.[477] The only exception is set out in T&C 122:5: *Thus came the voice of the Lord unto me, saying, All who have died without a knowledge of this gospel, who would have received it if they had been permitted to tarry, shall be heirs of the Celestial Kingdom of God. Also, all that shall die henceforth without a knowledge of it, who would have received it with all their hearts, shall be heirs of that Kingdom.* The Holy Spirit of Promise can extend to even single people who receive the word of the Lord by revelation here in mortality that they will be sealed and live in the eternal marriage covenant, even if they do not obtain that sealing while still mortal. Any promise from God confers this hope. What He commits to someone here, He is bound to deliver there.[478] The term "Holy Spirit of Promise" is used without adequate appreciation that it can be an office held by Divine appointment. Joseph Smith became the Holy Spirit of Promise through operation of the Divine appointment to hold the right. The office is held by more than just a single mortal man at one time and includes others who minister on earth, as well. These, at a minimum, include the Lord, John the Beloved, the Three Nephite Disciples, Elijah, other angelic ministers, as well as potentially others about whom nothing is known (*see* T&C 35:3).[479] This Holy Spirit of Promise is given its name because when one has received the Father and the Son, he becomes Their child of Promise, the inheritor of all the Father has, a member of His family. To reject this, as Joseph described it, is to deny the sun at noon-day. For to have been given the Holy Spirit of Promise, one has seen God and received from Him a Promise.[480]

Honor "An empowered promise from God" that can be claimed in the afterlife. It assures one of what he will receive from God because His oath and covenant establishes expectations.[481] To honor is to glorify God in word and action.[482]

Hope Something far greater, more profound, more strongly felt, more firmly based than just expectancy from vague desire.[483] Hope involves unshakable faith or confidence. Hope comes from "many revelations and the spirit of prophecy" and is based upon "witnesses" coming from beyond the veil to confirm the expectations. It causes faith which is "unshakable." It is hope which is powerful, controlling, and causes a thing to come to pass because it is now their right to receive the thing promised. God has conferred that right upon them.[484] Hope is more than a wish, as it requires one to secure a promise from God. It requires one to be at rest — secure in the knowledge the Lord has promised a glorious resurrection. Hope is waiting for the time of the Lord's promise to be fulfilled. Hope describes the state of mind of the recipient during the time interval after the promise, but before its realization. Hope involves unshakable faith or confidence. It is a concrete assurance, based upon a promise or covenant. Hope comes from knowing the Lord has promised one something. As sure as God's word cannot fail, one's hope is secure in Him. But men and women only obtain that hope from Him by getting Him to make a promise to them.[485]

Host(s) Heavenly Beings who surround the Throne of God. These are most correctly understood as members of the family of God the Father.[486]

House of God There is a need *to set in order the House of God* (T&C 83:4), which can only be accomplished through a temple where that work can be performed. The temple is not the "House of God" needing to be set in order. But a temple is required to accomplish the work for God's House, or family, to be set in order. As once described by God, *Organize yourselves, prepare every needful thing, and establish a house, even a house of prayer, a house of fasting, a house of faith, a house of learning, a house of glory, a house of order, a House of God, that your incomings may be in the name of the Lord, that your outgoings may be in the name of the Lord, that all your salutations may be in the name of the Lord with uplifted hands unto the Most High* (T&C 86:29).[487]

House of Israel The descendants of Jacob who have an active covenant with God, which excludes those descendants of Jacob who have abandoned the faith, broken the covenant, and gone off to serve false gods.[488]

House of Order God's house is a house of order, but that does not mean what many people think it means. God follows patterns. He establishes and ordains things according to one pattern and then takes them down again according to another. He does not vary.[489]

How Great Things The discussion should not be about *what* great things the Lord has done but *how* great things the Lord has done. This is the terminology that is found in the Book of Mormon. *What* doesn't matter anywhere near as much as *how*. *What* is essentially an exercise in voyeurism. *How* is an exercise in what one needs to do and how one comes about linking to, and participating in, what ultimately is the fullness of the Gospel of Jesus Christ.[490] "The archaic expression *how great things* is found in the King James Bible (six times), as in Mark 5:19 KJV (*and tell them how great things the Lord hath done for thee* [Mark 2:24]). In modern English, of course, we expect *what great things*, which is how Joseph Smith edited the title page for the 1837 edition. He made a similar change a little later: Unlike the change in the title page, Joseph directly marked this particular change in the printer's manuscript. In his later editing for the 1837 edition, Joseph discontinued making this change, thus leaving the remaining six occurrences of *how great things* unchanged in the text of the Book of Mormon (2 Nephi 1:1; Mosiah 11:26; Alma 29:20; Ether 1:19; and twice in Ether 3:8)."[491]

Humility Voluntary submission to the control or power of God or, in other words, obedience.[492] Children are by nature more humble than adults. They not only do not have a good working knowledge of practical skills, they are keenly aware of their own ignorance. As a result, children are inquisitive and eager to be taught. They not only don't know, they *know they don't know* and want to be given the chance to learn. They "seek" and "ask" and "knock." Children do, by nature, just as Christ bids all to do.[493] One is not teachable without humility. Humility and the capacity to accept new truth are directly related. Humbling oneself is not just an expression to wear on one's countenance. Rather, it is opening one's heart up to higher things.[494] "Can you accept truth if it is taught to you? Even if it contradicts your traditions? Even if it alienates you from family, friends, comfortable social associations, your neighbors (Matthew 9:24)?"[495] *See also* MEEKNESS.

Idol Anything that separates mankind from the Lamb of God. "Cast it aside, and come to Him. Why we have idols between us and the Lord is as different as one person is from another. Almost without exception, it comes as a result of a false tradition handed down. False traditions are based on each person's life experiences. No matter what they are or how they were acquired, whatever separates Christ from you must be set aside. Come to *Him* because only He can save you."[496]

If You Love Me Christ's words *If you love me, keep my commandments* appear several times in the Gospel of John. The words could be better translated to mean: "If you love me, act as a sentinel (or guard), ready to receive further instructions from me." The current King James translation was based on the recognition that the canon of scripture had closed and revelation had ended. Therefore, they took those things into account as they rendered their translation. [497] But recent revelation indicates that the canon of scripture is not closed; God *is* sending further instructions, and man must stand ready to receive it (*see* T&C 156–174). *See also* COMMANDMENT.

Ignorance Many prefer ignorance to light. They will not draw toward the light when it is revealed to them, and, therefore, cannot comprehend what the Lord is teaching. It makes no sense to them, for light is required in order to comprehend light; a person must be *willing* to increase in light, or he will be left in darkness and unable to apprehend any of what saves him. It remains a mystery. The way to darkness is broad and easy. It requires no effort. It welcomes one. It tempts mankind with its ease. It is popular, as there are *many who go in thereat*. Truth challenges. It requires change. It informs all of their faults and mistakes. It is difficult — man is called to rise above what the world is doing, what the world is saying, and what the world accepts as good and true. This tendency to want to be popular can twist a person away from truth quicker than any other corrupting influence here. "This is why Nephi cautioned about the latter-day churches that crave popularity and acceptance (1 Nephi 7:5). There will only be a *few who find it*. Even in the day in which we live, the measure will always be *few*. Not in a relative sense, but in an absolute sense. Few. Period. Only a small number."[498]

Another person's ignorance can never define one's own faith. Some people are unwilling to study their faith, even though they claim to practice it. If the restoration is truly of God, then it is important enough to warrant the closest of study. When any matter is studied with great care, issues will surface. Quandaries will arise. There will be gaps, problems, and failings. Human weaknesses will be exposed. Some things will get quite messy. The underlying truth, however, deserves a fair and full hearing. Study of the restoration which goes only far enough to discover the quandaries has not proceeded far enough. One should search into it deeply enough, prayerfully enough, and searchingly enough to find the answers. When one person has sought deeply and another has not, there is a gap between the understanding of the two which makes it problematic to have a common understanding. The one in possession of less is really not in a position to correctly judge the one in possession of more. Oddly, however, the one who has less is altogether more likely to judge the one with more, while the one with more is equipped to look more kindly upon the other. After all, the one with more has struggled from the lesser position.

Only fools judge a matter before they hear it. Such souls warrant one's kindly efforts to persuade, not their censure or condemnation. All carry foolishness, learning year by year, struggling to overcome the many things they've neglected in their study, prayers, and contemplation. God does not grade on a curve. Therefore, when anyone begins to think he's outshone his fellow man, he should reflect again on Moses' reaction to seeing the Man of Holiness: *Now for this cause I know man is nothing, which thing I never had supposed* (Genesis 1:2). No one has anything to boast of, even if he knows more than his fellow man. All know less than He who is *more intelligent than them all* (Abraham 5:4). "Whenever I contemplate the gulf between He who is Holiness and myself, and the great charity required from Him to condescend for me, I can hardly bear the thought of feeling triumph because of the ignorance of my fellow saints. How unkind. How foolish. How uncharitable. More than that, how very unlike the Lord whom we all claim to serve."[499] *See also* STIFFNECKEDNESS.

Image of God This includes the companionship between the sexes. Adam and Eve became in the image of God. This is at the core of redemption, the core of the work of God. This is what it means for God to complete His work and to have the continuation of the seeds.[500]

Iniquity Working at cross-purposes to God's work underway in a Dispensation. Iniquity may not involve violating a direct commandment. There is no record of Abraham issuing any commandments, but he was called of God and blessed, and therefore, anyone who worked at cross-purposes (i.e., took his wife from him, as happened on two occasions) was committing iniquity. God's work varies between Dispensations, so the actions which constitute iniquity also vary between Dispensations. In the current Dispensation, God is working to bring about a people of one heart and one mind, with no poor among them — Zion. So those who oppose equality and favor inequity commit iniquity — inequity is iniquity (two spellings of the same English word). Sin and iniquity overlap. However, there are times when a sin is not iniquity: when Christ's disciples plucked and ate wheat on the Sabbath or when David's warriors ate the shewbread that only the priests were to eat, neither of these sins were iniquity. There are also occasions when iniquity is not sin. When the people who heard Joseph preach failed to respond and accept his role as a messenger sent by God, there was no sin in that, but there was iniquity.

Christ was denounced as a "sinner" because He violated the commandments — repeatedly and openly. His explanation was not that He wasn't a sinner, but that the law was based on a higher set of principles that were more important than the law itself. And if the observant soul could see the higher principles, then they were to be preferred and followed. His Sermon on the Mount was an extensive exposition on the higher principles underlying the commandments — they were more important, so much so, that if one followed the commandments all his life but failed to notice the underlying principles, then he was truly ungodly and failed to understand the reason God provided the Law to Moses. When confronted about His sins, Christ did not really deny sinning. He instead posed questions about the rigorous focus on the Law to the exclusion of the underlying principle. In the case of His disciples plucking wheat and eating on the Sabbath, He did not reject the idea that it violated the Law but instead took an example from history to show that the life of man is more important. The Sabbath was made for man and not man for the Sabbath.

Paul wanted everyone to know that the Lamb was without blemish because He was sin-free. But the only reason Christ was sin-free was not because He kept the Law — He did not. It was because Christ saw something higher to be followed, and He followed and taught that higher set of principles — principles which bring about godliness, even holiness. Because He practiced holiness as a matter of principle, He was not merely ceremonially clean (which, by the way, He failed to accomplish), but He was, instead, *actually* clean. He was holy indeed, without the need of seeking holiness through the ceremonies of the Law of Moses.

To the extent that it did not involve a violation of higher principles, Christ also kept the Law and observed the Mosaic ordinances. More importantly (and *much* more importantly), He fulfilled the Law of Moses. He *was* the Paschal Lamb. He was the sacrifice for sin. The only way He qualified was because His life reflected consistently the higher principles upon which the Law was based. Had He failed to live consistent with those higher principles, He could not have qualified to fulfill the Law. He did not deny He sinned — Paul did that — but His sins were meaningless because His path followed everything commanded by the Father. What the Father said (to Him in His Dispensation) was what He did. Therefore, He was entirely justified and sanctified, albeit an offender of the Law of Moses. Therefore, He was without iniquity.[501]

Intelligence/s *The glory of God is intelligence, or in other words, light and truth* (T&C 93:11). *And [Christ] ministered unto [the Brother of Jared] even as he ministered unto the Nephites, and all this that this man might know that he was God, because of the many great works which the Lord had shewed unto him* (Ether 1:14). This is the definition of the glory of God. This is the definition of light and truth, to know these things about God.[502] *Whatever principle of intelligence we attain unto in this life, it will rise with us in the resurrection. And if a person gains more knowledge and intelligence in this life through his diligence and obedience than another, he will have so much the advantage in the world to come. There is a law, irrevocably decreed in heaven before the foundations of the world, upon which all blessings are predicated, and when we obtain any blessing from God, it is by obedience to that*

law upon which it is predicated.[503] How can mankind gain intelligence?
How does one gain knowledge? By "diligence and obedience." The
Lord speaks to man to cause him to act. Hearing the Lord's word
without giving it heed, diligence, and obedience yields nothing.[504]

God's glory can be described as either *intelligence* or *light and truth*.
This glory, light and truth, or intelligence is co-equal with God
Himself. *Intelligence, or the light of truth, was not created or made, neither
indeed can be* (T&C 93:10). It is a part of God Himself. He and it are
one. By extension, therefore, mankind is also one with Him. Joseph
does not leave the matter there. He goes on to equate mankind with
this same material, this same co-eternal light and truth: *Man was
also in the beginning with God. Intelligence, or the light of truth, was not
created or made, neither indeed can be* (ibid.). At his core, mankind is
part of God. All exist because they are made of the same material
from which God's glory, God's intelligence, or God's light and truth
are comprised. Joseph's translation of the Book of Abraham moved
from the singular "intelligence" to the plural in a description of
pre-mortal mankind: *Now the Lord had shown unto me, Abraham, the
intelligences that were organized before the world was; and among all these
there were many of the noble and great ones; And God saw these souls that they
were good, and he stood in the midst of them, and he said: These I will make
my rulers; for he stood among those that were spirits, and he saw that they
were good; and he said unto me: Abraham, thou art one of them; thou wast
chosen before thou wast born* (Abraham 6:1, emphasis added). When
organized into separate personalities, the intelligence changed
from the singular to the plural. With this change came creation (or
organization), and as a result, mankind came into being. Joseph
further revealed that in order to exist, mankind had to have the
freedom to choose. Without that freedom they would not exist at all.
They would still be singular, uncreated, and without an existence. *All
truth is independent in that sphere in which God has placed it to act for itself,
as all intelligence also; otherwise there is no existence* (T&C 93:10, emphasis
added). There is no existence unless man is free (and able) to choose
for himself. His existence flows from God's intelligence. He was
created from it. But to exist, he must be independent from God.[505]

Intercession A pleading, urging, or making of a petition in behalf
of oneself or another, even one's enemies; John 9 is considered the

great intercessory prayer. "Christ was [and is] the great Intercessor. In like measure, you must make intercession for those who fall short in your life. You should thank God for the opportunity that they give to you to show that charity. It may seem odd to do this when you start. But prayer and grace go together. You will find you are able to pray with sincerity for those in your life after you have spent time on your knees on their behalf. Grace begets grace. Do it, and you will grow as a result."[506] Just as Christ made intercession for all of mankind through the atonement (*see* 2 Nephi 1:6), so Nephi also makes intercession on behalf of his unbelieving brothers and *cried unto the Lord* (1 Nephi 1:9) for those who had rejected him. Nephi's conduct makes him a 'type' of Christ. Nephi shows himself to be faithful in the face of adversity. He has been charitable to the critical. As a result of this, he is ready to receive more.[507] Christ teaches man to love his enemies, bless those who are trying to do him harm, and pray for his persecutors. This is the only way to become like Him. He is an intercessor. Becoming an intercessor for others is part of one's development, through grace, to become as He is. It is through this that charity becomes a part of one's character (*see* Moroni 7:9), and charity is a necessary attribute in one's character (*see* 2 Nephi 11:17).[508]

Many "great souls" have interceded for their fellow man. Intercession for one's fellow man, including those who give offense, is one of the hallmarks of the saved soul. This is who Abraham was and why he became a friend of God. "I've hesitated to even discuss the exceptions to the rule because everyone wants the exceptions to apply to them. No one wants to comply with the rule. The higher way is, however, found in following the rule. It should be an absolute sacrifice, and a painful one at that, for the exception to be applied in your life. If an inspired condemnation is required at your hand and by your voice, then immediately afterwards you should make intercession with the Lord for those condemned. That is the way of those who know the Lord. Those who have been forgiven much — including those who have been forgiven everything — always love much in return (Luke 5:21)."[509] Once forgiven, man must forgive. He (or she) must take on himself (or herself) the role of the intercessor by accepting the shame and abuse of this world and must forgive and pray for those who give offenses. Through this, each comes to understand his Lord because he will be like Him.[510] Some few will forgive and plead for the weaknesses and failings of others. They will forgive and thereby be forgiven. They will obtain for themselves a judgment based only on mercy, for they will have shown mercy to others. This atoning act of love and intercession will be the hallmark by which the children of God are identified in the Day of Judgment (*see* Matthew 3:12). Only the peacemakers can be trusted to live in peace with one another. All others are unfit for the presence of God.[511] "Sometimes the relief other people need can only come from you. Under inspiration of the spirit, we can relieve the burdens of those around us."[512]

Iron Rod The *word of God* (1 Nephi 3:10; 1 Nephi 4:5), as seen in vision by both Lehi and Nephi; the path back to the tree of life is found in the revelations from God, as contained, in large measure, in the scriptures. Scriptures are of vital importance to mankind. Nephi has an angel instructing him, as well as Christ being shown to him, and the message includes this specific teaching about the importance of revelations and the scriptures.[513]

There are two different words used by Nephi regarding contact with the "iron rod" or word of God. Joseph Smith translated the two words as *cling* or *clinging* for one, with *hold* or *holding* for the other. The different word use raises the question of meaning. If they meant identical things, then the same word would have been translated. Therefore, there must be a reason for the different words. *And it came to pass that I beheld others pressing forward, and they came forth and **caught hold** of the end of the rod of iron; and they did press forward through the mists of darkness, **clinging** to the rod of iron, even until they did come forth and partook of the fruit of the tree* (1 Nephi 2:10, emphasis added). *Behold, he saw other multitudes pressing forward; and they came and **caught hold** of the end of the rod of iron. And they did press their way forward, continually **holding fast** to the rod of iron, until they came forth and fell down and partook of the fruit of the tree* (1 Nephi 2:12, emphasis added).

Some *catch hold*, then *cling*. Some *hold*, then *hold fast*. Both of these different approaches result in the persons reaching the destination, then partaking of the fruit. But they are situated differently as they move along the process. Some are *clinging* and some are *holding* as they move toward their destination. To *cling* implies something frantic, something charged with emotion, and something more desperate than to *hold*. *Holding* seems calm, thoughtfully committed, and more methodical than does *clinging*. From this, it's possible to conclude that there are at least two kinds of people who will make their way to partake of the fruit of the tree of life in this world. For one group, the process is unnerving, fearful, and emotionally wrenching. They cling on despite earth and hell. They fight to retain their grip, and they make heroic efforts in the opposition they face. They cling because they cannot relent, cannot relax, and know they face peril as they live their lives daily. For them their hopes are kept despite all their fears. They cling because they desire more than the opposition can deter them. For another group, the process is less emotional, but nonetheless filled with determination. They are not as charged with fear, but face what comes to them calmly and with the assurance that the Lord's word is in their hands and will be a refuge that will bring them to eternal life. There is another, more likely possibility, as well. There are not two groups, but only one. From time to time everyone faces moments of difficulty. The only way to stay with the rod is to cling. Then the seasons change, the storm relents, and calm returns. During those times when life improves, the person can continue to hold and move forward, but they have purchased the season of calm by the things they have endured in faith. Now they know it is only necessary to hold on, and all things will come to them. There is not a life that gets lived without challenge, difficulty, and seasons of despair. Everyone will at times be required to cling, and at other times have the ability to hold the course. Whether it is the one season or the other, however, at the end of the journey one may be able to lay hold on eternal life.[514]

Isle of the Sea Everything that is not part of the great Euro-Asian-African land mass. Although North America is currently regarded as a continent, in the Book of Mormon vernacular, it is an isle of the sea (*see* 2 Nephi 7:5). Further, most of Israel was relocated onto the isles of the sea (*see* 1 Nephi 7:2). So when the Lord affirms He speaks to those on the isles of the sea, He is confirming that there are multiple locations, involving multiple parties, each one of which has received sacred communication from Him.[515]

Jacob's Ladder A connection and transit between the Heavens and earth which Jacob (later named Israel) saw in a dream recorded in the Old Covenants: *And he dreamed, and behold, a ladder* [Heb. *cullam,* סֻלָּם]⁵¹⁶ *set up on the earth, and the top of it reached to Heaven. And behold, the angels of God ascending and descending on it. And behold, the Lord stood above it and said, I am the Lord God of Abraham your father, and the God of Isaac* (Genesis 9:20). Joseph Smith said, "Paul ascended into the third Heavens and he could understand the three principle rounds of Jacob's ladder — the telestial, the terrestrial, and the celestial glories or kingdoms, where Paul saw and heard things which were not lawful to utter. I could explain a hundredfold more than I ever have of the glories of the kingdoms manifested to me in the vision, were I permitted and were the people ready to receive them."⁵¹⁷ Joseph also said: "When you climb up a ladder, you must begin at the bottom, and ascend step by step, until you arrive at the top; and so it is with the principles of the gospel — you must begin with the first, and go on until you learn all the principles of exaltation. But it will be a great while after you have passed through the veil before you will have learned them. It is not all to be comprehended in this world; it will be a great work to learn our salvation and exaltation even beyond the grave."⁵¹⁸ The principles of the gospel are not supposed to be comprehended in one bite. Everyone progresses. The ladder that he's talking about climbing is, in fact, the ladder that is ordered and the one Jacob referred to. But whenever one begins that climb, he begins at the bottom. And so mankind finds themselves here — at the bottom of it. Notwithstanding finding themselves here, there are absolutely, invariably seven rungs on Jacob's ladder. ⁵¹⁹ No one can arrive at the throne of God in any other way than all have taken to arrive there. Everyone develops the same way, through the successive stages of Jacob's Ladder.⁵²⁰

In the afterlife there are different rungs on Jacob's ladder where different "Powers" are fixed: Angel, Archangel, Principality, Power, Dominion, Throne, Cherubim, or Seraphim — they may all be called "Powers of Heaven." These Powers have no desire to control or compel others to rise on Jacob's ladder. These are developmental stages of growth through which all must pass if they want to ascend nearer to God. Each individual on Jacob's ladder should be moving toward perfection.[521] Of course, some have elected to rebel and descend. But the ladder was ordained as a means for ascent. The great regret for man in the afterlife relates to his refusal to take advantage of the opportunity here to further his ascent.[522] What is the first rung on Jacob's Ladder? It is to have your calling and election made sure through the Holy Spirit of Promise. That is the beginning.[523] There are seven stages of development through which God's children must pass. It is not all to be done in this life. Christ is the prototype of the saved man, and He qualified by passing through these stages of development. When anyone arrives at the end of the journey through the seven rungs of Jacob's ladder, they will discover that the Mother was present throughout that journey. She is present all along the way through the seven pillars.[524] Scripture reveals a more complex afterlife, where ascent to God's Throne is more than a single step upward after this life.[525] Joseph Smith said, "It will be a great while after you have passed through the veil before you will have learned them."[526]

Jacob's Wrestle with the Angel A sacred embrace. "When one considers that the word conventionally translated as 'wrestled' (*yē'āvēq*) can just as well mean 'embrace' and that it was in this ritual embrace that Jacob received a new name and the bestowal of priestly and kingly power at sunrise [*see* Genesis 9:44], the parallel to the Egyptian coronation embrace becomes at once apparent."[527] *See also* SACRED EMBRACE.

Jesus Christ as the Father "Think of the word Father as *role* and not *identity*. If you take it as *role* and not *identity*, all the problems go away. If you hear the voice of God speaking to you, telling you Psalms 2:2, *You are my son; this day have I begotten you*, the voice you will be hearing will be Christ's. No one gets out of this world, back into the family of God in eternity, without Christ as their father. We're all the descendants of Adam, which means we're going to die. But if we become sons [and daughters] of God, we become sons [and daughters] of that God who won the victory over the grave, who becomes our Father, which is why the Book of Mormon calls Him *the very Eternal Father* — because Christ has to be your father in order to escape the doom which belongs to Adam. If you track the genealogy back of every one of us, you're going to find that the head of all that is a dead man who offended 'the Father.' When Christ worked out His salvation right down here, among us, we read in John — He's talking about Himself — He said, *I can of my own self do nothing. What I see the Father do, that do I.* [In] the closing verses of Matthew — after He's resurrected, after He's ascended back to the Father, after He's reported to the throne — He comes back and says, *All power is given unto me in Heaven and on earth* (Matthew 13:4). He no longer says, 'I need to follow what the Father did.' He says, in essence, 'I've completed the ascent. I am at the throne of God. I'm now the one who will rescue you. I have the power to rescue you. I have conquered death on your behalf.'

"Christ is 'the Father' when you think of it as *role* instead of personality or identity. When you get into personality or identity, you wind up with a mess on your hands. [In our prayers] there is no reason why that Father, to whom you address, should not be expected to have wounds in His hands and in His side and in His feet. When you hope to be rescued from the grave, He's going to be the Father that gets you out of there. You address the Father, but He has become the Father. The problem we have is that we want to assign a personality, we want to assign a role, we do not want to accept a status. We want personality instead of a role that gets played.

"Christ *is* the Father; Christ *was* the Son. He had to come in a subordinate position; He had to come into the world contaminated with blood; He had to have within Him the seeds of mortality in order to have the capacity to die because without the capacity to die He couldn't die. But His death had to be unjust so that it violated the law of justice. Justice had to be offended by the death of the Lord so that He, going into the grave, could say, 'An eternal wrong has been committed, because the wages of sin is death and I've committed no sin. I did not earn the wages of death, therefore I have the power to lay claim upon my life and take it up again, because that is the law of justice.' And justice had to surrender to His resurrection. So Christ comes out of the grave and is resurrected, and He wants to pull you out of the grave. And Justice says, 'No, she is a sinner.' And Christ says, 'Wait a minute, wait a minute, wait a minute; justice has been satisfied. I was entitled to eternally live. What you took away from me when you killed me, when you took my life, was eternal:

you robbed me of eternal life. Therefore I can claim her, too. Because the infinite of what you stole from me satisfied you infinitely. I am giving her a pass because, Justice, you offended me infinitely.' And Christ did this in order to bring us all back. But the only way we're getting out of here, after we shed these [bodies] and return from the grave, is through Him. And He becomes the Father.

"For as in Adam all die, even so in Christ shall all be made alive (1 Corinthians 1:63). He's going to give it as a free gift to everyone. The only question is: What will the quality of the afterlife then be? Because that's based upon a law that was predicated before the foundation of the world upon which infinite blessings are conferred."[528]

"The 'Father' of your eternal life will be Christ (T&C 18:1). He is your Father who is in Heaven, because your continuation after the grave will come through His sacrifice. He will literally provide you with the resurrected body you will inherit. This makes Him the Father (Mosiah 3:2.) Secondly, they are His teachings which will provide you with more than just resurrection. He will provide the further possibility of glory to you on the conditions He has made possible through obedience to Him. The one you follow, whose teachings you accept, whose ordinances you accept, is also your Father (1 Corinthians 1:17). The role of the Father is to raise His seed in righteousness. Christ's teachings are given in His capacity of a Father to all who will follow Him. Through His teachings you can have a new life here and now. You can be 'born again' as His seed (1 Peter 1:5). To do that you must first accept His role as your Father/ guide. Then you must further accept His role as Father/Redeemer. When you do that, He gives you a new life by His teachings and new life by His ordinances. Here, excluded from the presence of Heavenly Father Ahman, we have no way back except through Christ (Mosiah 1:15). He must become our Father to bring us back again into the Ahman's presence. Christ visits here. Christ labored here, lived among us, ministers still among us, and though resurrected, still walked alongside two of His disciples. He appeared in an upper room, cooked and ate fish on the lake's shore, and appeared to many. He will come to dwell here again. The Father Ahman, however, only appears in a state of glory, has not stood here since the Fall of Adam, and awaits the completion of the work of Christ before He will again take up His abode here. Christ is not the same person as Father Ahman. Christ becomes the Father of all who are redeemed through Him. Therefore, by redeeming you Christ has become your Father in Heaven. You will have many fathers, including Christ, Adam, Noah, Abraham, Isaac, Jacob, and in our dispensation, Joseph Smith as well. And all these will also be children of Father Ahman."[529]

Though Christ is a glorified, eternal God, reigning in Heaven and holding the power to exist from eternity to eternity, king Benjamin is informed by an angel that He will condescend to *dwell in a tabernacle of clay* (Mosiah 1:14). To be "exalted" is to already be in possession of what one hopes to acquire in mortality; that is, Christ was already exalted — He did not come here for His advancement, according to this angel, but He came and descended into a "tabernacle of clay" in order to serve us.[530] "Christ lives! He is the One who redeemed all of us. He has a rightful claim as the Father of us all. In the resurrection we come forth out of the grave as His children, because He purchased with His blood our continued life. We symbolize that future event when we are baptized by going under the water and coming up again. It symbolizes resurrection. It is to be born again a new creature in Christ. Baptism is a preliminary, ceremonial, necessary sign that we accept Him as our Father. He is real. I bear witness of Him. I have stood in His presence. I have spoken with Him. He speaks in plain humility."[531]

Judge/ment In 3 Nephi 5–7, Christ elevates the Law of Moses by raising the expectation for human conduct. He moves from mere outward conduct into the inner soul of the man. One is not doing as he should if all he does is refrain from killing. Instead, he needs to remove anger. The prior obligation ("said by them of old") focused only on one's conduct; now the focus is one's motivation. One can judge another based on conduct. They either do or do not do something. The conduct is observable and, therefore, capable of being judged. Now, however, Christ moves the battleground inside a person. It is now in the heart. On such terrain as that, man is incapable of knowing and, therefore, of judging.

With anything involving truth and rules of conduct, there are always some reasons to depart from the rule. Christ departed from this rule. First, however, it is necessary to know and understand the rule. The "judgment" which one is "in danger of" by being angry with one's brother is not the brother's anger, but God's. The judgment of God is provoked by those who are angry with their brother. One is not to be angry with his brother because that is the beginning of a whole sequence of events, the culmination of which may be killing. Anger leads to abuse. It leads to discourtesy, dishonesty, and cheating. It justifies miserable conduct because man thinks it right to give offense to another. It corrodes relationships and makes society sick. If this can be prevented in the heart, it can heal society. All must refrain from letting offenses turn into anger, dealing with them inside the heart, showing forgiveness and compassion.[532] The purpose of the Sermon on the Mount and the Sermon at Bountiful is not to equip man to judge others. It has no use for that. It is designed to change a person. "You need to become something different, something higher, something more holy. That will require you to reexamine your heart, your motivations, and your thoughts. It will require you to take offenses and deliberately lay them down without retaliation. When you do, you become someone who can live in peace with others. Living in peace with others is the rudimentary beginning of Zion. It will not culminate in a City set on the hilltop until there is a population worthy of dwelling in the high places, in peace, without poor among them. Christ's sermon is not merely a description of what kind of person He is. It is a description of what kind of person will qualify to live with Him."[533]

The context of *judge not, that ye be not judged* is framed by the statement that *with what judgment ye judge, ye shall be judged, and with what measure ye mete, it shall be measured to you again* (3 Nephi 6:2). We do "judge" one another, because we must. But the judgment should err on the side of forgiving. It should err in favor of trusting motives to be pure and intent to be good. All should be generous with their gratitude, evaluations, and suppositions. When they know someone is misbehaving, they should make allowances for those shortcomings, forgive them before they ask, and impute no retribution because of the offensive conduct. "This does not make us better than another, it makes us whole. It allows the Lord to forgive us for our own, much greater offenses against Him. For when we are generous, we merit

His Divine generosity. It is how we are healed. It is the means for our own salvation. Instead of thinking ourselves better than an offender, we should look upon them with gratitude, for they provide the means to obtain salvation — provided we give them forgiveness from all their offenses. This is why we should rejoice and be exceedingly glad. They enable us to obtain salvation by despitefully using us, as long as we measure them by the same standard that allows God to forgive us. What perfect symmetry: You measure to others using an instrument that will be used by God to measure back to you. So your ready forgiveness is how God will treat you. All those grudges can be replaced with petitions to God to forgive those who abused you. As you lay aside all those sins against you, committed by others, it will purge from you all your own sins. Straight and narrow indeed. But oddly appropriate and altogether within your control."[534]

The defect in judging is the position from which one proceeds. Man is blind. He has too many subjective problems in his background — training, education, culture, presumptions, prejudices, "things we just know to be true," ignorance, preoccupations, and impatience, all which interfere with perceptions. He acts on errors and reaches wrong conclusions. He measures with defective tools, then decides the matter from the wrong measure. Christ is reminding mankind that whenever he is inclined to correct another person, more often than not, he suffers from whatever defect he sees in others. That is why he noticed it. He sees it because it is really him. He is sensitive to the problem because he owns the problem. "First, whenever we see something amiss in another, start with the realization that we are seeing ourselves. Start inside. Ask, 'Why does this bother me? Am I really seeing myself in a mirror?' Then be grateful you saw another person display your problem. You now know what is wrong with you. Forgive them, fix you. The tendency to withhold patience is more often than not because their *mote* excites your notice through your own *beam*. A *mote* is a speck, a bit of sawdust. A *beam* is a board. Yours is the greater defect. For in you is not only the defect, but the tendency to judge others harshly. Both are wrong. When you have at last purged the defect, struggled to overcome and conquer the temptation or tendency, perhaps the price you pay to do so will make you humble enough to assist another. Not from the position as judge and condemner, but from the position of one who can help. When you 'see clearly,' then you may be able to *cast the mote out of thy brother's eye*. For now you see him as your *brother*. And in a kindly and affectionate manner you may act to reclaim him. Not as a judge, but as a brother. This is a continuing petition to make things better. But the only way you make them better is by starting inside. It is not for you to work on others, nor move outside your own range of defects, until you have first fixed what you lack. When you can proceed with charity to assist others to overcome what you have overcome yourself, then it is appropriate to approach your *brother* in kindness to help. Until then, stop judging and start removing *beams* from yourself."[535]

Justification The companionship of the Spirit that makes one justified by leading him to do what is right.[536] Christ possesses the knowledge to be able to justify all men and women. Moses explained the interrelationship: *For by the water you keep the commandment; by the spirit you are justified, and by the blood you are sanctified* (Genesis 4:9). It is the holy spirit that will justify each person.[537]

Key(s) Something used to open a lock; something that is important or central in importance. A "keystone" is the point in an arch that fits in the center, holding the arch together. Upon it all else rests. Keys are better viewed as a signal or a signpost along a pathway. Instead of "I hold *keys* and so I hold something of value," holding a key is better viewed as being given a strong guide or route to take. If the word is viewed using these meanings, it suggests that holding a key implies using it in action. The First Presidency and Quorum of the Twelve use their key positions to manage and maintain the worldwide LDS church organization. If not for that constant oversight, the organization of the church would lapse into disorganization. Their keys are indispensable to hold the entire structure together. Without them at the center, like a keystone, the building would collapse. Offices belonging to others are their responsibility. Each person receives keys that come to them in their own sphere. No one should be jealous of church positions; they do not matter and are not necessary.[538]

And this greater priesthood administers the gospel and holds the key of the mysteries of the kingdom, even the key of the knowledge of God (T&C 82:12).

"The word *keys* is horribly misunderstood. I have made it a practice to not use the word because of all the foolish and vain ideas that have accumulated around it. Joseph used the term in a variety of ways: for example, to mean authority, or opportunity, and in others it refers to a correct idea. This is the most important meaning. The term in the context of priesthood is completely absent from the Book of Mormon, and that book is the keystone of our religion, containing the fullness of the gospel. The only time the word keys is referenced in the Book of Mormon, it refers to a physical set of keys to unlock a door to the treasury controlled by Laban (1 Nephi 1:18). Although Joseph used the term often and meant many things by it, the challenge is to understand priesthood without being distracted by a poorly defined, and often used term. Mormon institutions now use the term most often to connote their exclusive right, license or control. The LDS *Handbook of Instructions* states the following, 'Priesthood keys are the authority God has given to priesthood leaders to direct, control, and govern the use of His priesthood on Earth.' This definition is the opposite of the way scripture directs priesthood be used (*see* T&C 139:5–7). The LDS *Handbook* approach turns this scripture upside down and backwards: by virtue of priesthood keys they have the right to direct, control and exercise influence over others. Mormon institutions in general all use their preferred meaning of the term *keys* to denounce anything or anyone they view as a rival. That is nonsense, and I avoid using the term because of widespread abusive practice."[539] If a Dispensation was given and the recipient failed to complete the work God assigned, then he acquires no key, no honor, no right, no authority from the Lord and therefore, has nothing to account for. The notion that someone can obtain keys without receiving a Dispensation from the Lord and successfully completing the work of God is a false idea that should be rejected. [540]

Keys are knowledge. A particular key is knowledge or instruction received from the Lord on how to do something. If one has the key, then one has the ability or power to do something. And conversely, if one is powerless to do or accomplish something (bind and loose, request ministering angels, command the elements or spirits, etc.), then they do not possess a key. "Then knowledge through our Lord and Savior Jesus Christ is the grand key that unlocks the glories and mysteries of the kingdom of Heaven…the key that unlocks the Heavens and puts in our possession the glories of the celestial world."[541] "There are many things which belong to the powers of the Priesthood and the keys thereof that have been kept hid from before the foundation of the world; they are hid from the wise and prudent to be revealed in the last times."[542] *Now the great and grand secret of the whole matter, and the summum bonum* [highest good] *of the whole subject that is lying before us, consists in obtaining the powers of the holy [Order of] Priesthood. For him to whom these keys are given there is no difficulty in obtaining a knowledge of facts in relation to the salvation of the children of men, both as well for the dead as for the living* (T&C 151:9). "The Melchizedek Priesthood…is the grand head, and holds the highest authority which pertains to [the Holy Order] and the keys of the Kingdom of God in all ages of the world, to the latest posterity on the earth; and is the channel through which all knowledge, doctrine, the plan of salvation, and every important matter is revealed from Heaven."[543] "In knowledge there is power. God has more power than all other beings because He has greater knowledge; and hence He knows how to subject all other beings to Him. He has power over all."[544] Joseph Smith also used the term *keys* to mean understanding, the greatest key being the ability to ask God and receive an answer (*see* T&C 147:12).[545]

Keys of the Kingdom To be able to ask and have God answer (*see* T&C 141:32; compare T&C 26:20; 82:12; 90:1; 131:5; and 151:12). Joseph Smith used the term *keys of the kingdom* to mean when a person can ask and receive an answer each time he asks. Those directed by God hold the keys of the kingdom because the kingdom belongs to God, and God must direct its affairs for it to be His.[546] Without revelation to obtain God's answer, Mormonism is just as adrift in uncertainty as apostate Christianity. They are like Laman and Lemuel who could not understand a revelation given to their father. In response to Nephi's inquiry as to why they did not ask God, they responded, *the Lord maketh no such thing known unto us* (1 Nephi 4:2). It takes revelation to understand revelation. That "key" is to sacrifice your life by obedience to God. Man must live humbly and meekly before God, obeying every word that proceeds from Him. They must do this, despite the rage of false religionists who will always condemn the things of God by pretending they, without revelation, can know what God meant, intended, or is doing. They are pretenders and are without authority. They fight against God. A man who has the "keys" must sacrifice all to know God.[547] Immediately following the two letters Joseph Smith wrote from Liberty Jail, he wrote the following (in one of the only talks he ever wrote out), *Thus we behold the keys of this Priesthood* [the priesthood that belonged to Noah before the flood, the priesthood that warned him about the coming flood and so on] *consisted in obtaining the voice of Jehovah, that he talked with him in a familiar and friendly manner, that he continued to him the keys, the covenants, the power, and the glory with which he blessed Adam at the beginning, and the offering of sacrifice which also shall be continued at the last time* (T&C 140:16). The keys of the Priesthood — the Priesthood that Noah held, the fullness of the Priesthood, the Holy Order, the version that came down then — consists in obtaining the voice of Jehovah, and He talked with him in a familiar manner. *Therefore it is given to abide in you, the Record of Heaven, the Comforter, the keys of the kingdom, the truth of all things, that which quickens all things — which makes alive all things, which knows all things, and has all power according to Wisdom, mercy, truth, justice, and judgement* (Genesis 4:9). It's given to abide in man; it is the Record of Heaven, the keys of the kingdom — the ability to get the voice of Jehovah to tell one the truth of all things, the answer to what one needs. If there is a group of people who claim to hold all of the keys who will tell you plainly that *the Lord maketh no such thing known unto us*, like Laman and Lemuel (but unlike Nephi, who says, "Have you asked God? He talks to me"), then one can know for a surety that those claimants do not have the keys. If God won't talk to them, they *cannot* have the keys.[548]

Kingdom of God The kingdom of God will always arrive as unwelcomed and unheralded as a thief in the night (*see* Revelation 6:8; 2 Peter 1:12; 1 Thessalonians 1:13).[549] "Whenever men can find out the will of God and find an administrator legally authorized from God, there is the kingdom of God; but where these are not, the kingdom of God is not. All the ordinances, systems, and administrations on the earth are of no use to the children of men, unless they are ordained and authorized of God; for nothing will save a man but a legal administrator; for none others will be acknowledged either by God or angels."[550] "Where there is no kingdom of God there is no salvation. What constitutes the kingdom of God? Where there is a prophet, a priest, or a righteous man unto whom God gives His oracles, there is the kingdom of God; and where the oracles of God are not, there the kingdom of God is not."[551] These are words for all of mankind and are as relevant today as they were when Joseph first spoke them.[552]

Kingdoms The afterlife is divided. More than one state exists immediately following death and lasting until the resurrection. These states are "Spirit Paradise" and "Spirit Prison." Following the resurrection from death, resurrected conditions are divided into progressively greater glory. The least condition of resurrected glory is called "Telestial" glory and is compared to that of the stars. The next highest resurrected condition of glory is called "Terrestrial" glory and is compared to that of the moon. The highest condition of resurrected glory is called "Celestial" glory and is compared to that of the sun. Each person receives the condition of glory that most accurately reflects the intelligence, or light and truth, they acquired by their heed and diligence to God during their experiences in this world. While these states of resurrected glory are temporary, they last an unknown period (of perhaps millions of years) until another opportunity or cycle of creation is merited for the person involved.

Another condition — one without any glory — is termed "Outer Darkness," where there is no light or glory and where the worm (the symbolic agent of decay) dies not and the fire (the symbolic agent of purification) is not quenched. Outer Darkness dissolves those who go there back into native spirit element, marking an end of all their potential. Outer Darkness is not considered a Kingdom but a condemnation, because there is no glory there.[553]

Know the Lord As foreseen by Jeremiah: *This shall be the covenant that I will make with the house of Israel: after those days, says the Lord, I will put my law in their inward parts, and write it in their hearts, and will be their God and they shall be my people. And they shall teach no more every man his neighbor and every man his brother, saying, Know the Lord — for they shall all know me, from the least of them unto the greatest of them, says the Lord* (Jeremiah 12:9). Getting to know the Lord is the definition of salvation (*see* John 9:19).[554] All are invited to come to know the Lord, see His face, and know that He is. *It shall come to pass that every soul who forsakes their sins, and comes unto me, and calls on my name, and obeys my voice, and keeps all my commandments, shall see my face and know that I am, and that I am the true light that lights every man who comes into the world, and that I am in the Father and the Father in me, and the Father and I are one* (T&C 93:1). "Can you imagine [how] different it would be if we were all able to say we know for ourselves, nothing doubting, our Lord? Can you imagine how all the problems we now face would evaporate overnight, if our quest was to grow from grace to grace until we too receive of the Father's fullness (T&C 93:7)? Most of what now afflicts us would become trivial, left behind as we grow in light and truth (T&C 36:4–5). To know the Lord is to have a covenant with Him."[555] All must come to know the Lord. The only way is to comprehend the Gospel of Christ, accept the invitation, prepare one's heart, mind, soul, and clean up, leaving behind sins, and come to face the Lord.[556] The Lord intends for all to return to Him; not in some future reunion following death, but here, in mortality. He wants all to "know Him."[557]

Know/ledge To have been visited by the Lord.[558] Faith was always intended to grow into knowledge.[559] Knowledge comes from contact with Jesus Christ (*see* Ether 1:14). This is the knowledge that saves and nothing else (*see* John 9:18). The idea that knowledge of Christ — through His personal appearance to each person — is now unavailable is an old sectarian notion and is false (*see* John 9:8).[560]
"Knowing God is Christ's definition of Eternal life and salvation. Joseph Smith clarified this does not mean to learn something about Him. Rather, it is to meet Him. It is to have Him minister to you, face to face, as one man speaks to another."[561] Since this is life Eternal, to *know* Him, would it be a simple and plain, but most precious teaching to urge people to part the veil of unbelief and behold their Lord? (*see* John 9:18).[562]

Lake of Fire and Brimstone Upon being judged, they go *into the place prepared for them* (2 Nephi 12:4). This place is for those who are grasped with "death and hell" and is called "a lake of fire and brimstone"— a lake, because it engulfs them so tightly they are flooded with the guilt; fire, because it is designed to purge and refine; brimstone, because of the bitterness of the experience. The torment there is "endless," meaning from God (*see* T&C 4:1–4). This purging does not confer blessings but merely balances out the claims of justice for those who would not accept mercy (*see* T&C 4:5).[563]

Law of Christ The law of Christ is found in the Sermon on the Mount (*see* Matthew 3). Christ gave many commandments, precepts, and teachings. He also gave a law.[564] "The greatest instruction that I know to have been given by God at any time, to any generation, is a rule of community found in the Sermon on the Mount and in the Sermon at Bountiful (*see* Matthew 3; 3 Nephi 5–6). This is how you and I should practice Christianity."[565] Early Christians were very diverse, but they agreed on two things: Christ's doctrine and Christ's law. Once Christians have these two essential teachings in common, they can have differences on other issues, just like the early Christians.[566] *See also* DOCTRINE OF CHRIST.

Law of Moses When the children of Israel refused to live a higher law, they were given the law of Moses. This law, in a general view, consisted of a collection of commandments, statutes, performances, rituals, sacrifices, and ceremonies. The law of Moses was "added" and then fulfilled. It was added when the dispensation intended to be delivered through Moses was rejected by Israel (*see* T&C 82:12–13), much like what happened with the early saints in Joseph Smith's time. The dispensation the Lord wanted to hand them (the saints of Joseph's time) was not received either (*see* T&C 141:10), so something less was added. The saints of this day get to partake in what they *were* willing to receive, but they were not willing to receive what they might have been given (*see* T&C 86:4).[567]

The ordinances are eternal. They do not and cannot change. When changed, the covenant is broken. God cannot and does not change His word. When men change it, they break the covenant and have no promise (*see* Isaiah 7:1). The addition of outward observances in the law of Moses was fulfilled in Christ's coming and sacrifice. Then, having been fulfilled, they were no longer necessary to observe (*see* 3 Nephi 5:22–23). When they were being observed, however, they did not change. From Moses to John, they were unchanged.[568]

King Benjamin explains something which ought to give everyone pause: *Yet the Lord God saw that his people were a stiffnecked people, and he appointed unto them a law, even the law of Moses* (Mosiah 1:16). The people who God claimed as *His* were a *stiffnecked people*. He didn't abandon them because of their spiritual stubbornness, nor did He reject them because they were suffering from their own pride and self-will. They were still "His." But because they were unable or unwilling to really come to Him and be redeemed from the Fall, He gave them something to trouble them — the law of Moses. This set of rules, sacrifices, ordinances, and observances included worship within a temple or House of God. There, in rich symbolism, they were reminded about the real thing — His presence. They were taught about His real nature. They were shown symbols that foreshadowed His coming into the world to be the bread of life, the light of the world, the sacrifice for sin, and the one through whose blood it was possible to enter back into the Holy of Holies. They had symbolic clothing, sacred language, Divine ritual, and sacred space given them. All this because they were a *stiffnecked people* who were unwilling to enter into His actual presence. These benighted and proud people then looked at all others and regarded them as less than "the chosen people" because the law of Moses given to them entrusted them with sacred space, sacred ritual, and sacred observances. These stiffnecked people made the law of Moses an end in itself. It was their special set of rites, their sacred space, their hidden rituals, participated in by only the "worthy" and "chosen few" that reassured them they were God's chosen people. And they were chosen. But they were chosen to be an example of foolishness, an example of pride, and ultimately, an example of those who reject God and kill His Son. They were chosen to show how to miss the mark while standing atop sacred ground dedicated to the God they claimed to worship. They were chosen to be foolish so that others in later times might be wise. They were chosen precisely because of their stiff necks — to show how God does not delight in the mere observances of outward rituals but expects our hearts to be made righteous. They illustrate how God rebuked the ancient chosen people for their failure to follow Him in the heart, rather than just in their empty ordinances (*see* 1 Samuel 7:9).[569]

The focus of the law of Moses was ritual purity, but Christ replaced that earlier ritual-based purity with internal purity.[570] Christ fulfilled all the law — not merely the law of Moses, which indeed pointed to Him (*see* Galatians 1:11), but also every part of the Gospel from Adam to Christ's earthly ministry (*see* Jacob 3:1; 5:2). All have testified of Him, and He has completed His ministry in strict conformity with all that was foreshadowed, all that was prophesied, all that was anticipated of Him. Just how completely He did this is not possible to understand with the current state of the scriptures. But He did fulfill all righteousness, complete every assignment, accomplish every task, and live in conformity with every prophecy concerning Him.[571]

Aaronic priesthood is a fairly durable kind of priesthood. It was what was involved in all kinds of rites and performances under the law of Moses (which were pretty easy to run afoul of and wind up in a state of uncleanliness or ceremonial condemnation, causing one to need renewal — even the High Priest would become unclean and have to renew), and all had to go through the Day of Atonement ceremonies; they had to purge from top to bottom; everyone was expected to purge with some regularity. Even a woman's regular monthly cycle resulted in ceremonial uncleanliness, requiring renewal. Childbirth was considered something that required a sacrifice and a ceremonial cleansing. Every time one turned around under the law of Moses, they had become unclean and had to fetch another animal, run up to the temple, offer sacrifice, and undo the ceremonial uncleanliness. The purpose of the Aaronic priesthood ministry was to bring one under condemnation regularly. Aaronic priesthood is pretty durable, precisely because of its functionality.[572]

When the Lord's people wanted religion but were unwilling to accept the fullness, He accommodated their desire and gave to them the law of Moses to keep them busy (*see* Mosiah 1:16). It is the nature of *stiffnecked people* that they prefer religious ceremonies and endless repetition of rituals to coming into the Lord's presence. King Benjamin was reminded by the angel that the purpose of the law of Moses was not to redeem anyone — it was merely a way to keep the people busy. In addition to the law of Moses, the Lord gave *signs* and *wonders* and many *types* and *shadows* to acquaint the people with the fact of *His coming* (Mosiah 1:16). These were not ends. They were all means. Why give the law of Moses? Why give *signs* and *wonders*? The people confused the symbols with the real thing. Because of the symbols, they thought they were chosen, elect, and holy. They thought they were a kingdom of priests, a royal priesthood. Instead, what they should have thought was that they were poor because the Lord was not dwelling among them; they considered themselves rich because they had *types and shadows*. They preferred the symbol to the reality. The true religion was only symbolized by the rites. By worshiping the symbols and not recognizing the truths which were their foundation, they became mere idolaters. It is one of the constant risks faced by God's people because the devil is always looking to convert the holy church of God into something perverted and evil (*see* Mormon 4:5). They could rejoice in their laws, rites, ordinances, and rituals. They could consider themselves better than the nations around them because they had God's program for salvation. All the program did was *harden their hearts,* because they became proud rather than humble. These religious and proud people did not understand that all their endless rites *availeth nothing* because it was the Lord alone who could redeem them (*see* Mosiah 1:16). They took their eyes off the Lord and put them on the religion. They did not understand the religion was nothing if it failed to point them to the Lord. How oft might the Lord have gathered them, indeed! It is astonishing that men would prefer religion to God; that they would prefer pride (which alienates them from God) to humility (which could bring them into His presence). Signs, wonders, types, and shadows are nothing if they fail to get mankind to look at the underlying reasons for them. They are not the real thing. They merely point to the real thing; for that, it is left between each individual and the Lord. Some few will see it as it really is. They will not be limited by the failures of the generation they live in. They can be saved in any generation because they see beyond the Lord in His types, shadows, signs, and wonders (*see* Alma 9:3).[573]

The law of Moses was fulfilled and will not return.[574] Christ introduced the concept that the law of Moses is now "fulfilled." Importantly, He says, *In me are all fulfilled* (3 Nephi 5:31). When He walked on the Road to Emmaus on the day of His resurrection, *beginning at Moses and all the prophets, he expounded unto them in all the scriptures the things concerning himself* (Luke 14:3). The rites and temple of the Dispensation of Moses testified to the details of His life. It ought to be noted that the things *under the law, in [Christ were indeed] all fulfilled*. His life was foreshadowed by the rites of Moses. His healing, His ministry, His history, and His sacrifice all were foreshadowed by the law of Moses. Since the Law pointed to Him, and He came to live His mortal life in conformity with that Law, it was now completed. The signpost was no longer necessary. The event had happened. When He says, "Old things are done away," it is not because they are terminated. It is because they were fulfilled. He completed the circle. He lived and died under the Law, fulfilling every jot and tittle of its requirements. Now it was time to push the meaning of the earlier Law deeper into the souls of His audience. *All things have become new*. It was a new beginning, a new Dispensation, a new message. The message was delivered by the Author of the law of Moses, not through an intermediary. The message came from the Author, in person.[575]

Liberally When the brother of Jared tried to solve the problem of interior lighting in eight barges, the Lord's answer had very little to do with the lighting problem (*see* Ether 1:11). The Lord's answer redeemed this prophet from the fall (*see* Ether 1:13), and the Lord *ministered unto him* (Ether 1:14), which would have included a great deal more than solving lighting issues. This is what liberally means. Revelations from the Lord go well beyond the question asked. Oftentimes, the issue that brings a prophet before God has nothing to do with the Lord's answer. The highly local question (which church to join, how to light a barge, where to hunt food, why some ancients had plural wives, what repentance is required, etc.) is largely irrelevant to readers of scripture. The liberally-given answers address matters of universal concern: apostasy and restoration; Priesthood restoration to Joseph; the fullness of God's revelations to mankind, including from the beginning to the end; calling and election; sealing authority; visions of eternity, etc. It is the liberally-given material which shows what the Lord really intends to bestow on mankind.[576]

Light Comprehension of the Doctrine of Christ is not based on command of a vocabulary or mastery of an argument. It is, instead, based on gathering light. Light is gathered by heed (obedience) and diligence alone.[577] By following the light one has already received, one grows in light (*see* T&C 36:4). This process leads to the "perfect day," where the light has chased away all darkness. This is how men and women, like Christ, can grow from grace to grace, until they receive a fullness, also (*see* T&C 93: 7). If one is unwilling to do this, then he may acquire a vocabulary with which to discuss the subject, but he will not have the light to comprehend it. Light can be shining all around a person, but if he does not acquire light within himself by his actions, he cannot comprehend the light (*see* JSH 13:11; 11:20; T&C 17:1; 23:1; 31:2; 86:8). "If [obtaining or gathering light] perplexes you, then ask God for understanding. He will tell you what to do. Follow His instruction. In this way you qualify to receive further light and knowledge by conversing with the Lord. He knows perfectly what you lack, and by the holy ghost within you will tell you what you must do. If you will not humble yourself and ask for this to be made known to you, then you cannot be brought into the light. Then the only result will be to perish in the dark. If you will follow the steps with the required real intent, acting no deception before God as you do, then you will receive the holy ghost. It will be unlocked to tell you what you lack and what you need to do. This inner light is a powerful source which can literally tell *you all things what ye should do* (2 Nephi 14:1). It is in the doing that you find the learning. It is in the act of following Him that you learn to be like Him. Obedience is the means by which you gather light. The commandments are revelations of the inner person you ought to become. They are how you grow in the flesh to comprehend God in the spirit. Your body is a veil that keeps you from Him. By subordinating the will of the flesh to the will of the spirit, you gain light and truth. Do it to understand it. Once you understand, you will be able to tell when someone speaks with the power of the spirit words of eternal life, or if they are, as Nephi puts it, *perishing in the dark* (2 Nephi 14:1). There are many who claim to speak on the Lord's behalf who declare false, vain, and foolish things. While they will be held to account for that, the point is not to condemn them. They may yet see the light, and repent, and return. The point is that you must avoid being misled by those who would lead you astray. The few humble followers of Christ are warned that they will be taught the precepts of men and must use caution to avoid being misled. Nephi is both pleading and warning in...2 Nephi 12:2. He wants you to go to the source and be directed from there. To have the words of Christ available to you. To hear the words of angels as you draw near to the light. If you do not, then it is because you refuse to follow the steps he has described. You must act to know. Without following through in your heart (which you cannot ever deceive) you can't draw near to the light. The discussion in *The Second Comforter* walks through line upon line that walk back into the light, and ultimately into Christ's presence. It is a modern manual to find Him."[578] The cares of this world — coping with Babylon — is all that is needed to keep one from acquiring light. Finding light requires a deliberate effort to notice it and take it in. When men and women are filled with light, the Heavens notice. In fact, it is the light within mankind that Heaven notices even from afar.[579] *See also* HEED AND DILIGENCE; GLORY; INTELLIGENCE; TRUTH.

Light of Christ Also known as Holy Spirit, intelligence, glory of God, power, or light and truth; the power by which man exists; and the mechanism that sustains all mankind from moment to moment and lends them the power to live and breathe. What is this relationship between God's power and the light of Christ? God's power proceeds forth from Him and sustains not only planets, stars, and the sun, but also all men and women so that they live. The light of Christ, which is in and through all things, is co-extensive with the Father's *glory* or *intelligence,* or in other words, *light and truth* (T&C 93:11).[580] All creation is sustained by the light of Christ. He keeps it organized by the light emanating from Him. This is why redemption is possible through Him. When He descended below it all, including death, He had the power to bring it all back to life with Him. He must permeate all things in order to lay ahold of all things and rescue all from destruction. "At this very moment we are in contact with Him through His Spirit. He is giving us life. He is not a distant God. He is an immediate and intimate God. He knows our thoughts because He gives us the ability and freedom to think. He knows how to judge us because everything we do uses His power. He lends us life and light. We have only the illusion of privacy. We have the freedom to act and choose, but our freedom operates inside His creation. Everything is dependent on His power."[581]

Light-mindedness Treating lightly things that are really important; not assigning the correct value to something that comes from God. "[Light-mindedness] doesn't have a single thing to do with a sense of humor or laughter…. I don't care how much you laugh, and yes, God has a sense of humor. When I'm all dour, and desperate, and pleading, very often the first response of the Lord is a quip about how inappropriately I'm behaving. The first message in the first talk of the 'ten talks' was to be of good cheer because our Lord is of good cheer. He takes seriously the things that will save us, but he really does enjoy our company and wishes that we likewise enjoyed one another's company as we ought to do."[582]

Living Water Christ instructs in 3 Nephi 5:8 about baptism: *And he said unto them, On this wise shall ye baptize, and there shall be no disputations among you. Verily I say unto you that whoso repenteth of his sins through your words and desireth to be baptized in my name, on this wise shall ye baptize them: behold, ye shall go down and stand in the water.* "This living ordinance should be performed in living water, if possible. Connect with God by using the things He provides. We believe and practice the Doctrine of Christ. We practice baptism by immersion in living waters — meaning lakes, rivers, streams, and oceans, where there is life."[583] Anciently the Jews practiced baptism in "living water," that is, in a naturally renewing body of water, like a river, lake, or ocean. Living water was part of the symbol.[584]

Lord's Anointed In the broadest sense, anyone who has been through an anointing in the temple.[585]

Lord's Supper *See* SACRAMENT.

Love There are two great forces at work in the universe. One is entropy — everything is getting colder, darker, and dissolving. This force is unrelenting and can be found everywhere in the physical world. Opposing it, however, is something that is creative, renewing, and equally unrelenting. This force that renews life, introduces new energy, and forms new systems is God's work — it is, in a word, love, or in the vernacular of the scriptures, it is charity.[586] *See also* CHARITY.

Lucifer "In our language we use the name Lucifer for an angel who was in authority before God, who rebelled, fought against the work of the Father, and was cast down to the earth. His name means *holder of light* or *light bearer*, for he had gathered light by his heed and diligence before he rebelled. He has become a vessel containing only wrath and seeks to destroy all who will hearken to him. He is now enslaved to his own hatred. Satan is a title which means *accuser*, *opponent*, and *adversary*; hence once he fell, Lucifer became, or in other words was called, Satan, because he accuses others and opposes the Father."[587] Lucifer pretends to be an angel of light because he once was one of the Powers of Heaven. He was *an angel of God who was in authority in the presence of God, who rebelled* (T&C 69:6). He still feigns to that authority, and fools are still misled into covenanting with him.[588] *See also* SATAN.

Maketh Flesh His Arm A way of saying the "strength of man," rather than the "strength of God." No man's precepts should be accepted when they do not originate in revelation from God. Without a connection to revelation and the holy ghost, the teachings are all the arm of flesh. If anyone wants to trust in that, he will be cursed (*see* 2 Nephi 12:6).[589] *See also* TRUST IN MAN.

Mansion The Greek word *monē* (μονή)[590] in John 9:6 was translated by Jerome in the late 4th century as *mansio* in the Latin Vulgate version of the Bible. Two verses later, in John 9:8, Jerome renders the same word *(monē)* as *abode*—an individual indwelling (*see* e.g., John 9:6; Enos 1:7; Ether 5:7; T&C 46:1.) Centuries later, the King James Version was influenced by the Latin translation and the word *mansio* retained its English cognate meaning of *mansion* from Latin *mansionem* (nominative *mansio)* "a staying, a remaining, night quarters, station." The word also was used in Middle English as "a stop or stage of a journey."[591] Although its meaning today has changed to describe a large, extravagant, and luxurious residence, its original connotation was a temporary stopping off place for travelers on their journey to an ultimate destination. "The Latin term *mansio* is derived from *manere*, signifying to pass the night at a place in travelling. On the great Roman roads the *mansiones* were at the same distance from one another as on those of the Persian empire. They were originally called *castra*, being probably mere places of encampment formed by making earthen entrenchments. In process of time they included, not only barracks and magazines of provisions...for the troops, but commodious buildings adapted for the reception of travelers of all ranks, and even of the emperor himself, if he should have occasion to visit them."[592] A mansion can be interpreted as a temporary place of rest or reward on the path of progression.

Marriage The gospel is all about marriage and family. The creation was for Adam, and creation was *not good* until Eve was given as a spouse and helpmeet for Adam. From this simple account of man's origin, one notes that everything from the stars above to the world itself led inexorably to the marriage of Adam and Eve. As a couple, the two were *the image of God*. The first commandment given to mankind was to *multiply and replenish the earth*. The account in Genesis testifies that God's creation of this world was to facilitate marriage of man and woman in order to produce a family. God performed the first marriage before death entered the world. At the creation, marriage was as eternal as man before the Fall. The restoration points to eternal marriage as man's glorious destiny. The restoration also began to make eternal marriage in the image of God again possible. Therefore, all the elements of the gospel point back to marriage as God's final purpose for mankind.[593] Marriage is a great venue for learning obedience, sacrifice, chastity, and consecration. Marriage is a laboratory to prove men and women and to see if they will give heed to God's direction.[594] Marriage, above everything else, is the image of God. This is what God intends to preserve into eternity. It is so much easier for God to take people who have the kind of marriage that is described in Jacob 2:11 and preserve them than it is to take someone who may know all the mysteries but whose marriage is in ruins and preserve them. The man and woman who have this kind of pure marriage are more godly.[595]

The Lord has reaffirmed in revealed scripture to this generation that: *Marriage was, in the beginning, between one man and one woman, and was intended to remain so for the sons of Adam and the daughters of Eve, that they may multiply and replenish the Earth. I commanded that there shall not any man have save it be one wife, and concubines he shall have none. I, the Lord your God, delight in the chastity of women, and in the respect of men for their wives. Marriage was established at the beginning as a covenant by the word and authority of God, between the woman and God, the man and woman, and the man and God. It was ordained by my word to endure for ever. Mankind fell, but a covenant established by my word cannot fail, and therefore in death they were not to be parted. It was my will that all marriages would follow the pattern of the beginning, and therefore all other marriages would be ordained as at the first. But fallen men refused my covenant, did not hearken to my word, nor receive my promise, and marriages fell outside my rule, disorganized and without me, therefore unable to endure beyond the promises made between the mortal man and the mortal woman, to end when they are dead.... Only those things that are by me shall remain in and after the resurrection. Marriage by me, or by my word, received as a holy covenant between the woman and I, the man and woman, and the man and I, will endure beyond death and into my Father's Kingdom, worlds without end. Those who abide this covenant will pass by the angels who are appointed, and enter into exaltation. Concerning them it shall be said, You shall come forth in the first resurrection, and if they covenant after the first resurrection then in the next resurrection, and shall inherit in my Kingdom their own thrones, dominions, principalities, powers, all heights and depths and shall pass by the angels to receive exaltation, the glory of which shall be a fullness and a continuation of their posterity for ever. Marriage is necessary for the exaltation of the man and woman and is ordained by me through the Holy Spirit of Promise, or in other words by my covenant, my law, and my authority. Like the marriage in Eden, marriage is a sacrament for a sacred place, on holy ground, in my presence, or where the Holy Spirit of Promise can minister. But rebellion has kept mankind from inheriting what I ordained in the beginning, and therefore women and men have been left to marry apart from me. Every marriage established by me requires that I be part of the covenant for it to endure, for Endless is my name and without me the marriage cannot be without end: for so long as I endure it shall also endure, if it is made by my word and covenant. But know also that I can do my work at any time, for I have sacred space above, and can do my work despite earth and hell....Whenever I have people who are mine, I command them to build a house, a holy habitation, a sacred place where my presence can dwell or where the Holy Spirit of Promise can minister, because it is in such a place that it has been ordained to recover you, establish by my word and my oath your marriages....Therefore the marriage covenant is needed for all those who would likewise seek to obtain from me the right to continue their seed into eternity, for only through marriage can Thrones and Kingdoms be established* (T&C 157:34–43).[596]

Martyr The kind of persecution which produces the "kingdom of Heaven" is martyrdom. Originally the word "martyr" meant "witness" (the Greek word for *martyr* is μάρτυς, *witness*), but so many of the early Christian witnesses were killed that it came to have the modern meaning of "one who dies for their faith." Martyrs were seen in John's vision below the altar of God (*see* Revelation 2:11). This means they were holy because of their sacrifice, the Heavenly altar being a symbol of them having shed their blood as witnesses. Joseph Smith and Hyrum joined those who qualified for such a witness. Blessed are those who are willing to endure persecution for His name's sake. For they are those who are willing to develop faith which cannot be obtained in any other way. It is through the sacrifice of all things that faith necessary for salvation is developed.[597] *See also* PERSECUTION.

Mary, the Mother of Christ Scriptures speak carefully about the existence and importance of a Heavenly Mother—a Divine Female whose greatest attribute is to bestow wisdom upon the whole of this creation. It is possible to completely miss Her presence.[598] The Father and the Son are masculine and therefore personified by the word "knowledge." The Mother and the Son's companion are feminine and are personified by the word "wisdom." These personifications reflect an eternal truth about these two parts of the One True God. Knowledge (masculine) initiates; Wisdom (feminine) receives, guides, and tempers. Knowledge can be dangerous, unless it is informed by wisdom. Wisdom provides guidance and counsel to channel what comes from knowledge. These are eternal attributes, part of what it means to be a male or a female. Creation begins with the active initiative of knowledge, but order and harmony for the creation requires wisdom. Balance between them is required for an orderly creation to exist. A great deal can be learned about Heavenly Mother by searching for the word "wisdom" in scripture. Very often the reference to "wisdom" is to Her distinctly, not merely an abstract attribute.[599]

What was Mary's role? Who was she? Is it possible she was "the mother of God" before she came into mortality? These are important questions that ought to be asked. If one can learn the answers, they would indeed be glorious. The Greek title "Mother of God," *Theotokos* (Θεοτοκοσ), has been used in Eastern Christianity since the Third Century (and perhaps as early as the Second Century). The title was exclusively associated with Mary. By the Fifth Century, the title became controversial, and the replacement term "Mother of Christ," *Christotokos* (Κριστοτοκοσ), was substituted. Since the pre-earth existence of man is not universally accepted in Christianity, most Christians have never considered even the possibility of a pre-earth identity for Mary. Despite this, she, like all mankind, existed before this world. If God the Father obeys the same commandments He imposes upon His children, then for Him to father a child with any woman other than His Wife would violate His decrees about adultery and chastity.[600] Before this creation, the Mother in Heaven was with the Father. She was beside Him when His work began. She was there when the plan was laid, the boundaries established, and the compass applied to establish order for the creation. All the Father knows, the Mother knows. All the Father established and ordered, the Mother established and ordered. They are One.[601] The Father is the source of glory and likened to the sun. The Mother reflects and shares this glory and is likened to the moon. She reflects God's glory, endures within it, and is empowered by it. She can participate with Him in all that is done wielding that glory. "Knowledge" is the initiator or force, and "wisdom" is the regulator, guide, apportioner, and weaver of that power. If not tempered and guided by wisdom, knowledge can be destructive. Wisdom makes the prudent adaptations required for order. The Father and Mother are One. But the Mother bridges the gulf between the Throne of the Father and fallen man. She made it possible for the Son of God to enter this fallen world for the salvation of everything in it. A great deal of reflection and study is needed to understand all this implies. This is an introduction of some basic information about the Mother of God or "the Mother of the Son of God after the manner of the flesh."[602] If "the condescension of God" included the Mother of God, as well as Her Son, then She was also a critical participant for providing the sacrificial lamb required for our redemption.[603]

"When She declares *whoso findeth me findeth life and shall obtain favor of the Lord*, (Proverbs 1:38), it should be taken literally. This does not mean we now pray to Her, for we are commanded to pray to the Father. But it does mean when we use the word *Father* to describe God, we finally regard God to be both *male and female* — the original *image of God*."[604] While acknowledging a Divine Mother is appropriate, singling Her out for worship is not. The words of the Divine Mother's Proverb and Mary's psalm both venerate and praise the Father. The role of God the Father is critical to acknowledge and understand for our salvation. Jesus Christ is the essential Savior and Redeemer whose atoning sacrifice is the means ordained by God to now rescue mankind from sin and death. Salvation depends on knowing, confessing, and worshiping Christ. Anything that distracts men or women from that can become an impediment to salvation. The Mother's greatest accomplishment has been to take the seed of God the Father and magnify it. She controls and weaves His seed into Their organized spirit offspring. From Their glory, or intelligence, She produces organized intelligences or spirits. One of the titles for the Heavenly Mother is "The Great Weaver" because She formed unorganized intelligence into organized spirits, becoming the Mother of All Living. All of mankind are intimately connected to Her, for they came from Her. Mortal women have inherited a similar power from Her. This inheritance empowers them to become mothers here. The capacity to fashion matter into another human being belongs only to Her daughters. All human life begins inside the womb of the woman, where the work of The Great Weaver is replicated for each one of Her children who has ever lived in this world.[605]

Meekness A difficult attribute to recognize, it is found in the relationship between man and God, not between man and man; to be meek is to follow the Lord's will, even when one doesn't want to do so, even when it brings one into conflict with friends, family, or community. Meekness is measured as between the servant and the Lord, not as between the servant and his critics.[606] Meekness, among other things, involves a conscious effort to avoid harming or offending others. It requires an absence of pride or self-will. It is not insistent upon being recognized or applauded. It denotes a willingness to suffer without complaint. Others may never recognize the meek, because meekness does not vaunt itself nor demand notice. There is great freedom in meekness. It relieves the meek from the burden of seeking their acclaim. It gives them the security of feeling God's approval for their course of living. It is private.[607] Meekness means a person voluntarily restrains himself and uses the absolute minimum control or authority over others. It is related to humility. Humility is voluntary submission to the control or power of God – in other words, obedience. Meekness affects a person's relationship with his fellow man. There is nothing showy or attention-grabbing about the meek. Instead, they are content to know they have a relationship and power with God. Unless God requires something to be done or revealed, the meek do not voluntarily put this authority on display.[608]

Melchizedek *And this Melchizedek, having thus established righteousness, was called the king of Heaven by his people, or, in other words, the King of peace. And he lifted up his voice, and he blessed Abram, being the high priest, and the keeper of the storehouse of God; him whom God had appointed to receive tithes for the poor. Wherefore, Abram paid unto him tithes of all that he had, of all the riches which he possessed, which God had given him more than that which he had need. And it came to pass, that God blessed Abram, and gave unto him riches, and honor, and lands for an everlasting possession; according to the covenant which he had made, and according to the blessing wherewith Melchizedek had blessed him* (Genesis 7:20–22). In 1844, the church-owned newspaper identified Shem as Melchizedek.[609] Joseph Smith explained that Melchizedek was not an earthly king, nor did he reign over a population.[610] Melchizedek is not a name but a title. It is a compound of two words. The first is *Malki* (מַלְכִּי), meaning "king," and *Zadok* (קדֶצ), meaning "righteous;" *Malki Tzedek* or *Malki Zedek* (מַלְכִּי־צֶדֶק) can mean "righteous king" or "king of righteousness."[611] As a comparison, the Dead Sea Scrolls portray their "Teacher of Righteousness" as *Moreh Zedek*. Joseph Smith asked, "What was the power of Melchisedick[?] twas not P. of Aaron &c. [but it was the power of] a king & a priest to the most high god. A perfect law of Theocracy holding keys of power & blessings. Stood as God to give laws to people. Administering endless lives to the sons and daughters of Adam."[612] Melchizedek was a king, and he was a high priest of the Most High God after the Order of the Son of God, i.e., a king and a priest. It is both a name-title and a new name given to Shem. Christ is the Great King and the Great High Priest. The name Melchizedek is really a name-title belonging to Christ. It was given to Shem because he was a worthy disciple of the Lord. The name-title became the designation of Priesthood. It was used as a substitute for the frequent repetition of the "Son of God."[613] The great priest Melchizedek is admired so much that the Priesthood was renamed after him because he was the last one to accomplish Zion. But when one examines carefully why Melchizedek qualified to obtain the Priesthood, one discovers it was because he "by faith" quenched the violence of fire, he subdued lions, by faith he achieved all these things – not by priesthood. By faith.[614] Melchizedek's city of peace came because those who heard him repented. They were taken into Heaven by their repentance. They, like Enoch's city, will return in the last days. The wicked will not survive their return. The next time there is a place where people of righteousness are taught and gathered, it will no longer be taken up to Heaven. Instead, it will allow Enoch's and Melchizedek's people to return. A holy city must be prepared to welcome that return.[615] *See also* SALEM.

Melchizedek Priesthood A form of priesthood Joseph Smith believed was conferred by the voice of God upon a recipient (*see* Genesis 7:18). It does not descend by birth but by the will of God. It holds the responsibility for administering spiritual blessings. First promised to Joseph Smith and Oliver Cowdery by John the Baptist, it was conferred by the voice of God for the first time at a conference in June 1831. Despite the evidence, the LDS church believes it was restored by Peter, James, and John sometime between May 16–28, 1829. The LDS church claims to be able to transfer this authority by the laying on of hands and, therefore, claims to have spread it throughout their adult male population. Until 1978, LDS Mormons refused to confer this priesthood on males of black African descent, but they changed their policy at that time and now ordain "all worthy males."[616] At a conference on June 3, 1831, a revelation to Joseph directed that twenty-three attendees were to be ordained to this heavenly priesthood. At the time of the conference, it was called "high priesthood" but later would be called Melchizedek Priesthood.[617]

Joseph Smith said, "All priesthood is Melchizedek, but there are different portions or degrees of it. That portion which brought Moses to speak with God face to face was taken away, but that which brought the ministry of angels remained. All the prophets had the Melchizedek priesthood and were ordained by God himself" (*TPJS*,

180–181).[618] When viewed not as a name but as a title, Melchizedek is a compound of two words: *Malki* (king) and *Zadok* (righteous) which means and is a reference to *the* "King of Righteousness," who is Jesus Christ, who possesses all Priesthood. Melchizedek priesthood or the priesthood of the King of Righteousness, viewed in this light, is the authentic Holy Order after the Order of the Son of God. Melchizedek priesthood is the priesthood of Jesus Christ. It is an association with the Son of God.[619] This complete *Melchizedek Priesthood comprehends the Aaronic, or Levitical priesthood and is the grand head, and holds the highest authority which pertains to the Priesthood, the keys of the Kingdom of God in all ages of the world to the latest posterity on the earth, and is the channel through which all knowledge, doctrine, the plan of salvation, and every important truth is revealed from Heaven* (T&C 140:2). The Melchizedek priesthood is given for blessing and giving life. If someone claims to hold Melchizedek priesthood, but he uses it to judge, condemn, control, compel, and assert authority over the souls of men, then it is a sign he holds no such authority. The office, the authority, and the keys of the Melchizedek priesthood are given by God to man to bless, to enlighten, and to raise one up by bringing light and truth, which is the glory of God or intelligence.[620] *See also* MELCHIZEDEK; HOLY ORDER.

Mercy Tenderness of heart which disposes a person to overlook error.[621] "If you want mercy from the Lord, you must give it to your fellow man. If you do not show mercy to your fellow man, the Lord cannot provide it to you. There is a law which binds the Lord to the same standard you set for yourself. It is an irrevocable law. Therefore, the Lord teaches us to show mercy so that we might merit mercy. We are the final beneficiaries of all the mercy we show to others. It really is true that that which ye do *send out shall return unto you again* (Alma 19:11). This is called 'karma' in another faith. It is a true principle. Perhaps it operates within a larger time frame than just this life, but it operates, nonetheless. Alma knew the truth and was teaching it to his son."[622]

Ministering Angel Ministering angels are an indispensable part of the Gospel of Jesus Christ. That is why those keys were restored so early on in this Dispensation and are so widely disseminated into the LDS Church membership (*see* JSH 14:1). There is a system by which men learn the mysteries of heaven and are saved. That system is set out in Alma 9:7: first, angels are sent to prepare men and women; second, they are allowed to behold the Lord's glory; third, they converse with the Lord, at which point they are taught the things that have been prepared from the foundation of the earth for their salvation. All of this is driven by the man or woman's faith, repentance, and holy works. This is in keeping with Joseph Smith's revelation about those chosen to become a member of the Church of the Firstborn. They are chosen by the holy angels, to whom the keys of this power belong (*see* T&C 74:8). If this isn't happening, then faith does not exist on the earth any longer (*see* Moroni 7:7).[623] Angels minister to "chosen vessels" or mortal messengers, as the Three Nephites did with Mormon and Moroni (*see* Mormon 4:2). Then these vessels testify and bear testimony so that the way is prepared *that the residue of men may have faith in Christ* (Moroni 7:6). These three visited with Mormon, but the people to whom Mormon ministered didn't see them. They ministered to Moroni, and those to whom Moroni ministered didn't see them. The chosen vessels also become as ministering angels.[624] Heaven's "chosen vessels" may seem most unlikely. In the cases of Alma the Younger and Saul of Tarsus, they were wicked when they were chosen. Yet both would later become ministering servants who preached righteousness to the residue of men.[625] Many people have received ministering angels. Men, women, and children have, can, and do receive angelic ministers (*see* Alma 16:26). When they minister to a man or a woman, it is to enable them — the ones being ministered to — to testify and help others to likewise have faith in Christ.[626] Angels minister to those with faith, who are supposed to then preach salvation to others.[627] *See also* ANGEL.

More Sure Word of Prophecy The testimony from Jesus, promising Eternal life. Christ provides it. It is in this sense that the "testimony of Jesus" is used in scripture. It is not something one possesses, speaks, or bears to another. It is something Christ delivers by His own voice — Christ testifies; hence the phrase "the testimony of Jesus." All those who seek His glory will need to acquire His testimony to them that they are saved. They must acquire His Word.[628] "Now for the secret and grand key: Though they might hear the voice of God and know that Jesus was the Son of God, this would be no evidence that their election and calling was made sure, that they had part with Christ, and were joint heirs with Him. They then would want that more sure word of prophecy, that they were sealed in the heavens and had the promise of Eternal life in the kingdom of God. Then, having this promise sealed unto them, it was an anchor to the soul, sure and steadfast. Though the thunders might roll and lightnings flash, and earthquakes bellow, and war gather thick around, yet this hope and knowledge would support the soul in every hour of trial, trouble and tribulation. Then knowledge through our Lord and Savior Jesus Christ is the grand key that unlocks the glories and mysteries of the kingdom of heaven.[629] The more sure word of prophecy means a man's knowing that he is sealed up unto Eternal life by revelation and the spirit of prophecy, through the power of the holy priesthood."[630]

Mormon "Before I give a definition, however, to the word [Mormon], let me say that the Bible in its widest sense, means 'good,' for the Savior says according to the gospel of John, *I am the good shepherd*; and it will not be beyond the common use of terms to say that good is among the most important in use, and though known by various names in different languages, still its meaning is the same and is ever in opposition to *bad*. We say from the Saxon, *good*; the Dane, *god*; the Goth, *goda*; the German, *gut*; the Dutch, *goed*; the Latin, *bonus*; the Greek, *kalos*; the Hebrew, *tob*; and the Egyptian, *mon*. Hence, with the addition of *more*, or the contraction, *mor*, we have the word Mormon, which means, literally, *more good*."[631]

Most Holy (Hebrew *qodesh,* קֹדֶשׁ).[632] Most holy does not mean "very holy"; it means "actively holy, imparting holiness."[633] (Cf. Exodus 14:5; 16:2,5; Leviticus 2:4.) The Law of Moses prescribed the death penalty for a variety of offenses. One of the ways to avoid the execution of the penalty was to go to one of the safe harbor cities. Another way was to come in contact with the altar, because the altar was considered most holy. Things that are most holy communicate holiness; one cannot profane them. If one comes in contact with something that is "most holy," while he or she is unholy, they don't make it unholy; the altar — or the thing that is "most holy" — makes *them* holy, because it is most sacred. "Part of the rites in the temple are intended to communicate to you things that are most holy. They are intended to make you holy. They are intended to make you a suitable recipient for an audience. They are intended to make you a suitable companion for a walk down a dusty road with the risen Lord who is trying to get you to notice exactly who it is that speaks to you."[634]

Mothers Mothers who minister to their children in patience and love will undoubtedly be among those whom the Lord will remember in the final day. The first parable, "The Busy Young Man,"[635] is about those little acts through which one finds their Lord. "The Weathered Tree"[636] is about the enduring power of a mother's love and how, like the Lord's own sacrifice, this often underappreciated calling has been and continues to be a lifetime of service. Mothers oftentimes do not take time to study because they are too busily engaged in the *actual work* of charity, love, and service. Some may not be able to construct a scripture-based explanation or exposition, but they recognize truth by the light that has been acquired within them by their fidelity to the Lord's system of conferring light and truth. "I have been far more impressed with mothers in Zion than with the tattered remains of what is now called Zion by the gentiles." [637]

Mutual Agreement In response to prayers and pleadings, the Lord answered with a definition of mutual agreement (as used in the Answer to Prayer for Covenant) this way: *As between one another, you choose to not dispute* (T&C 174:1). Simply put, even if men or women disagree, if they choose to not dispute, they have mutual agreement. *Pray together in humility and together meekly present your dispute to me, and if you are contrite before me, I will tell you my part* (T&C 157:54).[638] When the definition was given, it was accompanied by the realization the Lord could have disputed every day of His life with someone. He deliberately chose to not contend. He was not an argumentative personality.[639] "As between one another (that is, every one of us because every one of us is involved in a relationship with one another) you choose [to not dispute]. Mind you, Christ could have disputed, he could have corrected, he could have challenged every one of the ongoing religious and social conventions of his day.... How much of the gospel of Christ would not have been possible for Him to preach if He'd gone about contending? He chose not to. In that respect, perhaps His most godly example was the patience with which He dealt with those around him — kindly, patiently, correcting them when they largely came to Him with questions trying to trap Him, but affirmatively stating in the Sermon on the Mount how you could take any group of people and turn them into Zion itself, if we would live the Sermon on the Mount."[640] *See also* CONTENTION.

Mysteries of God   That knowledge which is hidden from the world and only made available through revelation to the faithful. Much of such knowledge may be learned but is not to be taught. One will have to apply the process of learning the mysteries in one's life if he or she intends to learn the mysteries themselves.[641] The scriptures tell us how to get the "mysteries of God." Learning these mysteries is the fullness of Christ's Gospel.[642] There is a system by which men learn the mysteries of heaven and are saved. That system is set out in Alma 9:7: first, angels are sent to prepare men and women; second, they are allowed to behold the Lord's glory; then they converse with the Lord, at which point they are taught the things that have been prepared from the foundation of the earth for their salvation. All of this is driven by the man or woman's faith, repentance, and holy works.[643] Joseph Smith said, *I advise all to go on to perfection and search deeper and deeper into the mysteries of godliness…. [As for myself] it has always been my province to dig up hidden mysteries, new things, for my hearers.*[644] This is the Book of Mormon theme. Search deeper, and find God.[645] *Ask that you may know the mysteries of God.* That is a commandment. Although given to Oliver Cowdery, it is a principle that is applicable to all of mankind (*see* T&C 3:3). The claim that one should stay away from the mysteries of God is false. Refusing to follow the command to *ask that you may know the mysteries of God* (JSH 13:26) denies the power of godliness and opposes the doctrine of salvation. It is anti-Christ.[646] "We make our own mysteries; we are not meant to be kept in darkness, and the mysteries of heaven will be unfolded to us as we make an effort to understand them."[647] Christ said that *the mysteries of the kingdom of heaven* are understood only by those who have been initiated and given that understanding (*see* Matthew 7:2). Mysteries can also be defined as solemn ceremonial ordinances or rituals which take place in a special setting. "Mysteries (from the Greek, *mystērion*, μυστήριον)…[are] confided only to the initiated and not to be communicated by them to ordinary mortals."[648]

Knowledge of the mysteries of godliness is obtained only through obedience to God. He ordained this method to make His greatest truths universally available to all His humble followers. If it were otherwise, men and women would all have to go to college to receive training for the ministry. Education is no real advantage in receiving light and truth from God. Humility is the only real, great advantage which any soul ever possesses (*see* T&C 159:31–32).[649] Alma's teaching that *it is given **unto many** to know the mysteries of God* (Alma 9:3, emphasis added) means what it says. This is God's promise in every age. Even if only few men or women are willing to receive it, that does not cancel the promise.[650] "The principle involving limited disclosure of things received in personal revelation is explained by Alma. If you are incapable of obeying these requirements, then you cannot receive any new mystery by revelation. Heaven will not permit any soul to receive mysteries if they cannot resist revealing them unwisely to others. The constraint — that they may be learned, but cannot be taught — is enforced by withholding them from those who will not abide by this constraint. If you are one of those who cannot respect this limitation, then the process will not work for you. Joseph said: 'The reason we do not have the secrets of the Lord revealed unto us is because we do not keep them, but reveal them; we do not keep our own secrets, but reveal our difficulties to the world, even to our enemies, then how would we keep the secrets of the Lord?'[651] The mysteries of God are His hidden but simple truths." [652] *See also* UNSPEAKABLE.

Naked and Afraid The reaction of any who come into God's presence in their fallen state (*see* Mormon 4:6). When Adam and Eve partook of the fruit and then Satan called their attention to the fact that they were naked, he was pointing out to them that they ought to be ashamed. Therefore, when they heard the voice of God speaking, they withdrew because of what the shame triggered within them — fear. They were ashamed to come into the presence of that being whom they knew to be just and holy, because now they were naked and afraid. Their "nakedness" before God came as a consequence of understanding the difference between what they were — sinful — and what God was — perfect.[653]

Names of God in Scripture Names serve not only as identification but as identity. Aspects and attributes of identity are often emphasized by the name itself. "Names are for identification, but they are more than that. Why is it necessary that all be done *in the name of the Son*…? Like the other elements of ordinance, it is a means of communication."[654] "To receive a new name is to receive a new role or persona, to be identified with a particular situation or association." [655] God's name is hallowed (*see* Matthew 3:29). *Hallowed* means "respected, acknowledged, reverenced, its authority held in awe."[656] (*See Beloved Enos*, 126–127, for a discussion of names and titles). Some of the names of God used in scripture are:

Abba The Father — or more personally, *my* father (Cf. Mark 7:11; Galatians 1:13; Romans 1:34).

Adonai A divine name, translated "Lord" or "Master." When a Hebrew reader came upon the unpronounceable tetragrammaton YHWH (יְהֹוָה), *Adonai* was substituted as the pronunciation. It occurs in the Old Covenants 434 times.[657]

Ahman God the Father (*see* T&C 75:1–2, The Testimony of St. John). *See also* FATHER AHMAN.

Alpha and Omega A name for Christ, as He said, *I am Alpha and Omega, Christ the Lord, yea, even I am he, the beginning and the end* (JSH 17:2; John 1:3, emphasis added). Alpha (A, α; ἄλφαis) is the first letter of the Greek alphabet, and Omega (Ω, ω; ωμέγα) is the 24th or last letter.

Christ A title meaning "anointed one." It is the anglicized form of the Greek word *Christos* (χριστός), which means "Messiah." Jesus Christ is a name with a title as is Jesus the Anointed (One) or Jesus the Messiah. *See also* MESSIAH.

El Translated as "God," singular. Many biblical names combine El with other words, e.g., Micha-el ("who is like God"), Samu-el ("name of God" or "God is heard"), and Rapha-el ("God is healer" or "God has healed"). *See also* EL, THE

El Elyon The Most High God; God the Father. It occurs in the Old Covenants 28 times.[658]

El Olam The everlasting or eternal God.[659]

El Shaddai Translated in the KJV as Lord God Almighty. It occurs in the Old Covenants 7 times.[660] The term "El Shaddai" could be the earliest Hebrew name for deity and may mean "god of the mountain(s) or high god." "The name could also mean a female destroyer or a nursing mother or even the guardian of the fields. Or all of them. The name has a feminine form."[661]

El, The Plural, referring to many of the El. *See also* EL.

Elohim A plural Hebrew noun (אֱלֹהִים) usually translated as "god." It occurs in the Old Covenants over 2,000 times.[662] Rendered as the Greek *Theos* in the Septuagint.[663] Those who inherit everlasting burnings are referred to as the "Elohim."[664] The image of God is both male and female. This is why the name-title "Elohim" is plural.[665]

End, The A name for Christ, as He said, *I am Alpha and Omega, Christ the Lord, yea, even I am he, the beginning and **the end**"* (JSH 17:2, emphasis added).

Father Ahman God the Father (*see* T&C 75:1–2; The Testimony of St. John). *See also* AHMAN.

God of Hosts Throughout scripture the Father is described as the God of Hosts. Seeing Him includes an accompanying "host," a "concourse of angels," a "train," or similar reference to others with Him. He appears with the heavenly Host because God has a family, including a spouse. There is no difference between the Father and His female Consort, the One about whom so little is said.[666] *See also* JEHOVAH SABAOTH.

Holy One of Israel The Lord God Almighty, the true Messiah and Redeemer who has a covenant relationship with those faithful to Him (*see* 2 Nephi 1:2). He is the *keeper of the gate…and…employeth no servant there* (2 Nephi 6:11). He is the One who keeps the gate, protects the way, and greets those along the way (*see* 2 Nephi 13:2–3).[667]

I AM Jehovah identifies himself to Moses as I AM (Exodus 2:5). Jesus makes a connection with declarations of *I am the good Shepherd* (John 6:26), and *before Abraham was, I am* (John 6:16).

Immanuel (Hebrew '*immanue'el*, עִמָּנוּאֵל) literally means "El (god) with us." Jesus Christ is the El (singular) and was identified by name in Matthew 1:5 and Isaiah 3:4.

Jehovah "The self-existing One," "eternal One," or Lord. It occurs ca. 6400 times in the Old Covenants. It is also translated "God."[668]

Jehovah is a Latinization of the Hebrew name, "Yahweh" (יְהוָה), and became the prevalent word for the God of the Old Testament during the Protestant Reformation. There are a number of variations of Jehovah in scripture: Jehovah-Ra'ah (the Lord is my Shepherd),[669] Jehovah-Nissi (the Lord is my banner, my altar),[670] Jehovah-Rapha (the Lord that heals),[671] Jehovah-Shammah (the Lord is there),[672] Jehovah-Tsidkenu (the Lord our Righteousness),[673] Jehovah-Jireh (the Lord will provide; the Lord sees),[674] Jehovah-Shalom (the Lord is Peace),[675] Jehovah-M'kaddesh (the Lord who sanctifies, consecrates you),[676] and Jehovah-Sabaoth (the Lord of Hosts).[677] The first seven are sometimes referred to as the "redemptive names" of God. *See also* JEHOVAH SABAOTH; GOD OF HOSTS; YAHWEH.

Jehovah Sabaoth The Lord of Hosts. Jehovah and Elohim occur with Sabaoth over 285 times. Not to be confused with Sabbath (Hebrew *shabbath*, שַׁבָּת; Greek σάββατον). *See also* GOD OF HOSTS.

Jesus The English name of Jesus originates from the Latin form of the Greek name *Iēsous* (Ἰησοῦς), a rendering of the Hebrew *yeshua* ("Jehovah saves") and similar to the name Joshua.

Jesus Christ ...*neither is there salvation in any other, for there is no other name under Heaven given among men whereby we must be saved* (Acts 2:5). *And moreover, I say unto you that there shall be no other name given, nor any other way nor means, whereby salvation can come unto the children of men, only in and through the name of Christ the Lord Omnipotent* (Mosiah 1:16).

Lamb of God During the first Passover, the Israelites marked their doorposts with the blood of a slain lamb as a sign to save them from destruction. Jews would later ritually sacrifice an unblemished lamb on the eve of Passover. Christ is the Lamb of God, the Paschal or Passover lamb as described by Paul (*see* 1 Corinthians 1:19) and provided by the Father as a witness (the Greek word for *martyr* is μάρτυς, *witness*) and as the literal symbol of the atoning sacrifice of the Son. *The Righteous is lifted up and the Lamb is slain from the foundation of the world* (Genesis 4:19). It is through the *blood of the Lamb* that one is made spotless (*see* Mormon 4:6). *The Lamb of God is the Son of the Eternal Father and the Savior of the world* (1 Nephi 3:24). *See also* CHURCH OF THE LAMB.

Lord Adonai, as well as Yahweh, was translated in the Septuagint as *kyrios* (κύριος), "the Lord." The Lord became synonymous with Jehovah. "The Lord" is the most common title for Jesus in the New Covenants.

Lord God Almighty These are three names used for God. Together, it is a three-fold assertion of divine authority. *Lord* refers to the Savior as Guide. *God* refers to Divine right and authority. *Almighty* refers to the irrevocable nature of the word used by God.[678]

Man of Holiness God the Father (*see* Genesis 4:9).

Messiah A title meaning the "anointed one," from the Hebrew *meshiach*, מָשִׁיחַ. *See also* CHRIST.

Only Begotten of the Father The singular reference to Jesus Christ as the sacrificial Son offering from the Father.[679]

Pater Father as begetter, progenitor, creator, as in an intimate relationship.

Redeemer Jesus Christ is the essential Savior and Redeemer whose atoning sacrifice is the means ordained by God to now rescue mankind from sin and death. "Our salvation depends on knowing, confessing and worshiping Christ."[680] *All mankind were in a lost and in a fallen state, and ever would be save they should rely on this Redeemer* (1 Nephi 3:2).

Rock of Heaven *And the Lord said, Blessed is he through whose seed Messiah shall come, for he says, I am the Messiah, the King of Zion, the Rock of Heaven, which is broad as eternity* (Genesis 4:20).[681]

Savior This title comes from the Old French word *sauver* (keep [safe], protect, redeem) and the Latin *salvare* (make safe, secure) and is a translation of the Greek word *sōtēr* (σωτήρ), which means "savior, deliverer, the one who extends salvation."[682] "The Father's testimony is that our salvation comes through Christ. For us the Father has provided a Savior. If we repent, we can come back into the presence of God and enter into our salvation and exaltation. But it is through the means provided for us: a Savior, who is Christ the Lord."[683] The doctrine of Christ is what the Father ordained as the means for salvation. Anyone who interferes with the process or offers another means for salvation cannot deliver (*see* Mosiah 1:16). Whether it is an institution or an individual, no one other than Christ can save. Hence His title as Savior.[684]

Son Ahman Jesus Christ, the Son of God (*see* T&C 75:3–4; The Testimony of St. John).

Son of God An acknowledged status meaning one has been accepted by God into His family (*see* T&C 18:1).[685] *The* Son of God is Jesus Christ (*see* JSH 14:17). Christ was *called the Son of God* because He *received not the fullness at first*. He was "called" to be the Son of God because that was not who He was before the call. He had to first qualify to be "called," as all must do. It should be self-evident: He *received not the fullness at first*. After being *called the Son of God,* it would still be a great while before He condescended to redeem (*see* The Testimony of St. John 12:10; T&C 93:4).[686]

Son of Man Jesus Christ refers to Himself as the "Son of Man," the "Son of the Man of Holiness," as well as "Son Ahman." (See Genesis 4:9,15,19, 21–23; 7:23–24; Matthew 11:9; Testimony of St. John 5:19; 6:16; 9:3–4.)

Spirit of Truth A formal name for Christ. *See* SPIRIT OF TRUTH.

Walker in the Path *Now, therefore, know that Jesus is the Messiah, the Walker in the Path who has proven for evermore that Father Ahman sent Him into the world to prove His Father's path* (Testimony of St. John 12:21).

Word, The *Therefore, in the beginning the Word was, for he was the Word, even the Messenger of Salvation, the Light and the Redeemer of the world, the Spirit of Truth, who came into the world because the world was made by him, and in him was the life of men and the light of men* (T&C 93:2; Testimony of St. John 12:8). Living by every word which proceeded from His Father, Christ personified the Father's teachings and literally became *the Word* of God.[687]

Yahweh Lord, Jehovah; also spelled YHWH (יְהֹוָה), without vowels, which was too holy to voice. As a result, *Adonai* is often substituted.[688] In prayer and conversation, modern Jewish culture will substitute *HaShem* (the Name) for *Adonai*. In most English translations, Yahweh is translated as "LORD" or "GOD" in small capitals. It is the most personal name that God gives Himself in the Old Testament. *See also* JEHOVAH.

Nation A title for a people or ethnicity, like the Israelites.[689] "Nations" does not refer to modern states, but to family divisions or subsets, like the ancient tribes of Israel. They were called nations. The terms "nations, kindreds, tongues, and people" have a family meaning; they specifically have the family of Israel — in its scattered condition — in mind. The gospel is intended primarily for one family of redeemed souls.[690] Nation can also be defined in another way. Not all of God's words are in the Bible. God has spoken to every nation — meaning He has spoken to every religious body of people. *For behold, the Lord doth grant unto all nations, of their own nation and tongue, to teach his word, yea, in wisdom, all that he seeth fit that they should have; therefore, we see that the Lord doth counsel in his wisdom, according to that which is just and true* (Alma 15:13).[691]

Natural Roots Those Fathers who still hold the rights under the original covenant (*see* Jacob 3:23).[692]

New Earth When the stars move from one age to another by the precession through the equinoxes, the new constellation was said anciently to be a new earth.[693] There is a different constellation that appears at sunrise on the vernal equinox, and that constellation tells you what age (Pisces, Aquarius, etc.) mankind is in. When that constellation changes from the previous constellation age (on the horizon at the vernal equinox), that's called a New Earth. There will be a New Heaven and a New Earth when Christ returns.[694]

New Heaven When the pole star changes, which happens about seven times every 25,900 years, anciently that change was called a New Heaven. Polaris represents a change to a new heaven.[695] There will be a New Heaven and a New Earth when Christ returns. All of these are given, as Christ said in Genesis 2:6, *for signs, and for seasons*, and everything testifies of Him.[696]

New Jerusalem A city of peace to be built in the Americas to fulfill prophecy. It is foretold in both the Bible and Book of Mormon and is part of the Mormon belief about events that will precede the Second Coming of Christ. The location of the city is believed by most Mormons to be fixed in Independence, Missouri. From other revelations, Biblical prophecies, and teachings of Joseph Smith there is reason to doubt that location.[697] Zion, the New Jerusalem, and the Kingdom of God all relate to each other and will be developed and functioning in the last generation before the Lord returns. If this does not happen, the whole earth will be cursed (*see* T&C 151:13; *see also* 3 Nephi 10:1; T&C 31:14; Genesis 4:22–23).[698] There is a new and different meaning in Christ's Book of Mormon prophecy to the Nephites (*see* 3 Nephi 10:2) that has come about because of recent events. Previously, Christ's words seemed to foretell that the lost and scattered remnants would build the Lord's House and the New Jerusalem; now it appears that there are covenant-receiving gentiles who are included – gentiles who repent and hearken to Christ's words and do not harden their hearts will be brought into covenant as His people. Christ mentions three distinct bodies. First, those who have accepted the covenant and are numbered among the remnant of Jacob to whom Christ gave this land for their inheritance. Second, the lost descendants of the remnant of Jacob on this land who will repent and return. Third, as many from the House of Israel who will repent and return. These three will build a city that shall be called the New Jerusalem and will come to know God while gathering and laboring to build it. Then they will go out to assist all of God's people in their lost and forgotten state, to be awakened to the work of God and gathered as one body of believers. And all who have any of the blood of Abraham, who are scattered upon all the face of the land, will come to be taught in the New Jerusalem. There the Power of Heaven will come down to be among them; the angels (and Enoch with his ten thousands) will come down; the Ancient of Days, or Adam (the first father), and Christ, also, will be in the midst of His people (*see* 3 Nephi 10:1). [699]

New Name The name of Jacob was given by man (his father); the name of Israel was given by God (his Heavenly Father). God giving someone a new name is a profound event. It signifies that person has a newness of life with Him. Receiving a new name from God also marks entry into His family, for when God gives a name, He is adopting into His family. He names someone because they belong to Him. [700]

Noble and Great There are two different groups that exist in this estate of mortality. One group is known as the *noble and great*, who are later identified as *the Gods*. The second group is those who are the spirits *organized before the world was* who are to "be proven" by the experience here in mortality. The mission assigned to each group is distinct – one is "proving," and the other is "being proven." These two very different groups are both here in this world, living as mortals. For those who are being "proven," this life is a probation. For the others, they are "proving" their fellow men. They are among those who have a calling to teach truth here. They are *noble and great* because they teach truth. They teach truth and know truth because they were of such a character before they came here that they had accepted, obeyed, and received the results of following truth. In a word, they were exalted before they were born here. Hence the need for the word "Elohim" to be plural (*see* Abraham 6:1; 7:1–3). However, there is a veil between this world and the pre-earth existence; the only way to know which group one belongs to is if someone on the other side of the veil reveals it.[701] The risks of mortality are the same for all who are here. The way back is the same no matter which group one belongs to, and either can acquire their exaltation or fall from it, depending entirely upon the kind of life they live here. Only the Lord knows and can tell someone of his or her pre-earth status. If one learns of that, it will only be through revelation.[702]

Numbers/Numbering, Large In the modern Hebrew Bible all numbers are written out in full, but for a long time the text was written without vowels. The absence of vowels made it possible to confuse two words which are crucial to this problem: *èleph* and *àlluph*. Without vowel points, these words look identical: *'lp. Èleph* is the ordinary word for "thousand," but it can also be used in a variety of other senses: e.g. family (Judges 3:2); clan or governor (Zechariah 1:25,33–34); or as a military unit. *Àlluph* is used for the chieftains of Edom (Genesis 3:3–43); probably for a commander of a military thousand; and almost certainly for the professional, fully-armed soldier.[703]

If *èleph* of these passages carries its normal meaning of "thousand," then many of the numbers appear extremely large. This difficulty has led many to discount the biblical numbers altogether or consider them to be intentional exaggerations. Though *èleph* usually meant "thousand(s)," the word clearly could also mean a part of a tribe (perhaps best translated "clan"). Given that *èleph* can mean "clan" and that Israelite soldiers may well have mustered and fought by clans, then *èleph* might stand for the soldiers who mustered from a particular clan. If correct, this suggests that the Bible may often refer to the number of tribal units rather than total numbers of troops.

Most of the large numbers that appear too large shrink down to a more believable but indefinite size if *èleph* means "clan" or the unit of troops drawn from the clan. It is perhaps more likely that Saul mustered 330 units of soldiers to rescue Jabesh Gilead rather than 330,000 soldiers.[704]

Numbers in the Book of Mormon are also used as a means to determine rank. In modern language, a military man may be identified by the title of "general" and by the star on his uniform. In the Book of Mormon, a "general" would be identified by the title "captain of 10,000." It does not mean that he has 10,000 men under his command. A captain of 100 does not mean that he has 100 men under his command. A captain of 50 does not mean that he has 50. It means that he holds a rank. When the pioneer companies were organized, they were divided into captains of 100, captains of 50, and captains of 10 — it was simply a way to identify a role, a rank, or a position; it was a way of dividing the people. "So, when you get to the end of the Nephite wars, with 'this and his 10,000' and 'that and his 10,000' and 'someone else and their 10,000' and they're all slain, it doesn't mean that you are reading about hundreds of thousands or millions who are dying. It means that someone in a position of rank and authority and all of those under his command were slain. What those numbers amounted to, we don't know."[705]

Oath and Covenant The oath and covenant is the Father's word that cannot be broken. It is not something one aspires to, but something that is accepted by following the conditions established by God. The Father is the One who *can* establish eternal covenants by His word because His word cannot be broken.[706] *See* T&C 82:17.

Office A position in an organization; not to be equated with the possession of priestly authority. Offices are created by people, and offices in the church are a matter of vote by the members, placing someone into a position (making offices of the church coincident with priesthood authority is another matter). Joseph Smith and Oliver Cowdery, for example, were elected to be the First and Second Elders of the church in 1830 — the Melchizedek Priesthood would not be restored until 1831. But they held the office of elder by virtue of the people accepting them by their vote. They could have elected them to be high priests or to any other office. Orson Hyde held the office of apostle (beginning in 1839) with, literally, no authority. Choose a title and have everyone vote; now one holds an office.[707]

Olive Tree Of all the material Jacob could have adopted as his prophecy, his selection of Zenos' allegory of the Olive Tree is telling. The account is a journey through various dispensations of the Gospel, tracking a bloodline of chosen people. To Jacob's credit, he realized the work of salvation was devoted primarily to rescuing the descendants of a chosen line beginning with Abraham. The allegory is a family story. The use of the olive tree is a deliberate symbol of a family and of the tree whose value was beyond question in the culture from which the allegory sprung. To understand the story, it is necessary to settle on meanings. The tree is a family line belonging to the *house of Israel* (Jacob 3:7). The work of the Lord of the vineyard and his fellow laborers is designed to cause the chosen family line to produce fruit worthy of preservation. The "fruit" is people, or more correctly, children raised in righteousness who comprehend and accept the Gospel and abide by its teachings.[708] *See also* FRUIT.

One Eternal Round There is no beginning, and there is no end; it is one eternal round.[709] "This round of creation is only part of the cycle. We are part of endless cycles. Now. Today matters a great deal. Therefore, what you do here matters, infinitely and eternally. Set aside doubts, and have faith. It is the only way to change your eternal destiny. We should all want to be baptized and to be cleansed from sin. But, the prototype of the saved man requires more. We may only receive limited grace in this life, but we must hold fast. We cannot receive more if we will not receive all that is offered us now. If we will receive what is offered now, we will be added upon for ever and for ever (Abraham 6:2). In other words, we move up the ladder by our heed and diligence in this cycle of creation. As we do, we will have so much the advantage in the next cycle."[710] Men and women can choose to move upward and be added upon, or they can choose to remain as they are, worlds without end. Now is part of eternity. Though mortal, all live in eternity and ought to take this opportunity seriously. The scriptures speak of things that happened "before the foundation of the world" or "in the first place" or "from the foundation of the world." These statements make it clear that what went on prior to this creation matters and affects mankind now. In the same way, what one accepts in this life, by his heed and diligence, affects what comes after. The course all are on has been ordained by God and is one eternal round (Alma 5:5; 17:8; JSH 10:2; T&C 18:1). Even if someone has proven himself before, he must prove himself again, now.

God has been at this a long time. Christ has been involved in many repeated cycles of creation. Moses was told: *And by the word of my power have I created them, who is my Only Begotten Son, who is full of grace and truth. And worlds without number have I created, and I also created them for my own purpose; and by the same I created them, who is my Only Begotten* [It is endless, and it is cyclical.] *For behold, there are many worlds that have passed away by the word of my power, and there are many that now stand, and numberless are they unto man; but all things are numbered unto me, for they are mine and I know them* (Genesis 1:6). This is God's great work. It has been going through cycles of creation, fall, redemption, judgment, and re-creation for ever. It is endless. Many unnumbered worlds have been, now are, and will yet be. The Lord told Moses just how vast this process is: *These are many and they cannot be numbered unto man, but they are numbered unto me for they are mine. And as one earth shall pass away, and the heavens thereof, even so shall another come. And there is no end to my works, neither to my words* (Genesis 1:7). This is a continual, endless cycle, worlds without end. Man falls into the cold realm of the temporal but is returned again to the spiritual. The process allows incremental development based on choices. When any cycle begins, man is spirit. When it is underway, man is temporal and physical. But when a cycle ends, man is spirit again. Humanity is nearing another turn of the wheel when wickedness ends. As modern revelation describes it, *For the hour is nigh and the day is soon at hand when the earth will be ripe, and all the proud and they that do wickedly shall be as stubble, and I will burn them up, that wickedness shall not be upon the earth.... For I will reveal myself from Heaven with power and great glory, with all the hosts thereof, and dwell in righteousness with men on earth a thousand years, and the wicked shall not stand* (T&C 9:3). Then, *when the thousand years are ended and men again begin to deny their God, then will I spare the earth but for a little season, and the end shall come, and the Heaven and the earth shall be consumed and pass away, and there shall be a new Heaven and a new earth* (T&C 9:7). The cycle repeats, but nothing is lost. The old passes away, but everything is kept to be used again, *both men and beasts, the fowls of the air and the fishes of the sea, and not one hair neither mote shall be lost, for it is the workmanship of my hand* (T&C 9:7).[711]

Oracle   A prophetic presence;[712] the revelations of God, which were given to mankind from Joseph Smith as the foundation, as the font from which all draw. "But it was always intended that there should arise in you the power of obtaining oracles for yourself."[713] The doctrines, commandments, revelations, and words of God are given as an oracle to guide mankind. The oracles are contained in the Book of Mormon, Lectures on Faith, and the revelations given by Joseph.[714]

Ordinance   "The ordinances are helps, symbols and requirements. *Helps* in that they establish milestones that memorialize passage from one stage of development to the next. *Symbols* in that they point to a deeper meaning or spiritual reality almost always grounded in the atonement of Jesus Christ. *Requirements* in that they mark the defined route taken by Christ as a mortal to fulfill all righteousness. The ordinances as symbols point to the real thing. The real thing is Jesus Christ and His Gospel."[715] Ordinances are the preliminary act, designed to bear testimony of the real event. They are not the real thing but are a "type" of the real thing. They must be seen through the eyes of faith (*see* Ether 5:3) to allow one to gain the faith necessary to obtain the real thing.[716] Ordinances are instituted to bring one to the point where one inherits in body and spirit the great blessings of the Doctrine of Christ. "They prepare you. Their effect is to qualify you, instruct you, advance you toward this goal of receiving the blessings found in the Doctrine of Christ. Once ordinances have been adopted, it is then unlikely you can ignore them, and [then] receive what is promised by the Doctrine of Christ."[717] "Ordinances instituted in the heavens before the foundation of the world, in the priesthood, for the salvation of men, are not to be altered or changed."[718] When the higher priesthood is present on the earth, everything done by it is an ordinance. God ordains by His power what is to happen. God ordains — and therefore, all He does is an ordinance, whether building up or taking down.[719] Latter-day Saints think "ordinances" are required for everyone, and they can receive them ad hoc to be saved. Heaven does not have unorganized crowds milling about, arriving fresh from receiving and accepting vicarious ordinances and claiming the right to be rewarded by entering Celestial glory. *If* anyone enters the kingdom of God, she will be there as part of God's family, not as a freelance believer. Those faithful who received the assurance before death that they would one day enjoy a glorious resurrection were unable to leave the spirit world with Christ, but remained behind to minister to others there. Mankind knows almost nothing, at this point, of the full scope of the original body of teachings, revelations, ordinances, and rites. Even all that came through Joseph is but a glimpse. Man is not worthy of the full view. The question is whether any will become meek and humble enough to endure giving it a hearing before they corrupt it with a flood of errors based on unbelief.[720]

Ordination (Priesthood) An invitation; not the same thing as receiving the power of the Priesthood. "When you walk through the lives of all these priestly men, you see there is a two-fold event. First is an ordination. Then later there is empowerment or ratification of the ordination by Heaven. Ordination involves men. Empowerment involves the Heavens. In the case of Nephi's brother Jacob, who was ordained by Nephi, we see the pattern set out. Jacob explains about his ordination by his brother, and then later confirms, he *firstly obtained mine errand from the Lord* (Jacob 1:4). There is a difference between the invite extended through ordination, and the blessing that comes when the power is conferred by Heaven."[721]

Other Sheep When Christ appeared as a resurrected being to the people who were gathered as a faithful body on the American continent and showed them the wounds in His hands, in His side, and in His feet, He told them, *Ye are they of whom I said, Other sheep I have, which are not of this fold; [I must go to them] and they [must] hear my voice, and there [should] be one fold and one shepherd* (3 Nephi 7:3). He explained that the disciples at Jerusalem didn't ask Him about it, and they didn't understand who He was talking about. They wrongly supposed that Christ meant He would speak to other sheep through the ministry of the people in Palestine, as they spread the message outward. Instead, He meant that He, Christ, would go, as a resurrected being, to scattered remnants of the House of Israel; that He would let them hear His voice, see Him, and He would minister to them. And that included, within the body of those that Christ intended to minister to, the people who were writing the Book of Mormon. And then He extended that and said, "I have still other sheep, in addition to you, and I'm going to go visit with them, also."

"And so, from the record of the Book of Mormon, in just one example, if you want to understand the obscure statement that Christ made, preserved in the New Testament, that He has other sheep to whom He's going to go minister, in order to understand that prophecy, you go to the last in time, the later to interpret the earlier, and the Book of Mormon supplies you that interpretation and explains: yes, Christ meant as a resurrected personage that He would go and He would appear. The record of Christ's appearance in his post-resurrected state in Palestine includes appearing first to two women. Then He spent the better part of the day walking on the road to Emmaus with two disciples — Cleopas and an unidentified other who wrote the record, Luke. Then He appeared to the twelve. Still later, He would appear to the apostle Paul. And then when He ascended, there were above 500 gathered together at the time that He ascended from the mount. And so there were multiple sightings, multiple witnesses, and multiple audiences to whom He ministered as a post-resurrected being. Then in the Book of Mormon He does exactly the same thing. He appears as a resurrected personage and He ministers."[722] Christ would like mankind to have this information. He wants all to know He is the God of Israel and, indeed, the God of the whole earth. He not only ministered in Palestine and visited the Nephites, but He visited all of His sheep, wherever they were located throughout the world. This is what the Book of Mormon was to prove. Although it is only a record of a single group of the "other sheep," it establishes there are "sheep" throughout the world to whom He paid a visit after His resurrection. In the title page of the Book of Mormon (now known as the Dedication in the Restoration Edition of scriptures), it says it was written *to shew unto the remnant of the house of Israel how great things the Lord hath done for their fathers, and that they may know the covenants of the Lord, that they are not cast off for ever. And also to the convincing of the Jew and gentile that Jesus is the Christ, the Eternal God, manifesting himself unto all nations.* This reference to "all nations" confirms the meaning of the term "other sheep," as

Christ elaborated to the Nephites. The term was intended to cover multiple groups of believers who had been separated from Palestine and not just a single third group of believers. Christ's ministry after His resurrection, therefore, may have involved many groups who both saw Him and heard His voice and, thereby, became part of His sheepfold.[723] The third chapter of Jacob, although an allegory, may be the most detailed account of these "other sheep."[724]

Outcasts of Israel *And he shall set up an ensign for the nations, and assemble the outcasts of Israel, and gather together the dispersed of Judah, from the four corners of the earth* (Isaiah 5:5). These are the Lost Ten Tribes of Israel, as well as others who have been led away by God, from time to time (*see* 2 Nephi 12:10; 3 Nephi 7:3), including the Book of Mormon people (*see* 1 Nephi 1:22; Alma 8:1).[725]

Patience As used in Mosiah 1:16, patience is not defined as it typically is; rather, it refers to the patience a child has as he grows into adulthood. There are many years ahead to reach adulthood — there is nothing the child can do to change that, nor do they attempt to do so. In much the same way, most adults have many years ahead of them before they become fit for the Second Comforter. Just like one cannot rush from childhood into adulthood but must progress by degrees through the many long months into many years, so too, men and women must progress from a smaller degree to a much larger one. Perhaps it takes decades to develop, as necessary, to receive an audience with Christ. Children persist in waiting, growing, and maturing. Their progression into adulthood is gradual. But that process is relentless and marches on through two decades of development and maturity. That is the patience spoken of in this scripture.[726]

Patriarchal Blessings Scripturally, fathers' blessings had legitimacy because they were spoken through the gift of the holy ghost. Three years previous to the death of Adam, he called together his posterity *into the valley of Adam-Ondi-Ahman, and there bestowed upon them his last blessing…and, notwithstanding he was bowed down with [great] age, being full of the Holy Ghost, predicted whatsoever should befall his posterity unto the latest generation* (T&C 154:19–20). That was the first patriarchal blessing. It was given by the power of the spirit, and it was prophecy. It would be appropriate to read "priesthood" out of that event and to read "holy ghost, power of the spirit, word of prophecy" into it. A patriarchal blessing that is delivered with no benefit of the spirit is just more ink on paper, but a blessing that is delivered by the power of the spirit, as a prophecy, is the word of the Lord, the mind of the Lord, and the power of God unto salvation, which cannot be broken. Later, when both Jacob (Israel) and Lehi called their children before them to bestow their final blessings, it was a reenactment of that event with the first father, Adam, in the valley of Adam-Ondi-Ahman. Jacob and Lehi were, likewise, bowed down with great age, knowing that they were going to soon depart this world; they had no personal investment in the outcome, but only intended to say what was for the blessing and benefit, through the spirit, of what would befall their children after them, things that they would not be around to witness; they confirmed by the spoken voice what it was that God had put into their hearts. A patriarchal blessing is generally given by someone like Lehi or like Jacob (in Genesis 12:14–26). They are calling upon all of the experience that they've had with the children throughout their lifetime, and then they're projecting forward by the power of the spirit. Sometimes what is prophesied to befall a child may be surprising to the one filled with the spirit who is pronouncing the blessing, but generally, that lifetime of experience with the child helps prepare the mind, the heart, and the connection of the father to Heaven. All of this, every bit of it, can occur with or without priesthood — people need not associate, and therefore limit, the power of the spirit to influence any person, without regard to rank, position, or office.[727] The identification of a Tribe of Israel in the Latter-day Saint patriarchal blessings does not restore the covenant, nor does it connect you to the "living vine," nor does it alter the status of being "gentile" by identification.[728]

Patriarchal Priesthood The right of dominion over the creation belonged to God. God gave that right to Adam and Eve. It does not automatically transfer to all their descendants. It was transferred from Adam to his first appointed heir, Seth. (Cain would have been the first heir, but because he rebelled, he lost his position. To prevent that loss, Cain slew the next heir, Abel, but it did not accomplish the ambition. Cain was, ultimately, replaced by Seth.) Seth was given the right belonging to the first Father, Adam, and through him down generations to Enos; then to his son, Cainan; and his son, Mahalaleel; and his son, Jared; and his son, Enoch; and his son, Methuselah; and his son, Lamech; and his son, Noah; and his son, Shem, who was given the new name of Melchizedek. This right is called the "patriarchal priesthood" — it is the right to hold dominion over the world as the steward, father, or patriarch over all creation (*see* T&C 154:9–20).[729] Joseph Smith explained that there are different portions or degrees of priesthood.[730] "The Melchizedek priesthood holds the right from the eternal God, and not by descent from father and mother; and that priesthood is as eternal as God himself, having neither beginning of days nor end of life. The second priesthood is Patriarchal authority. Go to and finish the temple, and God will fill it with power, and you will then receive more knowledge concerning this Priesthood. The third is what is called Levitical priesthood, consisting of priests to administer in outward ordinances, made without an oath and covenant. The holy ghost is God's messenger to administer in all those priesthoods" (*TPJS*, 323).[731] "Joseph never clarified he ranked these three from top, to middle, to bottom. It is possible he spoke of the middle first, then top next, and then the bottom (Levitical). We view the Patriarchal Priesthood as the highest because the Priesthood beginning with Adam was a single Holy Priesthood after the Order of the Son of God."[732] The Aaronic or Levitical Priesthood is an association with angels. The Melchizedek is an association with the Son of God. The Patriarchal is an association with the Father and makes one a son of God.[733] There are three levels of priesthood. There are three members of the Godhead. There is a different member of the Godhead associated with the three levels of salvation, the three levels of Divine ministration, and correspondingly, the three levels of priesthood. There is a priesthood that belongs to the Telestial order (or the world where we presently live). There is a priesthood that belongs to the Terrestrial order (or this world in its paradisiacal state during the Millennium). There is a priesthood that belongs to the Celestial order (or the final redeemed state which men hope to inherit in the Father's Kingdom). T&C 69 sets out these conditions of glory, and one can associate a level of priesthood with each. Doing so gives one a better grasp of the idea of *fullness of the Priesthood*. "The Patriarchal Priesthood is not defined in scripture. The most important point is that there is priesthood which exists, but is not contained within or conferred by [a] church. It comes from one source — the Father. To receive that, read *The Tenth Parable*[734] and you will have a description of how it unfolds." The Son is necessarily involved. He is the gatekeeper; He alone decides if a person is going to qualify. When the Son takes it as His work to bring a person before the Father, His ministry can take many years and is designed to cure what is wrong, fix all that is broken, and remove all that is impure in the candidate. Only when the Son can vouch for the individual is he brought before the Father. It is the Father who confers and ordains a man to the highest priesthood.[735] Patriarchal Priesthood is obtained by meeting God in *His* temple, not merely in a ceremony on earth. In the last days, this priesthood will again be called the Holy Priesthood after the Son of God. The Priesthood at the end of the world will be a mirror image of what was in the beginning.[736]

Pattern for Understanding Truth *And beginning at Moses and all the prophets, he expounded unto them in all the scriptures the things concerning himself* (Luke 14:3). This is the pattern adopted by the writers of the New Testament Gospels. Christ explained how to understand His ministry by using the law and prophets. The Gospels would not be written until decades after this, and they were composed following the Lord's pattern (found in the discussion that took place on the road to Emmaus) to vindicate Him as the promised Lord and Redeemer, and thereby, fulfilling scripture. This framework appears in Matthew, Mark, Luke, and John. They all wove into their records how Christ fulfilled the prophecies. Christ proved He came and suffered to fulfill the prophets. He opened the scriptures unto them so that they understood (*see* Luke 14:7). The Gospel writers followed this same pattern. "Our Lord could have testified by revealing 10,000 new truths to these two disciples [on the road to Emmaus]. He could have disclosed to them new visions and predictions. Instead, He expounded the scriptures concerning Himself. That is how He wants us to learn the truth. When the Lord first spoke to me, He expounded the scriptures. When He rose from the grave, except for these two disciples, His visit with everyone that day was brief, even perfunctory. With others He proved He had risen. But with these two, the Lord took hours, walking and talking in a discourse wherein *he expounded unto them in all the scriptures the things concerning himself* (Luke 14:3). They did not recognize Him, but they were moved by the content of His sermon. When they arrived at Emmaus, He entered the house because they asked Him to stay. If they had not asked, He would have passed by. The Lord does not force Himself upon us. We must invite. At the end of this encounter, *they said one to another, Did not our hearts burn within us while he talked with us by the way and while he opened to us the scriptures?* (Luke 14:4). It is not necessary to reveal any new thing in order to open eyes to everything the Lord has, and is, doing. Nothing apart from expounding the scriptures is required. He did not think it was necessary even when He arose from the dead. In the First Vision, Christ quoted or paraphrased Isaiah, Ezekiel, and Paul. Like His discourse on the road to Emmaus, in the First Vision our Lord expounded scripture. This is the condition of the world. Today is when mankind searches the earth and does not find the word of God, while the scriptures are available and ignored. When [Nephi] visited Joseph Smith, he quoted prophecies from Malachi, Isaiah, Peter, and Joel (*see* JSH 3:1–12). The pattern used by the Lord to reveal new truth is the same in every generation. The Lord is the same yesterday, today, and for ever. His path is straight and His course is one eternal round. Truth is best advanced by opening the scriptures."[737] *See also* STUDYING THE SCRIPTURES.

Peacemaker *And blessed are all the peacemakers, for they shall be called the children of God* (Matthew 3:12). More often than not, those who are "peacemakers" will be abused. They will have to endure aggression and give a soft word in return (*see* Proverbs 2:152). There will be no end to the peace which comes from Christ because there was no end to the suffering He was willing to endure (*see* Isaiah 4:1). When mankind hearkens to the Lord's commandments, they have peace like a flowing river (*see* Isaiah 17:3). This is because the Lord will fight for them, and they can hold their peace. The Lord will fight Zion's battles. When a man is right before God, even his enemies are at peace with him (*see* Proverbs 2:191), at least until his time comes and his mission is completed (*see* T&C 139:9; John 10:10). When the Lord was taken with violence and crucified, He was at peace (*see* Luke 13:19,21). He purchased peace through what He suffered. He alone can share that with all. Through Him, the "peacemakers" have found this peace. This is why they have become His "children," for He has begotten them (*see* Mosiah 11:28). In a world of violence and abuse, it is peace that many seek. But that peace comes only to the children of God and only because they know they are the children of God. At their rebirth, they are at rest from the cares of this dreary world and are informed by a better promise of things to come (*see* Alma 10:4; Moroni 7:2). Those who bring peace bring hope to this world. This world is filled with tribulation, but the Lord has overcome this world (*see* John 9:18). Many have experienced this peace and have become the children of God and then have been persecuted, hated, reviled, and killed. Peace is a gift from Christ, and His peace is for this world and the world to come (*see* John 9:9). But the promise of triumph is hereafter, when the world can no longer make any claim upon a child of God (*see* T&C 139:7). Though a man may declare peace, the world will not be at peace until the Lord slays the wicked (*see* Revelation 8:1). "Peace, as all other sacred things in our day, must be internal. We live in a day of overwhelming ignorance, foolishness, and wickedness. It is not possible to obtain peace except on the terms which allow it. If you live those, you will have peace. But the world will not live them with you…. To be a child of God and know peace is, in our day, to cry repentance and to bring others to Christ."[738]

Perfection The process of cooperating with God. People don't need to "accomplish something"; they only need to get their hearts right. Once their hearts are right, everything else follows in the ordinary course. In any event, life is not the time to enjoy exaltation; that comes later. Life is the time to overcome vanity, pride, and selfishness. It is the time to lose oneself. When one does that, it doesn't matter that he still has a great gulf between himself and perfection; he is, nonetheless, perfect. Submission is perfect. However, there is still a great work ahead of everyone seeking to attain exaltation. This life's agenda is very limited, even though the full effort involved will last many lifetimes. Men and women are not here to "get exalted." They are here to continue progression which began a long time before their current birth. At this moment, they are being "added upon" by what they experience here. At some point, they will have received what they need in this sphere and will be able to move on to the next stage of development. When they have gained everything they need from this life, they will have received "the fullness" from God. It is called "the fullness" because it is all that can be obtained here. It is not possible, however, to inherit everything God ultimately offers while here. For that, it will require a great work "even beyond the grave," as Joseph put it. Indeed, it isn't even possible to fully understand God while here in this life.[739]

Therefore, I would that ye should be perfect, even as I or your Father who is in Heaven is perfect (3 Nephi 5:31). In the Matthew text, Christ unequivocally limited this to His Father (*see* Matthew 3:26); here, "perfection" is achieved by both Christ and His Father. Assuming the Matthew text is correct, the difference is significant. It is another confirmation that anyone who is mortal, including the Lord, stands in jeopardy every hour (*see* 1 Corinthians 1:64). He simply could not claim perfection while in mortality because mortality is a time of change, challenge, and temptation. After all, He was tempted while mortal, just as every human soul is tempted (*see* Hebrews 1:11). Though He chose to give no heed to it, He was nevertheless tempted (*see* JSH 16:6). While mortal, He looked to the Father in all things (*see* John 5:5). After concluding His time in mortality and achieving the resurrection of the dead, He was given all power in Heaven and on Earth (*see* Matthew 13:4). Therefore, if the Matthew text is correct and the differences are accounted for, then the admonition of Christ for one's own perfection is not just an earthly endeavor. It is an invitation to follow Him and His Father into a loftier state, as well (*see* Abraham 6:2), one where the final realization will come only as one is able to endure greater glory than a mortal may possess (*see* Genesis 1:1). It is good to know this commandment is possible to accomplish (*see* 1 Nephi 1:10). It is hard to conceive of following the Son in this way. Yet it is He who pronounced it and He who has promised to share the throne of His Father with all who will come to Him (*see* Revelation 1:20).

"A harmonious symmetry of light, majesty, holiness, glory, and power are all around Him who is perfection. When I read the admonition to *[be ye therefore] perfect, even as I or your Father who is in Heaven is perfect* (3 Nephi 5:31), I can hardly grasp how that gulf between us could be bridged. I understand about the Lord's atonement. I have certainly been the beneficiary of it and will continue to be so. When I consider the infinite gulf between His and His Father's perfection, and my own imperfection, I am left completely stupefied at the idea it is even possible. Nevertheless, He gives no command which He does not provide means to obey.... He provides the means, and His Father ordained the laws by which it can be done, and they provide us with free will and the capacity to choose, but we must choose. We must accept. We must press forward holding Their hands in order to arrive at last, after an infinitely long journey, in the courts of Heaven itself, fit to reside there. Be ye therefore perfect. And start on that this moment. For you haven't another moment to spare."[740]

The word "perfect," as used in the New Testament, comes from the Latin Vulgate *perfectus,* meaning "complete, finished" and is a translation of the Greek *teleios* (τέλειος), which means: "having attained the end, complete, perfect, full-grown, mature, initiated into the mystic rites, the initiate, consecrated, having finished the course, etc."[741] and can be interpreted ritually as completing *the* ascent. "The word perfect (*teleios*) does not mean perfect digestion, perfect eyesight, perfect memory, and so on; it is a special word meaning keeping the *whole* law."[742] "In a ritual setting, among the connotations of this word, this term refers to preparing a person to be presented before God 'in priestly action'.... Early Christians continued to use this word in this way in connection with their sacraments and their ordinances. Hugh Nibley saw that the meaning of the word *teleios* is namely 'living up to an agreement or covenant without fault: as the Father keeps the covenants he makes with us...the completely initiated who has both qualified for initiation and completed it is *teleios*, literally "gone all the way," fulfilling all requirements, every last provision of God's command.'"[743]

Persecution Persecution is what happens when an idea cannot be opposed on its merit. Persecution is the product of fear, typically experienced by those lacking knowledge. There are two great competing forces in the whole of creation: love and fear.[744] *And blessed are all they who are persecuted for my name's sake, for theirs is the kingdom of Heaven* (3 Nephi 5:19). "It is not just persecution, but persecution *for [His] name's sake* that makes you blessed. When you are doing what you should for His name's sake, you are likely to provoke persecution. He will later explain this is almost inevitable. It won't be because you are provoking it by your obnoxious behavior. It is because people will question your sincerity and commitment. The world expects hypocrites. They regard everyone with suspicion. And, let's face it, most charlatans adopt religion as one of their cloaks. The kind of persecution which produces the *kingdom of Heaven* is, of course, martyrdom.... Blessed are those who are willing to endure persecution for His name's sake. For they are those who are willing [to] develop faith which cannot be obtained in any other way. It is through the sacrifice of all things that faith necessary for salvation is developed. Sometimes we bring persecution upon ourselves because we are unwise. The Lord addresses that. We are to take offenses, but not give them. When we unwisely give offenses and cause persecution, that is not for His name's sake. There is a balance between wisdom and righteousness."[745]

And blessed are ye when men shall revile you, and persecute, and shall say all manner of evil against you falsely, for my sake (3 Nephi 5:19). The world's first reaction to followers of Christ will be skepticism, which will result in an attempt to measure the follower's sincerity. Until he's been tested by the world, there is no reason for the world to believe anything he has to say. They will revile him, thinking he is just another fraud. They will persecute him as a charlatan, even though he is His disciple. They will say all manner of evil against him falsely, all the while thinking they are only giving the follower what he deserves. This is how the world decides if he is actually following Him. They have seen and heard no end of those who have claimed to follow Him, and this man is no different in their eyes; that is, until he has actually followed Him — borne their criticism, returned good for evil, and shown how devoted he is. When he has proven his devotion, then some few will soften their hearts. Others will remain unwilling to admit the truth, even when it is apparent he is His. This is the way in which Christ lived His life. The teachings in the Sermon on the Mount and at Bountiful are an explanation of Him. They are an explanation of the lives of any who follow Him. To follow Him and to learn of His ways always requires experiencing some of what He experienced. While He assumed a full measure of these teachings, His followers are only required to experience some of what He did, which allows them to understand Him. But these teachings are meant to be lived. They are meant to be applied and tested. If a person tests them, he or she will discover Him through them. They will also come to know and understand the prophets who went before, some of whom will, invariably, come to succor their fellow Saints. This is always the pattern when the fullness of the Gospel of Jesus Christ is lived on the earth.[746] *See also* MARTYR.

Pestilence *And now behold, this is the will of the Lord your God concerning his saints — that they should assemble themselves together unto the land of Zion, not in haste lest there should be confusion, which brings pestilence* (T&C 50:6). Pestilence is not just bugs and vermin; it is also confusion, disorder, and chaos.[747]

Pharaoh A title that originally meant "great house" or "great family"; Pharaoh was the "father" over Egypt who taught and led them. Over time, however, this title came to mean a "king" or "tyrant" who controlled people.[748] Given the Egyptian preoccupation with the afterlife, the name is likely related to an expectation for the eternities and not merely a description of the office held in mortality.[749]

Plan of Salvation The plan of education; the plan of knowing God and the principles of godliness.[750]

Possess Your Soul *And seek the face of the Lord always, that in patience you may possess your souls, and you shall have eternal life* (T&C 101:6). To possess one's soul is to have body and spirit inseparably connected in a resurrected and immortal state. T&C 86:2 explains: *Now, verily I say unto you that through the redemption which is made for you is brought to pass the resurrection from the dead. And the spirit and the body is the soul of man, and the resurrection from the dead is the redemption of the soul.* To possess one's soul, therefore, is to have the resurrection. T&C 38:6 builds on this by saying that while in that resurrected state, one will *inherit eternal life*. This means "to receive exaltation." So the concept that these words are covering is the concept of exaltation and receiving, in the resurrection, a Celestial inheritance.[751]

Power of God "The Father's power was not used only to create us, but continues to preserve us. We do not have a moment from our birth to our death in which we are not reliant upon God for the continuance of our existence. God *created [us] from the beginning* and

is *preserving [us] from day to day* (Mosiah 1:8). Without Him, we would not be 'preserved,' or in other words, we would not stay created or organized. We would dissolve into the original, pre-creation, primordial constituent parts. We would be 'uncreated' if we lost His 'preserving' power. The full extent of our dependence upon the Father becomes clear when we are told He is *lending [us] breath*. This preserving power is also described in T&C 86:1: *And the light which now shines, which gives you light, is through him who enlightens your eyes, which is the same light that quickens your understandings, which light proceeds forth from the presence of God to fill the immensity of space: the light which is in all things, which gives life to all things, which is the law by which all things are governed, even the power of God who sits upon his throne, who is in the bosom of eternity, who is in the midst of all things.* The full extent of God's involvement in our daily existence cannot be overstated; it is not limited to an original launch, or 'big bang.' He did not just wind up a watch and let it run on its own. He is the power behind *all things* and *gives life to all things* through His 'power.' This description puts God at the center. However far the concentric circles may proceed from Him in all directions, He remains in the center 'throne' from which His power continues to provide the *light* which sustains it all. This involvement is immediate, continuing and intimate."[752]
See also HOLY SPIRIT.

Power of Godliness The ability to open the heavens in order to be given assignments, confirm revelation, and receive blessings from God. All power is tied to heaven. When the powers of heaven are withdrawn from someone, then their authority comes to an end, and they have no power. The power of godliness must be gained through Jesus Christ, access to Whom is available to all men and women on equal terms.[753] Godliness is different from virtue; it is even different from righteousness. Godliness requires one to become godlike in one's sentiments and in one's meekness before Him. "Whether men understand you or attribute motives to you, the relationship is between you and the Lord. Godliness is when your walk here is along the path He has chosen for you."[754] The *power of godliness* (T&C 82:12) is inseparably connected with the ordinances (*see* T&C 139:5). Without the power of godliness, the current rites are much like the apostate world Christ condemned in His initial visit with Joseph Smith (*see* JSH 2:5). The *power of godliness* and *the authority of the priesthood* are connected with *see[ing] the face of God, even the Father* (T&C 82:12).[755]

Powers of Heaven A title referring to a specific group with status on the other side of the veil; a proper noun, not just an abstraction. In the afterlife there are different rungs on Jacob's ladder where different Powers are fixed: Angel, Archangel, Principality, Power, Dominion, Throne, Cherubim, and Seraphim — they may all be called Powers of Heaven. These Powers have no desire to control or compel others to rise on Jacob's ladder. Each rung is a developmental stage of growth through which all must pass if they want to ascend nearer to God. Each individual on Jacob's ladder should be moving toward perfection.[756]

Pray/er The worthy speech that ascends to Heaven that is uttered by the faithful.[757] There is no magic formula for communicating with God; no list of what is to be said or repeated; no vain — meaning ineffective — repetitions. He "gets it" even before man speaks. The act of prayer is a formal way of showing God the following: respect, by doing what He has asked; devotion, by showing submission to Him; obedience, by keeping the commandment to *pray always* (2 Nephi 14:3); and companionship, by taking the time to be alone with Him. "You take thought about what you care for, but they are not what the Lord knows you need. Your cares are merely the tiniest of obstacles given you to remind you to pray. The Father operates on a much grander scale, dealing with the salvation of souls. He will use the man or woman of prayer as the means of accomplishing a great deal more than they imagined. Pray. Ask simply. It is not necessary to be elaborate or long-winded. State clearly what you believe you need. Accept what then comes in His answer. Trust He knows more than you. Trust He can give you what you need, even if you hadn't even thought about it as a need."[758] "Talk like you are addressing your most intimate friend and have nothing to hide. Tell Him about your regrets, hopes, frustrations, concerns, fears, and confusion. Before long you will discover that whatever you care about, God also cares about. He can give perspective that changes everything. Prayer should not recognize the distance between us and God but should become the way we close that distance."[759] *See also* VOICE OF GOD.

Pray Always To retain a personal connection with heaven; particularly, to retain that connection through the holy ghost and through Christ's Spirit that one seeks to always have. If this is a lively connection, one is able to avoid being "sifted." If it lapses into darkness, one is vulnerable to being taken captive.[760]

Priest One who has authority to perform ordinances, as described in the Book of Mormon.[761] It is also an office in the Mormon movement that was established by a visit from John the Baptist with Joseph Smith and Oliver Cowdery, May 15, 1829, prior to the organization of a church. Mormons believe priests have the authority to baptize, as well as preach, teach, exhort, and expound.[762]

Priestcraft A new message that does not include knowledge about how the audience may come to God themselves; the primary intent is always to make others dependent on the messenger. It is foolishness to separate information about what the Lord is doing from instruction on how to become redeemed. It is vanity to spread new and personal revelation about the afterlife, God, man, prophecy, visionary encounters, and spiritual experiences if the primary reason does not focus on instructing how the audience can come to God themselves. It is dangerous to trust teachings that fail to give man guidance on how to find God for himself. "If all that is delivered is a message about some great experience, the experience was probably not intended for you. It is the way to find God that will save you, not someone else's new and exciting spiritual manifestation. Still, people will go to great trouble and spare no effort to find someone who will only give a titillating peek behind the veil but who will do nothing to instruct you on how you can meet God here, be redeemed from the fall of man, and come back into God's presence."[763] Pandering for popularity is at the heart of priestcraft.[764] Priestcrafts are where people seek approval of the world but not the best interest of Zion (*see* 2 Nephi 11:17).[765] Any man who tries to put himself between another person and heaven, claiming that he alone should be the source of religious beliefs and education, is practicing priestcraft and will, in the end, lead both himself and his followers to damnation.[766] All churches, if the Book of Mormon is true, are filled with corruption and priestcraft.[767] The obligation to hold up a light is circumscribed by His direction that [*He is*] *the light which ye shall hold up* (3 Nephi

8:8) — nothing and no one else. He is the lifeline. Therefore, when anyone offers to preach, teach, exhort, and expound, He must be at the center of this prophesying, or they are engaging in priestcraft.[768] "When gentiles pursue any end other than establishing Zion, the Book of Mormon calls it priestcraft. That is what the gentiles have accomplished with the Book of Mormon thus far."[769]

Priesthood An association between mankind and those on the other side of the veil. It is a brotherhood. It is also, potentially, a sisterhood. It is a fellowship wherein mortals are connected with the "Powers of Heaven."[770] There are two brotherhoods. One is between men (or women), and it is here among mortals. There is a second one between mortal man and the Powers of Heaven. It is the fellowship, association, or priesthood with the Powers of Heaven that gives to man the power.[771] Priesthood is not a franchise, nor is it given to control others. Priesthood, in its highest form, is an opportunity to serve and bless others. (That is not true of priesthood in lesser forms.) This high priesthood is a call to save, redeem, and rescue others from destruction. Man can condemn himself with only very little authority. But to raise mankind up and offer salvation is a greater work requiring greater authority.[772] Men do not make priests; God does. Men do not make prophets. God has reserved that right for Himself (*see* Numbers 7:22). God calls them, whether or not men accept or recognize them.[773] Priesthood, in its most meaningful sense, involves the Holy Order after the Order of the Son of God.[774] The Lord has revealed that only a very few of those who ever receive even a little priestly authority will be saved (*see* T&C 139:5–8). Priesthood authority cannot be abused. When it is attempted, the authority comes to an abrupt end.[775] The focus of attention on priesthood skews what may be most important; it distorts the whole picture: All of the miraculous things that Melchizedek accomplished — quenching the violence of fire, closing the mouths of lions, causing rivers to run out of their course — all of those things were accomplished by Melchizedek without the priesthood. When Paul listed the things that got accomplished by faith, he was not talking about priesthood, ordination, office, or authority. Most of what people think belongs to the franchise called "priesthood" really should be viewed as the evidence (or the absence) of faith. Priesthood has a really limited bundle of rights and responsibilities that, at its most basic level, involves baptism and blessing the sacrament.[776]

Priesthood is connected to Heaven. Without a connection to Heaven, there is no priesthood. The "Powers of Heaven" are the angels themselves. Priests must have angelic accompaniment to claim priesthood. And angels cannot be manipulated by the world ambitions of men or their self-will.[777] The power of the priesthood cannot be controlled by men. It comes from Heaven or it does not come at all. There has never been an institution or church entrusted with the power of Heaven. The power of the priesthood comes only one way, and, as the revelation to Joseph Smith states, men do not have any right to either confer it, or prevent it from being conferred. Heaven alone determines if a man will be permitted to act as one of Heaven's chosen high priests (*see* T&C 139:5). Ordination invites. God alone confers His power.[778] The purpose of priesthood is to accomplish two things: first, to have valid ordinances; second, to obtain answers or direction. One can have the first with nothing more than Aaronic priesthood. However, the Holy Priesthood after the Order of the Son of God can give the second.[779] *See also* HOLY ORDER.

Priesthood, Blessings of the The result of a recipient receiving an authorized priesthood holder's administration. The blessings of the priesthood endure even after the death of the priesthood holder. Although Joseph Smith died in June 1844, the blessings he conferred while here endured until early in the 20th Century.[780] *See also* PRIESTHOOD, POWER IN THE.

Priesthood, Power in the The acknowledgement of heaven that a priest's acts are authorized, such as in baptism and blessing the sacrament. Not every act done by men claiming authority from God is acknowledged by God; only those with power in the priesthood belong to Him, hence the Lord's saying, *And many will say unto me in that day, Lord, Lord, have we not prophesied in your name, and in your name have we cast out devils, and in your name done many wonderful works? And then will I say, You never knew me. Depart from me, you that work iniquity* (Matthew 3:47).[781] It is necessary to reconnect with heaven itself to have not just authority but also power in the priesthood.

That connection of power in the priesthood comes from the hand of God, not from another man. The powers of the priesthood are inseparably connected with the Powers of Heaven and the hand of God (*see* T&C 139:5).[782] The Lord's ordination among the Nephites required only His word to be spoken, and power was conferred (*see* 3 Nephi 5:8). The word used in His conferral of priestly right was *power* and not *authority*. One should consider the difference. What does it mean for the Lord to speak to a man and tell him that he has power from the Lord? Is there a difference between having the *authority* to baptize and having the *power* to baptize as conferred by Christ?[783] Power in the Priesthood is, literally, the result of knowing and following the Lord. His friends hold His authority. His friends act within the same pattern, follow the same law, observe the same principles, and excite the same opposition as He did.[784] Power in the Priesthood also includes any endowment conferred directly by the Lord upon a person to accomplish an act, deliver a message, perform a mission, or labor on the Lord's behalf with His authorization.[785]

Principalities In the afterlife there are different rungs on Jacob's ladder where different Powers are fixed: Angel, Archangel, Principality, Power, Dominion, Throne, Cherubim, or Seraphim — they may all be called "Powers of Heaven."[786]

Principles and Rules "What is the difference between 'principles' and 'rules?' Assuming you define 'principles' as the underlying reason for the commandment, then you're also speaking about what the Apostle Paul called the *spirit of the law* as opposed to the *letter of the law*. He said, *The letter kills, but the spirit gives life* (2 Corinthians 1:9). I think he was right. Any rule can be abused. Any rule can become broken even when it is being kept. Rules can become harsh taskmasters, inflicting punishment when they were designed to bless. The underlying principle, however, always seeks to bless. The underlying principle was designed as a blessing. When the rule begins to oppress, then [it] should be abandoned in favor of the principle. Rules have and do change. But principles remain constant. The brutality of the rules was exposed by Christ when He healed on the Sabbath. He did that specifically to demonstrate the futility of ignoring the principle while only adhering to the law/rule. In the English common law tradition there were cases 'at law' and cases 'in equity.' They divided the Courts into separate forums, where courts of law could not do equity. But courts of equity could ignore the provisions of law, modify them, or establish a higher principle which resolved fairly a dispute despite some legal impediment to the relief sought. That tradition follows the Lord's example. Principles ennoble. Rules preoccupy."[787] *See also* VIRTUE; RIGHTEOUSNESS.

Promised Land Every time the full covenant is given, it includes a promised land. The Americas are the land God covenanted to give His people. The gentiles must repent and accept His gospel, not adulterate or change it, to be part of His covenant people.[788] *Notwithstanding our afflictions, we have obtained a land of promise, a land which is choice above all other lands, a land which the Lord God hath covenanted with me should be a land for the inheritance of my seed. Yea, the Lord hath consecrated this land unto me and to my children for ever, and also all they who should be led out of other countries by the hand of the Lord* (2 Nephi 1:1). This was a covenant made by God to Lehi, as a dispensational head. The beneficiaries of the covenant included Lehi's family and those who came with them, as well as generations of Lehi's family who came thereafter. The covenant is made with the dispensation head to allow others to likewise be saved.[789] "We are all equal. We all accept the Book of Mormon as a covenant for us to be numbered among the Lord's covenant people. This land in particular, is a land of promise to those who serve the God of this land, who is Jesus Christ (*see* Ether 1:7). The time is coming when those who are not the Lord's people will be swept off this land."[790] There is a land inheritance given as part of the covenant, and therefore, if the covenant is kept, there is a right to remain on the land when others will be swept away.[791] The Lord said in the renewed covenant ordinance: *I will raise you up and protect you, abide with you, and gather you in due time, and this shall be a land of promise to you as your inheritance from me* (T&C 158:13).

Prophet The late 12th century English word *prophet* comes from the Latin *propheta* and the Greek *prophetes* (προφήτης) which literally means "to speak forth, speak out, one who speaks forth."[792] A prophet is one who has the spirit of prophecy, which is the testimony of Jesus.[793] *The testimony of Jesus is the spirit of prophecy* (Revelation 7:10). John the Beloved spoke of the importance of a personal testimony of Christ by directly connecting it with the gift of prophecy. To have a saving testimony of Him is to become a prophet. It is no wonder, then, that Moses wished all men were prophets (*see* Numbers 7:19). All are invited to receive testimonies of Christ and are, therefore, invited to become prophets.[794] When Moses reestablished the direct connection between the chosen people and God, the Lord explained to Moses: *Hear now my words: If there is a prophet among you, I the Lord will make myself known unto him in a vision and will speak unto him in a dream* (Numbers 7:22).[795] All the prophets had the Melchizedek Priesthood and were ordained by God himself.[796] The existing hierarchy between Moses and Jesus Christ could not have ordained the prophets of the Old Testament because that hierarchy did not have the authority to do so. The portion of the priesthood authority which let men speak face to face with God was bestowed by God directly upon the prophets, independent of the mainstream of the people and their leadership.[797] Christ takes ownership of the prophets by declaring, "I send unto you prophets!" There can be no mistake about this claim of personal ownership.[798] The prophet's role is always to cry repentance. Priests may preside and kings may rule, but the prophet's voice is always crying repentance. Prophets have almost never presided over a congregation (other than occasionally a small inner-circle). They always speak from the sidelines, crying for a return to God's ways.[799] True prophets may teach, but they do not supplant.[800] "Now if any man has the testimony of Jesus, has he not the spirit of prophecy? And if he has the spirit of prophecy, I ask, is he not a prophet? And if a prophet will, he can receive revelation. And any man that does not receive revelation for himself must be damned, for the testimony of Jesus is the spirit of prophecy" (*WJS*, 230, spelling corrected, 291n1; *TPJS*, 312). *See also* TESTIMONY OF JESUS.

Public Rites (Ordinances) "Because of the potential and actual abuse by some priesthood holding men, I asked the Lord to extend priesthood to women. I was told as to public rites, *priesthood is confined to men because of the Fall and the conditions ordained at that time.* Until things are reversed at the Millennium, it will remain for men alone to perform the public ordinances thus far given to us. This order is not going to change until the Millennium. I asked the Lord that if only men were to hold priesthood for our public ordinances, then could only women vote to sustain them. This pleased the Lord, for it was already in His heart. But He added: *There shall be a minimum of seven women to sustain the man in any vote, and if the man is married, his wife shall be one of them.* If you have already been ordained, then you have the right to continue to minister to your family as a matter of right. But outside your family it is different. Even though already ordained, a community needs to recognize and authorize anyone to minister for them. For any who would like to qualify to minister outside his family, he must meet in a community and obtain a sustaining vote of a minimum of seven women. When that is done, all seven who vote to sustain should sign a certificate."[801] This refers to "public rites" and not to those rites and performances the public are excluded from knowing. The Holy Order conveys blessings and information that is withheld from the world. But men and women jointly obtain the Holy Order.[802] *See also* ORDINANCES.

Pure in Heart *And blessed are all the pure in heart, for they shall see God* (3 Nephi 5:17). This is a remarkable promise – if one would like to see God, then he must first purify his heart. It is interesting that what must be "pure" is the heart. There are so many other things that one might measure. But what the Lord looks upon to determine purity is the "heart." This is not just ritual purity, which had been the focus of the law of Moses. Christ is replacing the earlier, ritual-based purity with internal purity. He speaks about the heart, rather than the hands and feet. Christ is speaking about beholding God, unlike the retreat Israel took from the offered opportunity at Sinai (*see* T&C 82:12–14). He is returning to the time of Moses, when a higher way might have been chosen. Purity of the heart is a borrowed benefit from the Savior. Man cannot become clean before God without the necessary offering of a sacrifice. The law of Moses taught this, but Christ actually brought it to pass (*see*, e.g., Alma 16:37). Christ's atonement cleanses mankind (*see* Alma 10:1; Ether 6:3). Through repentance, all can turn to Christ and listen to and follow Him. Until then, one is not even facing the right direction in life. "Some reminders of how the heart may be purified: Let virtue constantly prevail in your thoughts. Pray to the Father with a devoted heart. Repent and call upon God with a contrite spirit, asking the atonement to be applied to your sins. Fast and pray often, that you may become humble. Follow what light you have to receive more light, until you have the 'perfect day' in which you are a vessel of light."

There is almost nothing about man that can become perfect in this life. The only thing that can approach perfection, however, is one's intent. One can mean to follow God at all times — even if the dilemmas of life make it impossible to actually do so, one can still intend to follow Him. Often, one may not even know if what he is doing pleases God, let alone how to resolve conflicting interests or commandments. One may even be making a mistake, but if his intent is right, his heart may be pure. This is one of the reasons man is commanded to not judge another. Others may be weak, foolish, and error prone, but if they *intend* to be doing the right, then God alone can measure their hearts and decide whether they are approved. It would take a God to know if the person's life, training, understanding, and intent are pure before Him. "I suspect there are those we look upon as deluded and even evil, but the Lord views them with compassion and understanding. He may find their hearts to be perfect even before the heart of the proud who claim they have and follow the truth. Though a person may misunderstand a great deal, still, if they have love for their fellow man, relieve suffering where they can, give patience to the foolish, and water to the thirsty, they may be perfect before God."[803] Impurity is like a compound that exists within each person, a compound that could be identified by the Lord and burned away. He is like the fuller's soap or the refiner's fire, where impurity is removed and something pure and clean is left behind. To survive that burning purge there must be so little to burn away that the injury from the burn will not threaten life. This is a useful way for each person to examine what is inside them and a useful way to reconsider their thoughts.[804]

Rabbi A title which means "acknowledged teacher."[805]

Raise Up Seed Jacob 2:6–8 does not point to a justification for plural wives and concubines, which the Book of Mormon vehemently condemns, but refers to raising up a righteous branch (specifically from the fruit of the loins of Joseph) or raising up seed unto the Lord of Hosts (*raise up seed unto me*). A righteous seed are those who accept Christ as their father, become the begotten sons and daughters of God, and who are connected with Him by adoption, affiliation, or association. Other instances in the scriptures where the phrase "raise up" is used is in combination with the following: a *mighty nation* (1 Nephi 7:3); *one mighty* (2 Nephi 2:7); a *righteous branch* (2 Nephi 2:2); a *Moses* (2 Nephi 2:5); a *seer* (2 Nephi 2:3); and a *great nation* (Ether 1:4). When the term "raise up" is used in connection with "seed," it is very specific, i.e., *that they might raise up seed unto the Lord in the land of promise* (1 Nephi 2:2) and *raise up unto me a righteous branch.... For if I will, saith the Lord of Hosts, raise up seed unto me, I will command my people* (Jacob 2:7-8). *See also* SEED OF CHRIST, OR HEIRS OF THE KINGDOM.

Rebaptism Believing in Christ precedes baptism. In fact, belief in Christ causes baptism. The one results in the other. Without faith in Him, there is no need for baptism. This then makes the first step belief in Christ, with baptism the second step. "I've heard of those who obtain a testimony of Christ in adulthood, but who were baptized many years earlier at age eight. If belief in Christ is supposed to precede baptism, but in fact follows it, does that recommend repeating the ordinance? Does Christ's establishment of an order to these things, by the commandment of the Father, matter? If it matters, then why not try it? If tried and it 'tastes good,' then you have your answer. And if nothing changes, then you also have learned something, as well. I was fortunate to be able to follow the proper sequence. I was 19 years old when I came to the [truth]. I try to follow the proper sequence with my own children by teaching them before baptism and testifying of Christ to them in a way calculated to produce faith in Him. I would take no offense, however, if one of my children were to later want to be rebaptized as an affirmation of their continuing belief in Christ. I can't see why anyone would take offense."[806]

On Sunday, March 20, 1842, Joseph Smith preached about baptism and rebaptized about 79 church members and at least one new convert. The first baptism was the convert. *Wilford Woodruff's Journal* records: "President Joseph Smith went forth into the river & Baptized with his own hands about 80 persons for the remission of their sins & what added Joy to the scene the first person Baptized was Mr L. D. Wason a nephew of sister Emma Smith was the first of her kindred that have embraced the fulness of the gospel."[807] On the next Sunday, Woodruff recorded: "After the meeting closed the congregation again assembled upon the bank of the river & Joseph the seer went into the river & Baptized all that Came unto him & I considered it my privilege to be Baptized for the remission of my sins for I had not been since I first Joined the Church in 1833. I was then Baptized under the hands of Elder Zerah Pulsipher. Therefore I went forth into the river & was Baptized under the hands of JOSEPH THE SEER & likewise did Elder J Taylor & many others..." (*Wilford Woodruff's Journal,* March 27, 1842).[808] In these two journal entries one sees that rebaptism was taught and practiced by Joseph Smith, John Taylor, and Wilford Woodruff. If other contemporaneous records are consulted, it is clear that rebaptism was universal in the early days of Mormonism. One did not partake of the sacrament to renew baptismal covenants; they were rebaptized.[809] The purpose of baptism grew from remitting sins and joining the church to include rebaptism as a means for rededication and purification, as well as rebaptism for the healing of the sick. Emma Smith was rebaptized in October 1842 for her health.[810] Nephi had authority to baptize before Christ came. When Christ came, He gave Nephi the authority to baptize again. Nephi baptized a group of people, then he *baptized the same group of people a second time – he rebaptized them.* Rebaptism is a sound gospel principle and is practiced every time God sends a message. The correct way to accept and proceed is to renew baptism, just like the people in the Book of Mormon did.[811] The Lord renewed this commandment (for all to be baptized) on September 9, 2014. "He expects us to follow His pattern and obey this to receive a remission of sins."[812]

"Even if you have been baptized previously, be baptized in this new dispensation. The Lord has renewed this commandment for our time and baptism is a sign of acceptance of what God is doing in each generation. He expects us to follow His pattern and obey this to receive a remission of sins. This baptism is not membership in any organized church or religion. It is a sign between you and God that you sincerely believe in Jesus Christ and wish to follow Him. If you've not been baptized, or would like to be baptized again, there are those who have authority to administer this ordinance. To the thousands who have been rebaptized: This is a sign you are not an idolater and will not be destroyed at the Lord's coming."[813] *See also* BAPTISM.

Redeem Jerusalem To re-establish the promised heirs upon their own land and bring again Zion. *And when the words of the prophet Isaiah shall be fulfilled, which say: Thy watchmen shall lift up the voice, with the voice together shall they sing, for they shall see eye to eye when the Lord shall bring again Zion. Break forth into joy, sing together ye waste places of Jerusalem, for the Lord hath comforted his people, he hath redeemed Jerusalem. The Lord hath made bare his holy arm in the eyes of all the nations and all the ends of the earth shall see the salvation of God* (3 Nephi 7:6). In this profound insight and declaration by Christ, readers learn Isaiah was *not* speaking of the return to the Middle East for these coming events to unfold. Instead, the "waste places of Jerusalem" are nowhere near Jerusalem — they are in another place, far away, where the residue of Jerusalem's scattered people are wasted and then restored again. "Waste places" is plural; according to Christ's interpretation, they are scattered throughout the world. One is in the Americas, on an *isle of the sea* (2 Nephi 7:5). There is also something odd about this passage — after the removal of the gentiles, there is joy, rejoicing, singing together, seeing eye to eye, and a return to Zion. This emotional setting seems at odds with what mankind anticipates. It would seem that destroying the gentiles and experiencing the trauma of those days would produce mourning and lamentation. It does not. Instead it produces singing in joy. Whatever bottle-neck of destruction is needed to bring that triumph to pass will be worth it. So great will be the peace that follows that it will wipe away all tears; truth, saving doctrine, and being fed by Christ's own message will end all laments, as described in Revelation 2:16, *for the Lamb who is in the midst of the throne shall feed them, and shall lead them unto living fountains of waters, and God shall wipe away all tears from their eyes*. ("3 Nephi 16:17–20," June 27, 2010, blog post). *See* NEW JERUSALEM; ZION.

Redemption To be brought back into the presence of God. Ether 1:13 confirms: *When he had said these words, behold, the Lord shewed himself unto him and said, Because thou knowest these things, ye are redeemed from the Fall. Therefore, ye are brought back into my presence; therefore I shew myself unto you.* This is the gospel of Christ. Eternal life requires all to know Him.

Ether affirms the brother of Jared was redeemed when Christ came to him. Christ redeemed him from the Fall: *Because thou knowest these things, ye are redeemed from the Fall* (ibid.). Christ defines redemption. Reconciliation comes through Christ, with Christ, and by Christ. He has the power to redeem all.[814] "The monetary metaphor is by far the commonest [one for redemption or reconciliation], being the simplest and easiest to understand. Frequently the word *redemption* literally means to buy back, that is, to reacquire something you owned previously. Redemption, or atonement, restores one to a former, happier condition…. By redemption, someone has paid a price to get you off."[815] It is impossible to become altogether clean in this fallen world. Man can do his best, but in the end, he's going to find he is lacking. The scriptures admit this. The proposition is so fundamentally understood among most saints that it goes without saying: All are in need of redemption from an outside power, someone with greater virtue and power than man has, who can lift mankind from their fallen condition into something higher, cleaner, and more godly. This is the role of Christ. His atoning sacrifice equipped Him to accomplish this.[816] As explained by Alma, the redemption which comes from faith in Christ is what empowers one's repentance, so that he or she can take advantage of His atonement by forsaking their sins (*see* Alma 16:34). This is a difficult process, involving constant attention to His mercy, which redeems all mankind (*see* Alma 16:35).[817] How humble it is for the Lord to be willing to accept the reluctant, tardy, and slow to repent. Nevertheless, He is willing to accept even them. He suffered for all and will redeem as many as will come to Him. Ultimately, the outcome will depend upon how committed they are to the process of repentance, for to repent is to come to Him. They decide if His open arms will be where they finally embrace Him.[818]

The God of the Telestial Kingdom (in which man is presently situated) is the holy ghost. The God of the Terrestrial Kingdom (which the Millennium will reflect) is Jesus Christ. The God of the Celestial Kingdom is God the Father (*see* T&C 69). The holy ghost brings man to Christ; Christ brings man to the Father, and the Father extends the promise of exaltation by making one a son or daughter of God. The plan of redemption brings men and women from their current, fallen state back to a state of awareness of their condition, and then by cleansing them, elevates them in light and truth. The primary God with whom men and women interact here in this world is the holy ghost. However, the association with Christ is promised by Him in John 9. Joseph Smith explained that when the promise given by Christ (in that chapter of John) is realized, then the Father and Son will visit with the person from time to time.[819] In a universal sense, modern revelation confirms that all will be "redeemed," except the sons of Perdition (*see* T&C 69:7,24). *And by Adam came the Fall of man. And because of the Fall of man came Jesus Christ, even the Father and the Son; and because of Jesus Christ came the redemption of man. And because of the redemption of man which came by Jesus Christ, they are brought back into the presence of the Lord. Yea, this is wherein all men are redeemed, because the death of Christ bringeth to pass the resurrection, which bringeth to pass a redemption from an endless sleep, from which sleep all men shall be awoke by the power of God when the trump shall sound; and they shall come forth, both small and great, and all shall stand before his bar, being redeemed and loosed from this eternal band of death, which death is a temporal death* (Mormon 4:7). The plan of salvation provides blessings and benefits for all of mankind, with the hope that all will be added upon here. Therefore, redemption reflects the adding of celestial, terrestrial, and telestial estates available through the atonement.[820] The holy ghost is the instrumentality by which redemption itself comes. The spirit is the guide which will lead back to the Lord's presence. Without the guide, the doctrine of Christ is incomplete.[821] The Gospel of Jesus Christ is true, authentic, and holds the means for redeeming mankind.[822]

Redemption causes the redeemed to work for the salvation of others. The reason some obtain the kind of redemption Nephi obtained (*see* 2 Nephi 15:2) is because they are of a character to work for the redemption of others. There is no reason to withhold the promise of eternal life from them, because others will be redeemed as a result of their redemption. They will labor, preach, teach, intercede, seek, pray, and work tirelessly to bring others to the tree of life. They become fellow-servants with Christ and labor alongside Him in the work of redeeming others. This is one of the reasons for the parable of "The Busy Young Man"[823] in *Ten Parables*.[824] *See also* ATONEMENT.

Re'em The word used by Joseph Smith to replace "unicorn" in the scriptures. It refers to an extinct species of wild ox — likely the aurochs or the Arabian oryx.[825]

Reins A Biblical term that is often translated or used as heart or mind, that literally means *kidneys* (pl.) or loins, from the Hebrew *kilyah*, (כִּלְיָה)[826] and the Greek *ephros*, (νεφρός) meaning kidney, fig. the (inmost) mind. The reins are the seat of the inward feelings, emotions, and passions of man.[827]

Remember Often used in the Book of Mormon to mean "keep" (*see* 1 Nephi 3:2). Nephi used it in his record as a way of being asked if he kept the covenants of the Father, so far as they applied to him.[828] The angel was inquiring about Nephi's worthiness to receive more and was asking, in other words, "Do you follow the Father's commandments?" When Nephi responded, "Yes," the angel said, "Then I will show you more."[829]

Remnant In 3 Nephi 9:11, the Lord calls the Nephite audience and their posterity, *this people who are a remnant of the house of Jacob…this my people*. It is important to know that the Lord describes them with this identity as *my people* throughout His sermon and prophecy. This careful limitation of the reference to the Lord's *people* should not be applied broadly. It does not include gentiles. Mankind should not change His meaning. He is speaking about a single, identified group as *my people*, and it is those standing before Him, as well as their descendants.[830] Speaking to Nephi, the angel stated, *Behold, saith the Lamb of God, after I have visited the remnant of the house of Israel (and this remnant of whom I speak is the seed of thy father)…* (1 Nephi 3:23). Notice that the definition of the remnant to whom the prophecies apply has now been given. The distinction between the "gentiles" and the remnant is apparent here.[831] Nephi refers to the remnant variously as: descendants of his father, Lehi (*see* 1 Nephi 3:23); descendants of his brethren (1 Nephi 3:24); his family's descendants or *our seed* (*see* 1 Nephi 4:3); and a mixture of Nephi's descendants who are among his brother's descendants (*see* 1 Nephi 3:22). Although it would be impossible, without revelation, for someone to determine which of these lines a person might belong to today, the Lord, nevertheless, revealed in 1828 that these various divisions remain identified to Him (*see* JSH 10:7). No doubt, in time He will restore to the remnant descendants this knowledge of their sacred paternity and eternal identity. Their blood may be mixed, but the remnant remains. Nephi may have referred to them more often as descendants of his *brethren*, but they have within them some of his blood, as well. In the day of redemption and restoration, the promises will all be fulfilled. The whole of the family of Lehi will be represented in the remnant.[832]

Repent/ance A "change" requiring believers to turn away from the world and toward God. It is the change in life that follows from seeing things in a better, truer light. There is another, higher way to live available to everyone. But to move upward, people must make changes in their lives to incorporate more light and truth. By living a higher way, they are repenting. This process is not a single event. It does not happen once. It should happen over and over as all increase the light in their lives.[833] Repentance is granted by God (*see* Alma 10:4; 19:15; Acts 6:9). It involves acquiring light and truth — meaning intelligence. Repentance is abandoning a foolish error, a vain tradition, or a false belief and replacing it with truth.[834] Penitence is another way to describe repentance (or the process of change and growing beyond sins that limit your happiness). It comes as you allow Christ to "succor" you through the power of the atonement. Through penitence, people do away with the darkness in their lives and add light instead.[835] Repentance is turning away from all other distractions to face God.[836]

To repent is to turn to Him. To turn to Him is to face Him, listen to Him, heed Him, and pay attention to what He is, says, and does. It is to seek to be in contact with Him. If one is in contact with Him, He will teach him all things he should do (*see* 2 Nephi 14:1). "Constant contact between you and [God] can and will occupy your desires, thoughts and deeds. But turning to face Him is left to you. He cannot enter where He is not invited. He may want to be a part of your life more than you want Him to. It is your choice to let Him in. Hearing alone will not save you. Doing is the thing which saves."[837]

Rest of the Lord One enters the "rest of the Lord" as soon as the promise of Eternal life is made by Him. It is His rest one inherits in the last day. The words of the promise are enough to guarantee the inheritance. Therefore, once the promise is made, it is true enough that one has entered into the rest of the Lord.[838] The glory of God is intelligence. The "rest of the Lord" is the fullness of His glory, or in other words, light and truth of a perfect day.[839] The only thing that stills the mind of man and brings rest from the trouble of this world is the atonement of Christ. That is why it is called the "rest of the Lord."[840] "What is the rest that He offers? It is to become part of the 'living vine' and to have Him take up His abode with you (*see* Alma 11:7)."[841] On the other side of the test of one's faith is the "rest of the Lord." But that doesn't mean that the insecurities of mortality are removed. Only one thing changes: the one that is chosen will now know God — but he will still need to go to work and pay the bills.[842] It does not mean retirement, nor does it excuse him from this life's labors, difficulties, challenges, or struggles. But he will know that God lives and that his life is acceptable to Him.[843]

Restoration or Apostasy Religion moves through two stages. In the first, God reveals Himself to man. This is called "restoration." It restores man to communion with God, as in the Garden of Eden. In the second, man attempts to worship God according to His last visit. This stage is always characterized by lack and inadequacy. This is called "apostasy." Apostasy always follows restoration. Abraham, Moses, and Isaiah ascended the bridge into God's presence. Through Jesus Christ, God descended the celestial bridge to live with man. Those examples all show God wants to reconnect with man. Unfortunately, the participants in a restoration leave only an echo of God's voice unless they remain connected with God through continual restoration. Every restoration risks a lapse back into lack and apostasy. Whether the echo is preserved through a family (as in ancient Israel) or through churches (as in Christianity), some organization acts as a substitute for God's presence during apostasy. Unfortunately, organizations can only imitate God's involvement. Though Moses guided Joshua into the abundance of restoration obtained by Joshua's own direct contact with God, Israel forfeited their opportunity to do the same thing. Earlier, Abraham established a restored dynasty in Isaac, Jacob, and Joseph. Abraham's was the greatest success since the time of Adam. Apostasy is the rule, restoration the exception. It is a curious failure since God declared His works and words never cease. Institutions cannot control God. As faith in God is institutionalized, it becomes part of this world and, necessarily, influenced by cultural, social, legal, and economic pressure. These forces erode faith. Religious institutions are where the ideal comes into conflict with the less-than-ideal. LDS Mormonism illustrates this dynamic. Through compromises of its ideals, the pattern unfolds in modern time. Religion has always frustrated good men. Churches fail to practice the ideal. This frustration produces reformers who reject the inevitability of spiritual famine and who long for the return of a revelatory God.[844] Either on a collective or personal basis, the path requires motion. Man remains in motion all the time. There is no stasis, no holding a position. He advances (that is, experiences restoration), or he recedes (that is, experiences apostasy). There is no avoiding movement.[845] It is not possible for an individual, nor a collection of individuals, to remain static. They are either involved with restoring truth or are in apostasy from it; they are never merely "preserving" it. Those who claim to merely preserve the truth given them are concealing the fact of their apostasy. They are soothing their conscience. Caretakers simply cannot exist.[846] Mankind should not be misled by the language of revelations about the restoration through Joseph Smith being "the last": *...which kingdom is coming forth for the last time* (T&C 90:1); *...this Priesthood given for the last days, and for the last time, in the which is the Dispensation of the Fullness of Times* (T&C 124:7). These references (and more) should be understood as "most recent" — as in the same language of T&C 69:5: *...this is the testimony, last of all, which we give of him: that he lives.* Just as this language does not mean there will never be a testimony of Christ after February 1832 — only that theirs was the latest — likewise, the other use of "last" in the revelations means "most recent."[847]

Restoration, The The restoration is not the property of an institution. Although dozens of churches claim the role of succeeding to Joseph Smith's "true and living" church, the restoration belongs to everyone. Whether one belongs to some denomination claiming Joseph as a founder or one is a traditional Christian, the things restored through Joseph Smith came from God as a gift to all. Because of this, everyone has the responsibility to remember and respect the inspired work of Joseph Smith. The restoration is God's call to action and offer to renew His direct contact with mankind. If there is any chance of remembering the restoration, it is now. Until the restoration is remembered, there can be no completion.[848] God's work is the same yesterday, today, and for ever. Those who would like to throw mankind about by every wind of doctrine are merely teaching the commandments of men as if they were doctrine. They are not. "God spoke through Joseph and expects us to remember and study what was given. God will do no more to move the restoration forward until we repent. The first order of repentance is to remember what God gave to us through Joseph. If we do that, we will find God is willing to resume the restoration and move it forward to completion. When we fail to honor what was given, God will simply wait for another generation more humble and meek than ours."[849] "The third and fourth generations have passed. The atrophy of the restoration has now brought it to an end. The Lord intends to complete what He began through Joseph. God gave us prophecy, telling what would happen, and signs have confirmed the gentile failure. We live at the end of one era and the beginning of another."[850] God's house is a house of order. He does it according to patterns. It is not God's purpose to abandon the restoration, but it is His purpose to preserve it, which at this moment is in terrible jeopardy. The restoration must be rescued and preserved. Those who cannot detect the terrible changes it has undergone and is now undergoing are blind, indeed. Shall God forget the work He began through Joseph? Shall the downward course be permitted without Him raising His hand to save it? Or should a kind and merciful God give mankind a chance to preserve it, with His assistance, if they choose to act? There are many willing to act. They only need some indication from God of how to do so. Thankfully, the pattern was given through Joseph Smith.[851] "We should follow all that has been given to us in scripture. We should be completing the restoration, not throwing anything away. We are trying to preserve, return, and renew. Nothing given through Joseph should be discarded if it is useful, laudable, worthy, desirable, or came through the restoration. God's purpose is to preserve, not abandon, the restoration."[852]

The Restoration had elements which, necessarily, involved creation, renewal, restoration of light, and newness. It was, after all, a "new" and everlasting covenant coming into play. "I do not think Joseph drove the agenda. Nor do I think that we can drive the agenda when it comes to what Heaven is working out for mankind. Instead it is the Lord's agenda, with His timing, and our responsibility to conform to it. However, it was restored for a 'last' time, with judgment to follow after a period of probation. The time of the gentiles is drawing fast to a close, or has closed and is now merely moribund and in need of a funeral. We are numbered among the gentiles. So for us, the harmonic to which we should conform involves that portion of the cosmic ring involved in closing, ending, judgment, and loss. This closing down, as all cycles, will be followed again with renewal, for those who survive. The timing will shift again, and a happy new day will dawn with all the possibilities of creation anew. Of course, even inside the decline, there are elements of renewal and rebirth on an individual basis. While Noah was preparing the ark there were still those who received eternal rebirth as [Genesis] confirms. But the agenda is the Lord's. Always has been and always will be. We get invited to the party, but the party is His. Therefore, I continue to entertain the conviction that despite the seasons and times assigned to us, we are supposed to realize the 'signs of the times' which are upon us and conform our own petitions and conduct to the larger picture within which we are living. When we do, we get a response. When we don't, we get silence."[853]

Restoring Knowledge There are at least three stages in the process of restoring knowledge. The first stage is to receive it. Receiving it is not the same thing as the second stage, which is to comprehend it. It is possible that a man receive something without understanding what it was that he received. Time and careful, solemn, and ponderous thoughts are required to untangle what has been received in order to comprehend what it is that one has been given. But it is altogether something of a different order of magnitude, completely separate from that, to teach it. One can receive it and comprehend it, but he may not be able to teach it. When it finally does get taught, undoubtedly it will be taught in the manner Joseph Smith was beginning to work on in Nauvoo but never finished — that is, by ceremony and by covenant. And this, too, by something given by God. It will only be established in a House that is acceptable to Him. If anyone wants to know what Joseph Smith was doing in his efforts—in a whole new effort—he has to understand the birthright, sealing power, and organizing again on the earth the kingdom of God. He was trying to bring back the actual family. But he was taken at the incipient stage, because all that he was sent here to do was to lay the groundwork, to lay the beginning, to come as an Elias. Joseph came to call to the world and to give them, if they will pay attention to it, a basis for study to learn and potentially qualify for the Lord to resume the restoration and bring it to a completion.[854]

Resurrection/Burial In a discourse given by Joseph Smith on April 16, 1843 in the unfinished Nauvoo temple (the walls being only four to twelve feet high), he placed great importance on this subject and related a small portion of a vision he experienced that is to provide comfort and reassurance. Recorded by two eyewitnesses, no other accounts of this vision exist: "He wished all of the saints to be comforted with the victory they were to gain by the resurrection. It is sufficient to encourage the saints to overcome in the midst of every trial, trouble, and tribulation. Though thunders roar and earthquakes bellow, lightnings flash and wars are upon every hand, yet suffer not a joint to tremble nor let not your heart faint. For the great Elohim will deliver you and, if not before the resurrection, will set you eternally free from all these things: from pain, sorrow, and death. I have labored hard and sought every way to try to prepare this people to comprehend the things that God is unfolding to me. In speaking of the resurrection I would say that God hath shown unto me a vision of the resurrection of the dead and I saw the graves open and the saints as they arose, took each other by the hand, even before they got up or while getting up, and great joy and glory rested upon them."[855] "Would you think it strange that I relate what I have seen in vision in relation [to] this interesting theme[?] Those who have died in Jesus Christ may expect to enter in all that fruition of joy when they come forth, which they have pursued here. So plain was the vision I actually saw men, before they had ascended from the tomb, as though they were getting up slowly, they took each other by the hand. And it was my father and my son, my mother and my daughter, my brother and my sister. When the voice calls, suppose I am laid by the side of my father. What would be the first joy of my heart? Where is my father, my mother, my sister? They are by my side.

I embrace them and they me. It is my meditation all the day, and more than my meat and drink, to know how I shall make the saints of God to comprehend the visions that roll like an overflowing surge before my mind…. O how I would delight to bring before you things which you never thought of, but poverty and the cares of the world prevent. But I am glad that I have the privilege of communicating to you some things, which if grasped closely will be a help to you when the clouds are gathering and the storms are ready to burst upon you like peels of thunder. Lay hold of these things and let not your knees tremble nor your hearts faint. What can earthquakes do, wars and tornadoes do? Nothing. All your losses will be made up to you in the resurrection, provided you continue faithful. By the vision of the Almighty I have seen it. More painful to me [is] the thought of annihilation than death. If I had no expectation of seeing my mother, brother, and sisters, and friends again, my heart would burst in a moment and I should go down to my grave. The expectation of seeing my friends in the morning of the resurrection cheers my soul and make[s] me bear up against the evils of life. It is like their taking a long journey and on their return we meet them with increased joy. God has revealed His Son from the Heavens and the doctrine of the resurrection also. And we have a knowledge that these we bury here, God bring[s] them up again, clothed upon and quickened by the spirit of the great God."[856]

Revelation The word revelation comes from the Latin *revelare* (reveal, uncover, disclose, literally "draw back a veil, unveil") and from Latin *velum* ("a veil"). "To be saved you must know God. God will speak to each of us about what is important in our lives. All things past, present, and future are continually before the Lord. God's revelations have depth and layers beyond the human mind because they originate from a higher source. The most important thing to know is the Lord's will for you. The pattern is to study scripture, ask God to help you understand, then listen to God's answer. God would like to talk directly to you. The scriptures have a message from God for you."[857] "The greatest help given to us to solve the contradiction between praying to God and the answer being exactly what we wanted, exactly what we expected, and exactly what makes us right and everyone else wrong; the greatest guide is the scriptures. They provide us a lifeline for measuring any inspiration we think we obtain from God. But that's not enough if it's not coupled together with prayerful, ponderous thought, and time and experience. Compare these statements from Joseph Smith about this topic: 'The spirit of revelation is in connection with these blessings [having your calling and election made sure and the privilege of receiving the other Comforter, etc.]. A person may profit by noticing the first intimation of the spirit of revelation; for instance, when you feel pure intelligence flowing into you, it may give you sudden strokes of ideas, so that by noticing it, you may find it fulfilled the same day or soon; (i.e.) those things that were presented unto your minds by the Spirit of God, will come to pass; and thus by learning the Spirit of God and understanding it, you may grow into the principle of revelation, until you become perfect in Christ Jesus' (*DHC* 3:381, June 1839; *TPJS*,151; *WJS*, 5-6).That seems to suggest that answers can come suddenly, quickly, perhaps even easily. But Joseph also said this: *A fanciful and flowery and heated imagination beware of; because the things of God are of deep import; and time, and experience, and careful and ponderous and solemn thoughts can only find them out. Thy mind, O man! if thou wilt lead a soul unto salvation, must stretch as high as the utmost heavens, and search into and contemplate the darkest abyss, and the broad expanse of eternity–thou must commune with God* (T&C 138:18; *TPJS*, 137, March 1839). That second quote is taken from a letter that Joseph Smith composed while he was in Liberty Jail in which he had plenty of time to fashion the language. The first quote, sadly, is taken from a source which may not be reliable or accurate. The source for that first quote is Willard Richard's Pocket Companion in which he quoted something which, if Joseph Smith said it, Joseph said it while Willard Richards was in England on a mission and he could not possibly have heard it. He doesn't even attribute it to Joseph Smith. But when the Documentary History was being compiled they used the Willard Richards Companion to take that language and attribute it to a talk given by Joseph in 1839 because most of the stuff in the Pocket Companion can be tracked to Joseph, and therefore they conclude this one likewise fit that same category. The second one is clearly, unambiguously from Joseph Smith and describes the process. It's almost poetry, the way Joseph describes what he went through there.

But it is poetry describing the actual bona fides of Joseph receiving answers from God. God's most important inspiration for the most challenging subjects is often not hasty, quick and without effort at our end. Consider the advice to Oliver Cowdery that he must *study it out in [his] own mind* first before asking God to tell him the answer. Many people want a quick, perfunctory response from God with no forethought. What they receive in turn is a quick, perfunctory answer. God is almost always, for the most difficult challenges, not a 'short order cook' although there are certainly false spirits who are willing to be just that.... It requires humility to approach God and ask Him for His answer and yet more humility to know it is from Him and not [one's] own ego, presumptions, hopes, desires, wants and conceit."[858] "A man is saved no faster than he gets knowledge, for if he does not get knowledge, he will be brought into captivity by some evil power in the other world, as evil spirits will have more knowledge, and consequently more power, than many men who are on the earth. Hence it needs revelation to assist us, and give us knowledge of the things of God."[859] The scriptures are designed to reveal *and* conceal. They are able to reveal even very hidden and mysterious things to the understanding of mankind when one understands what is being discussed. Until the reader has been prepared for this understanding, reading the messages will not necessarily result in greater insight. It is almost as if one has to know the answer first or have it revealed to him. Then, while in possession of the truth, he can see that prophets and seers have been speaking about these matters since the beginning of time.[860] "You *must* understand doctrine. You *must* study the scriptures. But more important than anything else, you *must* seek to gain further light and knowledge by conversing with the Lord directly. Harmony of the whole is dependent upon His direct guidance and blessings. You simply cannot move forward a piece here and a bit there, while neglecting the whole composite picture of the Gospel. He will open it to your view. He will show you how one part is related to another, and that to another still, so that it all moves forward together. It is not to all be comprehended at once. It is to be gained a little bit of the whole here, a further harmony of things there, until the whole moves forward together. Always moving in balance, in harmony, and as a complete magisterial revelation of God's will."[861] The riches of eternity are offered by the Lord to all and to each one directly. It does not come from learning "secrets" from someone else. It comes by following the path. "You do not need anything more than a description of the path. Follow it. Until you follow it, the Heavens will remain shut against you. As soon as you follow it, you will have the results you would like to have. Curiosity about sacred details that the scriptures repeatedly warn are not lawful to put into writing here in this fallen world reveals an immaturity that should be overcome. If you want the details, learn them from the Lord. Directly. Without an intermediary. Teachers are commissioned by the Lord to reiterate the path by which they are to be obtained. He does not send someone to do the work for you. Indeed, you either do the work for yourself or it remains undone — for ever."[862] Revelation from Heaven is also a revelation of oneself. For as one sees Him, he sees most clearly how very limited and dependent he is upon Him. One cannot be prideful after seeing himself alongside Him (*see* T&C 159:6).[863] Joseph Smith said, "All things whatsoever God in his infinite wisdom has seen fit and proper to reveal to us, while we are dwelling in mortality, in regard to our mortal bodies, are revealed to us in the abstract, and independent of affinity of this mortal tabernacle, but are revealed to our spirits, precisely as though we had no bodies at all."[864]

Righteousness Conformity to the Divine Law.[865] God measures differently than does man. Being "righteous before God" may not mean the same thing one thinks "righteousness" means. Man wants outward signs, symbols, dress, grooming, and conformity. God looks at the intent of the heart.[866] Righteousness comes by obedience. Obedience requires action. Without conforming conduct to the Lord's commandments, it is impossible to enter into the kingdom of heaven.[867]

Rights Belonging to the Fathers Melchizedek inherited from his father the right of "dominion" that was originally given by God to Adam. He was the "father" over all mankind and in that capacity was a "king" or a "ruler," though he exercised that right given to him as did Adam — as a father-figure and not as a tyrant. Abraham came to him to obtain this same right belonging to the first fathers or the right that descended from Adam. This is the "rights belonging to the fathers" which Abraham was so overjoyed to have obtained, because he was then the rightful father of "many nations," by reason of his position in the family of God. This, however, did not confer authority that was respected or acknowledged by men in that day, but it was respected by God.[868] *See also* THE FATHERS.

Rock The Book of Mormon contains Christ's Gospel. It also contains His rock and His salvation. What is the rock contained within it? The better translation of Christ's colloquy with Peter would have included the Lord identifying Peter not as a rock but as a seer stone. And upon the stone or seership would the Lord build His church [*see also* CEPHAS]. The Book of Mormon is more a Urim and Thummim than a book. It is a tremendous source of subject matter upon which to ponder, oftentimes drawing a veil at critical moments while inviting the reader to ponder, pray, and ask to see more. Used in that fashion, the Book of Mormon can open the heavens and make any person a seer. The words of a prophet are best understood by another prophet. If one can come to understand the Book of Mormon's words, he or she can become a prophet (or more correctly, a seer) before whom scenes of God's dealings with mankind — past, present, and future — will be put on display. Another way to interpret the rock is found in *Eighteen Verses* (p. 49), which discusses the meaning of 1 Nephi 1:3. The meaning of the rock —Ma'at— before Lehi (who wrote in Egyptian and would therefore understand meanings) was the stone of judgment, the symbol of truth, which signifies "reality," on one hand, and "light," on the other. Facsimile 2, figure 4 in the Book of Abraham, for example, shows the image of the Horus Hawk atop a rock and on the heavenly boat.[869] Mankind has its own symbolic meanings associated with a rock. One of the clearest is Christ's declaration that His names include the title "Rock of Heaven." In vision, Enoch saw and heard the Lord declare: *I am the Messiah, the King of Zion, the Rock of Heaven* (Genesis 4:20).[870] "The 'rock' upon which we build is the Father, Son and holy ghost. There is abundant evidence of other 'gods' and of 'goddesses.' It is beyond dispute that the 'image of God' includes both male and female. It is inescapable, therefore, that the God we worship includes a Father and a Mother. However, we are only to seek after the Father, Son and holy ghost as the 'rock' upon which our salvation is to be built."[871]

Ruach There are instances in which Hebrew uses the feminine directly to describe God. For example, the spirit of God, Ruach Elohim (רוח אלהים) is a feminine noun. Likewise, when referring to the "presence of God" Hebrew uses the feminine.[872] The word *Shekhinah* was coined as a proper noun to replace a phrase literally meaning "he caused to dwell." That phrase is better understood to convey "the presence of God" and therefore the word *Shekhinah* was adopted.[873] God's presence includes the feminine.[874] *Ruach* means breath, wind, spirit.[875] Joseph Smith expands our insight into the word: "The 7th verse of c 2 of Genesis [KJV] ought to read 'God breathed into Adam his spirit or breath of life.' But when the word 'ruach' applies to Eve it should be translated lives." (*See* Genesis 2:11.)[876] It appears that into Adam was breathed the breath of life. Into Eve, however, was breathed the breath of *lives*.

Ruler A teacher of truth. "We were spirits before we were born (Abraham 6:1–3). We were all there when some were chosen to be rulers, or in other words, teachers."[877] To rule is to be responsible to teach all those in one's dominion.[878] A ruler is a teacher responsible for instructing others (*see* 1 Nephi 1:9).[879] The account in Genesis explains that Eve (and by extension her daughters) was put under Adam's rule. Adam was handed responsibility and accountability for Eve. These are the words in the parable: *Thy desire shall be to thy husband, and he shall rule over thee* (Genesis 2:18). Adam was made accountable to "rule" in the fallen world. All the mistakes, mismanagements, failings, wars, and difficulties of mortality are the responsibility of the appointed "ruler." Adam would not have been accountable for Eve unless she was made subject to his "rule." Once under Adam's rule, the redemption of Adam became also the redemption of Eve. Therefore, Adam (and the sons of Adam) and Eve (and the daughters of Eve) were all rescued through Christ's atonement for mankind.[880] In the Book of Mormon, the term "ruler" was synonymous with teacher (*see* e.g., Jacob 1:2).[881] In Paul's Epistle to the Hebrews, the use of the word "rule" in context means the assigned role to teach. *Remember them who have the rule over you, who have spoken unto you the word of God* (Hebrews 1:59). He repeats it twice: *Obey them that have the rule over you, and submit yourselves; for they watch for your souls as they who must give account, that they may do it with joy and not with grief*

(Hebrews 1:61); *Salute all them that have the rule over you, and all the saints* (Hebrews 1:64).[882] *See also* TEACH.

Sabbath Day A day set apart by the Lord as a remembrance of the creation and His redemptive power (*see* Exodus 12:7; Deuteronomy 2:10). During the creation, God established a plan for six days of labor and one day of rest. That one day of rest was to be continually observed and would later be memorialized in the law of Moses. But on that first day of rest, Adam and Eve were sent out from the Garden of Eden, and instead of resting, they labored. The reckoning of the week was disturbed by the fact that a day was lost, and the calendar resulted in a day's disparity because of the fall of Adam and Eve. Christ was resurrected on what was called the "first day of the week" because it was the first day of the week as reckoned from the fall of Adam. Christ's atonement was intended to fix the fall of Adam — to put everything back right again — and to repair the damage that had been caused. Therefore, even though Christ's resurrection appears to have come one day late, it was actually just on time. He repaired not only the damage done in the original fall, but He repaired the Sabbath as well. Hence the day of Resurrection was observed as the day of rest and was called the first day of the week (instead of the seventh) because that's how time had been reckoned from the fall of Adam until the resurrection of Christ. Many observe the Sabbath on the day on which Christ was resurrected as a symbol of his repair of the premature fall and the loss of the original day of rest, going back to the time of Adam and Eve. The original Christians would let one worship on Saturday and would let another worship on Sunday, because as long as one kept the doctrine of Christ and accepted the law of Christ, men and women could figure it out together over time, and eventually one would persuade the other, perhaps not by argument and debate, but by the quiet example that persuades the heart that there's something more to be preferred in one than in the other.[883]

On Sunday, August 7, 1831, the Lord gave instructions about the Sabbath: *And that you may more fully keep yourself unspotted from the world, you shall go to the house of prayer and offer up your sacraments upon my holy day. For verily, this is a day appointed unto you to rest from your labors, and to pay your devotions unto the Most High. Nevertheless, your vows shall be offered up in righteousness on all days and at all times, but remember that on this, the Lord's day, you shall offer your oblations and your sacraments unto the Most High* (T&C 46:3). The following November His command was restated: *And the inhabitants of Zion shall also observe the Sabbath day to keep it holy* (T&C 55:6). It is noteworthy that immediately following the command to teach one's children, there is a warning to observe the Sabbath day to keep it *holy* [consecrated, set apart, distinct from other days].[884] The Lord gives mankind agency in keeping the Sabbath day holy; circumstances for one may be different from another, *and it is not meet that [He] command in all things.... Men should be anxiously engaged in a good cause, and do many things of their own free will, and bring to pass much righteousness* (T&C 45:6).

Sacrament (Lord's Supper) Christ instituted the sacrament during the Passover meal. It was His "last supper" with His closest followers. All the accounts agree on the purpose: to remember the body and blood He would sacrifice on behalf of mankind. When the Lord appeared to the Nephites, He proclaimed He had fulfilled the law (*see* 3 Nephi 7:2). All the rites and sacrifices added through Moses pointed to His great sacrifice of His body and blood. The purpose of the sacrament is to remember Christ, His body that was broken to fulfill the required sacrifice, and His blood that was shed for man's redemption.[885] When the bread is broken and blessed, those who qualify (by having repented and been baptized) receive it as a gift or token from Christ — it is His body. This is to be done *in remembrance of [His] body* (Moroni 4:1). It is through His body that He, the living sacrifice, shows the way to all. "A loving God has died for us. His body is a testimony of life, obedience, sacrifice, cruelty, forgiveness, death, resurrection, immortality, power, and glory. When you remember His life, you should remember all that is associated with it."[886]

When the Lord visited the Nephites, He *commanded that they should eat* (3 Nephi 8:6). This is more than an invitation; it is more than an offering. It is a commandment. What is it about partaking of His sacrament, eating in remembrance of the body of Christ, that must be done? Why would people who had seen, touched, and knelt at the feet of the risen Lord need to partake of the bread as a "witness" and "remembrance" of Him? How did this add to what they had already received? Why is the sacrament sacred enough to be celebrated by the Lord with people who are in His very presence?[887] When people share food with one another, they become part of the same material. When a meal is shared, life is shared. They become one of the same substance. The substance which binds the followers of Christ is that which symbolizes the "body of Christ." Christ "broke" the bread before it was blessed. What does breaking the bread symbolize about Christ? How is His broken body intended to unite His followers with one another, as well as to unite them with Him? Why is the broken bread distributed to those who *shall believe and be baptized in my name*? (3 Nephi 8:6). Does the order matter? Can a person be baptized before they believe, later come to believe, and then receive the sacrament correctly? Or must they come to believe first, then receive baptism second, before it is proper to partake of the sacrament? The Lord's commandments are simple. They can be done by anyone. But they are specific and should be followed in the same manner the Lord instituted them. This is the *strait* path that He says is *narrow* and has *few…that find it* (3 Nephi 13:2). Perhaps it is not found, because men and women proceed with inexactitude to do what He has laid out before them with exactness.[888]

"The sacrament should be taken in the way God commanded. Partake of the sacrament in your families and in your gatherings. Christ commanded it. Follow the pattern in 3 Nephi 8:6–7 and Moroni 4:1. *Kneel down with the church* (Moroni 4:1; JSH 16:24) is how the scriptures direct it to be done. Use wine. If you are opposed to alcohol or have a medical condition that prevents you from using wine, use red grape juice. Use the symbol of the blood of our Lord. Red wine is bitter for a reason. Drinking that bitter wine in remembrance of His blood is symbolic and appropriate."[889] Grape juice changes, through fermentation, into something that affects the senses. The crushed grape — like blood spilled and then allowed to ferment — is a symbol of the great work of the Lord.[890]

Only one who has authority is to bless the sacrament. This suggests something about the sanctity of the sacrament when it is performed in the correct manner. It should be viewed as a "higher ordinance" because of the more exclusive reservation of the "power" conferred by the Lord. This should say something about the manner in which all ought to proceed when blessing and partaking of the sacrament.

The disciples partook first, and after having partaken, they passed it to the multitude. This illustrates the practice of receiving it before being able to pass it to others. It is not possible to pass along what has not first been received. This is true of all the Lord's ordinances. It is one of the reasons Alma rebaptized himself the instant he first began to baptize others (*see* Mosiah 9:8). Those who bless are to be sanctified by partaking, then they pass the sacrament as sanctified ministers. Those who are passing are not more important than the others, but they need to be purified first, so that those to whom they minister may receive the ordinance from those who are already clean.

If the priest performing the sacrament ordinance gets a word wrong or adds a word while pronouncing the blessing, he should repeat the entire sacrament prayer. This shows one's willingness to follow the ordinance with exactness. It should be performed in every particular as the Lord has instructed. When it is performed this way, the promise of having His spirit to always be with them is realized.

He gave unto the disciples and commanded that they should eat. And when they had [eaten] and were filled, he commanded that they should give unto the multitude. And when the multitude had eaten and were filled… (3 Nephi 8:6). The disciples ate until they were *filled*. Does this mean their stomachs were sated? Does it mean their souls were affected? Does it mean both? How were they *filled* by partaking of the bread? Did they need to first be filled themselves before they would be permitted to minister to others? Was that why the Lord required them to first partake, then be filled, before they were commanded to minister to the others? When they ministered to the multitude, what was it they gave to the multitude? Was it the bread alone? Was it also something that had filled them? And then the multitude takes part in eating the bread and *were filled*. This raises the question of how they were filled. Were their stomachs filled because of the amount they ate? Did they eat until they were filled, or did they get filled on just a small amount of bread? Or was this a spiritual filling where each heart was touched and each person's countenance before the Lord filled with light?[2891]

The sacrament is intended to be a *testimony unto the Father that ye do always remember [Him]* (3 Nephi 8:6). This is again identified as a *witness unto...the...Father* (Moroni 4:1), rather than a witness unto anyone else. It is not even a witness unto Christ. Nor is it a witness unto one another. It is a witness unto the Father.[892] The act of testifying is not composed merely of the act of eating the bread. To actually testify to the Father one must first, repent; second, be baptized; third, receive the bread after it has been properly blessed with power; and fourth, remember His body and the ten things symbolized through it — namely, His body as a testimony of life, obedience, sacrifice, cruelty, forgiveness, death, resurrection, immortality, power, and glory. Remembering His life means remembering all that is associated with it. This is the acceptable sacrifice the Father will receive as a *testimony* of Christ. When the sacrament is performed in this way, they will receive power to *have his spirit to be with them*.[893] The sacrament also reminds one of the promised wedding feast. In addition to remembrance of Christ's shed blood and slain body, it foreshadows a final feast with the Lord to celebrate His success in redeeming those who accept His invitation.[894]

"These are simple steps. They are possible to be performed. When they are, the Father receives the act as a testimony before Him of the truth that you do always remember His Son. It will be recorded in Heaven, and will be a witness for your salvation in the Day of Judgment. Since the result is to have His spirit to be with you, it should be a simple matter to determine by reflection if you have His spirit as your companion. If you can feel that He is always with you, then you have an acceptable testimony to the Father. If you do not, then perhaps you should revisit the steps He has provided to see what you might improve. Having Christ's spirit to be with you is significant enough proof that you should know the truth of the matter. Since you know the means by which to judge, see that you judge the matter correctly. Note the prayers all refer to Christ's spirit. This is something apart from the holy ghost. It is Christ's spirit which is to always be with them."[895] "[Having Christ's spirit always with you] is more intimate than touching His side, hands and feet. This is to have His spirit within your touch at all times. You become an extension of Him, properly taking His name upon you. For you are then, indeed, a Christian. He will christen or anoint you, not with the symbol of oil, but with the reality of His spirit. This anointing is the real thing, of which the oil was meant only to testify. The holy ghost was intended to become a companion at the time of baptism. The Spirit of Christ is intended to become a companion in your very person as well. When there are two members of the Godhead represented in your living person, then it is the Father who receives this testimony of you, about you, by you, and for you. You become His, for these three are one."[896]

Sacred Embrace The Book of Mormon account of the risen Lord began with an embrace (*see* 3 Nephi 5:6). The first wound that was felt when the people came to the Lord at Bountiful was an embrace. It was the wound on His side. "The first place He brings you is to Himself, standing in His presence, beside Him, in an embrace, in plain humility, as if any of us were good enough to stand in His presence. That is where it begins. Then His hands, and then as it fully dawns upon you the enormity of the gulf between you and Him, where you end up is kneeling at His feet. It's the wounds on the feet you see last."[897] In 3 Nephi 8:6 the Lord reminded the Nephites that they should remember the body *which [He had] shewn unto [them]*. Partaking of the sacrament in the way that He instituted was to remind them of the sacred embrace and ceremony of recognition they had just participated in with the risen Lord. The Lord could give no greater testimony of what He had done, who He was, and how He served them than by showing to them His risen body still bearing the marks of crucifixion.[898] "In a ceremony of recognition and sacred embrace, you will find that the rites of the LDS temple are a wonderfully accurate preparation for the real event."[899] *See also* CEREMONY OF RECOGNITION.

Sacred Information Almost without exception, people who are unable to keep things *sacred* will never receive exposure to the *most sacred*. When a person treats sacred information in an appropriate way, they *prove* (Abraham 6:2) themselves to be worthy of weightier information. When *it is given unto [them] to know the mysteries of God… they are laid under a strict command that they shall not impart — only according to the portion of his word which he doth grant unto the children* *of men, according to the heed and diligence which they give unto him* (Alma 9:3). That which is holy belongs to those who make themselves holy through their repentance. When the price has been paid, the person is now trusted, and the mysteries have been shown unto them, they possess pearls of great price. Such things do not belong to "swine" who are unclean, unrepentant, unwilling to do what is needed to qualify for the Lord's presence, unthankful, and unholy (*see* 3 Nephi 6:2; T&C 25:2). Entrusting the things that are, in truth, *most sacred* to those who are not qualified will arouse their anger. They will "turn and rend" the humble followers of God (*see* Helaman 2:35) because they will have been shown something that excites their envy, jealousy, hatred, and fear. They know God's chosen has something they lack. They harbor resentment because of what they cannot easily obtain. Therefore, one must carefully measure what is given to others. The final arbiter of the decision to impart is not made by man; it is made by the Lord. Those who are eager to share with others any tidbit of information they learn about the sacred are not helping anyone and may forfeit things themselves. Why would they do such a thing? Is it to make themselves look good — therefore, because of vanity? Is it to try to help others? If it is to help, then the information should not be shared; the manner in which the information is gained should be shared. Teaching another the way to receive sacred information for themselves is charitable. Showing off sacred information is worse than foolish — it will bless no one and will destroy both the unprepared audience and the unwise speaker.[900]

Sacrifice This world is the place of sacrifice. All of humanity came here to make sacrifices. They wanted to come here, knowing it would require sacrifice to produce the faith necessary for salvation — and all gladly came. According to the Lectures on Faith, Christ is the great *prototype of the saved man*. He came and gave Himself as a sacrifice, and mankind is to follow Him if they are to be saved. Men and women came here to lay everything on the altar: their desires, appetites, passions, and everything with which the Lord has blessed them. Abraham put his beloved son on the altar, intending to kill him and then burn his remains because God asked it of him. He did not refuse. However bitter, terrible, and painful the request, the Lord asked it of Abraham, and he proceeded to offer it. No one obtains the faith necessary for salvation unless they are prepared to sacrifice all things to God. Faith for salvation cannot otherwise be obtained (*see* Lectures on Faith). [901] "Now I do not expect anyone to be asked to sacrifice their only child. Nor to be told to kill someone and take their possessions. What I expect is that in the context of the life someone has lived or is living, they will be asked to do, or not do, something which is so specific to them that they alone will understand why it is a sacrifice to them. If asked of another, it may be completely insignificant. But when asked of them, it will be exactly what the person will struggle to place on the Lord's altar. Hence the term sacrifice with its partial meaning of parting with something involving great value to them. However, it is not possible to rule anything in or out — the Lord alone will know you and what is required for you to obtain this faith. The requirements for obtaining this kind of faith are the same for every man or woman who has ever lived. Without making the sacrifice it is not possible to obtain the faith."[902]

Sacrifice is necessary if a person is to have faith. Men and women can believe a lot of things, but if they're going to have faith, it is the order of Heaven that they have to make sacrifice to demonstrate that faith.[903] *And in the last days, before the Lord comes, he is to gather together his saints who have made a covenant with him by sacrifice* (Lectures on Faith 6:9). This is not a covenant *to* sacrifice. One can go make a covenant *to* sacrifice every day the LDS temple is open. Making a covenant *to* sacrifice is not at all the same thing as making a covenant *by* sacrifice. It's only through actually sacrificing that it is possible for the Lord to make a covenant with man: *Our God shall come, and shall not keep silence: a fire shall devour before him, and it shall be very tempestuous round about him. He shall call to the Heavens from above, and to the earth, that he may judge his people. Gather my saints together unto me; those that have made a covenant with me by sacrifice* (Psalms 50:1).[904] Sacrifice is directly related to faith — obtaining faith *requires* sacrifice. It can be had in no other way. When sacrifice is an end in itself, it produces nothing. Sacrifice must be directed toward the correct end, or it fails to produce faith. If sacrifice were in itself an end, then self-denial, self-abuse, and the most extreme practices of asceticism would be noble. But they are not. Rather, they are self-centered and selfish. There is nothing noble about these extremes. They never produce great faith. From Moses to Jesus Christ there was sacrifice performed as a daily rite in Jerusalem (excepting only temporary interludes, including the Babylonian captivity). In spite of performing daily sacrifices, the people most directly involved had no visitations from angels, had no revelations, received no audience with God, and performed no miracles. When Christ came to fulfill the law of sacrifice, the ones performing the sacrifices were the least willing to accept Him. The sacrifices they had and were performing had no faith-producing effects for them. Sacrifice must, therefore, be connected with a proper understanding of how it relates to something higher. Sacrifices are not intended to teach one *how to* sacrifice; they are intended to teach an underlying truth. If there is no understanding of that underlying truth, then the act of sacrifice can become a meaningless end in itself. Almost any principle of the Gospel can become a misleading end in itself. The Gospel is a harmony of principles correctly weighed and measured. It is a symphony, and not a single, bloated, and distorted note. The underlying truth sacrifice teaches is simple. All great truths are simple. If they were not, then they could not be obtained by the weak, simple, and childlike — and, of course, it was and is to such persons that the Gospel has always been primarily directed. Sacrifice is a tool that is given to change one's heart and realign one to being less materialistic and more spiritual. Men and women can only let in "one light" at a time — they are so constituted to be able to focus on only one thing at a time. One must necessarily choose between all other things and that one thing. Christ is teaching, through sacrifice, how to choose God above all else. Sacrifice allows men and women to show, by their choice, that what they lay upon the altar is not more treasured to them than God's will for them. By laying themselves and their emotional needs on the altar and sacrificing the things this world values, they are saying and proving they choose the other world to this one. They value the things of the spirit above the material things of this existence. It is another affirmation that they would prefer to have their existence filled with things of the spirit, rather than filled with the materialism of the world.[905] "I used to think having the right heart must precede action to be of any worth. What I have found instead is that action can lead the heart. Christ's

Sermon on the Mount is a call to action. Do the things asked by Him and the heart will follow. The mind can lead the heart. The heart does not always have to go first."[906]

Saint The English word saint is derived from the Latin *sanctus* (holy). The typical use of the Greek word *hagios* (ἅγιος) in the KJV (which is defined usually as holy, sacred, pure, sanctified, consecrated, or separated) is *holy* in 161 instances, *saint(s)* 61 times, and *Holy One* 4 times.[907] "Saints" are *supposed* to be identified as baptized followers of Christ—holy, sacred, consecrated, and pure—and in the scriptures they often are, but historically they have also fallen short of that description. Sanctification is the process of becoming a saint. *For the natural man is an enemy to God…and will be for ever and ever but if he yields to the enticings of the holy spirit, and putteth off the natural man, and becometh a saint through the atonement of Christ the Lord* (Mosiah 1:16).[908] It is a godly aspiration to become a saint or belong to the body of saints. Sainthood is not defined in the scriptures the same way modern religions portray formally-recognized and canonized individuals—although some (including Mother Teresa and St. Francis of Assisi) have been exemplary role models for Christians and non-Christians alike. In an age of darkness and apostasy, the Lord spoke with St. Francis and sent angels to minister to him. He is appropriately referred to as a Saint. He lived the Sermon on the Mount. It is perhaps St. Francis who, above all others, proves a mortal may walk in the Lord's steps. Christ did it first and more completely than any other would. But St. Francis surely followed.[909] Many religious organizations—including The Church of Jesus Christ of Latter-day Saints, headquartered in Salt Lake City, Utah (the largest denomination claiming Joseph Smith as their founder), as well as the Community of Christ, headquartered in Independence, Missouri (the second largest denomination)—equate the term "saint" with the term "member" and believe them to be synonymous. *See also* SANCTIFICATION.

Salem The Hebrew is *shâlêm* (שׁלם), "peace."[910] Salem is used consistently throughout the Joseph Smith Translation of the Bible (*see* Genesis 7:14,20; Psalms 76:1), and the Book of Mormon confirms that *Melchizedek was a king over the land of Salem* (Alma 10:2), which may be interpreted as a land of peace. Joseph Smith said that the word *salem* should be correctly rendered *shalom,* meaning peace.[911] "It is understood by many by reading [Hebrews 1:17] that Melchesedeck was king of some country or nation on the earth, but it was not so. In the original it reads king of Shaloam, which signifies king of peace or righteousness, and not of any country or nation."[912] "Salem is designed for a Hebrew term. It should be Shiloam, which signifies righteousness and peace."[913] "Since the King James Version of the New Testament comes from Greek manuscripts, the transliteration of Σαλήμ (given as Salem) in [Hebrews 1:17] is correct."[914] *See also* MELCHIZEDEK.

Salvation Getting to know the Lord (*see* John 9:19).[915] The teachings of the Savior most clearly show the nature of salvation and what He proposed to the human family when He proposed to save them — He wanted to make them like unto Himself, and He was like the Father, the great prototype of all saved beings: *And for any portion of the human family to be assimilated into their likeness is to be saved; and to be unlike them is to be destroyed: and on this hinge turns the door of salvation* (Lectures on Faith 7:16). *For salvation consists in the glory, authority, majesty, power and dominion which Jehovah possesses, and in nothing else; and no being can possess it but himself or one like him* (Lectures on Faith 7:10). "Salvation means a man's being placed beyond the powers of all his enemies" (*TPJS*, 301).[916] Being saved means to have increase.[917] "There isn't going to be any man or group of men who save you. There is literally a single way and a single source. That is Christ (Mosiah 1:16). Whether you are able to receive salvation or not is entirely dependent on how you respond to Him, not to other people (2 Nephi 6:11)."[918] There is no collective salvation. Each person comes to Him one at a time. Even when He redeems a group, He visits with them individually (*see* 3 Nephi 5:5–7).[919] "To speak of Christ is necessarily to speak of salvation. To understand Christ is to understand salvation. Salvation requires of us what was required of Christ. We cannot be different from Christ and be saved, because salvation depends upon being precisely what He is and nothing else. Despite how plainly this is put, we still seem not to comprehend."[920] "Remember, when you climb up a ladder, you must begin at the bottom and ascend step by step until you arrive at the top; and so it is with the principles of the Gospel — you must begin with the first, and go on until you learn all the principles of exaltation. But it will be a great while after you have passed through the veil before you will have learned them" (*TPJS*, 348; *WJS*, 350). Christ came to complete His salvation and attain to the resurrection of the dead. All men and women will need to do likewise to be saved.[921]

The prototype of the saved man is Jesus Christ. If any man will be saved, he must be precisely what Christ is and nothing else, because Christ attained to the resurrection. All men and women are going to be resurrected, but it was Christ who attained to the resurrection for their benefit. On the other side of mankind's resurrection, they won't hold the keys of death and hell — He will. "He'll use them for your benefit, but ultimately you are going to have to hold the keys of death and hell if you are going to be precisely what the prototype of the saved man is or else not be saved."[922]

Therefore, come unto me and be ye saved. For verily I say unto you that except ye shall keep my commandments which I have commanded you at this time, ye shall in no case enter into the kingdom of Heaven (3 Nephi 5:23). "There goes the argument that all you need do to be saved is 'confess Jesus.' It doesn't work that way. You must keep His commandments. If you don't, then *ye shall in no case enter into the kingdom of Heaven*. It is not possible to *come unto [Him]* and *be saved* without also keeping His commandments. It is the only true measure of coming to Him. And *except ye shall keep [His] commandments…ye can in no case enter into the kingdom of Heaven*. Entry is barred unless you follow Him. If He needed baptism to enter, then clearly we do as well. Righteousness comes by obedience. Obedience requires action. Without conforming conduct to the Lord's commandments, it is impossible to enter into the kingdom of Heaven."[923]

Sanctification The baptism of fire and the holy ghost is for sanctification. It is done upon the body and the Spirit within each person.[924] The work of this "baptism of fire" is always sanctification. It brings the recipient into greater contact with God. The end of that increasing contact is to receive the Son, through whose blood all can be sanctified (*see* Genesis 4:9). Once sanctified, one is prepared for the presence of the Father (*see* Alma 21:3; 1 Nephi 3:5).[925] It is the companionship of the Spirit that makes one justified by leading him or her to do what is right. It is the resulting application of Christ's blood on one's behalf that sanctifies (*see* Genesis 4:9). One cannot receive sanctification without first receiving baptism and then also the holy ghost.[926] "In effect, you receive holiness through the sanctifying power of the Holy Spirit. This in turn makes your own spirit holy."[927] Man is unworthy to enter into God's presence and, therefore, requires a power higher than his own from which to borrow purity. This purifying agent is the holy ghost (*see* 3 Nephi 9:3–4). Christ will administer the final rites and confer the final blessings only upon the pure (*see* 3 Nephi 9:4–5). The reference to "blood" as sanctifying is a reference to the Lord (*see* Genesis 4:9). He alone sanctifies.[928] Christ sanctifies mankind; they don't sanctify themselves.[929] "To be purified, to be sanctified by the Lamb — removing from you, and taking upon Himself the responsibility to answer for whatever failings you have — this is not ritual purity. This is purity in fact. To be sanctified is to be qualified to stand in the presence of God without sin, clean of all blood and sin — righteous forever. He is Christ's, and Christ is the Father's, and all that each of them will be is the same; for we shall see Him as He is, because we will be like Him. To be like Him is to be sanctified."[930]

Satan A title that means "accuser," "opponent," and "adversary"; hence, once he fell, Lucifer became — or in other words, was called — Satan because he accuses others and opposes the Father (*see* Revelation 4:3; 8:6). The Lord rebuked Peter and called him Satan because he was wrong in opposing the Father's will for Him, and Peter understood and repented. There are those who have been Satan, accusing one another, wounding hearts, and causing jarring, contention, and strife by their accusations.[931] Satan was (and is) an angel. He is described as *an angel of God who was in authority in the presence of God* (T&C 69:6) *and was cast down* (T&C 157:7). Such a being does not look vile. Visually, he may appear to have light and glory. Although a liar, he uses his appearance as a pretense to be an angel of light. Moses was able to discern between Satan and an actual messenger from God, but that had nothing to do with the appearance of Satan. It was because of the content of the message. Moses distinguished between his message and the Lord's. The Lord's was a message of glory, which is intelligence, or in other words, light and truth. Satan's message takes one into a dark and dreary waste.[932] *See also* ACCUSE; LUCIFER.

Scales of Darkness Joseph restored a faith demanding that men and women awake and arise. They must ask God to remove the scales that blind them (*see* 2 Nephi 12:12). The blinding "scales" are a darkness *and* an incorrect weight and measure. There is no reason to err, because all men and women can ask God for the answer. If one's judgment is not just, their dark scales will condemn them. Care is required to correctly distinguish between what is God's and what is the devil's.[933]

School of the Prophets A theological training program where lectures were prepared to instruct early members of the Mormon priesthood on how to acquire faith. The series of lectures was formalized and adopted as scripture — titled "Lectures on Faith" — and included in the 1835 canon.[934]

Scripture Inspired writings containing information either directly quoting the Lord or containing lessons, experiences, events, or words of instruction that honor God. To be acknowledged, a conference must adopt the writing as part of a canon. People who are in a living covenant with God always have an open canon and expect additional scripture.[935]

Sealed in Their Foreheads "[To] seal the servants of God in their foreheads, etc. …means to seal the blessing on their heads meaning the everlasting covenant thereby making their calling & election sure."[936]

Sealing Power There are three kinds of sealing authority. The first is given at the founding of a dispensation. As a dispensation head, the first form of sealing power is given to establish a covenant for the benefit of those living then and thereafter. Joseph Smith was given a dispensation. This first form of priesthood is only given to men by God. The second is embedded in authoritative ordinance. All dispensations must follow the covenant giver's ordinances or preserve the ordinance as established through the dispensation head. For as long as the ordinances are kept intact, the covenant is in effect. The condition of being faithful remains part of the ordinance, and the ordinance must be practiced faithfully and cannot be changed, or it is broken. If these conditions are met, the covenant is sealed by the Holy Spirit of Promise, and the blessing is secured. This second form of sealing power is not dependent on the presence of a dispensation head and can be a limited sealing authority. This form of sealing is conditional. God is not bound by anything that is one iota different from His word. It can be passed from man-to-man, from generation to generation, and remains in full force and effect for so long as the covenant is unbroken. The third kind of sealing power goes beyond either of the first two. It is given only in rare circumstances and for highly specific purposes. With it, man has the authority to control the elements. This was held by Christ and given to Enoch, Melchizedek, Moses, and Elijah. This was the reason Christ declared that no man could take His life, but He could both lay it down and take it up again. Every individual with this authority must choose to give their lives up willingly. Their lives cannot be taken. This third form is extremely rare and involves an extraordinary combination of mortality and immortality, in which God has faith in a man. All those given this third form of sealing power have only one objective: saving the souls of men. [937]

Second Comforter *See* COMFORTER, THE SECOND

Seed of Abraham Those who hearken to the same God that Abraham hearkened to. The seed of Abraham have an obligation and a ministry to bear testimony that the God of Abraham lives and that He is *the* God over the whole earth; they also testify that His work began with Adam and won't wrap up until the second coming of Christ in judgment on the world — to save and redeem those that look for Him. The Lord explains what Abraham's descendants are going to inherit: *And thou shalt be a blessing unto thy seed after thee, that in their hands they shall bear this ministry and priesthood unto all nations. And I will bless them through thy name; for as many as receive this gospel shall be called after thy name and shall be accounted thy seed, and shall rise up and bless thee, as unto their Father. And I will bless them that bless thee and curse them that curse thee. And in thee (that is, in thy Priesthood) and in thy seed, (that is, thy Priesthood) — for I give unto thee a promise that this right shall continue in thee and in thy seed after thee* (Abraham 3:1). The record of Abraham was given in order to understand the covenant that God made with Abraham and to vindicate the promise that's made in the Book of Mormon. If the Book of Mormon was translated by the gift and power of God, the Book of Abraham was translated no differently, only by the gift and power of God. It includes information that's vital for men and women to understand so they can inherit the same gospel that was given to Abraham. In so doing, they can lay hold upon the same blessings that were given to Abraham and realize that the covenants that were made with the Fathers can be understood, activated, and realized — and they can obtain those same blessings here in the last days. Joseph's work had to necessarily include recovery of the covenants with Abraham. One may regard himself as a gentile, but the covenant that was made with Abraham makes one a descendant of Abraham if he hearkens to that same God and receives that same gospel. If gentiles are willing to receive what God has offered, then they're numbered among the house of Israel (*see* 1 Nephi 3:25; 3 Nephi 9:11). The Book of Mormon reveals that God made a covenant with Abraham in the beginning and at the end; God intends to vindicate the covenant that was made with Abraham by changing gentiles into the house of Israel — by covenant. Abraham looked forward to having seed that would be countless, despite only having one son. "The time will come when everyone who receives this gospel — that is, the gospel that Abraham had in his possession, a gospel that is unfolding in front of your eyes today — that [gospel] will continue to unfold until all of its covenants, rights, obligations, privileges, [and] understandings will all roll out. The Restoration will be completed, but the promise was made to Abraham that whenever the gospel is on the earth, those who receive it will acknowledge Abraham as their covenant father, the father of the righteous."[938]

Seed of Christ Those who accept Christ as their father; those who receive Him to be their parent and His offspring; and those who become the begotten sons and daughters of God. They are also referred to as *heirs of the Kingdom*. They are spirit children of God the Father, but they have to come here and become born again — become the seed of Christ, who is both the Father and the Son. Those who benefit from all this and who are the seed of the Savior are those who are connected with Him by adoption, by affiliation, and otherwise.[939] *And thus God breaketh the bands of death, having gained the victory over death, giving the Son power to make intercession for the children of men, having ascended into Heaven, having the bowels of mercy, being filled with compassion toward the children of men, standing betwixt them and justice, having broken the bands of death, having taken upon himself their iniquity* *and their transgressions, having redeemed them and satisfied the demands of justice. And now I say unto you, who shall declare his generation? Behold, I say unto you that when his soul has been made an offering for sin, he shall see his seed. And now what say ye? And who shall be his seed? Behold, I say unto you that whosoever has heard the words of the prophets, yea, all the holy prophets who have prophesied concerning the coming of the Lord, I say unto you that all those who have hearkened unto their words, and believed that the Lord would redeem his people, and have looked forward to that day for a remission of their sins, I say unto you that these are his seed, or they are heirs of the kingdom of God* (Mosiah 8:7–8). Salvation is tied to accepting prophets actually sent by Christ, not pretenders He has not spoken with. Joseph taught, "Whenever men can find out the will of God and find an administrator legally authorized from God, there is the kingdom of God; but where these are not, the kingdom of God is not."[940] If man can find anyone sent by God, there is the kingdom of God. This is a true principle. Someone is sent to declare a message. Any who hear and hearken will become His seed. This is how men and women obtain faith, and faith brings them to meet God. "We will find redemption, hear His voice, and become holy because His word is in us. We will have no doubt about our salvation because He will declare it in His own voice to us."[941] *See also* RAISE UP SEED.

Seer The concept captured by the title "seer" involves sight. Seeing is the hallmark of the seer. They have vision.[942] A seer is someone who has knowledge of things which cannot be seen with the natural eye.[943] When Joseph Smith received the Urim and Thummin from an angel, he was told: *the possession and use of these stones were what constituted seers in ancient or former times…* (JSH 3:3; *see also* Mosiah 5:13). When anyone has possession of such an instrument, they are, by definition, a seer; the instrument itself allows the possessor to see the past, present, and future. However, it is not necessary to possess this instrument to be a seer.[944] Whenever hidden knowledge is revealed to a person, the recipient is a seer. Whether they have a Urim and Thummim or not, anyone receiving Divine revelation of future or past events has the gift of seership.[945] It remains the calling of a seer to reveal things which are secret or hidden.[946] Seers have a responsibility to teach others or, if their contemporary generation rejects them, to leave a written testimony for future generations.[947]

Any people who have a seer among them gain knowledge of things as they are, as they were, and as they are to come.[948] Mankind needs living seers, or they are cut off from one of the gifts intended to guide them.[949] Seership and exaltation are connected.[950] "There is no reason you cannot also receive the gift of seership to guide you as occasion requires. The knowledge of some things requires you to behold the past, present and future."[951] Seership is a voluntary process; anyone who is willing to follow the path to get there may climb the mountain and see into the distance.[952] Seership is something that all ought to expect will be included in the Lord's tutelage while they are here.[953]

Selflessness Surrendering all to God. "The Lord frees us through selflessness. It is the great escape from our earthly prison. We must lose ourselves if we want to find Him. We must surrender our will to His to find the same freedom that He enjoyed. This does not mean surrender to *men*. It means surrender to Him. He never asked us to follow another man. We are supposed to be selfless in responding to the Lord's demands, not to the demands of any man or men. The difference is profound."[954]

Self-Reliance King Benjamin struck the perfect balance on the subject of self-reliance. His example was his greatest sermon. King Benjamin refused to tax or oppress his people, although he could have done so as the monarch. Instead, he labored with his own hands and spent his life serving his people. He governed to end the servitude that had been allowed under the law of Moses. Long before Christ would do so, king Benjamin freed men from slavery. But it came at a social cost. Servitude was limited under Moses' law to six years; in the seventh year, the servant was freed (*see* Exodus 13:1). So without servitude to repay debt, some were forced to beg. For the sake of the impoverished, king Benjamin taught his people to give to beggars. He expected his people to notice them and not allow them to petition in vain for relief of their needs. He forbade withholding from beggars because of the convenient thought that beggars deserved their direful condition. According to king Benjamin, all are beggars (*see* Mosiah 2). No one is (or can ever be) anything more than a beggar, dependent upon God. God gives everyone the power to live. He gives them the power to breathe and the ability to move and do what they will. God lends all of this to man so he can choose according to his own wishes. Since all are beggars, utterly dependent on God for their very existence, they have nothing to brag of and no legitimate claim to self-reliance. That recognition is what motivated king Benjamin, though a monarch, to humbly labor for his own support. In this modern day of abundance, men and women are easily misled into thinking the blessings of their productive society permit them to be self-reliant. Of course, abundance is only temporary. The principles upon which current society's prosperity was built have been discarded. Therefore, one's *riches [will become] slippery* (Helaman 5:8), as the fruit of true principles vanish from those who dishonor the foundation upon which that prosperity was conferred. In the coming scarcity of the last days, safety will only be found in Zion. Zion will require the laborer to labor only for Zion, not for himself (*see* 2 Nephi 11:17), and together all will perform the required great labor to build and sustain the society. No one can expect to eat or be clothed in Zion if he or she does not work to produce the necessities. Benjamin's talk provides a framework for Zion.[955]

"The hopelessness of man's presumed independence from God is stressed in His statement that by taking thought none of us *can add one cubit unto his stature* [Matthew 3:37; Luke 8:23; 3 Nephi 6:1]. Our lives are not ours. They belong to Him. We have no independence from Him. We are NOT self-existent beings. We borrow all we are and have from Him. Even, as it turns out, the dust from which we are made belongs to Him. If God gives us air to breathe, power to exist, the capacity to move, and sustains all of us from moment to moment, then how little faith is required to rely on Him to provide His disciples with food and raiment? The purpose of putting a man in such a dependent state before God is not to find out whether God can take care of him. God already knows what a man needs before he should even ask. But the man will, by becoming so dependent upon God, acquire a broken heart and a contrite spirit, always quick to ask, quick to listen, quick to do. Vulnerability makes a man strong in spirit. Security and wealth make a man incorrectly believe in his independence from God. He wants His disciples to be dependent upon Him. He wants them praying, and then grateful to Him for what He provides. He wants them, in a word, to become holy."[956]

Seraphim One of the classes of the Powers of Heaven, seraphim dwell in everlasting burnings. They are the glorious ones in flames of glory (*see* T&C 123:22).[957] The Hebrew verb *śārāph* means "to burn" and may be applied to their extraordinary brightness and fiery appearance. Seraphim are the burning, fiery ones, and the word literally means "fiery snakes or serpents." A number of biblical verses associate seraphim with snakes or serpents. The Lord sent *fiery serpents* [seraphim] *among the people* and ordered Moses to *make a fiery serpent* [saraph] *and set it upon a pole* (Numbers 10:7). Seraphim are described as Heavenly beings that stand above the throne of God, proclaiming holiness, and who are able to minister to mortals (*see* Isaiah 2:1–2).

Servant *See* ANGEL.

Seventy A quorum established in 1835 whose primary responsibility was missionary work. The quorum was originally established to be equal in authority to the First Presidency and Quorum of the Twelve and was comprised of seventy members. Following the death of Joseph Smith, the Seventy were considered inferior to the Quorum of the Twelve and First Presidency and acquired administrative authority beyond missionary responsibility. They are considered part of the General Authorities of the LDS Church and preside over all the church under the direction of the First Presidency and Twelve.[958]

Sheol *Hades*, the Greek, or *Sheol*, the Hebrew, these two significations mean "a world of spirits." *Hades*, *Sheol*, paradise, and spirits in prison all mean the same thing. It is a world of spirits.[959]

Shew An archaic spelling of the word *show*, including its noun and verb forms of *shewed*, *shewn*, and *shewing*, which is never pronounced "shoo," even in combination with *shewbread*. "In almost every instance [within the Book of Mormon], the earliest textual sources prefer the archaic verb shew rather than the more modern show. In the early transmission of the text, some of these examples of shew were accidentally replaced by the more expected show. In fact, it is possible that in the original text there were no examples of show, only shew.[960]

Shewbread The ancient temple had ascending levels of holiness that were symbolically separated by degrees on the basis of who was excluded. The fewer the number of people permitted to enter, the greater the associated holiness. In ascending degrees of holiness, the outer court area (where sacrifices and killings took place) was the first degree of holiness. All Israel was welcomed there. The second degree of holiness was the area immediately inside the temple building called the Holy Place. In it there was a table for shewbread (sometimes referred to as "showbread" in scripture), an altar of incense, and the menorah or seven-branched candlestick. In this area the priests alone were permitted to enter.[961] The shewbread consisted of twelve unleavened loaves that were placed every Sabbath in the temple on the table beside the altar of incense and eaten by the priests at the end of the week (*see* Exodus 25:30; Matthew 12:4). Tyndale's use of the word shewbread or showbread was based or influenced by Luther's German translation of earlier texts into *Schaubrot,* translating from the Latin *panes propositiones,* as well as the Greek *artai enopioi* and Hebrew *lechem panim* (lechem "bread" + panim "face, presence"). Old English bible translations used the expression *offring-hlafas* ("offering loaves").[962] Shewbread is literally the bread set before the face of the Lord or bread of the presence. "This had been consumed every Sabbath by the priests, and was their 'most holy portion' eaten in the holy place."[963]

Signs Faith is not produced by signs, but signs follow those who believe (*see* T&C 50:3). That is why Pharaoh was never impressed by the things God did through Moses — signs are inconsequential if one does not have faith. Signs are not controlled by men but are God's to give as God determines (*see* T&C 50:3). They should not be the subject of boasting (*see* T&C 82:22). "Some of the most remarkable signs that have been given to me are only silently recorded in my journal. Signs exist — they have been given to testify of this work. Many of the signs recorded in the lives of believers may be unknown to you, but there are signs in rich abundance among believers today." The adulterous are the ones who seek signs, according to our Lord, and He said it twice — Matthew's account includes Him saying it to two different audiences on two different occasions (*see* Matthew 6:15; 8:15). Adulterers are sign seekers.[964] When signs attract followers, the resulting congregation of followers are all vulnerable to the sin of adultery. This is one of the reasons why so many were adulterers in Nauvoo, as well as later in Utah and today among various splinter groups. It is a plague that can only be avoided by removing adulterous thoughts from the heart.[965] Contrary to what many have heard all their lives about "signs," they are and always have been part of the true Gospel. They invariably follow faith but do not and never have produced faith (see T&C 50:3). There are examples of signs throughout God's dealings with those who follow Him (see, e.g., Helaman 5:10; Ezekiel 12:4; Exodus 7:1; and Acts 2:1). Men and women are supposed to see signs, so that they may know God is with them.[966]

Signs of the Times Mankind is approaching the moment in which the Lord is about to return (see Matthew 11). All of the signs that He speaks of will occur in one single generation, and the signs have begun to appear. This means those now alive are living within a generation in which a great deal is to occur. As it was in the days of Noah, so is it about to be — on the one hand, dreadful things are coming; but it also means that prophets are again going to be among man, people with messages that come from the Lord.[967] There is a great difference between recognizing the "signs of the times" and knowing the detail of how prophecy will be fulfilled. An example of the difference is found in Matthew. Matthew tells of "wise men" who studied the scriptures, watched the signs in the Heavens, recognized a "star" that testified of the birth of the Messiah or newborn "king of the Jews," traveled a great distance (perhaps as long as two years) to worship Him, facilitated fulfilling prophecy by their presence in Jerusalem, and were visited by God in a dream. Despite all the wise men were able to know, they did not know where to find the newborn king. They mistakenly went to Herod's people to inquire about Christ's birth. They did not know, and God did not reveal to them, that Christ would be born in Bethlehem. It is unlikely they would have willingly acted to fulfill the Jeremiah 12:7 slaughter of children, yet Matthew credits their involvement with fulfilling this prophecy (see Matthew 1:11). Can men unwittingly fulfill prophecy? Can anyone, even wise men who are well-studied in scripture and prophecy, ever fully understand prophecy? One of the lessons from this scriptural account is that all "wise men" whose diligence and faithfulness lead them to understand God's hand is at work may still not understand how or where God will act. There remain "mysteries" which God will accomplish but men cannot understand beforehand. If the wise men knew He had been born but could not identify where Christ's birth happened (despite all else they were able to do), then how can anyone know how God will accomplish His "strange act" in the last days? Prophecies are not given so man can know details beforehand. They are given so that when they are fulfilled, one may understand that God knows the end from the beginning (*see* Isaiah 17:1).[968] The heavenly signs in the lights of the firmament are testifying and confirming many of the events currently happening on the earth. Very few today are giving them any notice.[969] These "signs" in the lights of heaven are meant to be seen and understood by the unaided human eye from the surface of the earth.[970]

Sin A violation of a commandment (*see also* INIQUITY). The sins that offend God are not the errors, weaknesses, and foolishness of the past. He is offended when one is forgiven by Him and then returns to the same sin. That shows a lack of gratitude for His forgiveness. Even then, however, there are addictions, compulsions, and weaknesses that people sometimes struggle with for years, even decades. "When the sin is due to some difficulty based on biology, physiology or an inherent weakness that we fight for years to overcome, then His patience with us is far greater than our own. He will help in the fight. He will walk alongside you as you fight. He does not expect you to run faster than you have strength. When, because of age or infirmity, a troubling weakness is at last overcome, He will readily accept your repentance and let you move forward clean, whole and forgiven. That is His ministry — to forgive and make whole."[971] The only one who can forgive sin is Christ. He requires men and women to forgive one another but will Himself determine whose sins He will forgive (*see* T&C 51:3). He is the only gatekeeper for forgiveness (*see* 2 Nephi 6:11).[972] The Greek word *hamartia* (ἁμαρτία) defines *sin* as missing the mark; not hitting the target; a mistake.[973] "Sin is waste. It is doing one thing when you should be doing other and better things for which you have the capacity. Hence, there are no innocent idle thoughts. That is why even the righteous must repent, constantly and progressively, since all fall short of their capacity and calling."[974] *See also* TRANSGRESSION.

Single to God When God occupies a place of priority in one's life; He is central. It does not mean one neglects his family nor his labors.[975] *See also* T&C 86:12.

Slow of Speech *And when Enoch had heard these words, he bowed himself to the earth before the Lord, and spoke before the Lord, saying, Why is it that I have found favor in thy sight, and am but a lad, and all the people hate me, for I am slow of speech; wherefore am I thy servant?* (Genesis 4:2). Being "slow of speech" does not mean Enoch was inarticulate or somehow impaired. He was not at all "slow." He was a brilliant man. He was an articulate man. He was a most capable man. He wrote the record which Moses preserved in his account and Joseph Smith restored to us by revelation. He was always envisioned anciently as the Great Scribe. He was thought by antiquity (by the Egyptians) to be the one who brought wisdom, who brought knowledge (Thoth). This phrase clearly means something else. He is "slow of speech" because he would rather think about things than talk about them. He would rather consider a matter carefully than speak quickly about it. He would rather be left alone than to make public declarations. He would rather have his privacy, his family, and a few close intimate friends than he would to minister to people who don't give a damn about what he has to say. He would have preferred to avoid contact with those who think he is a wild man come among them, because they believe he has no business delivering the message. He was trusted by the Lord precisely because the message was the Lord's, and Enoch would not add to it because he craved attention. In other words, being "slow of speech" is a qualifier for Enoch as the Lord's messenger, not a handicap.[976]

Small Means When God undertakes to accomplish something, *there is nothing that the Lord God shall take in His heart to do, but what He will do it* (Abraham 5:4). Often the means used by the Lord to accomplish His "strange act" and to perform His "strange work" (*see* T&C 101:20) are very small indeed. *Now ye may suppose that this is foolishness in me, but behold, I say unto you that by small and simple things are great things brought to pass, and small means in many instances doth confound the wise. And the Lord God doth work by means to bring about his great and eternal purposes, and by very small means the Lord doth confound the wise and bringeth about the salvation of many souls* (Alma 17:8). It is almost always the case that the Lord uses simple things to confound the mighty.[977] The Lord has a way of bringing great things to pass through small measures.[978] Is not the pattern always the same? Does not God manifest Himself to the world through the weak things first (*see* T&C 54:4)? He uses such small means they are unseen except through faith. Only when the small means accomplish what God foretold are they mighty to save. Only the scriptures are able to define what matters and how God's hand is moving to fulfill His promises.[979] God uses "small means" and "simple things" to accomplish His greatest influence.[980]

Son of Perdition An angel can fall from grace only by being cast out of Heaven (*see* 2 Nephi 1:9). When an angel falls, he becomes a devil. For these, it would be better if they had never known Christ, for they have decided to crucify Him anew. After having had the holy spirit make great things known unto them, they have turned against the Lord by their knowing rebellion against Him (*see* T&C 69:7). They are sons of perdition, and the Heavens weep over them (*see* T&C 69:6–7). These are they who know the battle is and always has been the Lord's, and they either align themselves with Him or against Him.[981] *See also* UNPARDONABLE SIN.

Sons and Daughters of God Before the world was created, everyone was a child of God. However, in the fullest sense of the term, the real gospel objective is to elect whether or not one will *become* sons and daughters of God. This new acknowledged status means being accepted by God into His family.[982] Christ said of Himself in Ether 1:13: *Behold, I am he who was prepared from the foundation of the world to redeem my people. Behold, I am Jesus Christ. I am the Father and the Son. In me shall all mankind have life; and that eternally, even they who shall believe on my name. And they shall become my sons and my daughters.* This is the way men and women may become sons of God. The One who redeems them becomes their Father, and therefore, He who is the Only Begotten of the Father in turn begets many sons and daughters (*see* T&C 69:5).[983] "The Father declares what is right and true, and His Son obeys. Thus, the Son became the Word of God because He did what the Father asked Him. Do you want to be a son or daughter of God? Do what He asks. This is what we must do to worship Him."[984] Abinadi declared Christ would be *called the Son of God* (Mosiah 8:5). He explained He was "called" because He *subjected the flesh to the will of the*

Father. "We cannot be the Son of God the Father unless we subject our will to Him. We are His 'Son' when we are like Him because we obey Him. This was how Christ defined Himself."[985] Abinadi understood God. *And now I say unto you, who shall declare his generation? Behold, I say unto you that when his soul has been made an offering for sin, he shall see his seed. And now what say ye? And who shall be his seed? Behold, I say unto you that whosoever has heard the words of the prophets, yea, all the holy prophets who have prophesied concerning the coming of the Lord, I say unto you that all those who have hearkened unto their words, and believed that the Lord would redeem his people, and have looked forward to that day for a remission of their sins, I say unto you that these are his seed, or they are heirs of the kingdom of God. For these are they whose sins he hath borne; these are they for whom he has died, to redeem them from their transgressions. And now, are they not his seed? Yea, and are not the prophets, every one that has opened his mouth to prophesy that has not fallen into transgression? (I mean all the holy prophets ever since the world began.) I say unto you that they are his seed* (Mosiah 8:7).[986] The Holy Order after the Order of the Son of God makes those who inherit it, by definition, the sons of God. Therefore, in a way, calling it the Holy Order after the Order of the Son of God is a way of identifying the recipient as someone who has become one of God's sons.[987] Even though a couple may be mortals in the flesh, they are by definition "sons of God" if they belong to the Order. It is the nature of this Holy Order that it is conferred upon the man and woman jointly (*see* 1 Corinthians 1:44).[988]

Soothsayers Those who make predictions by using means other than true prophecy. Modern application of soothsaying may exist in business, government, economics, weather — especially long-term weather — politics, etc.[989] It is foretelling for gain, profit, popularity, or influence without God's commission and direction.[990]

Soul/Spirit/Body of Man The definition of "soul" — given through Joseph Smith years prior to his translation of the Book of Abraham — was the "spirit and the body" together: *And the spirit and the body is the soul of man* (T&C 86:2). Christ, as well as the "noble and great," were all embodied and therefore resurrected beings before this world. They were "souls." *Now the Lord had shewn unto me, Abraham, the intelligences that were organized before the world was, and among all these there were many of the noble and great ones. And God saw* *these souls, that they were good, and he stood in the midst of them* (Abraham 6:1).[991] Joseph Smith said, "God made a tabernacle and put a spirit into it, and it became a living soul. (Refers to the old Bible.) How does it read in the Hebrew? It does not say in the Hebrew that God created the spirit of man. It says, 'God made man out of the earth and put into him Adam's spirit, and so became a living body.'"[992] (Cf. Genesis 2:11: *And I, the Lord God, formed man from the dust of the ground and breathed into Adam his spirit or the breath of life, and man became a living soul, the first flesh upon the Earth, the first man also.*) "In tracing the thing to the foundation and looking at it philosophically, we shall find a very material difference between the body and the spirit. The body is supposed to be organized matter, and the spirit by many is thought to be immaterial, without substance. With this latter statement we should beg leave to differ and state that spirit is a substance, that it is material, but that it is more pure, elastic, and refined matter than the body — that it existed before the body, can exist in the body, and will exist separate from the body, when the body will be moldering in the dust, and will in the resurrection be again united with it. Without attempting to describe this mysterious connection and the laws that govern the body and spirit of man, their relationship to each other, and the design of God in relation to the human body and spirit, I would just remark that the spirits of men are eternal, that they are governed by the same priesthood that Abraham, Melchizedek, and the apostles were: that they are organized according to that priesthood which is everlasting — *without beginning of days or end of years* [Hebrews 1:17] — that they all move in their respective spheres and are governed by the law of God, that when they appear upon the earth they are in a probationary state and are preparing, if righteous, for a future and a greater glory."[993]

Speak with the Tongue of Angels To have knowledge and inspiration that reckons from heaven itself; to be elevated by "fire" which purges sins and purifies — in effect, to receive holiness through the sanctifying power of the Holy Spirit. This, in turn, makes one's *own spirit* holy. "Your spirit or your ghost is within you, connected to heaven to such a degree through this process that you are in possession of a 'holy spirit' or a 'holy ghost' within you."[994] To speak with a new tongue is to speak worthily of sacred things. It is to correctly weigh the truth of a matter, to know by the power of the spirit that what is said is true and in conformity with God's will, and then to speak it. It is to render sacred the vessel by the things it holds. To speak with a new tongue is to be able to speak with the tongue of an angel because one has become an angel — or a companion of angels, anyway. It is to elevate one's thoughts so that what then proceeds forth from the mouth is because of what is in one's thoughts. It is to reveal truth by the things one is authorized or commissioned to speak. It is to have a right to speak in the name of the Lord by His consent, His authority, and His will. It is to [know], nothing doubting (Ether 1:14) that He is one's Lord. It is to say, without hypocrisy, without guile, without hesitation, and in truth that the power of salvation is found in Christ and has made one His, that He has entrusted one with words of life, and that salvation can be found only in Him and His words. It is to have the Word of God within one. "You cannot speak with the tongue of angels without having knowledge of certain things given you. The clarity with which you can declare truth is distinct from what others say or claim to know. Light and truth, which is intelligence or the glory of God [see T&C 93:11], is not a mystery, but an understood and appreciated experience where darkness has fled and God's own glory has been upon you [see Genesis 2:2]." [995] *See also* GIFT OF TONGUES.

Spirit Matter At one time, Joseph said the Father was "a spirit," and at another time, He was said to "have a body as tangible as man's." Similarly, Jesus Christ was resurrected and unquestionably had a tabernacle consisting of "flesh and bone" that could be handled (*see* Luke 14:6). He ate fish and broke bread with His disciples (*see* Luke 14:7; John 11:7–8). These were physical acts. Yet He also appeared in the upper room on the day of His resurrection without entering through the shut door (*see* John 11:4). He ascended into Heaven (*see* Acts 1:3) and then descended from Heaven in the sight of a multitude (*see* 3 Nephi 5:3). These are not typical of physical bodies, as mankind knows them. When it comes to resurrected and glorified beings, the bodies are not the same as man's own physical, coarse constitutions. Nevertheless, God is composed of matter: "There is no such thing as immaterial matter. All spirit is matter, but it is more fine or pure, and can only be discerned by purer eyes; We cannot see it; but when

our bodies are purified, we shall see it is all matter."[996] Therefore, it
is equally true that God is a spirit, and that He also possesses a body
"as tangible as man's." How "quickened" is the body when He shows
Himself? Or, in this coarse environment, how great a glory has He
set aside to show Himself here?[997]

Spirit of Christ *You pray each time you partake of the sacrament to always
have my spirit to be with you. And what is my spirit? It is to love one another
as I have loved you* (T&C 157:51).

Spirit of Truth Capitalization and context of how this term is used
result in three different meanings:

spirit of truth — the light given to everyone; a description of something
sought after to help guide or answer;

Spirit of truth — an event in which the holy ghost ministers (as in an
ordinance), or when Christ takes ownership over something as
His; and

Spirit of Truth — a proper noun; a formal name for Christ, in the
context of scripture.[998]

Stiffneckedness When a person is 1 — in error and 2 — decidedly
committed to remaining so. He won't budge, won't humble himself,
and won't ask the Lord to remove his scales of darkness. He remains
a devoted disciple of unbelief, leading to wickedness that is borne
upon the shoulders of his ignorance.[999] *See also* IGNORANCE.

Strange Act Mankind is working their way back in a great chiasm
of history as the Lord counts things back to the beginning, and it
all draws to the end. He calls it His *strange act* (*see* T&C 101:20; Isaiah
8:4). Everything will happen as foretold. Man cannot and is not
supposed to be able to see it beforehand. They are only supposed
to witness it unfold before them. They cannot comprehend God's
strange act. Those who take the spirit for their guide will not be
deceived or hewn down.[1000] "We are nowhere near Zion, and only a
small fraction of what needs to be recovered has been given. Unless
this generation is patient enough to allow God to do His *strange act*,
and humble enough to support what He provides as He provides
it, another future generation will need to accomplish Zion."[1001] If
the wise men knew He had been born but could not identify where
Christ's birth happened, despite all else they were able to do, then
how can anyone know how God will accomplish His "strange act"

in the last days? Remember the modern caution in T&C 101:20: *What I have said unto you must needs be, that all men may be left without excuse, that wise men and rulers may hear and know that which they have never considered, that I may proceed to bring to pass my act, my strange act, and perform my work, my strange work, that men may discern between the righteous and the wicked, says your God.* Prophecies are not given so one will know details beforehand. They are given so that when they are fulfilled, one may understand that God knows the end from the beginning *(see* Isaiah 17:1).[1002] As a Gospel dispensation is unfolded, the Lord will always violate rules that man thinks exist involving timing and sequence. He will confer things which apparently belong long into the process and will do it, apparently, independent of the established requirements. But His strange act is not man's. He will do as He wills.[1003]

Stretched Forth His Hand *And now it came to pass that after Abinadi had spoken these words, he stretched forth his hands and said, The time shall come when all shall see the salvation of the Lord, when every nation, kindred, tongue, and people shall see eye to eye and shall confess before God that his judgements are just* (Mosiah 8:12). Mosiah 7:17 helps one to understand what *he stretched forth his hand(s)* means: *The Lord hath made bare his holy arm in the eyes of all the nations.* Abinadi is demonstrating the Lord's action, thereby affirming he is His messenger. He had been given the sign to testify and used it to declare he was a true messenger. Later in the Nephite history, the prophet Alma concluded his testimony of Melchizedek by using the same sign to evidence his authority: *And now it came to pass that when Alma had said these words unto them, he stretched forth his hand unto them and cried with a mighty voice, saying, Now is the time to repent, for the day of salvation draweth nigh!* (Alma 10:3). He used this sign because he was authorized to do so, and he understood what the declaration meant. Although those who were there may not have understood, it was a sign that he was a true messenger. Man cannot be saved in ignorance. Once the key of knowledge is lost, mankind is lost and cannot be saved until that key is returned. Prophets sent with messages who testify to an ignorant people use signs that the Lord recognizes and authorizes, but they may not be noticed or understood by those who hear the message. Nevertheless, the testimony becomes binding when the Lord's seal is put upon it.

This often involves a required sign to be given, or in other words, for hands to be stretched forth.[1004]

Still, Small Voice The gift of the holy ghost is conferred after baptism. It is intended to be a guide and to lead one into greater light and truth. It is the still, small voice which helps by whispering or giving impressions. It is a subtle and quiet tool, intended to help one develop sensitivity and reverence. It is the first comforter that is promised to the faithful.[1005]

Studying the Scriptures The scriptures are a great source of inspiration and revelation. Through them one can gain experience in listening to the spirit. They tutor the seeker, not just in doctrine, but in hearing the voice of inspiration, as well. "Through scripture study you can develop a greater spiritual sensitivity. If you have not begun to do that, you will need to start. Find time to be alone. Take the time to study, not just read, the scriptures. Pray before you begin. Think about the phrases used, and don't try to digest whole chapters at once. Be silent, so that you can hear the still, small voice. If there is some serious sin in your life, repent of it. Let the Lord know you are doing so because you want the spirit as a guide in your life. He will respond. You will find He is no respecter of persons. He will send His spirit to any sincere seeker for truth. And when He does, it will be as a result of you seeking the light and obeying the commandments. The Comforter's purpose is to guide you into greater truths. There is a library of truth waiting to be discovered inside the scriptures. Use this library and experience the inspiration it offers."[1006] If someone is not willing to receive the contents of the revelations already recorded in the scriptures — by studying them and learning such mysteries as they contain — then what makes that person think he can qualify to receive revelation of yet greater things? Why would Heaven violate the rules of its own economy and do for that person what he can do for himself? No miracle is required to teach many of the mysteries of Heaven. They are already in the scriptures and in the ordinances. But if they are ignored with a refusal to receive what is in them, there is little reason to part the veil and teach more. "We prove our need to be taught by Heaven when we have done our part to study what Heaven has already revealed. When we have exhausted the available information here, we are permitted to receive more because we ask and we are ready to receive. You can know a person is ready to receive because they have paid heed to what has been delivered to mankind already. Nephi has done this. This is why we find ourselves gaining a new flood of light from him. As we will see, however, not all scripture is of equal value. When it comes to the scriptures, the Book of Mormon is plainly the best source for learning the mysteries of God. Within its pages is the fullness of the Gospel, set out in plainness like no other volume. Joseph Smith was perhaps understating the matter when he proclaimed 'the Book of Mormon was the most correct of any book on Earth, and the keystone to our religion, and a man could get nearer to God by abiding by its precepts than by any other book' (DHC 4:461; also TPJS, 194). In addition to other important matters, as Nephi's visionary encounter with the Second Comforter will teach us, the scriptures from all other sources have been corrupted."[1007] "There are two things that will bring you closer to God than anything else. First, personal scripture study. Learn from them when you have time. Your private study will be more important than what others tell you about the scriptures. Second, personal prayer. Your private time spent in prayer will have the power to shape your life. If you study the scriptures when you are alone, and you pray in private, these two things, more than anything else, will draw you to God."[1008] *See also* PATTERN FOR UNDERSTANDING TRUTH.

Submissive/sion Acceptance of the Father's will in preference to your own. This does not say one should submit to men. There is nothing about following a man in the concept of submission. *For the natural man is an enemy to God, and has been from the fall of Adam, and will be for ever and ever, but if he yields to the enticings of the holy spirit, and putteth off the natural man, and becometh a saint through the atonement of Christ the Lord, and becometh as a child: submissive, meek, humble, patient, full of love, willing to submit to all things which the Lord seeth fit to inflict upon him, even as a child doth submit to his father* (Mosiah 1:16).[1009] As used here, submission is not just an unanchored term, abstractly applied to anyone or anything. It is submission to God.[1010]

Suddenly Surprisingly; in an unexpected way; being caught off-guard. "I declared what I was going to do, I did it, and you got caught off-guard." (*See* e.g., Isaiah 17:1.)[1011]

Suffer For Their Own Sins As to who will "suffer for their own sins" and yet enter into the Celestial Kingdom, there are at least two categories: The first is those who have received their calling and election but who return to sin (but not an unpardonable sin). These are required to "pay the price" for this misconduct. The second is those who are "sealed up" through the faithfulness of their parents and claimed as children of promise as a matter of right (because of the sealing upon the parents). Such children will need to either qualify in their own right, or if inheritors of the promise through the merit of their parents' sealing, they will have to suffer to become clean in order to inherit what is sealed upon them by this right.[1012] It is a mistaken idea that once someone's calling and election has been made sure they are required to suffer for their own sins, because they have knowledge they are redeemed. This is a twisted view, designed by the adversary to discourage those who might otherwise seek and find. It is not that the atonement ceases to operate for the redeemed. The atonement continues to cover the on-going sins of these redeemed souls which arise from their foolishness, mistakes, errors of comprehension, and the things they don't understand yet. Christ does not require them to do what they don't know is a requirement yet. As the gentle and kind Lord, He will forgive all they do that is wrong, while He reveals through greater light and knowledge a higher path.[1013]

Surety, Christ as Surety is a word dating back to c. 1300, "a guarantee, promise, pledge, assurance," from Old French *seurté*, from Modern French *sûreté*, from Latin *securitatem*, "freedom from care or danger, safety, security," meaning "one who makes himself responsible for another."[1014] It was the power of the Son that was responsible for all creation. There is a dichotomy when the Son is saying He has to rely on the Father for all that He does and is, and yet He's very clearly the One that is responsible for this creation and is the life and the light of this creation — and it is through His sustaining power that all exist. The Father empowered the Son to use the Father's power to accomplish this. All had to be done through the Son because the Son was going to come down into the creation, reverse the process, and atone. The creation had to be made with the power of Christ in order for Christ to be able to redeem the entirety of the creation.

Christ acts as the *surety* to guarantee that if this creation goes amok, He will sacrifice Himself in order for that to be reversed and restored again. Christ operates by the power of the Father to accomplish the creation and the redemption, and by accomplishing the redemption, He's able to reverse the process and restore it again. Once He had finished the process of the atonement, He had finished the course, He had lived the life that allowed Him to lay claim upon the resurrection (because the "wages of sin" is death, but He did not earn those wages), He had the right to eternal life. In fact, it's because He had the right to eternal life that the atonement itself was infinite. What He gave up was infinite life by taking upon Himself death. Christ guaranteed, as a surety, that this whole mess would be fixed by His willingness to attain to the resurrection and put himself in this position. Because the Father's power was what came through and because the Father had attained to the resurrection, it was impossible for the Father's plan to fail — the Father has already taken care of redeeming all the creations under His hand.[1015]

Sustain To openly signify support and approval by vote or affirmation (e.g., when seven women sustain a man to use his priesthood outside his own family for the benefit of the fellowship); to support as true, legal, or just; or to allow or admit a proposal as valid. Not used in the sense of providing temporal support or relief or supplying sustenance. The LDS tradition is to ordain to the priesthood at age twelve, and that has become the standard. There is compelling evidence that both Jesus and John were initiated into the temple at age twelve before the Passover in essentially what would today be called a *bar mitzvah*. It was important for Jesus to be at the temple at the age of twelve for that initiation. For a youth to be ordained, at least seven women must vote to sustain him to be a priest, which would, of necessity, include the mother because she would be most acquainted with his daily walk.[1016]

"And again, the husband is to hold priesthood to baptize and bless the sacrament of bread and wine in the home, and the husband and wife are to bless their children together. For the husband to use authority to administer outward ordinances outside his own family, his wife must sustain him."[1017] Sustaining of priesthood within a fellowship is by women, and removing authority to act within a community or fellowship is, likewise, to be done by the vote of women. [1018] *See also* WORTHY/UNWORTHY; COMMON CONSENT.

Symbols God intended symbols to convey glory, honor, and a gift or endowment upon the people who received them. The symbols are not the real thing, but they teach and point to the real thing that is required for salvation. Symbolism substitutes one thing to represent another. There is always *this* that stands in the place of *that*. The value of the symbol is in teaching about *that* by employing *this* as a teaching tool. In temple symbolism, the *this* used has no real value, but *that* holds eternal value. If an unbelieving person obtains access to *this* temple symbol but fails to understand its relationship to *that* which is eternal, they have nothing of value. Likewise, when the symbol of *this* has no meaning for those who believe in the temple, then it fails to have any value for the believer as well.

God's highest truths frequently use symbols. Christ used parables to teach about *that* by using the familiar to substitute as a representation. He explained that this was to prevent those who were unworthy of the symbol from comprehending the truths. Seeing, they *see not,* and hearing, they *hear not* (*see* Matthew 7:2; Mark 2:13). Merely getting *this* without understanding *that* is worthless.

Temple rites are a gift from God that is filled with *this* for *that*. Ignorance leads to apostasy because the ignorant cannot see that *this* holds powerful value to teach about *that*. Even the greatest symbols can become nothing when they are not understood and are discarded by the ignorant. Then *they shall return again to their own place, to enjoy that which they are willing to receive, because they were not willing to enjoy that which they might have received. For what does it profit a man if a gift is bestowed upon him, and he receive not the gift? Behold, he rejoices not in that which is given unto him, neither rejoices in him who is the giver of the gift* (T&C 86:4).[1019]

Synagogue A public worship place of the Jews; the building in which worship is done. From the Greek *sunagóge* (συναγωγή) literally "a bringing together, an assembling."[1020] *See also* CHURCH.

Take Away Our Reproach The prophecy of being *called by thy name,* as a fulfillment of Isaiah 1:12–13 and 2 Nephi 8:8, refers to the name of Christ. Seven women sustaining a man to priesthood precedes the ordinance of baptism itself. When baptized, one takes upon him or her the name of Christ. It is the name of Christ through baptism that will take away one's reproach or, in other words, provide the remission of sins, as mentioned in Isaiah 1:13.[1021]

Take the Name of the Lord in Vain Attributing something to God without His authority or authorization;[1022] not swearing, but rather, when one claims to speak for the Lord when they do not; whenever someone proclaims their own agenda in the name of the Lord. All ought to speak in the Lord's name the words of Eternal life. Unfortunately, many pretended saints instead speak idle words, gratify their pride, and exercise their vain ambition while using the Lord's name only in vain.[1023] The Lord has instructed us: *Wherefore, let all men beware how they take my name in their lips, for behold, verily I say that many there be who are under this condemnation, who use the name of the Lord and use it in vain, having not authority* (T&C 50:14). The expression "My God, people!" is akin to Joseph Smith's exasperated comment to James Arlington Bennet: "Great God! When shall the oppressor cease to prey and glut itself upon innocent blood!"[1024] This is not "taking the name of God in vain" because first, in both cases, God's name is not used; second, neither involves advancing untruth while vainly attempting to empower falsehood by attributing it to God; and third, it dramatically calls attention to the importance of the surrounding statement and, hopefully, makes it all the more memorable. These are serious matters deserving one's complete attention.[1025]

Taken Captive by the Devil To *know nothing concerning [God's] mysteries* (Alma 9:3). When a person knows nothing concerning God's mysteries, they are then *taken captive by the Devil and led by his will down to destruction*. When they are taken captive by their ignorance, they are bound *by the chains of hell*. The result of ignorance of God's mysteries is "destruction" and "captivity." The ignorant will remain devoted to falsehoods, blind leaders, and guides who give no truthful accounts of their awful situation because they do not understand truth.[1026] They are all left without repentance, because repentance requires knowledge.[1027] *See also* CHAINS OF HELL.

Teach/Teacher To impart light and truth to another.[1028] In the Book of Mormon, teachers were ordained by the power of the holy ghost *to preach repentance and remission of sins through Jesus Christ by the endurance of faith on his name to the end* (Moroni 3:1). *See also* RULER.

Temple Where Heaven and earth meet, both symbolically and literally.[1029] The purpose of a temple (meaning an actual temple that is commissioned, ordered, blessed, accepted, and visited with His presence) is to substitute for the temporary ascent of a mortal into God's presence. A real temple becomes "Holy Ground" and the means for making available to faithful people in every state of belief and hope the opportunity to receive, by authorized means, the same covenant, obligation, association, expectation, and sealing through an authorized and binding arrangement in sacred space. This is the same thing they can receive from God directly if they enter into His presence while still in the flesh. In effect, the temple becomes an extension of heaven. God, angels, and mankind are able to associate there as in Eden. It is a return to Eden, where God walks *in the cool of the day* (Genesis 2:17). The ordinances or rites of the temple are presented in ritual form. This is required. God's House is a House of Order because it is reoriented to point away from this world in order to reflect the order of heaven and the actual eternal ascent into His presence. The volume of information conveyed by God would be too vast to set out in non-ritual form. In ritual, it is possible to convey a great body of information with symbolism, metaphor, relationships, and types that work on the mind of man the same way that visionary experiences directly with God convey. The mind is expanded, and the ritual allows something of God's viewpoint to be transmitted into the mind of man. The temple has only one real purpose: to convey God's promise to exalt those who experience it, provided they abide the conditions for exaltation. It portrays the real, second Eternal form of ascent in a way that gives the initiate a promise: that if they walk in the path shown them, they will arrive at the Throne of God in the afterlife.[1030] The whole temple message can be summarized in one brief statement: We are to be prepared in all things to receive further light and knowledge by conversing with the Lord through the veil. The ceremony of the temple is not the real thing. It is a symbol of the real thing. The real thing is when a person actually obtains an audience with Jesus Christ, returns to His presence, and gains knowledge by which they are saved.[1031] The temple is a revelation of the process by which one may pass through the veil to God's actual presence.[1032] The purpose of a temple is to allow the communication of great knowledge and greater knowledge to restore what has been lost since the time of Adam, in order for people to rise up and receive the Holy Order.[1033] A temple in Zion is to be a place where He can come to dwell and not merely to manifest Himself to some.[1034]

Isaiah's prophecy concerning the last days' temple clearly identifies it as a house where man will be instructed in God's path (*see* Isaiah 1:5). It will be a facility where the God of Jacob will teach His pathway of ascent back to the Throne of God. Mankind will learn the laws governing that pathway.[1035] The purpose of the coming last days' temple in Zion is to allow the communication of great knowledge and greater knowledge, and to restore what has been lost since the time of Adam.[1036] In the "Answer to Prayer for Covenant" the Lord explained: *Whenever I have people who are mine, I command them to build a house, a holy habitation, a sacred place where my presence can dwell or where the Holy Spirit of Promise can minister, because it is in such a place that it has been ordained to recover you, establish by my word and my oath your marriages, and endow my people with knowledge from on high that will unfold to you the mysteries of godliness, instruct you in my ways, that you may walk in my path. And all the outcasts of Israel will I gather to my house* (T&C 157:41). The main requirement of temples is to organize the living into a family. The organization cannot happen outside a temple. That is the only place God will allow the restoration, rites, ordinances, and covenant to be ministered. Heaven and earth will reunite and angels will attend to many of the required things when an acceptable temple has been built. "We think a temple can be built following a pattern based on current ordinances. There is no understanding of the ordinances necessary to organize the family of God again. Trying to fit the original full plan of God for mankind into our incomplete and corrupt model, and make it conform to our expectations will not work. There has not been a full restoration as yet."[1037]

Temptation All can fill themselves with the mind of God, and if they do so, they will find themselves, as the scriptures recite, having *no more disposition to do evil, but to do good continually* (Mosiah 3:1). This kind of repentance comes as a consequence of the things one knows, as a consequence of the light and truth within one. It causes temptation to disappear because one gives it no heed. This is how the Lord overcame all temptations.[1038] *He suffered temptations, but gave no heed unto them* (JSH 16:6). When someone "gives heed" to his temptations, he loses the battle our Lord won. It is possible to live in a world filled with sin and avoid becoming embroiled in the errors. "Do not let your eyes focus on the wickedness you see around you, but look up to Heaven and the example of Heaven's God, where there is no corruption."[1039]

Testify *Therefore, hold up your light, that it may shine unto the world. Behold, I am the light which ye shall hold up, that which ye have seen me do. Behold, ye see that I have prayed unto the Father, and ye all have witnessed. And ye see that I have commanded that none of you should go away, but rather have commanded that ye should come unto me, that ye might feel and see; even so shall ye do unto the world. And whosoever breaketh this commandment suffereth himself to be led into temptation* (3 Nephi 8:8). "When admonished earlier to *let your light so shine before this people, that they may see your good works and glorify your Father who is in Heaven* (3 Nephi 5:21), what the Lord meant is that it is He who should be held up. He alone. Not you, or your good intentions, your conspicuous acts or philanthropy. Not you at all. Him."

The obligation to hold up a light is circumscribed by God's direction that He is *the light which ye shall hold up* — nothing and no one else. He is the lifeline. Therefore, when anyone offers, preaches, teaches, exhorts, and expounds, He must be at the center of the prophesying, or the one "prophesying" is engaging in priestcraft (*see* 2 Nephi 11:17). The Lord *prayed unto the Father* (3 Nephi 8:4) in the Nephites' presence. His example points to how prayer is to occur and to whom it is addressed. They all witnessed this and knew for themselves how it was to be done. He did not tell any of those who were present to go away. He brought the same message to all. He gave them His example of liberality: *Ye see that I have commanded that none of you should go away, but rather have commanded that ye should come unto me* (3 Nephi 8:8). No one was refused. All were welcomed. Whether those in the multitude thought someone was unworthy or whether there were some with conflicts, it did not matter. All were invited. None were refused. They were all *commanded that [they] should come unto [Him]*.

"What is the reason we are commanded to come to Him? It is so *ye might feel and see*. So that you might know Him. So that you can also be a witness of His physical evidence of suffering, crucifixion and death. The wounds He bears could not be received without death. His body testifies that He died. His body also testifies of His resurrection. Despite the wounds which memorialize His suffering and death, He lives! He stands before you in life! He has risen! As you testify of Him, you must invite others to likewise come that *[they] might feel and see* Him. This is how witnesses of Him are commanded to *do unto the world*. This is their ministry, their burden, their witness, and their command from Him. When they fail to testify, teach, and proclaim, they *break this commandment and suffer themselves to be led into temptation*. This is why the Lord required at my hands the book *The Second Comforter*. That is how He directs all those who are *commanded to come unto Him, that they might feel and see*. It will not be in vague innuendo or veiled language. It may not be in a published book, and may well be in private. But they will all be required to invite others to likewise *come unto Him* that everyone *might feel and see* our Risen Lord. He is accessible. He invites. More than that, He commands. All are commanded and *none of you should go away*. We think it a great thing when someone testifies of Him. Yet He wants all to *come* so that everyone *might feel and see* Him."[1040]

Anyone who has had the Lord appear to them should testify as a witness to that fact. That is paramount. It is important for witnesses to declare He lives, and that they have seen Him. What is not appropriate for disclosure are details that go beyond what the Lord has chosen to make public already through the scriptures or ordinances. He controls that. Though He may reveal much to a person and place them under a different standard than what is given openly to mankind, that is His decision. Until He commands, the line is drawn between witnessing He lives — which is required — and disclosing what He alone reserves for Himself to reveal — which is forbidden. "I have said and I do believe our Lord has a continuing ministry. But that is His, not mine. Like anyone with a testimony of the Lord, I testify to help my fellow man increase in faith in Jesus Christ. I have an obligation to do so. We all do."[1041] Everyone has a duty to testify of the truth and to teach one another the doctrines of the kingdom. Therefore, all are under some obligation to declare what they believe, explain why, and defend it using the scriptures and declarations of the prophets.[1042]

Testimony of Jesus When Christ has promised one Eternal life, he can know with a surety he has Eternal life. Until then, all remain at risk and in jeopardy every hour they are here (*see* 1 Corinthians 1:64). When one knows he is sealed up to Eternal life, he has the more sure word of prophecy or the testimony of Jesus (*see* WJS, 201–202; WWJ, 2:230–231; T&C 86:1). These are they who have been told by the voice of God from heaven that they have Eternal life.[1043] *The testimony of Jesus is the spirit of prophecy* (Revelation 7:10). To have a saving testimony of Him is to become a prophet. It is no wonder, then, that Moses wished all men were prophets (*see* Numbers 7:19). All are invited to get testimonies of Christ and are, therefore, also invited to become prophets.[1044]

What if someone were to declare today *that the Lamb of God is the Son of the Eternal Father and the Savior of the world, and that all men must come unto him or they cannot be saved* (1 Nephi 3:24)? What if they were to declare in sober words that the Lamb of God lives still? That He had appeared to and spoken with the one making the declaration? Would there yet be those who would hear and repent? Would that message be drowned out by the chorus of foolish and vain things being spoken in the name of Jesus Christ by those who, despite having real intent and sincere desire, have not been given power to declare His words? Would such a message only be another bit of entertainment for the bored and curious to give but passing notice? Could the world be given such a message and warned but fail to see what it is they are being offered for one last time before the harvest is to begin? "If so, would we notice? Should someone choose to come, *they must come according to the words which shall be established by the mouth of the Lamb; and the words of the Lamb shall be made known in the records of thy seed, as well as in the records of the twelve apostles of the Lamb* (1 Nephi 3:24). How must they come? The Book of Mormon suggests it must be through the gate of revelation (Moroni 10:2). Without revelation you cannot obtain the testimony of Jesus, which is the spirit of prophecy (Revelation 7:10). Or, in other words, unless you find prophets who can bear testimony of Him, you have not yet found the means for salvation."[1045] The whole text of the Book of Mormon comes down to experience after experience, being retold by people who, during their lifetime, had this opening up of the Heavens to them, and they came into contact with Jesus Christ and recognized who He is and what His role is. "The testimony of Jesus is not something that comes from *you* (i.e., 'I have this [testimony,] and let me tell it to you'). The testimony of Jesus is something that He gives to you as His confirmation to you that you have part in His kingdom. To receive the testimony of Jesus is to receive from Him the promise that He will give you eternal life. The Book of Mormon is filled with accounts of people that had had that experience and that's — at one point — an expected and normal part of the Christian experience. It became very rare, unexpected, and in fact is denounced by many denominations as something that doesn't happen, can't happen, ought not happen. And if you think that you've come into contact with a divine being, then you've been misled because, well, Jesus is busy. He can't be troubled with your lot...don't think that you're going to have an encounter with Jesus. However, my view is that Christian salvation is based upon the testimony of Jesus, to you, of your salvation. I also think that it doesn't matter when you live or what the circumstances were; if you were true and faithful to Him, you will have that experience.... I believe it to be an authentic part of every Christian's life."[1046] *See also* PROPHET.

Testing the Spirits Not all "spiritual experiences" can be trusted to have come from God. *True spirits* do the following: testify of Christ; lead to repentance; are consistent with existing scripture; edify and enlighten the mind; are understandable and do not cause confusion; cause light to grow within; turn one toward Christ, not men; never cause pride; make one a better servant; increase one's love of his fellow man; clothe one with charity for the failings of others; conform to the true whisperings of the holy ghost that had been previously received; leave one humble and grateful for God's condescension; make one want to bring others to the light; are grounded in love toward God and all mankind; and lead one to rejoice. On the other hand, *false spirits* will: deny Christ; cause pride; make one believe he is better than others because of the experience; contradict the scriptures; appeal to carnality and self-indulgence; cause confusion; lead to ambition to control others; make one intolerant of others' failings; seek self-fulfillment rather than service; appeal to one's vanity and assure him that he is a great person; bring darkness; repulse the holy ghost; prevent one from repenting and forsaking sins; interfere with serving others; and focus on oneself rather than the needs of others. "Do not think all spiritual experiences can be trusted. There is no difference between the activities of deceiving spirits today and those in Kirtland, as well as those in the New Testament times. If you follow the Lord you must still test the spirits and only follow those which point to Christ (1 John 1:18). Even Joseph Smith had to ask God about some of the phenomena going on in Kirtland before he knew which were of God and which were deceiving."[1047] There are many unclean spirits who will deceive mankind. Unless one is anchored in what is taught in the scriptures and requires all truth to measure up to that, he or she can be deceived. That is as true now as then. Some people are so thrilled by having any spiritual experience that they accept anything. Lying spirits appeal to one's pride and vanity. God will chasten and require one to be meek and serve both Him and one's fellow man. Lying spirits will tell a man that he is some great and mighty person. God will remind him that only He is strong, but He uses the weak things of this world to accomplish His work. No one can take credit but Him for whatever is accomplished.[1048]

Three Witnesses Oliver Cowdery, Martin Harris, and David Whitmer. They claimed an angel showed to them the plates from which the Book of Mormon was translated. Their testimony is in the front of every published copy of the Book of Mormon. In 1835, these three men chose and ordained the first quorum of twelve apostles.[1049]

Thrones One of the rungs on Jacob's ladder, found in the afterlife, where different "Powers" are fixed. Angel, Archangel, Principality, Power, Dominion, Throne, Cherubim, or Seraphim — they may all be called "Powers of Heaven."[1050]

Times of the Gentiles Joseph Smith was instructed by a heavenly messenger on Sept. 23, 1823 that the fullness of the gentiles was soon to come in (see JSH 3:4). Modern revelation states that the times of the gentiles is that time when the fullness of the gospel will come among the gentiles (see T&C 31:6–7). The times of the gentiles will be fulfilled in that generation *when the gentiles shall sin against my gospel, and shall reject the fullness of my gospel* (3 Nephi 7:5), and *they receive it not* (T&C 31:6). The Lord will then *bring the fullness of my gospel from among them. And then will I remember my covenant which I have made unto my people, O house of Israel, and I will bring my gospel unto them* (3 Nephi 7:5).

Tithing An offering to the Lord; one tenth of one's surplus after all responsibilities and needs have been taken care of.[1051] The primary purpose of collecting the tithes and the yield upon it is to bless and benefit the lives of those in need. "Assist the poor directly, looking for God's guidance in so doing. Have no poor among us. Help provide for those who need housing, food, clothing, healthcare, education, and transportation. Take the money the Lord intended for the poor, and administer it for the poor."[1052] (*See* T&C 173:1).

Transgression Both "sin" and "transgression" are used when describing "offending the laws ordained before the foundation of the world." Transgression is used primarily when the offense is done in innocent ignorance. Sin is used primarily when the offense is done deliberately, knowing that an eternal law is being violated. Transgression requires repentance, just as does sin. However, repentance from transgression involves recognition, understanding, and change; whereas repentance from sin requires sincere soul searching, confession, and recognition that the deliberate violation of an eternal law is a serious character flaw requiring greater self-control, discipline, and commitment to follow Christ.[1053] *See also* SIN.

Translation *And men having this faith, coming up unto this Order of God, were translated and taken up into Heaven* (Genesis 7:19). Even the translated will undergo a change akin to death (*see* 3 Nephi 13:3). Those born in the Millennium will likewise undergo this same experience (*see* T&C 50:11).[1054] "Now the doctrine of translation is a power which belongs to this Priesthood. There are many things which belong to the powers of the Priesthood and the keys thereof, that have been kept hid from before the foundation of the world; they are hid from the wise and prudent to be revealed in the last times. Many have supposed that the doctrine of translation was a doctrine whereby men were taken immediately into the presence of God, and into an eternal fullness, but this is a mistaken idea. Their place of habitation is that of the terrestrial order, and a place prepared for such characters He held in reserve to be ministering angels unto many planets, and who as yet have not entered into so great a fullness as those who are resurrected from the dead. See [Hebrews 1:49], *Others were tortured, not accepting deliverance, that they might obtain a better resurrection*. Now it was evident that there was a better resurrection, or else God would not have revealed it unto Paul. Wherein then can it be said a better resurrection. This distinction is made between the doctrine of the actual resurrection and translation: translation obtains deliverance from the tortures and sufferings of the body, but their existence will prolong as to the labors and toils of the ministry, before they can enter into so great a rest and glory. On the other hand, those who were tortured, not accepting deliverance, received an immediate rest from their labors. See [Revelation 5:5], *And I heard a voice from Heaven saying unto me, Write: Blessed are the dead who die in the Lord from henceforth, yea, says the spirit, that they may rest from their labors. And their works do follow them*. They rest from their labors for a long time, and yet their work is held in reserve for them, that they are permitted to do the same work after they receive a resurrection for their bodies. But we shall leave this subject and the subject of the terrestrial bodies for another time, in order to treat upon them more fully."[1055] Though Christ rose again the third day, yet He was not spared death by being translated. God does not take any man off the earth through translation unless they have a calling to minister. The city of Enoch did receive a calling to minister to others.[1056] People continued to be translated to Enoch's city right up to the flood. Shem remained through the flood but held a promise that he could join Enoch's people, and later God vindicated the promise, and Melchizedek's people were, likewise, able to "flee" (*see* Genesis 4:23). The period of translation into the city of Enoch ended at Melchizedek except for only one-at-a-time events relating to dispensations and assignments requiring further work. Moses, for example, needed to return for the events on the Mount of Transfiguration. So he was taken. Elijah was needed for a last-days return to open a corridor between Heaven and earth. So he was taken. These were not comparable to the earlier cities being taken into Heaven but were specific assignment-related events, requiring them to be involved with later work within the gambit of the assignment given to them by God.[1057]

Trust in Man Reliance on man to save; man's theories, hopes, or vain formulas for finding the path to God. "Nephi puts it into two opposing camps. There are only two. There are either inspired teachings, given by revelation and confirmed by the holy ghost, or they are man's understanding. The first will save you. The other will curse you. There is no happy marriage of these opposing positions. You cannot have both. This sword cuts both ways and forces you to make a decision. Your eternity will be affected by the decision. So either you find the right way and follow it, or you are relying upon men and will in the end be cursed."[1058] (*See* 2 Nephi 12:6.) *See also* MAKETH FLESH HIS ARM.

Truth *Knowledge of things as they are and as they were and as they are to come* (T&C 93:8).[1059] You can only know the truth by having it revealed to you from heaven itself (*see* T&C 69:29).[1060] "We must know the truth. The truth informs us how things are (now, today, in our current peril). The truth informs us of how things were (revealing exactly what happened, without mythical or political overlay, with its disappointments and tragedies candidly depicted). The truth informs us of the things to come (even if the prophecies and promises dash our hopes, crush our vanity and expose our foolishness). Without the truth it is impossible to repent. In order to take people captive, all that is required is for people to be content with their ignorance. The greatest threat to salvation does not come from teaching false doctrine but instead comes from ignoring doctrine altogether. Substituting platitudes and truisms for careful, ponderous and solemn investigation of the deep things of God is sufficient to keep people in the chains of captivity. It isn't necessary for the devil to convince you of lies, only for him to make you content in your ignorance or fearful of the search for truth."[1061]

Twelve Apostles Based upon the New Testament model of Christ's twelve apostles, it was an ecclesiastical body formed in 1835. Members were originally chosen and ordained by the Three Witnesses to the Book of Mormon. This quorum was originally equal to the First Presidency (3 men), the Seventy (70 men), and High Councils (local bodies of 12 men), all of whom were considered to equally hold the keys over the church. Upon the death of Joseph Smith, his successor, Brigham Young, changed the way the quorums were organized and made this quorum superior to all others. They are currently considered to exclusively hold "all the keys" in the LDS church, and the senior (longest-serving) member automatically becomes the president of the LDS church upon the death of his predecessor.[1062]

Unbelief As used in the Book of Mormon, it means one does not understand and has not accepted true doctrine.[1063] The word unbelief means to accept false doctrine or to have an incomplete and inaccurate understanding of correct doctrine. Unbelief is often used in conjunction with losing truth, forsaking doctrine, and "dwindling." The phrase *dwindling in unbelief* is the Book of Mormon's way to describe moving from a state of belief, with true and complete doctrine, to a state of unbelief, where the truth has been discarded. Miracles end because men dwindle in unbelief.[1064]

Under the Earth As used in Genesis 4:9, this is referring to the cycles of the "wandering stars" or planets. It does not refer to the subterranean composition of the earth's mantle.[1065] When an object in the firmament moves below the horizon, it is "under the earth."[1066]

Unity Oneness and undivided; having the same spirit dwelling in them.[1067]

Unpardonable Sin "All sins shall be forgiven, except the sin against the holy ghost; for Jesus will save all except the sons of perdition. What must a man do to commit the unpardonable sin? He must receive the holy ghost, have the Heavens opened unto him, and know God, and then sin against Him. After a man has sinned against the holy ghost, there is no repentance for him. He has got to say that the sun does not shine while he sees it; he has got to deny Jesus Christ when the Heavens have been opened unto him, and to deny the plan of salvation with his eyes open to the truth of it; and from that time he begins to be an enemy."[1068] "A man cannot commit the unpardonable sin after the dissolution of the body."[1069] *And he that receives my Father receives my Father's kingdom, therefore, all that my Father has shall be given unto him. And this is according to the oath and covenant which belongs to the priesthood* (T&C 82:17). The oath and covenant is the Father's word that cannot be broken. It is not something one aspires to but accepts by following the conditions established by

God. It is received by an oath and covenant from the Father who CAN establish eternal covenants by His word, because His word cannot be broken. *Therefore, all those who receive the Priesthood* [Priesthood is singular — there is a single fullness given by the Father], *receive this oath and covenant of my Father.* This is not about abstractions, quorums, groups, churches, organizations, orders, or associations of men on this side of the veil. This is about a direct, covenantal relationship established by the Father with those who have "*The* Priesthood." *The* Priesthood is a fullness *which he* [the Father] *cannot break* [because if He were to break this once He has made this covenant, He would cease to be God], *neither can it be moved.* Once the Father has made this covenant and conferred these rights, earth and hell cannot make it otherwise. *But whoever breaks this covenant after he has received it, and altogether turns therefrom, shall not have forgiveness in this world, nor in the world to come* (T&C 82:17). This powerful curse applies only to the few who reject a covenant established directly by God the Father with them. This is not merely an ordination to church office. If a priest of this kind, after being called His son, were to turn away from the Father, he would be in a state of willful rebellion against God who sustains all creation. Those with this Priesthood have been in His presence. This is not at all the same thing as an elder drifting into inactivity and disaffection. Those with this Priesthood stand in the light of the noonday sun and deny that light. In these circumstances, it is rebellion against knowledge.[1070] *See also* SON OF PERDITION.

Unspeakable Christ's gospel includes things one may not yet understand. The Apostle Paul referred to hidden truths as "unspeakable" because they are not yet understood. Paul referred to those in possession of hidden knowledge as *stewards of the mysteries of God* (1 Corinthians 1:14). This hidden knowledge is true but remains a "mystery" for those who are not shown it by God. One servant of God may know but be forbidden from revealing a matter, while another is later commanded to reveal it. Therefore, because one has a Bible, one should not assume it contains all of God's words, that He has not revealed more, or that He will not reveal more. An infinite and eternal God has spoken many things and will yet reveal more things. Some truths are already in scripture but hidden from view by God's decree. Christian scriptures declare, *It is the glory of God to* *conceal a thing, but the honor of kings is to search out a matter* (Proverbs 4:1). So all should search out matters God has concealed to see more of His glory.[1071] *See also* MYSTERIES.

Urim and Thummim Lights and perfections. It appears from early Church history the term Urim and Thummim was not used until 1835; prior to that, the term applied to the instrument was "interpreters."[1072] *The place where God resides is a great Urim and Thummim. This earth, in its sanctified and immortal state, will be made like unto crystal and will be a Urim and Thummim to the inhabitants who dwell thereon, whereby all things pertaining to an inferior kingdom, or all kingdoms of a lower order, will be manifest to those who dwell on it; and this earth will be Christ's. Then the white stone mentioned in [Revelation 1:12], will become a Urim and Thummim to each individual who receives one, whereby things pertaining to a higher order of kingdoms will be made known; and a white stone is given to each of those who come into the celestial kingdom, whereon is a new name written, which no man knoweth save he that receiveth it. The new name is the key word.*[1073]

Veil "You were a spirit before you were born. You were there when some were chosen to be 'rulers,' or in other words, teachers. You have within you a spirit that was in that group. You saw and participated in what went on, and have that somewhere still inside you. It is kept from you by the 'veil of flesh' now covering your spirit (Hebrews 1:32). Somewhere within you lies the 'record of Heaven.' Or more correctly, the Record of Heaven. If you gain access to it, it has the capacity to teach you the 'truth of all things.' Within it is such an abundance of truth that the things of God are not hidden from you, neither far off. It is not in Heaven, so that you ask: Who will go to Heaven to bring it to us. It is not beyond the sea, that you should ask, Who can go to bring it to us? But it is very close to you, in your own mouth, in your own heart, that you can do what is asked of you."[1074] Obedience is the means by which all men and women gather light. The commandments are revelations of the inner person one ought to become. They are how one grows in the flesh to comprehend God in the spirit. The body is a veil that keeps man from Him. By subordinating the will of the flesh to the will of the spirit, one gains light and truth.[1075] "The first step along the path is to make it through the veil. Not the veil in a temple, or in a rite offered by men to one another. We must be brought through the veil back into the Lord's presence. That is the step which stops most of our progress. By and large we don't believe it possible. We make no attempt because we think it is not available, or we should not be trying to become more than our leaders, or we are not qualified, or some other false teaching which hedges up our progress."[1076] Perhaps the greatest idea to man's mind is that all CAN converse with God through the veil, preliminary to entering into His presence. In that idea is found the promise of communication with God, followed by Him allowing one to visit with Him through the veil. Every soul who has faith in that and acts consistent with their faith will obtain the most glorious assurances from God. They will not be barren or unfruitful in their knowledge.[1077] When the Lord determines a man's "righteousness" is acceptable before Him, then He redeems that man by parting the veil and bringing him into the company of the redeemed (*see* T&C 69:19).[1078] "It is a thin veil, not a wall, that separates you from God. Do not let it become insurmountable. It was always meant to be parted."[1079]

In a temple ceremony, a veil is used as a symbol to separate the initiate from the Lord. This veil is a symbol of the division between heaven and earth, between time and eternity, or between the sacred and the commonplace. Beyond the veil are the angels, gods, and spirits. Here there are mortals. Passing through that veil happens in one of two ways. One way is to gain knowledge of God's mysteries and to live true and faithful to them. Passing through the veil is symbolized in the temple ceremony, but the reality of it actually happened in the case of the brother of Jared. *And because of the knowledge of this man, he could not be kept from beholding within the veil. And he saw the finger of Jesus, which when he saw, he fell with fear, for he knew that it was the finger of the Lord. And he had faith no longer, for he knew, nothing doubting. Wherefore, having this perfect knowledge of God, he could not be kept from within the veil. Therefore, he saw Jesus, and he did minister unto him* (Ether 1:14). Temple rites explain that anyone who arrives at the veil boundary who has been true and faithful in all things is entitled to converse with the Lord through the veil. Once the Lord is satisfied they possess the required attributes, then they can enter into His presence. The second way of passing through the veil is explained by Alma: *Behold, it has been made known unto me by an angel that the spirits of all men, as soon as they are departed from this mortal body, yea, the spirits of all men, whether they be good or evil, are taken home to that God who gave them life* (Alma 19:6).

The ceremony employs two veils to symbolize the separation between mortality and eternity, the sacred and the profane. The boundary veil is used during the ceremony to test the initiate before permitting the individual to enter into the presence of the Lord. The second veil is used to symbolize the role of the woman. Except for what happens in the womb of the woman, everything in mortality is subject to entropy. Women have the ordained power to produce new life. Everything else decays and dies. Her power defies the universal effects of entropy.[1080] Mothers are the physical veil between pre-earth spirits and physical bodies inhabited in mortality. They clothe children in the veil of flesh. This power used to be honored in the LDS temple veiling of women. This power to give life has been regarded in almost all societies as something sacred and holy. In this current coarse and vulgar society, the idea has been rejected, as a matter of law, that women engage in a sacred and holy labor when bearing children.[1081]

The ceremonial boundary veil that acts as the divider between worlds represents the physical boundary at which the initiate must stop when being tested by heaven. This testing takes place before they are permitted to pass from earth to heaven, from time to eternity, and from the commonplace to the sacred. In direct contrast, the veil of the woman represents the transition of pre-earth eternal spirits into mortality, when the sacred becomes embodied. She, along with God, veils in flesh the spirits from beyond the veil. *You have clothed me with skin and flesh, and have knit me together with bones and sinews* (Job 4:10). Therefore, the woman's veil represents the inverse of the other veil. The boundary veil symbolizes losing the flesh to leave mortality, and the woman's veil endows the immortal spirit with mortal flesh. Like her heavenly counterpart, the woman represents creation. This process, like that which is beyond the boundary veil, is sacred. Both veils symbolize the sacred. Woman is veiled in temple ceremony to show that in a fallen world, trapped by decay and death, creation continues through her. Life springs anew, and what is sacred and pure is born into mortal life. It is not proper to remove the ceremonial veiling from the woman unless the intention is to abort the symbol of new life and creation. It destroys the symbol of the sacred power given to woman.[1082]

Virtue Virtue is almost always passive, constraining from abrupt and improper behavior. It contains and limits. It is a strong barrier against misconduct. It has protocols and expects behavior to be mild. It is not the same as righteousness. Righteousness will often require or impose action — sometimes action that exceeds mere virtue. Nephi was constrained to kill Laban. Elijah mocked the false priests. Christ rebuked the Scribes and Pharisees as unclean "whited sepulchers" filled with rot and decay. These kinds of righteous actions are not ungoverned or spontaneous. They are carefully controlled and are undertaken only when the priesthood holder, whose thoughts are virtuous and disciplined, is led by the power of the holy ghost to rebuke sharply.[1083] Virtue can be offended by righteousness. Righteousness controls, and virtue surrenders. Whenever it is necessary to do so, virtue yields every time to righteousness.[1084]

Voice of God Every person who has ever lived is one-of-a-kind. All can "hear" God's voice, but how it comes to each person may be different from how it comes to anyone else. The description frequently found in scripture is merely that *the word of the Lord came* to the prophets (*see*, e.g., Ezekiel 5:2; Hosea 1:1; Jacob 2:3; and T&C 115:1). It can come to the mind; it can be "heard" in the mind; it is sometimes sensed in the impressions; it can come as a dream; or it can be a conviction that comes with palpable certitude. However it comes — and in any individual case it may do so in an altogether unique way — it comes from a source outside of man. It is often surprising and not at all what was expected. It can be inconvenient, requiring what one would not voluntarily seek. These are not just "emotions" or "feelings"; rather, there is an intelligence to it which originates from outside of the person and delivers a message — not feelings, but a message. After receiving the "word," confirmation follows. The confirmation allows a person of faith to see evidence or support for their belief and trust in God. Again, when it comes to the confirming sign that follows faith, the variety of forms is unique to the person.

First, however, remember that all are unique and will have unique experiences in relating to God. Given the care with which each person has been organized as an individual creation, how can anyone expect communication with the Lord to be standardized? Why would the way in which He speaks with one person be identical to the way in which He speaks to all others? Why wouldn't He carry on a conversation with each of His children in ways adapted to the individual child? As one recognizes His "voice" through the eyes of faith, he or she will begin to realize it comes from Him. The ordinary contains the extraordinary. "You must see the extraordinary in the ordinary before the truly extraordinary opens up to you. You must have faith before you are shown signs."[1085]

There are a variety of ways in which one receives communications from the Lord. When it progresses from initial stirrings to the "voice" which one hears within, one should not assume it will be a uniform experience. The "voice" is clearly not one's own and introduces ideas or concepts that are clearly not one's own. A person can have a dialogue with this "voice" in which his or her ideas are juxtaposed with those coming from the other. It is not audible, but one hears it inside. It is clearly not one's own voice, but that of another.[1086]

The great difference between prophets and others is not in God's willingness to speak but in the refusal to listen. Some listen, and they are prophets. Others do not and struggle to believe the prophets. God, however, has and does speak to all. "We are unique, and God's ways of speaking to each of us is as unique as each of us. We do ourselves a great disservice when we attempt to fit ourselves into a singular, stereotypical persona seeking only a singular way for God to talk with and to us. We make ourselves into something we aren't, in the search to find what cannot be found that way. If we demand only the extraordinary before we will recognize His voice, we run the risk of looking in the wrong way for Him. His voice is there. He speaks to all of us. But we can miss it if we are not attuned to listen. You may never be able to hear God speak to you in the way in which others hear Him. If you determine He must speak to you in a specific way and not in any other way, you can go a lifetime without ever having a conversation with Him. He longs to speak with each of us. Within each of us there is something uniquely attuned to Him. How He reaches out to you may be as singular and unique as you are, and you can be assured He is reaching out. In fact, God is rather noisy if you will allow Him to be. We were never intended to live without a direct connection to Him. How each of us receives contact with God, how we hear His voice, and what gifts we possess are unique. There is no single, universal way for one to *hear [His] voice…and know that [He] is* (T&C 36:8). And so it is a mistake to ignore your own unique talent for 'hearing' your Father in Heaven. He did not send you here powerless to hear Him. But it will require you to develop the capacity. Relying merely upon your 'feeling' or 'emotions' alone is insufficient; you must learn to hear His voice. All of the prophets…from Moses to Gideon to Elijah, received contact from God. They were certain Who it was that spoke to them. They obtained intelligence, heard His voice, and learned from Him. None of them relied upon mere 'feeling' but instead 'heard' words from Him. He spoke with them just as He did with Nephi."[1087] (*See Nephi's Isaiah*, chapter 18 for a more detailed discussion.) *See also* PRAY.

Washing Away of Sin The anointing of the spirit.[1088]

Watch To be observant and detect elements of control, dominion, and compulsion; to become vigilant in separating the will of men from the will of God. It is to keep the Lord's teachings in mind and to measure any person's teachings, actions, and persuasions against the standard the Lord has explained.[1089] (*See* 3 Nephi 8:8.)

Waxing Strong To be increasingly determined or committed.[1090]

What/Which is Right *Therefore, ye must always pray unto the Father in my name. And whatsoever ye shall ask the Father in my name, which is right, believing that ye shall receive, behold, it shall be given unto* you (3 Nephi 8:8). The whole meaning of this promise is captured in the qualification that it must be that "which is right." If one acquires an understanding of what "is right," then by asking for it, one submits to the Father's will. Even if one would shrink from it, beg that it may pass from him, or cower at the thing required,when one *asks the Father in [Christ's] name* for whatsoever *is right*, despite his desire for things to be otherwise, he is going to become one with Them. Then he will be like Them and learn the great truth that the will of the Father IS indeed "whatsoever is right." Joseph Smith explained it: "When the Lord has thoroughly proved him, and finds that the man is determined to serve Him at all hazards, then the man will find his calling and his election made sure; then it will be his privilege to receive the other Comforter, which the Lord hath promised the Saints."[1091] The way Heaven knows a man has arrived at that point is by the offered prayers. When they seek to do the will of the Father, and the requests are "what is right," then the Heavens cannot withhold anything from that man. Indeed, the Lord will prompt the right questions by what the Lord says to that man, so that the knowledge of that man will reach into the Heavens (*see* Ether 1:12–14). Therefore, one must not only *pray always unto the Father in Christ's name*, but one must also grow in understanding, humility, and meekness so as to *ask the Father* for that *which is right*. This is a process. [1092]

What Lack I Yet? Complicated or intricate skills are taught one step at a time. There should be in the mind of the student only *one* thing to do. There is always only *one* thing to do. There is never more than the single thing to be addressed, and it is the thing most wrong at the moment. Once that is addressed and corrected, then it is possible to move on to the next thing, where again, there is only one thing to do — and it is the next thing in the sequence. When the next skill is acquired, then there is still only one thing to do. So it is here. "There is only one thing for you to do. You will know what you need to do within the context of your own life. But whatever it is that most hinders you is the one and only thing you have to do. When it is resolved, then you move on to the next thing. Sometimes we all have blind spots about our own shortcomings. If you cannot figure out what the thing you most need to resolve is, then ask the Lord. He has always been willing to answer the sincere inquiry of 'What lack I yet?' The answer to that question is the one thing you should work on. But never work on three, or thirty, or fifty things at once."[1093]

White and Delightsome "When the Book of Mormon speaks of white and delightsome, its translator means, 'shining, glittering in gladness,' not *Caucasian*. The Old English version of Genesis speaks of elf-sheen, and I suppose that is what our Book of Mormon implies: shining, glittering, lucid being. There is no racism here, but a promise of becoming like Ahman, and to reside gladly in Ahman, the name of Him giving us the name of a realm where his children gather and find rest."[1094] The earliest extant versions of the Book of Mormon use "white" and "delightsome"; "pure" was first substituted for "white" in the 1840 edition.[1095] "Notice, in the Book of Mormon that peculiar thing: 'a white and delightsome people' and 'a dark and loathsome people'. It doesn't refer to skin color at all [only to countenance], but there's a lot about race in the Book of Mormon. [Speaking of the text of an Egyptian who lived a short time before Nephi, *The Autobiography of Kai*, he refers] to himself as *ḥd-ḥr* (white of countenance), *nfr bi-t* (excellent of character), *pḥꜣ ḥ-t* (clean of body and in moral habits). And he shunned everything that was *snk-wt*. The word is very interesting. It means 'black of countenance,' and it also means 'greed or anything that is evil.' He [Kai] used those peculiar terms. He was *ḥd-ḥr*. He has a picture of a white face (white of countenance). And he was clean of body, and he eschewed *snk-wt* (what is greedy or what is dark of countenance)."[1096]

White Garments   To have the blood and sins of one's generation removed from him; to be purified; to be sanctified by the Lamb — removing from the individual and taking upon Himself the responsibility to answer for whatever failings he has. This is not ritual purity. This is purity in fact. *Therefore, they were called after this Holy Order and were sanctified, and their garments were washed white through the blood of the Lamb. Now they, after being sanctified by the holy ghost, having their garments made white, being pure and spotless before God, could not look upon sin save it were with abhorrence. And there were many, an exceeding great many, who were made pure and entered into the rest of the Lord their God* (Alma 10:1). This describes those who are qualified to stand in the presence of God without sin; they are clean of all blood and sin — righteous for ever. "He is Christ's, and Christ is the Father's, and all that each of them will be is the same; for we shall see Him as He is, because we will be like Him. To be like Him is to be sanctified."[1097] These people are sanctified by the holy ghost as a result of having their garments made white. They are pure and spotless before God. This is the reason they can enter His presence. He has accepted them because, just like Him, they are without sin. They were not perfected by their own acts. The earlier reference to their repentance makes that clear. They become pure and spotless before God because they have done what was asked of them to become clean. They have repented.[1098] "Christ sanctifies us, we don't sanctify ourselves. Our 'righteousness' is borrowed from Him. It can be symbolized in this way. He provides a white robe, we put it on, and then He looks upon the whiteness and purity of the robe we received from Him and treats us as if the borrowed robe is our condition. We owe Him for that. He is willing to proceed with us as if we merited the robe. (*See* 2 Nephi 6:5.)"[1099]

White Stone "Then the white stone mentioned in [Revelation 1:12] will become a Urim and Thummim to each individual who receives one, whereby things pertaining to a higher order of kingdoms will be made known. And a white stone is given to each of those who come into the Celestial Kingdom, whereon is a new name written, which no man knoweth save he that receiveth it. The new name is the key word."[1100] Since the white stone and new name mentioned in it are referring to the state of exaltation and inheritance, and since the promise which the Second Comforter (Christ) is working to obtain for those to whom He ministers is the promise of exaltation, that equivalency may also be made. The difference is that those described in this statement are in a future state in which they have actually inherited the condition of exaltation, have entered into the Celestial Kingdom to dwell there, and possess the white stone on which their new name is written; whereas the promises Joseph speaks of in reference to the Second Comforter[1101] and the promises in T&C 86:1 are given to a mortal and are to be realized fully in the future.[1102]

Whole Enos 1:1 concludes with the remarkable comment from the Lord to Enos: *Wherefore, go to, thy faith hath made thee whole.* The idea captured by the word "whole" is akin to the idea of being completed. Enos is no longer a work in process. He has run a good race, finished the course, and can enter into the rest of the Lord.[1103]

Wicked At His return, the Lord intends to destroy the wicked. Included in the "wicked" are those who are telestial and, therefore, cannot endure His presence. These are those who worship men instead of God; they reject a true prophet when one is sent to them; they are liars, adulterers, whoremongers, and all who love and make lies (*see* T&C 69:27). These are those who have taken our Lord's name in vain, having not authority (*see* T&C 50:14), and all those who have preached for hire and practiced priestcraft (*see* 2 Nephi 11:17). It was because of priestcraft that the Jews could not recognize Christ, and therefore they rejected and killed Him (*see* 2 Nephi 7:1). The false priests always rail against the true ones. In the last days, false prophets will outnumber the true ones (*see* Mark 6:4). Zion will require that all this wickedness comes to an end.[1104]

Will of the Father If one acquires an understanding of what "is right," then by asking for it, one submits to the Father's will. Even if one would shrink from it, beg that it may pass from him, or cower at the thing required,when one *asks the Father in [Christ's] name* for whatsoever *is right* (3 Nephi 8:8), despite his desire for things to be otherwise, he is going to become one with Them. Then he will be like Them and learn the great truth that the will of the Father is indeed "whatsoever is right."[1105]

Willing to Submit The final quality in Mosiah 1:16 of being *willing to submit* again reminds one of Christ. His knee bent to the Father in all things. And although every knee will ultimately submit to Him, many of those kneeling at the last day will do so from fear or regret, although most will do so from gratitude. Submitting to Him now — when there is no great persuasion to do so and all of the world may be aligned against His ways — stands as proof one really is willing to submit. Christ asked: *And why do you call me, Lord, Lord, and do not the things which I say?* (Luke 5:13). Calling Him Lord is not enough. Willingness to submit requires a willingness to be inconvenienced.[1106]

Wisdom In scripture, wisdom is feminine (*see*, e.g., Proverbs 1:38; Mosiah 5:14). In Hebrew it is called *chokmah* (חָכְמָה), (phonetically khokmaw´) which is a feminine noun.[1107] In Greek it is *sophia* (σοφία) which is, likewise, a feminine noun.[1108] "The role of the man is to become knowledge, so as to be able to fulfill a role that is eternal. The role of the woman is to become wisdom, because creation will only move forward if guided by wise counsel and prudent adaptations. Only together do they become complete and therefore *one*. Alone they are barren and unfruitful but joined they are infinite, because they continue. Knowledge alone may provide the spark of creation, but it is potentially dangerous when merely energetic. Creation must be wisely assisted to avoid peril. Wisdom alone is not an agent of action. Knowledge can initiate action, but wisdom is necessary to guide and counsel. The physical is a mirror of the spiritual. The seed of man provides the spark of life, but it is the womb of women where life develops. Likewise, the role of the woman in nurturing new life here is akin to the role of wisdom in eternity. Together, man and woman become whole, capable of creating and then nurturing a new creation."[1109]

Wisdom is the correct application of knowledge. Nothing in this world is more desirable than acquiring wisdom — understanding and putting knowledge to wise use. Zion will require the wisdom to use pure knowledge in meekness, humility, and charity. Zion will require Her influence. Wisdom and prudence go together as companions. "Prudence" means good judgment or common sense and is the quality of assessing things correctly and making a sound decision in light of the circumstances and persons involved. Prudent judgment is not hasty or unfair.[1110] *See also* MARY, THE MOTHER OF CHRIST.

Woe When one "woe" is pronounced upon a people, it is a warning of condemnation in this life. It is more concerning when three "woes" are pronounced upon a people — the connotation being a condemnation that will last beyond this life and into eternity.[1111] A three-fold condemnation goes beyond this life and will follow those to whom they apply into the hereafter. A three-fold woe is pronounced by a power that cannot be altered.[1112]

World "The world and earth are not synonymous terms. The world is the human family."[1113] What is the end of the world? The destruction of the wicked.[1114]

Worlds Without End If men and women will receive what is offered now, they will be added upon for ever and for ever. In other words, each person moves up the ladder by his or her heed and diligence in this cycle of creation. As they do, they will have so much the advantage in the next cycle. They can choose to move upward and be added upon or choose to remain as they are, worlds without end. Now is part of eternity. Though mortal, man lives in eternity and ought to take this opportunity seriously. The scriptures speak of things that happened *before the foundation of the world* (1 Peter 1:4; Testimony of John 9:20; T&C 138:19) or *in the first place* (Mosiah 1:9;

Alma 9:10) or *from the foundation of the world* (Matthew 7:8; T&C 138:19; Revelation 6:11). These statements make it clear that what went on before "this creation" *did* matter and *do* affect mankind now. In the same way, what is accepted in this life by one's heed and diligence affects what comes after. This current course of life has been ordained by God and is *one eternal round* (LOF 3:15; T&C 2:1; JSH 10:2). Even if one has proven before, he must prove himself again, now. God has been at this a long time. Christ has been involved in many repeated cycles of creation. God's great work has been going through cycles of creation, fall, redemption, judgment, and re-creation for ever. It is endless. Many unnumbered worlds have been, now are, and will yet be. This is a continual, endless cycle, worlds without end. "Ever notice how the pre-earth and the Millennium seem alike? Ever wonder what *worlds without end* means? Ever considered how God's work *never ends*, and yet it has definite increments separating one cycle from the next? God's works are endless. We are His greatest work. He intends to give us immortality and eventual eternal life. How long it will require depends on how long it takes us to become like the prototype of the saved man."[1115] *See also* FOR EVER.

Worthy/Unworthy "If the man is married, his wife must be among the seven women who vote to sustain a man to be ordained and minister outside his own family. If his wife will not sustain him, he is unworthy to provide priesthood service for the fellowship. There is nothing implied in the word regarding a man's standing before God. Within the community of fellowship, until his wife is prepared to support him acting outside the family, his effort should be within his family. The word unworthy is not a statement of condemnation but only of qualification. It was the word the Lord used, and therefore, I do not feel at liberty to change it."[1116] *See also* SUSTAIN.

Wrath There are two levels of wrath. One is temporal — here and now. The wicked are often punished here by letting them pursue their own evil course until it destroys them. Repentance, in that sense, relieves them of the physical, emotional, social, military, economic, and interpersonal disasters they bring upon themselves by their ruinous pursuit of destructive behavior. The other is eternal — meaning coming after this life. That second wrath is a result of leaving this life with accountability for what happened here and the lack of preparation for the moment when "judgment" is rendered. That "judgment" consists of the unrepentant finally facing reality. "When you are in His presence you can accurately measure the difference between what you are and what He wanted you to become — i.e., like Him. The gulf is so great that you would rather be in hell than in the presence of a just and holy being when you are stained with the blood and sins of your generation (Mormon 4:6)."[1117] God withdrawing is how His wrath manifests itself. "If He withdraws from you, that should be felt keenly as an absence and rejection."[1118]

God's wrath is "poured out" and takes a specific form: *wars and rumors of wars among all the nations and kindreds* (1 Nephi 3:29). People go to war. The *wicked shall slay the wicked* (T&C 50:8; Proverbs 2:37; Mormon 2:1). The wicked get to destroy one another, but they do not get to destroy the righteous (*see* 1 Nephi 7:4). The angel makes a point of stating what Nephi is beholding in 1 Nephi 3:29: *Behold, the wrath of God is upon the mother of harlots.* How is this God's wrath? The answer is that when God is angry, He withdraws His spirit (*see* Helaman 2:34; 5:3). And when He withdraws His spirit from one, He generally pours it out on another (*see* Helaman 2:34). When His spirit withdraws, men are left to their natural, carnal state, filled with envy, jealousy, covetousness, ambition, and greed. When the Heavens become silent, the judgments of God follow (*see* Revelation 2:17; T&C 86:20).[1119]

Wrest The mingling of scripture with the philosophies of men, resulting in error.[1120] Wrest comes from the Old English word *wræstan*, which meant "to twist or wrench."[1121] The term is further defined by the Greek word *strebloó* (στρεβλόω), which connotes "wrest" with "to pervert" or "to torture language to a false sense."[1122] In modern language, wrest means "to distort; to turn from truth or twist from its natural meaning." This is how it is used in the Book of Mormon: *Behold, the scriptures are before you; if ye will wrest them it shall be to your own destruction* (Alma 10:12). *For behold, some have wrested the scriptures and have gone far astray because of this thing* (Alma 19:9). The Lord warns that: *Satan does stir up the hearts of the people to contention concerning the points of my doctrine, and in these things they do err, for they do wrest the scriptures and do not understand them* (JSH 10:20). The verb *wrest* also means to forcibly take something from another's grasp.

Joseph Smith described how John the Baptist "wrested the keys, the kingdoms, the power, the glory from the Jews, by the holy anointing and decree of heaven."[1123] "When Christ came the first time, God took down [or wrested from the Jews] a previously established hierarchy using an orderly process, informing us about His house of order. He ordained John to bring it to an end, which put him on a collision course with the hierarchy. John the Baptist *was ordained by the angel of God at the time he was eight days old unto this power: to overthrow the kingdom of the Jews, and to make straight the way of the Lord before the face of his people, to prepare them for the coming of the Lord* (T&C 82:14). For His return, we should expect something similar to His first coming. That is, an orderly take down of a competing hierarchy using someone ordained to accomplish that end that is put by God on a collision course with the targeted power structure."[1124]

Zion A prophesied last-days community of saints to which the City of Enoch will return, and where Christ will dwell. Originally expected by Mormons to be located in Independence, Missouri, it was later relocated to Nauvoo, Illinois. Late in his life Joseph Smith changed the location to "the whole of North and South America," predicting it will cover the entire land mass at some point during the Millennial reign of Jesus Christ.[1125] Zion consists of people living in harmony with God. It is defined in revelation as *the pure in heart* (T&C 96:5–7; T&C 101:3; Genesis 4:14–16,19), but prophecy also confirms it will be an actual location and a place of gathering.[1126]

Zion and a New Jerusalem will exist before the Lord's return in glory (*see* T&C 31:6; 58:3; 31:14–16). God will bring it as His work. Mortal man will labor with Him, but the Lord will be given credit for accomplishing it. No institution exists with the capacity to accomplish Zion. It will be so entirely foreign to this world that the people who come there will be required to adopt a new society, a new way of thinking, a different way of interacting, an entirely new law, a form of government that does not presently exist, an order to their lives that alters everything, and a form of righteousness that is only possible for a society with a new structure.[1127] The law of Moses did not produce Zion. The New Testament Primitive Christian church did not produce Zion. Modeling after either of these, as the church established by Joseph Smith did, has likewise not produced Zion.

Zion will be produced by a journey begun in equality, pursued by equals, with no man able to command another man's actions. Persuasion, meekness, unfeigned love, and pure knowledge are the only tools necessary for Zion.[1128]

Zion is something that has only been accomplished in the known history of the world by two communities. It is prophesied that there will be a third. What is to be created is something so foreign to this world that there is nothing in the world which can be used to judge its progression. Even the scriptures do not give a blueprint to follow. If they contained the necessary information, Zion would have been established long ago. "God alone will establish Zion. His instructions are vital and necessary for us. Once He instructs us, the Scriptures can then be used to confirm that His direction to us now is consistent with what He prophesied, covenanted, and promised would happen. But the path to Zion is to be found only by following God's immediate commands to us. That is how He will bring it. He will lead us there. There is no magic, there is no sprinkling fairy dust that will take you to where God is. It does not and cannot happen that way. He will lead us, teach us, command us, guide us, but we have to be the ones who become what He commands. We have to be the ones who do what he bids us do."[1129] The single, all-encompassing topic of Denver Snuffer's ministry is Zion. "If you go back to the very first book, *The Second Comforter: Conversing with the Lord through the Veil*, and you read everything I have written beginning there until now...what you will discover is that I have given one continuous exposition. Admittedly it's long, admittedly it fills millions of words in English, but it is a single exposition. I have been addressing one subject from the beginning until now; it is all one great whole."[1130]

The counterpart to the world (or Babylon, as the scriptures have nicknamed the world) is Zion.[1131] The criteria or the description of Zion can be read in Genesis. *From that time forth there were wars and bloodshed among them, but the Lord came and dwelt with his people and they dwelt in righteousness* (Genesis 4:14). This is an interesting contrast. There are wars and bloodshed, on the one hand, but then there is the Lord dwelling among people who are living in peace and righteousness, on the other hand. *And the fear of the Lord was upon all nations, so great was the glory of the Lord which was upon his people* (ibid.). It was the *glory of the Lord...upon his people* that intimidated the wicked. The Lord doesn't show Himself to the wicked except to destruction, but the Lord shows Himself unto those who are prepared. The *glory of the Lord upon [them]* is what others find intimidating. And that was the case with these people of Enoch's Zion. *And the Lord blessed the land, and they were blessed upon the mountains and upon the high places, and did flourish* (ibid.). That is literal — Zion is not located in a valley, either in the past or in the future. Zion belongs on a high place. The prophecies make this clear. *And the Lord called his people Zion because they were of one heart, and one mind, and dwelt in righteousness, and there were no poor among them* (ibid.). Of these, the words *and the Lord dwelt [among them]* are the most important. But He could not do so unless they were united. Becoming one and rising up to receive the proper order of things is but a prelude to the Lord's presence.[1132] "The Lord will fight the battles for Zion, when Zion exists. You will not need to have a weapon's budget in Zion's camp. It doesn't happen that way. The battle to be fought is fought by the Lord. The prophecy given through Joseph Smith about the last days predicts the wicked decide they will not take on Zion, because Zion is too terrible. They will reach that conclusion entirely because of the presence of the Lord there (T&C 31:14). It is not because of munitions. In fact, that same description includes a statement about Zion's residents. They are those who will not take up arms against their neighbor, but instead flee to Zion. They are the only ones that aren't killing others."[1133]

Zion will include people who are willing to receive revelations from God and obey commandments. God does this to bless His people. *Blessed are they whose feet stand upon the land of Zion, who have obeyed my gospel, for they shall receive for their reward the good things of the earth, and it shall bring forth in her strength. And they also shall be crowned with blessings from above, yea, and with commandments not a few and with revelations in their time — they that are faithful and diligent before me* (T&C 46:1). In other words, if any are privileged to stand upon the land of Zion, God will speak to them. He speaks two things for their benefit: first, *commandments*, and those will be *not a few,* because they will need a great deal of direction if they are going to be His people; and second, *revelations in their time,* because they will be ignorant of many mysteries He expects them to one day comprehend. Therefore, one of the characteristics of these people will be their willingness, even alacrity, to receive commandments and revelations.[1134] Apparently, the people who are to settle in the New Jerusalem and cause Zion to reappear will need to know not only how to act, but to have the basis to know *why* they are to act according to the Heavenly pattern — which is not needed for the world but absolutely essential to the creation of Zion.[1135]

"Being 'one' is required of us for Zion to return. Zion is required for the Lord to dwell among us again. He is going to return to a Zion, no matter how few may be involved. He will come even if only two or three gather in His name (Matthew 9:14). Zion may be small, but it will nonetheless be Zion before He can visit with her."[1136] The significance of Zion is its spiritual endowment. It is the Power of Heaven and not the voting bloc. It is not their big numbers which intimidate the ungodly. Even a handful is sufficient. Righteousness is a power in itself.[1137] Zion is the Lord's work. Getting it will not depend on the goodness or desires of men and women but on their submission to the Lord who intends to accomplish it. "*We* can't force it, cause it, bring it, or hope it into existence. What we can do is submit to the Lord in a way that encourages Him to continue to use us for His purposes."[1138] Zion, like our Lord, will receive little attention or regard from the world. The people who will recognize that its foundation is being laid will be very few. While the Jews, Christians, saints, and philosophers look to constantly replenish themselves from the east (*see* Isaiah 1:7), God will begin His work quietly in the mountains of the west (*see* T&C 58:3).[1139]

GLOSSARY **ENDNOTES**

1   "144,000, Part 2," Nov. 7, 2012, www.
    denversnuffer.com/blog. (Subse-
    quent references to the weblog will
    only mention blog post.)

2   "A Clarifying Question," March 27,
    2015, blog post.

3   *A Man Without Doubt* (Salt Lake City:
    Mill Creek Press, 2016), 165.

4   *Preserving the Restoration* (Salt Lake
    City: Mill Creek Press, 2015), 180.

5   Ibid., 179.

6   *Teachings of the Prophet Joseph Smith*,
    comp. Joseph Fielding Smith (Salt
    Lake City: Deseret Book, 1976), 322,
    herein cited as *TPJS*; *The Words of Jo-
    seph Smith*, comp. Andrew F. Ehat
    and Lyndon W. Cook (Provo, UT:
    Religious Studies Center, Brigham
    Young University, 1980), 244, herein
    cited as *WJS*; *Joseph Smith Papers* (Salt
    Lake City: The Church Historian's
    Press, 2008–ongoing), *Journals* Vol.
    3:86, herein cited as *JSP*.

7   *Preserving the Restoration*, 181.

8   "Cursed: Denied Priesthood," Jan.
    07, 2018, Sandy, UT, 11, transcript
    of Q&A.

9   "1 Nephi 13:31–32," June 29, 2010,
    blog post.

10 "Alma 13:17–18," June 15, 2010, blog
    post.

11 *TPJS*, 301; *WJS*, 202; *JSP*, *Journals* Vol.
    3:17–18, Editorial Note; 17 May
    1843; "Joseph Smith Discourse," 17
    May 1843–A, in William Clayton
    Journal, p. [16], *JSP*, https://www.
    josephsmithpapers.org/paper-sum-
    mary/ discourse-17-may-1843-a-as-
    reported-by-william-clayton/1; CHL.
    This is the source for D&C 131:6.
    Section 131 of the LDS Doctrine and
    Covenants first appeared as canon
    in the 1876 revision prepared by
    Orson Pratt under the direction of
    Brigham Young.

12 "Accountability," Nov. 2, 2012, blog
    post.

13 "But if" is a Hebraism for "unless."

    See Royal Skousen, *Analysis of Tex-
    tual Variants of the Book of Mormon* 6
    vols. (Provo, UT: Foundation for An-
    cient Research and Mormon Studies,
    2004–2009), 2:1173–1174.

14 "King Benjamin's Wisdom," Jan. 25,
    2014, blog post.

15 "Alma 13:31," June 21, 2010, blog post.

16 "Answer to Moroni 8:8," Dec. 14,
    2011, blog post.

17 *The Second Comforter: Conversing
    with the Lord Through the Veil* (Salt
    Lake City: Mill Creek Press, 2006),
    274–275. Herein cited as *Second Com-
    forter*.

18 The entire sermon from which this
    has been taken was dictated by Jo-
    seph Smith to his scribe, Robert B.
    Thompson, who read it to the saints
    in general conference and is "appar-
    ently the only discourse for which
    the Prophet ever prepared a text."
    See *WJS*, 50, 5 October 1840, note 1.

19 "Our Divine Parents," March 25,
    2018, 36, paper.

20 "The Holy Order," Oct. 29, 2017, 3,
    paper.

21 Ibid., 5.

22 *TPJS*, 157; *WJS*, 8–9.

23 "The Holy Order," Oct. 29, 2017, 2n8,
    paper.

24 Ibid., 2; Email to Scripture Commit-
    tee, April 3, 2019.

25 Ibid., 42.

26 Jonathan Stapley, "Adaptive Sealing
    Ritual in Mormonism," *Journal of
    Mormon History*, Vol. 37, No. 3, Sum-
    mer 2011, 53–117.

27 *Passing the Heavenly Gift* (Salt
    Lake City: Mill Creek Press, 2011),
    481–482.

28 "The Holy Order," Oct. 29, 2017, 43,
    paper.

29 Email, Dec. 16, 2018.

30 "3 Nephi 12:31–32," Oct. 14, 2010,
    blog post.

31 "The Restoration's Shattered Prom-
    ises and Great Hope," address given

32 "Adultery, Part 3," Dec. 18, 2018, blog post.

33 "3 Nephi 12:31–32," Oct. 14, 2010, blog post.

34 *The Second Comforter*, 415–416.

35 *TPJS*, 157, 167; *WJS*, 39.

36 *Preserving the Restoration*, 161.

37 "Mosiah 3:23," June 12, 2012, blog post.

38 Ibid.

39 D&C 130:5. Section 130 of the LDS Doctrine and Covenants first appeared as canon in the 1876 edition prepared by Orson Pratt under the direction of Brigham Young. Its inclusion here is for reference. For original sources see *JSP, Journals* Vol. 2:323–326, (Dec. 1841–April 1843), 2 April 1843. Willard Richards didn't accompany Joseph Smith on his four-day trip to Ramus, IL, and reconstructed the Joseph Smith Journal entry from the Journal of William Clayton. See *JSP*, Journals Vol. 2:403–405, Appendix 2, 1–4 April 1843. *WJS*, 169, 267n3; 171, 268n15.

40 *Passing the Heavenly Gift*, 331n419.

41 "Follow-up Question," Jan. 3, 2012, blog post.

42 "The Holy Order," Oct. 29, 2017, 16, paper.

43 *Preserving the Restoration*, 75.

44 Ibid., 76.

45 "2 Nephi 33:5–6," Sept. 6, 2010, blog post.

46 "Answers to Last Week's Questions," May 12, 2012, blog post.

47 "D&C 132, conclusion," April 9, 2010, blog post.

48 "Pretensions of Public Piety," Sept. 7, 2015, blog post.

49 *Passing the Heavenly Gift*, 410.

50 "Forward or Backward," April 16, 2010, blog post.

51 "Jacob 5:38–41," April 4, 2012, blog post.

52 Hugh Nibley, *Temple and Cosmos* (Salt Lake City: Deseret Book, 1992), 395, 397.

53 "The Holy Order," Oct. 29, 2017, 18, paper.

54 *JSP, Documents*, Vol. 3:43n259.

55 *Preserving the Restoration*, 49n138.

56 "Was There An Original," address given at Sunstone Symposium, Salt Lake City, July 29, 2016, paper, 18–19; 18n78. The LDS Historian's Office acknowledges it meant, "A title indicating one sent forth to preach; later designated as a specific ecclesiastical office." See *JSP, Documents*, Vol. 1:495; Glossary, s.v. "Apostle."

57 "Was There An Original," address given at Sunstone Symposium, Salt Lake City, July 29, 2016, paper, 18–19; 18n79,80. "On this day the council of the seventy meet to render an account of their travels and ministry, since they were ordained to that apostleship." *JSP, Journals* Vol. 1:139.

58 *Passing the Heavenly Gift*, 61.

59 "Adam's Religion," December 21, 2015, blog post.

60 Margaret Barker, *The Hidden Tradition of the Kingdom of God* (London: Society for Promoting Christian Knowledge, 2007), 26.

61 *TPJS*, 348; *WJS*, 350.

62 *TPJS*, 346–347; *WJS*, 344–345, 350; *Wilford Woodruff's Journal, 1833–1898: Typescript*, 10 vols., ed. Scott G. Kenney (Midvale, UT: Signature Books, 1983), 2:384. Herein cited as *WWJ*.

63 "Why a Temple?" April 29, 2016, blog post.

64 *The Second Comforter*, 92.

65 Ibid., 99.

66 Ibid., 111–113.

67 Ibid., 116.

68 *Ten Parables* (Salt Lake City: Mill Creek Press, 2008), 93.

69 "3 Nephi 14:7–8," Oct. 28, 2010, blog post.

70 "3 Nephi 1419 11," Oct. 28, 2010, blog post.

71 James Strong, *Strong's Expanded Exhaustive Concordance of the Bible* (Nashville: Thomas Nelson, 2009), H3722.

72 Ibid., G2643.

73 Hugh Nibley, *Approaching Zion* (Salt Lake City: Deseret Book, 1989), 567.

74 Ibid., 605.

75 "3 Nephi 11:31–32," Sept. 27, 2010, blog post.

76 "Forsake, come, call, obey, keep, see, and *know*," July 12, 2011, blog post. Edits by email to Scripture Committee, Mar. 5, 2018.

77 Instructions to Scripture Committee, May 31, 2018.

78 *Preserving the Restoration*, 347n932; *WJS*, 344–345, 350, 357; *WWJ*, 2:384.

79 Ibid., 304.

80 Ibid., 21.

81 *Essays: Three Degrees* (Mill Creek Press: Salt Lake City, 2013), "The Mission of Elijah Reconsidered," 64.

82 "King Benjamin's Self Reliance," Jan. 23, 2014, blog post.

83 Hugh Nibley, *Approaching Zion*, 14–16.

84 500th Year Reformation Talk Five, 3–4, Sandy, UT, Sept. 7, 2018, transcript of recording.

85 "3 Nephi 11:26," Sept. 25, 2010, blog post.

86 "3 Nephi 11: 24–25," Sept. 24, 2010, blog post.

87 "3 Nephi 11:26," Sept. 25, 2010, blog post.

88 "2 Nephi 31:17," Aug. 27, 2010, blog post.

89 "God's Many Works," Part 5, Aug. 17, 2012, blog post.

90 "3 Nephi 11:36," Sept. 29, 2010, blog post.

91 *WJS*, 185.

92 *Second Comforter*, 240.

93 Email to Scripture Committee, Jan. 31, 2018.

94 "3 Nephi 11:37–38," Sept. 29, 2010, blog post.

95 *TPJS*, 346–347; *WJS*, 358.

96 "3 Nephi 11:27," Sept. 26, 2010, blog post.

97 "3 Nephi 11:5," Sept. 28, 2010, blog post.

98 *Passing the Heavenly Gift,* 51–52.

99 *Second Comforter*, 54.

100 "Nephi's Brother Jacob, Part 6," March 16, 2012, blog post.

101 "3 Nephi 11:31–32," Sept. 27, 2010, blog post.

102 *Strong's Concordance*, G1985.

103 D. Michael Quinn, *The Mormon Hierarchy: Origins of Power* (Salt Lake City: Signature Books, 1994), 69.

104 *Preserving the Restoration*, 260n684.

105 Ibid., 260.

106 *Beloved Enos* (Salt Lake City: Mill Creek Press, 2009), 49.

107 Ibid., 125–126.

108 *Essays: Three Degrees*, "The Mission of Elijah Reconsidered," 83–84.

109 *JSP, Journals* Vol. 2:403–405, Appendix 2, 1–4 April 1843; *WJS*, 170, 267n15, 268n14.

110 *The Second Comforter*, 182–183.

111 Ibid., 289n236.

112 "The Holy Order," Oct. 29, 2017, 11, paper.

113 "Blood crying for vengeance," May 24, 2010, blog post.

114 "2 Nephi 33:15," Sept. 9, 2010, blog post.

115 "2 Nephi 28:22," Aug. 3, 2010, blog post.

116 "3 Nephi 18:24–25," Nov. 15, 2010, blog post.

117 "1 Nephi 13:38," July 2, 2010, blog post.

118 *Strong's Concordance*, G4698.

119 *Preserving the Restoration*, 98.

120 Ibid., 34–35.

121 "3 Nephi 12:19," Oct. 10, 2010, blog post.

122 "3 Nephi 12:30," Oct. 13, 2010, blog post.

123 "3 Nephi 13:26–32," Oct. 25, 2010, blog post.

124 *Preserving the Restoration*, 383.

125 "Answers to Last Week's Questions," May 12, 2012, blog post.

126 *Preserving the Restoration*, 159.

127 "3 Nephi 11," Sept. 22, 2010, blog post.

128 "3 Nephi 11:24–25," Sept. 24, 2010, blog post.

129 "Alma 13:28," June 19, 2010, blog post.

130 "Alma 13:28," June 19, 2010, blog post; edited for Glossary Dec. 8, 2018.

131 "Follow-up Question," Jan. 3, 2012, blog post.

132 *History of the Church of Jesus Christ of Latter-day Saints*, 7 vols., ed. B. H. Roberts, 2nd ed. Rev. (Salt Lake City: Deseret Book, 1957), (May 21, 1843; 5:401–403). Herein cited DHC.

133 *Nephi's Isaiah* (Salt Lake City: Mill Creek Press, 2006), 71, 71n115.

134 *Eighteen Verses* (Salt Lake City: Mill Creek Press, 2007), 175.

135 Ibid., 175n123.

136 "Alma 13:13," June 13, 2010, blog post. See *WJS*, 209, as cited in *Eighteen Verses*, 32n19.

137 "3 Nephi 18:31–32," Nov. 16, 2010, blog post.

138 *The Second Comforter*, 371–372.

139 Ibid., 176.

140 Ibid., 18–19.

141 Ibid., 19n17.

142 The Testimony of St. John 1:12. (A newly revealed account. Cf. John 1:6).

143 *The Second Comforter*, 169–170

144 *Preserving the Restoration*, 298n777.

145 "Weightier Matters," Oct. 4, 2012, blog post.

146 *Preserving the Restoration*, 361.

147 Restoration Archives recording, Nov. 24, 2018; See Podcast Episode 46: "Charity – Part 1," Nov. 25, 2018.

148 *Preserving the Restoration*, 173.

149 *Strong's Concordance*, H3742.

150 "Jacob 5:60–63," April 12, 2012, blog post.

151 "Blessed are the peacemakers," May 3, 2010, blog post.

152 "3 Nephi 20:25–27," Sept. 20, 2010, blog post.

153 "God's People," June 20, 2012, blog post.

154 *Come, Let Us Adore Him* (Salt Lake City: Mill Creek Press, 2009), 40–41. (See Ch. 3 for a complete explanation of this topic).

155 "Other Sheep Indeed," expanded paper of address given at Sunstone Symposium, Salt Lake City, UT, July 19, 2017, 15–16.

156 Address at the Unity in Christ Regional Conference, Spanish Fork, July 30, 2017, 1–3, transcript of talk.

157 *The Second Comforter*, 171.

158 Ibid., 155–156; 360–361.

159 Denver Snuffer, Jr., "The Holy Order," Oct. 29, 2017, 16, paper.

160 "3 Nephi 18:11," Nov. 10, 2010, blog post.

161 "Come Unto Christ," Dec. 29, 2015, blog post.

162 "3 Nephi 18:16," Nov. 12, 2010, blog post.

163 *Strong's Concordance*, G1577.

164 Online Etymology Dictionary, https://www.etymonline.com/word/church.

165 "Peoplehood," May 8, 2010, blog post

166 Email to Scripture Committee, Jan. 31, 2018.

167 Email to Scripture Committee, Jan. 31, 2018.

168 Hugh Nibley, *Teachings of the Book of Mormon*, 4 vols. (American Fork, UT: Covenant Communications, 2004), 3:51–52; quoted in comments to blog post "1 Nephi 14:3–4," July 6, 2010.

169 "1 Nephi 14:3–4," July 6, 2010, blog post.

170 *The Second Comforter*, 3–4.

171 *Passing the Heavenly Gift*, 51n46.

172 D&C 130:3. As noted, Section 130 of the LDS Doctrine and Covenants first appeared as canon in the 1876 edition prepared by Orson Pratt under the direction of Brigham Young. Its inclusion here is for reference. For original sources see *JSP, Journals* Vol. 2:323–326, (Dec. 1841–April 1843), 2 April 1843. Willard Richards didn't accompany Joseph Smith on his four-day trip to Ramus, IL, and reconstructed the Joseph Smith Journal entry from the Journal of William Clayton. See *JSP, Journals* Vol. 2:403–405, Appendix 2, 1–4

April 1843. *WJS*, 169, 267n3, 268n14.

173 "White Stone and a New Name," March 23, 2010, blog post.

174 *The Second Comforter,* 383.

175 Ibid., 108.

176 *WJS*, 169, 267n3; 171, 268n15. D&C 130:3. Section 130 of the LDS Doctrine and Covenants first appeared as canon in the 1876 edition prepared by Orson Pratt under the direction of Brigham Young. For original sources for D&C 130:3–7 see *JSP, Journals* Vol. 2:323–326, (Dec. 1841–April 1843), 2 April 1843 and *JSP, Journals* Vol. 2:403–405, Appendix 2, 1–4 April 1843.

177 "Why Wait," May 4, 2010, blog post.

178 *The Second Comforter*, 44.

179 *Strong's Concordance,* H4687.

180 Ibid., G1785.

181 *Essays: Three Degrees,* "The Mission of Elijah Reconsidered," 63.

182 *The Second Comforter*, 289–290.

183 Ibid., 294–295.

184 Ibid., 295–296.

185 Ibid., 298.

186 "Keep the Commandments," March 1, 2010, blog post.

187 "3 Nephi 12:2," Oct. 2, 2010, blog post.

188 "Remembering the Covenants" Conference, Aug. 4, 2018, Centerville, UT, 6, transcript of recording.

189 Noah Webster, *An American Dictionary of the English Language,* 2 vols. (New York: S. Converse, 1828), s.v. "Consent."

190 "Reorganizing A Stake," Dec. 6, 2015, blog post.

191 "The Mormon Legal Mind," Comments made at Sunstone Symposium panel discussion by Denver Snuffer, Aug. 1, 2015, transcript, 20.

192 *Preserving the Restoration*, 158.

193 *Passing the Heavenly Gift*, 418.

194 "Sacrament and Tithing," Jan. 4, 2016, blog post.

195 "Organize Yourselves," Sept. 19, 2016, blog post.

196 *Beloved Enos*, 8–9.

197 *Strong's Concordance*, H6942.

198 "2 Nephi 32:9," Sept. 3, 2010, blog post.

199 *Preserving the Restoration*, 288.

200 "That We Might Become One," Jan. 14, 2018, 4, transcript of talk.

201 Ibid., 6–7.

202 *Preserving the Restoration*, 387.

203 See also "Answer to Prayer for Covenant," July 27, 2017, 6.

204 "Covenant People," July 21, 2017, blog post.

205 "Covenant," April 6, 2017, blog post.

206 *Preserving the Restoration*, 78.

207 Ibid., 21.

208 D&C 130:20. Section 130 of the LDS Doctrine and Covenants first appeared as canon in the 1876 edition prepared by Orson Pratt under the direction of Brigham Young. For original sources see *JSP, Journals* Vol. 2:323–326, (Dec. 1841–April 1843), 2 April 1843. Willard Richards didn't accompany Joseph Smith on his four-day trip to Ramus, IL, and reconstructed the Joseph Smith Journal entry from the Journal of William Clayton. See *JSP, Journals* Vol. 2:403–405, Appendix 2, 1–4 April 1843. *WJS*, 169–170, 267n6; 172–173.

209 *40 Years in Mormonism Lecture 4, "Covenants,"* 7.

210 Ibid., 12.

211 "Book of Mormon as Covenant," talk given at the Book of Mormon Covenant Conference in Columbia, SC, on Jan. 13, 2019; Podcast 54: "Abraham, Part 1," Jan. 27, 2019.

212 "More Ancient Than the New Testament," Feb. 26, 2012, blog post.

213 *40 Years in Mormonism Lecture 4, "Covenants,"* 14.

214 *40 Years in Mormonism Lecture 6, "Zion,"* 19–20.

215 *Preserving the Restoration*, 365.

216 Ibid., 373.

217 Ibid., 377.

218 Email to Scripture Committee, Jan. 31, 2018.

219 Email to Scripture Committee, Oct. 29, 2017.

220 "A Student of the Lord," April 19, 2010, blog post.

221 Ibid.

222 *TPJS* p. 322; *WJS*, 247.

223 *The Second Comforter*, 182.

224 "Remembering the Covenants" Conference, Aug. 4, 2018, Centerville, UT, 4, transcript of recording.

225 500th Year Reformation Talk Three, 15, Atlanta, GA, Nov. 16, 2017, Q&A.

226 *Strong's Concordance*, G1249.

227 500th Year Reformation Talk Two, 6, Dallas, TX, Oct. 19, 2017.

228 "God's Many Works, Conclusion," Aug. 18, 2012, blog post.

229 *Beloved Enos,* 88.

230 "A parting thought," Nov. 17, 2012, blog post.

231 "Questions and Answers," Feb. 9, 2010, blog post.

232 "Joseph Smith Papers 2," Oct. 4, 2016, blog post.

233 "3 Nephi 12:46–47," Oct. 17, 2010, blog post.

234 *TPJS*, 375; *WJS*, 382, 39.

235 "Miscellaneous," July 21, 2012, blog post.

236 "A Question About 'Seeds of Doubt,'" July 13, 2012, blog post.

237 "3 Nephi 12:17–18," Oct. 12, 2010, blog post.

238 "Follow-up Question," Jan. 3, 2012, blog post.

239 "Cursed: Denied Priesthood," Jan. 07, 2018, Sandy, UT, 23, transcript.

240 "The Holy Order," Oct. 29, 2017, 2, paper.

241 Email to Scripture Committee, Oct. 3, 2018.

242 "3 Nephi 21:26," July 21, 2010, blog post.

243 "3 Nephi 11:28–30," Sept. 27, 2010, blog post.

244 *Cassell's New Latin Dictionary*, ed. D. P. Simpson (New York: Funk & Wagnalls, 1960), s.v. "dives," 199.

245 *Preserving the Restoration*, 517–518.

246 "2 Nephi 31:18," Aug. 29, 2010, blog post.

247 "3 Nephi 11:39," Sept. 30, 2010, blog post.

248 "Forward or Backward," April 16, 2010, blog post.

249 Hugh Nibley, *The Prophetic Book of Mormon* (Salt Lake City: Deseret Book, 1989), 462–463.

250 See also "Answer to Prayer for Covenant," July 27, 2017, 7.

251 "Things to Keep Us Awake," expanded paper of address given in St. George, UT, March 19, 2017, 19.

252 *Strong's Concordance,* G1404.

253 *The Second Comforter*, 71–73.

254 "Sorting Things Out," July 22, 2012, blog post.

255 *Passing the Heavenly Gift*, 52.

256 *A Man Without Doubt*, 170.

257 *JSP, Documents* Vol. 1:320, citing JS History Vol. A1:118.

258 "Laying On Hands,"Aug. 19, 2014, blog post.

259 "Hyrum Smith - Part 2," July 18, 2012, blog post.

260 "Power in the Priesthood," May 18, 2012, blog post.

261 Commentary added to Glossary Dec. 8, 2018.

262 Joseph Smith Jr., John Whitmer, "Letter to the Church in Colesville, 2 December 1830," 205–206, *JSP, Documents* 1:214–219.

263 *Nephi's Isaiah*, 85.

264 Ibid., 85n132.

265 "1 Nephi 14:10," July 8, 2010, blog post.

266 *The Second Comforter*, 419.

267 *Nephi's Isaiah*, 26.

268 *TPJS*, 335; *WJS*, 327–336; *WWJ*, 2:359–360; *JSP, Journals* Vol. 3:200n878.

269 *TPJS*, 337; *WJS*, 329, 333–335; *WWJ*, 2:361.

270 *TPJS*, 340; *WJS*, 331; *WWJ*, 2:365.

271 "Things to Keep Us Awake," expanded paper of address given in St. George, UT, March 19, 2017, 16–17.

272 "Reply to Questions," Oct. 20, 2011, blog post.

273 See descriptions of the *axis mundi*

in Mircea Eliade, *The Sacred and the Profane: The Nature of Religion*, trans. Willard R. Trask (New York: Harcourt, Brace & World, 1963), 33–37, 44, 52–54, 177.

274   Email to Scripture Committee, June 30, 2018.

275   *A Man Without Doubt*, 169.

276   *A Man Without Doubt*, 13.

277   "2 Nephi 31:15," Aug. 27, 2010, blog post.

278   "3 Nephi 15:9–10," Nov. 4, 2010, blog post.

279   "2 Nephi 33:4," Sept. 5, 2010, blog post.

280   *The Second Comforter*, 401.

281   Ibid., 401n340.

282   *DHC* 4:7; *WJS*, 33.

283   "Our Divine Parents," March 25, 2018, 37–38, paper.

284   *Preserving the Restoration*, 430n1146.

285   "The Power of Words: 50 Words – Words that Lift, Inspire, Motivate, Elevate, and Transform Us," Aug. 24, 2009, video, https://www.youtube.com/watch?v=iQCL-roJ9wuM.

286   Ibid., 254.

287   Ibid., 254.

288   *The Second Comforter*, 165.

289   Ibid., 165n138.

290   Ibid., 177–178.

291   "1 Nephi 14:5," July 6, 2010, comment to blog post.

292   *The Second Comforter*, 54–60.

293   *Passing the Heavenly Gift*, 52.

294   Ibid., 52n50.

295   *The Second Comforter*, 54–60.

296   *Preserving the Restoration*, 329.

297   *Eighteen Verses*, 73–74.

298   Ibid., 312.

299   Ibid., 350.

300   "Follow and Receive," Jan. 30, 2015, blog post.

301   "Pretensions of Public Piety," Sept. 7, 2015, blog post.

302   "Signs Follow Faith," March 3, 2019, talk given at Centerville, UT, transcript, 3.

303   "Things to Keep Us Awake," expanded paper of address given

in St. George, UT, March 19, 2017, 18.

304   "The Restoration's Shattered Promises and Great Hope," address given at Sunstone Symposium, Sandy, UT, July 28, 2018, paper, 15.

305   "3 Nephi 12:6," Oct. 5, 2010, blog post.

306   Hugh Nibley, *Eloquent Witness: Nibley on Himself, Others, and the Temple,* ed. Stephen D. Ricks (Salt Lake City: Deseret Book, 2008), 325–326.

307   "Last Week's Comments," May 19, 2012, blog post.

308   *The Second Comforter*, 92n72.

309   "Zion Will Come," Moab, UT, April 10, 2016, 7–8.

310   "The Temple," 19, Oct. 28, 2012, transcript of talk.

311   *Eighteen Verses*, 312.

312   "Ignorance Enshrined," Feb. 22, 2013, blog post.

313   "2 Nephi 28:20," Aug. 2, 2010, blog post.

314   "Recent Conversations," Nov. 25, 2011, blog post.

315   "The Trick to Avoiding Apostasy," June 22, 2012, blog post.

316   "Jumping out a Window," Feb. 24, 2010, blog post.

317   *Eighteen Verses*, 312.

318   See *Preserving the Restoration*, 518–524; 500th Year Reformation Talk Two, 8, Dallas, TX, Sept. 21, 2017.

319   "The Holy Order," Oct. 29, 2017, 4–5, paper.

320   *TPJS*, 157; *WJS*, 8–9.

321   *TPJS*, 149; see also *WJS*, 4; 17n1; JS, Discourse, Commerce, IL, between 26 June and 2 July 1839; in *Willard Richards Pocket Companion,* pp. 15–22; *Willard Richards, Journals,* CHL, JSP, https://www.josephsmithpapers.org/paper-summary/discourse-between-circa-26-june-and-circa-2-july-1839-as-reported-by-willard-richards/3

322   *WJS*, 17n5.

323   WJS, 344–345; 350, 358; WWJ, 2:384.

324   Preserving the Restoration, 306–308.

325   "2 Nephi 31:13," Aug. 26, 2010, blog post.

326   "2 Nephi 31:13," Aug. 26, 2010, blog post.

327   "2 Nephi 31:15," Aug. 27, 2010, blog post.

328   TPJS 346–347; Preserving the Restoration, 347n932; WJS, 344–345, 350, 357; WWJ, 2:384.

329   "2 Nephi 31:10–11," Aug. 25, 2010, blog post.

330   Email to Scripture Committee, Jan. 31, 2018.

331   Preserving the Restoration, iv; ivn4.

332   "Knowledge and Indifference," Jan. 17, 2012, blog post.

333   "God is no respecter of persons," April 27, 2010, blog post.

334   Preserving the Restoration, 296.

335   Come, Let Us Adore Him, 226.

336   Preserving the Restoration, 14

337   Ibid., 105.

338   Strong's Concordance, H6617.

339   "Our Divine Parents," March 25, 2018, 5, paper.

340   Ibid., 7.

341   Ibid., 6.

342   Preserving the Restoration, 144–145.

343   Ibid., 34–35.

344   Ibid., 124n324.

345   40 Years in Mormonism Lecture 7 "Christ: The Prototype of the Saved Man," 4.

346   "Fruit," March 10, 2018, blog post, emphasis his.

347   The Second Comforter, 235.

348   Eighteen Verses, 284.

349   Eighteen Verses, 283.

350   The Testimony of St. John 3:4, cf. T&C 93:4.

351   The Testimony of St. John 12:10, cf. T&C 90:13–4

352   Preserving the Restoration, 19.

353   The Second Comforter, 11.

354   Ibid., 114.

355   "The Holy Order," Oct. 29, 2017, 2–3, paper.

356   JSP, Documents Vol 2: July 1831–January 1833, 85.

357   "Keep the Covenant: Do the Work" Sept. 30, 2018, 2, transcript of talk.

358   "Things to Keep Us Awake," expanded paper of address given in St. George, UT, March 19, 2017, 3; Preserving the Restoration, iv.

359   "Alma 13:11," June 12, 2010, blog post.

360   Commentary added to Glossary Dec. 8, 2018.

361   500th Year Reformation Talk Two, 19–20, Dallas, TX, Oct. 19, 2017, Q&A, transcript.

362   Nephi's Isaiah, 74n121.

363   Passing the Heavenly Gift, 331.

364   Ibid., 95n110.

365   Ibid., 332.

366   "1 Nephi 14:6," July 7, 2010, blog post.

367   "1 Nephi 13:33–34," June 30, 2010, blog post.

368   "1 Nephi 14:1–2," July 5, 2010, blog post.

369   "3 Nephi 16:11," June 24, 2010, blog post.

370   Preserving the Restoration, 146.

371   Ibid., 147.

372   "God's Many Works, Part 5," Aug. 17, 2012, blog post.

373   "God's Many Works, Conclusion," Aug. 18, 2012, blog post.

374   WJS, 170, 173, 268n5. The original Willard Richards entry reads, "But the Holy Ghost is a personage of spirit — and a person cannot have the personage of the H.G. in his heart he may receive the gift of the holy Ghost. It may descend upon him but not to tarry with him" (JSP, Journals Vol. 2:326, Appendix 2, 1–4 April 1843, 405).

375   "BFHG, Part 2," Aug. 21, 2012, blog post.

376   "Laying On Hands," Aug. 19, 2014, blog post.

377   "Clarifying Distinctions," Oct. 7, 2015, blog post

378   Hugh Nibley, Eloquent Witness: Nibley on Himself, Others, and the Temple, 334–335.

379 "2 Nephi 31:14," Aug. 26, 2010, blog post.

380 See 1835 D&C 3:2–3; *Preserving the Restoration*, 164–165; "The Holy Order," Oct. 29, 2017, 6,10, paper.

381 "Organize Yourselves," Sept. 19, 2016, blog post.

382 *Essays: Three Degrees*, "The Mission of Elijah Reconsidered," 88.

383 "Gifts come from God," June 2, 2010, blog post.

384 *Second Comforter*, 139–140.

385 *Preserving the Restoration*, 119.

386 Ibid., 353.

387 Hugh Nibley, *Eloquent Witness: Nibley on Himself, Others, and the Temple*, 326–327.

388 Podcast 60: "Third Root," March 30, 2019.

389 Ibid., 14.

390 "Some of Christ," Feb. 9, 2012, blog post.

391 *Strong's Concordance*, G2098.

392 "First Principles of the Gospel," March 24, 2010, blog post.

393 "Process Not Event," March 28, 2010, blog post.

394 *Preserving the Restoration*, 307–308.

395 Ibid., 343.

396 "3 Nephi 21: 25," July 20, 2010, blog post.

397 *WJS*, 171, 267n3; D&C 130:3. Section 130 of the LDS Doctrine and Covenants first appeared as canon in the 1876 edition prepared by Orson Pratt under the direction of Brigham Young. For original sources for D&C 130:3–7 see *JSP, Journals* Vol. 2:323–326, (Dec. 1841–April 1843), 2 April 1843 and *JSP, Journals* Vol. 2:403–405, Appendix 2, 1–4 April 1843.

398 *WJS*, 254; *JSP, Journals* Vol. 3:109.

399 "The Whole Not the Parts," Dec. 28, 2011, blog post.

400 "3 Nephi 11:24–25," Sept. 24, 2010, blog post.

401 "Cursed: Denied Priesthood," Q&A, Jan. 7, 2018, 22, transcript of talk.

402 *40 Years in Mormonism Lecture 4*, "Covenants," 6.

403 "Cursed: Denied Priesthood," Q&A, Jan. 7, 2018, 22, transcript of talk.

404 "The Power of Words: 50 Words – Words that Lift, Inspire, Motivate, Elevate, and Transform Us," Aug. 24, 2009, video, https://www.youtube.com/watch?v=iQcLroJ9wuM.

405 "3 Nephi 12:20," Oct. 11, 2010, blog post.

406 Ibid., 332.

407 Ibid., 330.

408 *TPJS*, 51; *DHC*, 2:8; from "The Elders of the Church in Kirtland, to Their Brethren Abroad," Jan. 22, 1834, published in *Evening and Morning Star*, Feb. 1834, 135.

409 "2 Nephi 32:4–5," Sept. 1, 2010, blog post.

410 *The Second Comforter*, 303.

411 *Preserving the Restoration*, 361.

412 "Nephi's Brother Jacob, Part 5," March 15, 2012, blog post.

413 "1 Nephi 14:3–4," July 6, 2010, blog post.

414 "1 Nephi 14: 10," July 8, 2010, blog post.

415 "1 Nephi 14:8–9," July 8, 2010, blog post.

416 "The Holy Order," Oct. 29, 2017, 3, paper.

417 Ibid., 11.

418 Ibid., 16.

419 Ibid., 24.

420 Ibid., 30.

421 *TPJS*, 310; *WJS*, 213, 215; *WWJ*, 241.

422 "Our Divine Parents," March 25, 2018, 21, paper.

423 Ibid., 22.

424 *Nephi's Isaiah*, 17.

425 "Other Sheep Indeed," expanded paper of address given at Sunstone Symposium, Salt Lake City, UT, July 19, 2017, 9, 9n20.

426 "3 Nephi 20:25–27," Sept. 20, 2010, blog post.

427 *Preserving the Restoration*, 32–33. (See also "The Mission of Elijah Reconsidered," in *Essays: Three Degrees*, 2013).

428 "The Mission of Elijah Reconsidered," paper, Oct. 14, 2011, 27–28.

429 *Passing the Heavenly Gift*, 8; see also 19, 87, 95, 212, 287, 346, 359; Hebrews 1:15.

430 Commentary added to Glossary Jan. 31, 2019.

431 "Concourses of Angels," March 13, 2010, blog post.

432 *Preserving the Restoration*, 386.

433 *TPJS*, 51; *DHC*, 2:8; from "The Elders of the Church in Kirtland, to Their Brethren Abroad," Jan. 22, 1834, published in *Evening and Morning Star*, Feb. 1834, 135; *WJS*, 346; *WWJ*, 386.

434 "The Restoration's Shattered Promises and Great Hope," address given at Sunstone Symposium, Sandy, UT, July 28, 2018, transcript, 7.

435 *TPJS*, 357; *WJS*, 353.

436 "The Kingdom of Heaven contrasted with Hell," Feb. 1, 2010, blog post.

437 "Constantine and Correlation," May 7, 2010, blog post.

438 "Isaiah 53:5," May 13, 2010, blog post.

439 "1 Nephi 14:7," July 7, 2010, blog post.

440 "1 Nephi 14: 3–4," July 6, 2010, blog post.

441 "The Power of Words: 50 Words – Words that Lift, Inspire, Motivate, Elevate, and Transform Us," Aug. 24, 2009, video, https://www.youtube.com/watch?v=iQcLroJ9wuM.

442 Email to Scripture Committee, Jan. 9, 2018.

443 "Holy Ghost vs. The Holy Spirit," April 28, 2010, blog post.

444 "God's Many Works, Part 5," Aug. 17, 2012, blog post.

445 "God's Many Works, Part 4," Aug. 16, 2012, blog post.

446 "Holy Ghost vs. The Holy Spirit," Aug. 10, 2012, blog post.

447 Ibid.

448 *TPJS*, 328. *WJS*, 256; *JSP, Journals* Vol. 3:114.

449 Emails to Scripture Committee, May 21–22, 2017.

450 *TPJS*, 149; *WSJ*, 4.

451 "2 Nephi 31:18," Aug. 29, 2010, blog post.

452 "The Temple," Oct. 28, 2012, transcript of talk, 15.

453 Hugh Nibley, *Teachings of the Book of Mormon, Semester 3* (Provo, UT: FARMS, 2004), 331, 332.

454 *The Second Comforter*, 49.

455 *TPJS*, 166–167; *WJS*, 38.

456 "The Holy Order," Oct. 29, 2017, 8, paper.

457 Ibid., 7.

458 Ibid., 5.

459 Ibid., 1.

460 Ibid., 1.

461 Ibid., 5n13.

462 Ibid., 6.

463 Ibid., 6.

464 Ibid., 4.

465 Ibid., 3.

466 Ibid., 10.

467 Ibid., 44.

468 Ibid., 4.

469 Ibid., 32.

470 Ibid., 10.

471 Ibid., 7n18.

472 Ibid., 41.

473 Ibid., 8.

474 "Holy Ghost vs. The Holy Spirit," April 28, 2010, blog post.

475 "Question on Sealing," Feb. 29, 2012, blog post.

476 "Cursing and Abominations," June 28, 2012, blog post.

477 *Eighteen Verses*, 71.

478 *Eighteen Verses*, 71n49.

479 "Question on Sealing," Feb. 29, 2012, blog post. (See also T&C 158:39 Answer to Prayer for Covenant).

480 "God's Many Works, Conclusion," Aug. 18, 2012, blog post.

481 *Preserving the Restoration*, 352.

482 "Remembering the Covenant," 500th Anniversary of the Christian Reformation, video, Sept. 1, 2018.

483 *Eighteen Verses*, 64.

484   Ibid., 67.

485   Ibid., 312.

486   Email to Scripture Committee, Jan. 31, 2018.

487   "Keep the Covenant: Do the Work" Sept. 30, 2018, 14, transcript of talk.

488   Email to Scripture Committee, Jan. 31, 2018.

489   *Preserving the Restoration*, 481.

490   *40 Years in Mormonism Lecture 2,* "Faith," 1.

491   Royal Skousen, *Analysis of Textual Variants of the Book of Mormon*, 1:32–33.

492   *Beloved Enos*, 98.

493   *The Second Comforter*, 234.

494   "Alma 13:28," June 19, 2010, blog post.

495   Ibid.

496   "1 Nephi 14:6," July 7, 2010, blog post.

497   "If you love me, receive instruction from me," June 7, 2010, blog post.

498   "3 Nephi 14:13–14," Oct. 29, 2010, blog post.

499   "A fair and full hearing," Sept. 9, 2011, blog post.

500   *Preserving the Restoration*, 387.

501   Scripture committee meeting notes and emails, Oct. 25–26, 2017.

502   *Preserving the Restoration*, 359.

503   D&C 130:18–19. Section 130 of the LDS Doctrine and Covenants first appeared as canon in the 1876 edition prepared by Orson Pratt under the direction of Brigham Young. Its inclusion here is for reference. For original sources see *JSP, Journals* Vol. 2:323–326, (Dec. 1841–April 1843), 2 April 1843. Willard Richards didn't accompany Joseph Smith on his four-day trip to Ramus, IL, and reconstructed the Joseph Smith Journal entry from the Journal of William Clayton. See *JSP, Journals* Vol. 2:403–405, Appendix 2, 1–4 April 1843. *WJS*, 169–170, 267nn5–6; 172–173, 268n4.

504   *Preserving the Restoration*, 331.

505   *Beloved Enos*, 14–15.

506   *Second Comforter*, 192.

507   Ibid., 67.

508   "3 Nephi 12:43–45," Oct. 16, 2010, blog post.

509   "3 Nephi 12: 21–22," Oct. 11, 2010, blog post.

510   "Forgiving to be Forgiven," Aug. 3, 2001, blog post.

511   "2 Nephi 30:2," Aug. 16, 2010, blog post.

512   *Preserving the Restoration*, 92.

513   *The Second Comforter,* 120.

514   "Catch hold or cling," May 28, 2010, blog post.

515   "2 Nephi 29:6–7," Aug. 11, 2010, blog post.

516   *Strong's Concordance*, H5551.

517   TPJS, 304–305; DHC: 5:402.

518   TPJS, 348; WJS, 358.

519   *40 Years in Mormonism Lecture 2,* "Faith," 6.

520   "Mosiah 3:10," June 1, 2012, blog post.

521   *Preserving the Restoration*, 173.

522   Ibid., 173n445.

523   "First Rung," Nov. 5, 2013, blog post.

524   "Our Divine Parents," March 25, 2018, 24, paper.

525   *Preserving the Restoration*, 177.

526   TPJS, 348; WJS, 358.

527   Hugh Nibley, *The Message of the Joseph Smith Papyri: An Egyptian Endowment*, 2nd ed. (Salt Lake City: Deseret Book, 2005), 434.

528   Remarks to a Sandy, UT, fellowship, Feb. 22, 2015; Podcast 17: "Prayer – Part 1," May 6, 2018.

529   "Ether's Reference to Christ as Father," Feb. 27, 2012, blog post.

530   "Mosiah 3:5–6," May 25, 2012, blog post.

531   "Zion Will Come," April. 10, 2016, 18, transcript of talk

532   "3 Nephi 12:21–22," Oct. 11, 2010, blog post.

533   "3 Nephi 12:26–26," Oct. 12, 2010, blog post.

534   "3 Nephi 14:1–2," Oct. 26, 2010, blog post.

535 "3 Nephi 14:3–5," Oct. 27, 2010, blog post.

536 "2 Nephi 31:8–9," Aug. 24, 2010, blog post.

537 *Eighteen Verses*, 268.

538 "'Keys' as Challenge," Sept. 14, 2012, blog post.

539 "The Holy Order," Oct. 29, 2017, 1, paper.

540 Ibid., 2.

541 *TPJS* 298–299; *WJS*, 201; *WWJ* 2:331.

542 *DHC*, 4:209.

543 "The Holy Order," Oct. 29, 2017, 5–6, paper; *TPJS*, 166–167; *WJS*, 38.

544 *TPJS*, 288; *WJS*, 183, 187; *JSP, Journals* Vol. 2:345.

545 "Signs Follow Faith," March 3, 2019, talk given at Centerville, UT, recording.

546 "Signs Follow Faith," March 3, 2019, talk given at Centerville, UT, recording.

547 "Was There An Original?" expanded paper of address given at Sunstone Symposium, July 29, 2016, 44n178.

548 Instructions to Scripture Committee, May 31, 2018.

549 *Preserving the Restoration*, 191.

550 *DHC* 5:256–259.

551 *TPJS*, 272; *WJS*, 156, 159; *WWJ*, 2:213.

552 *Preserving the Restoration*, 191.

553 Email to Scripture Committee, Feb. 9, 2018

554 "3 Nephi 14:6," Oct. 27, 2010, blog post.

555 *Preserving the Restoration*, 81.

556 Ibid., 249.

557 Ibid., 14.

558 "1 Nephi 14:5," July 6, 2010, comment to blog post.

559 "Faith, Belief, Knowledge," March 16, 2010, blog post.

560 "The Whole Not the Parts," December 28, 2011, blog post. See also D&C 130:3. Section 130 of the LDS Doctrine and Covenants first appeared as canon in the 1876 edition prepared by Orson Pratt under the direction of Brigham Young. Its inclusion here is for

reference. For original sources see *JSP, Journals* Vol. 2:323–326, (Dec. 1841–April 1843), 2 April 1843. Willard Richards didn't accompany Joseph Smith on his four-day trip to Ramus, IL, and reconstructed the Joseph Smith Journal entry from the Journal of William Clayton. See *JSP, Journals* Vol. 2:403–405, Appendix 2, 1–4 April 1843. *WJS*, 169, 267n3. See note 14.

561 *Passing the Heavenly Gift*, 463–464.

562 "3 Nephi 13:31–32," June 29, 2010, blog post.

563 "2 Nephi 28:23," Aug. 3, 2010, blog post.

564 500th Year Reformation Talk One, 10, Dallas, TX, Oct. 19, 2017.

565 Ibid., 10.

566 500th Year Reformation Talk Two, 10, Dallas, TX, Oct. 19, 2017.

567 "Clearing Off Some Pending Questions," July 14, 2012, blog post.

568 "Themes From Email," May 29, 2014, blog post.

569 "Stiff Necks, Ancient and Modern," Feb. 27, 2014, blog post.

570 "3 Nephi 12:8," Oct. 6, 2010, blog post.

571 "3 Nephi 12:17–18," Oct. 9, 2010, blog post.

572 "Cursed: Denied Priesthood," Jan. 07, 2018, Sandy, UT, 10–11, transcript.

573 "Mosiah 3: 14–15," June 5, 2012, blog post.

574 "2 Nephi 31: 21," Aug. 30, 2010, blog post.

575 "3 Nephi 12:46–47," Oct. 17, 2010, blog post.

576 "Answer: Reading Scripture," June 30, 2012, blog post.

577 *WJS*, 169, 172–173, 267n5, 268n4. D&C 130:18–19. Section 130 of the LDS Doctrine and Covenants first appeared as canon in the 1876 edition prepared by Orson Pratt under the direction of Brigham Young. For original sources see *JSP, Journals* Vol. 2:323–326, (Dec.

1841–April 1843), 2 April 1843. Willard Richards didn't accompany Joseph Smith on his four-day trip to Ramus, IL, and reconstructed the Joseph Smith Journal entry from the Journal of William Clayton. See *JSP, Journals* Vol. 2:403–405, Appendix 2, 1–4 April 1843.

578 "2 Nephi 32:4–5," Sept. 1, 2010, blog post.

579 "3 Nephi 13: 22–23," Oct. 22, 2010, blog post.

580 "God's Many Works, Part 3," Aug. 15, 2012, blog post.

581 *Preserving the Restoration,* 338.

582 St. George Conference, Q&A, March 19, 2017, 14, transcript.

583 500th Year Reformation Talk One, 7, Dallas, TX, Oct. 19, 2017.

584 "3 Nephi 31:33–34," Sept. 28, 2010, blog post.

585 "Last Week's Comments," May 19, 2012, blog post.

586 "Provo Tabernacle," Dec. 17, 2010, blog post.

587 T&C 158:7–8 *Answer to Prayer for Covenant.*

588 *40 Years in Mormonism Lecture 5,* *"Priesthood,"* 44.

589 "2 Nephi 28:31," Aug. 7, 2010, blog post.

590 *Strong's Concordance,* G3438.

591 Online Etymology Dictionary, https://www.etymonline.com/word/mansion#etymonline_v_6820

592 James Yates, "Mansio," in William Smith, *A Dictionary of Greek and Roman Antiquities* (John Murray: London, 1875), 729. http://penelope.uchicago.edu/Thayer/E/Roman/Texts/secondary/SMIGRA*/Mansio.html

593 *Preserving the Restoration,* 385.

594 Ibid., 391.

595 Ibid., 415.

596 "Answer to Prayer for Covenant," July 27, 2017, 5–6.

597 "3 Nephi 12:10," Oct. 7, 2010, blog post.

598 "Our Divine Parents," March 25, 2018, 1, paper.

599 Ibid., 5.

600 Ibid., 12.

601 Ibid., 23.

602 Ibid., 14–15.

603 Ibid., 20.

604 Ibid., 24.

605 "Our Divine Parents," March 25, 2018, 27, paper.

606 "Power in the Priesthood, Part 3," May 22, 2012, blog post.

607 *The Second Comforter,* 234.

608 *Beloved Enos,* 98.

609 *Preserving the Restoration,* 121, 121n289, *Times and Seasons,* 5:746, Dec. 15, 1844.

610 Ibid., 127n309, citing *WJS,* 246.

611 *Strong's Concordance,* H4442. The Greek form is Μελχισεδὲκ, G3198.

612 *WJS,* 244, August 27, 1843, spelling in the original; *JSP, Journals* Vol. 3:86.

613 *Preserving the Restoration,* 164–165. See also "The Holy Order," Oct. 29, 2017, 6,10, paper.

614 "The Doctrine of Christ," Sept. 11, 2016, 2, transcript of talk, Q&A.

615 *Preserving the Restoration,* 129.

616 *A Man Without Doubt,* 174.

617 "The Holy Order," Oct. 29, 2017, 33, paper.

618 *WJS,* 59; T&C 140:2.

619 *Preserving the Restoration,* 180.

620 Ibid., 183.

621 "The Power of Words: 50 Words – Words that Lift, Inspire, Motivate, Elevate, and Transform Us," Aug. 24, 2009, video, https://www.youtube.com/watch?v=iQCLroJ9wuM.

622 "3 NE 12:7," Oct. 5, 2010, blog post.

623 "Angels," March 6, 2010, blog post.

624 "The Holy Order," Oct. 29, 2017, 16, paper.

625 Ibid., 16n62.

626 Ibid., 16n63.

627 Ibid., 16.

628 *Passing the Heavenly Gift,* 431.

629 *TPJS,* 298; *WJS,* 201; *WWJ* 2:331.

630 *TPJS*, 301; *WJS*, 202; *JSP, Journals* Vol. 3:17–18, Editorial Note.

631 Joseph Smith, Letter to the Editor, *Times and Seasons* 4:194, May 15, 1843.

632 *Strong's Concordance*, H6944.

633 Margaret Barker, "Temple and Liturgy, June, 2009, 7, paper: http://www.margaretbarker.com/Papers/

634 "Christ's Discourse on the Road to Emmaus," Fairview, UT, April 14, 2007, 37, transcript.

635 *Ten Parables,* 1.

636 Ibid., 37.

637 "2 Nephi 33:7–9," Sept. 7, 2010, blog post.

638 Scripture Committee, "Committee G&S Update," guideandstandard. blogspot.com, Nov. 30, 2017.

639 "That We Might Become One," Jan. 14, 2018, 4, transcript of talk.

640 Ibid., 7–8.

641 Ibid., 11n10.

642 *The Second Comforter,* 11.

643 "Angels," March 6, 2010, blog post.

644 *WJS,* 366; JS, Discourse, Nauvoo, Hancock Co., IL, 12 May 1844, JS *Collection,* CHL. "Discourse, 12 May 1844, as Reported by Thomas Bullock," p. [1], *JSP*, https://www.josephsmithpapers.org/paper-summary/discourse-12-may-1844-as-reported-by-thomas-bullock/1

645 *Preserving the Restoration*, 20.

646 Ibid., 20.

647 Hugh Nibley, *Eloquent Witness: Nibley on Himself, Others, and the Temple,* 439.

648 Joseph H. Thayer, *Thayer's Greek-English Lexicon of the New Testament* (Peabody, MA: Hendrickson Publishers, 2000), s.v. *"mystērion,"* No. 3466, 420. See also *Strong's Concordance*, G3466.

649 *The Second Comforter,* 416.

650 Ibid., 131–132.

651 Ibid., 17–18; See also *DHC* 4:479; *TPJS*, 195; *WJS*, 81.

652 "The Restoration's Shattered Promises and Great Hope," address given at Sunstone Symposium, Sandy,

UT, July 28, 2018, transcript, 7.

653 *Essays: Three Degrees*, "The Mission of Elijah Reconsidered," 62–63.

654 Hugh Nibley, *Temple and Cosmos* (Salt Lake City: Deseret Book, 1992), 60.

655 Hugh Nibley, *Eloquent Witness*, 364.

656 Ibid., 245.

657 *Strong's Concordance*, H136.

658 Ibid., H5945.

659 Ibid., H5769.

660 Ibid., H7706.

661 Margaret Barker, *The Mother of the Lord, Vol. 1: The Lady in the Temple*, (London: Bloomsbury, 2012), 133.

662 *Strong's Concordance*, H430.

663 Ibid., G2316.

664 *Preserving the Restoration,* 199.

665 Ibid., 386.

666 Ibid., 386.

667 Ibid., 118.

668 *Strong's Concordance*, H3068.

669 Ibid., H7462.

670 Ibid., H3071.

671 Ibid., H7495.

672 Ibid., H3074.

673 Ibid., H3072.

674 Ibid., H3070.

675 Ibid., H3073.

676 Ibid., H6942.

677 Ibid., H6635.

678 "2 Nephi 28:15," July 30, 2010, blog post.

679 Email to Scripture Committee, Feb. 23, 2018.

680 Our Divine Parents," March 25, 2018, 27, paper.

681 *The Second Comforter*, 408n348.

682 *Strong's Concordance*, G4990.

683 "3 Nephi 11:31–32," Sept. 27, 2010, blog post.

684 "3 Nephi 11:35," Sept. 28, 2010, blog post.

685 Email to Scripture Committee, Feb. 23, 2018.

686 *Preserving the Restoration*, 311.

687 *Eighteen Verses*, 160.

688 *Strong's Concordance*, H3068.

689 "2 Nephi 29:6–7," August 11, 2010, blog post.

690 "Beloved," March 4, 2011, blog post.

691 "The Restoration's Shattered Promises and Great Hope," address given at Sunstone Symposium, Sandy, UT, July 28, 2018, transcript, 9.

692 "Opening Remarks," Covenant of Christ Conference, Boise, Idaho, Sept. 3, 2017, 3.

693 "Signs of the Second Coming, "April 7, 2016, blog post.

694 500th Year Reformation Talk Three, 16, Atlanta, GA, Nov. 16, 2017, Q&A.

695 "Signs of the Second Coming, "April 7, 2016, blog post.

696 500th Year Reformation Talk Three, 16, Atlanta, GA, Nov. 16, 2017, Q&A.

697 *A Man Without Doubt*, 175.

698 "All or Nothing, 5," Nov. 4, 2016, blog post.

699 "Keep the Covenant: Do the Work" Sept. 30, 2018, 13–14, transcript of talk.

700 *Nephi's Isaiah*, 77.

701 *Essays: Three Degrees*, "First Three Words," 21–25.

702 Ibid., 56.

703 David Alexander and Pat Alexander, *Eerdmans' Handbook to the Bible* (Grand Rapids: Eerdmans, 1992), 191.

704 Boyd Seevers, *Warfare in the Old Testament: The Organization, Weapons, and Tactics of Ancient Near Eastern Armies* (Grand Rapids: Kregel Academic, 2013), 53–55.

705 "Book of Mormon as a Covenant," Jan. 13, 2019, 3–4, transcript of talk.

706 *Preserving the Restoration*, 162–163.

707 "Cursed: Denied Priesthood," Q&A, Jan. 7, 2018, 12–13, transcript of talk.

708 "Jacob Chapter 5," March 23, 2012, blog post.

709 *TPJS*, 354; *WJS*, 346, 352, 359; *JSP, Journals Vol.* 3:220; *WWJ*, 2:385.

710 *WJS*, 169, 172–173, 267n5, 268n4. *D&C* 130:18–19. Section 130 of the LDS Doctrine and Covenants first appeared as canon in the 1876 edition prepared by Orson Pratt under the direction of Brigham Young. Its inclusion here is for reference. For original sources see *JSP, Journals* Vol. 2:323–326, (Dec. 1841–April 1843), 2 April 1843. Willard Richards didn't accompany Joseph Smith on his four-day trip to Ramus, IL, and reconstructed the Joseph Smith Journal entry from the Journal of William Clayton. See *JSP, Journals* Vol. 2:403–405, Appendix 2, 1–4 April 1843.

711 *Preserving the Restoration*, 320–322.

712 *Come, Let Us Adore Him*, 17.

713 *40 Years in Mormonism Lecture 5*, "*Priesthood*," 24.

714 *Preserving the Restoration*, 90.

715 "*Godliness*," March 23, 2010, blog post.

716 "2 Nephi 31:5," Aug. 23, 2010, blog post.

717 "2 Nephi 31:21," Aug. 30, 2010, blog post.

718 *TPJS*, 308; *WJS*, 210; *JSP, Journals* Vol. 3:32 *WWJ*, 2:240.

719 *Preserving the Restoration*, 349.

720 "Plural Marriage," March 22, 2015, Sandy UT, 33–34, paper.

721 *Essays: Three Degrees*, "The Mission of Elijah Reconsidered," 83.

722 500th Year Reformation Talk Five, 3, Sandy, UT, Sept. 7, 2018, transcript of recording.

723 *The Second Comforter*, 95–96.

724 Ibid., 96n76.

725 Commentary added to Glossary Dec. 15, 2018.

726 *The Second Comforter*, 235.

727 "Cursed: Denied Priesthood," Jan. 07, 2018, Sandy, UT, 19, transcript of Q&A.

728 "Jacob 5: 52," April 9, 2012, blog post.

729 "All or Nothing, 4," Nov 2, 2016, blog post.

730 *TPJS*, 180–181; *WJS*, 59; *T&C* 140:2.

731 *WJS*, 244–245; *JSP, Journals* Vol. 3:86–87.

732 *Preserving the Restoration*, 185.

733 *Preserving the Restoration*, 180.

734 *Ten Parables*, 93.

735 "Fullness of Priesthood," Jan. 2, 2012, blog post.

736 *Preserving the Restoration*, 193.

737 Ibid., 299–300.

738 "3 Nephi 12:9," Oct. 6, 2010, blog post.

739 *Eighteen Verses*, 282–283.

740 "3 Nephi 12:48," Oct. 18, 2010, blog post.

741 Bauer, Arndt and Gingrich, *A Greek-English Lexicon of the New Testament and Other Early Christian Literature* (Chicago: University of Chicago Press, 1957), s.v. "τέλειος," 816–818. See also *Strong's Concordance*, G5046.

742 Hugh Nibley, *Approaching Zion*, 438.

743 John Welch, *The Sermon on the Mount in the Light of the Temple* (Farnham, England: Ashgate Publishing, 2009), 118; 118n115.

744 "The Restoration's Shattered Promises and Great Hope," address given at Sunstone Symposium, Sandy, UT, July 28, 2018, paper, 7.

745 "3 Nephi 12:10," Oct. 7, 2010, blog post.

746 "3 Nephi 12:11–12," Oct. 7, 2010, blog post.

747 "The Restoration's Shattered Promises and Great Hope," address given at Sunstone Symposium, Sandy, UT, July 28, 2018, transcript, 21.

748 "Keep the Covenant: Do the Work" Sept. 30, 2018, 3, transcript of talk.

749 *Eighteen Verses*, 61n44.

750 *Preserving the Restoration*, 16.

751 "What Does It Mean to Possess Your Soul?" April 25, 2010, blog post.

752 *Eighteen Verses*, 157–158.

753 "Godliness," March 23, 2010, blog post.

754 "Questions From This Week," Feb. 23, 2013, blog post.

755 "Received of His Fullness, Part 3, "July 6, 2012, blog post.

756 *Preserving the Restoration*, 173.

757 *Preserving the Restoration*, 101.

758 "3 Nephi 13:7–8," Oct. 19, 2010, blog post.

759 "Prayer," June 14, 2017, blog post.

760 "3 Nephi 18:17–18," Nov. 12, 2010,

761 Email to Scripture Committee, Jan. 31, 2018.

762 *A Man Without Doubt*, 178.

763 "Joseph The Prophet," June 26, 2011, blog post.

764 "3 Nephi 21:26," July 21, 2010, blog post.

765 "3 Nephi 21:19–20," July 18, 2010, blog post.

766 "The process is everything – the answer is nothing," May 4, 2010, blog post.

767 "Weep for Zion for Zion has fled," June 4, 2010, blog post. Revised in Email to Scripture Committee, Jan. 31, 2018.

768 "3 Nephi 18:24–25," November 15, 2010, blog post.

769 "Scripture, Prophecy and Covenant," March 27, 2017, 6, paper.

770 *Preserving the Restoration*, 173–174.

771 Ibid., 177.

772 Ibid., 172.

773 "Discussion of the Gentiles and the Remnant," July 24, 2010, blog post.

774 "The Holy Order," Oct. 29, 2017, 10, paper.

775 *Come, Let Us Adore Him*, 188–189.

776 "Cursed: Denied Priesthood," Q&A, Jan. 7, 2018, 13, transcript of talk.

777 "The Restoration's Shattered Promises and Great Hope," address given at Sunstone Symposium, Sandy, UT, July 28, 2018, paper, 12.

778 "The Restoration's Shattered Promises and Great Hope," address given at Sunstone Symposium, Sandy, UT, July 28, 2018, paper, 11–12n29.

779 *Preserving the Restoration*, 187.

780 "Power in the Priesthood," Jan. 23, 2019, blog post.

781 Commentary added to Glossary Jan. 22, 2019.

782 "Discussion of the Gentiles and the Remnant," July 24, 2010, blog post.

783 "'Power' or 'Authority'", June 4, 2010, blog post.

784 "Power in the Priesthood," *Part 3*, May 22, 2012, blog post.

785 Commentary added to Glossary Jan. 22, 2019.

786 *Preserving the Restoration*, 173.

787 "Principles and Rules," Feb. 10, 2010, blog post.

788 *Preserving the Restoration*, 149.

789 Ibid., 200.

790 "Opening Remarks," Covenant of Christ Conference, Boise, Idaho, Sept. 3, 2017, 2.

791 Ibid., 7.

792 *Thayer's Greek-English Lexicon of the New Testament)*, s.v. "προφήτης," No. 4396, 553.

793 Email to Scripture Committee, April 1, 2018.

794 *Come, Let Us Adore Him*, 2–3.

795 Ibid., 51–52.

796 *TPJS*, 180; *WJS*, 59.

797 *Come, Let Us Adore Him*, 69.

798 Ibid., 212, emphasis his.

799 "Nephi's Brother Jacob, Part 8," March 20, 2012, blog post.

800 *Come, Let Us Adore Him*, 70.

801 *Preserving the Restoration*, 509–510.

802 "The Holy Order," Oct. 29, 2017, 7, paper.

803 "3 Nephi 12:8," Oct. 6, 2010, blog post.

804 "3 Nephi 12:27–29," Oct. 13, 2010, blog post.

805 The Testimony of St. John 1:12.

806 "3 Nephi 31:33–34," Sept. 28, 2010, blog post.

807 *WWJ*, 2:163.

808 *WWJ*, 2:165.

809 "Rebaptism," Nov. 21, 2015, blog post.

810 "Was There An Original," address given at Sunstone Symposium, Salt Lake City, July 29, 2016, paper, 8–9.

811 "Rebaptism," May 6, 2015, blog post.

812 *Preserving the Restoration*, 516.

813 "God's Great Work," Nov. 21, 2014, blog post.

814 *Preserving the Restoration*, 343.

815 Hugh Nibley, *Approaching Zion*, 556, 557.

816 "Forsake, come, call, obey, keep, see, and *know*," July 12, 2011, blog post.

817 "Mosiah 3: 7, continued," May 29, 2012, blog post.

818 "2 Nephi 28:16–17," July 31, 2010, blog post.

819 "Current State of Things," April 12, 2010, blog post.

820 Email to Scripture Committee, Dec. 30, 2018.

821 "2 Nephi 31:8–9," Aug. 24, 2010, blog post.

822 "I Am a Mormon, Part 5," May 15, 2012, blog post.

823 *Ten Parables*, 1.

824 "2 Nephi 33: 11–12," Sept. 8, 2010, blog post.

825 *Strong's Concordance*, H7214.

826 *Strong's Concordance*, H3629.

827 Ibid., G3510.

828 "1 Nephi 14:8–9," July 8, 2010, blog post.

829 "1 Nephi 14: 8–9," July 8, 2010, blog post.

830 "3 Nephi 21:2–3," July 13, 2010, blog post.

831 "1 Ne 13:33–34," June 30, 2010, blog post.

832 "2 Nephi 28:1–2," July 25, 2010, blog post. See also blog posts "*The* Remnant," April 13, 2010 and Remnant, Parts I–X, Sept. 10–22, 2010.

833 *Eighteen Verses*, 197.

834 *Preserving the Restoration*, 98.

835 *Eighteen Verses*, 308.

836 "The Temple," Portland Temple Symposium, Oct. 9, 2010, transcript of notes from talk.

837 "3 Nephi 14:26–27," Nov. 2, 2010, blog post.

838 "Alma 13:29," June 20, 2010, blog post.

839 *Preserving the Restoration*, 239.

840 "How beautiful upon the mountains," March 4, 2010, blog post.

841 *Passing the Heavenly Gift*, 465.

842 *The Second Comforter,* 44.

843 Ibid., 400.

844 *Preserving the Restoration*, 423–424.

845 "The Restoration's Shattered Promises and Great Hope," address giv-

en at Sunstone Symposium, Sandy, UT, July 28, 2018, transcript, 9.

846 "Restoration and Apostasy," Jan. 22, 2011, blog post.

847 *Preserving the Restoration*, 482n1298.

848 Ibid., vii–viii.

849 Ibid., 107.

850 Ibid., 480.

851 Ibid., 502.

852 Ibid., 519.

853 Email, March 10, 2010.

854 "Plural Marriage," March 22, 2015, Sandy UT, 47, paper.

855 *WWJ*, 2:226–227, spelling corrected; "Discourse, 16 April 1843, as Reported by Wilford Woodruff," p. [25–27], *JSP*, https://www.josephsmithpapers.org/paper-summary/discourse-16-april-1843-as-reported-by-wilford-woodruff/1; *WJS*, 197–198.

856 "Discourse, 16 April 1843, as Reported by Willard Richards," p. [143–147], *JSP*, https://www.josephsmithpapers.org/paper-summary/discourse-16-april-1843-as-reported-by-willard-richards/9, spelling corrected; *WJS*, 194–197; *JSP, Journals* Vol. 2:358–361.

857 *Preserving the Restoration*, 10.

858 "That We Might Become One," Jan. 14, 2018, Clinton, UT, transcript, 2–4.

859 *TPJS*, 217; *WJS*, 113–114; *WWJ*, 2:170.

860 "The importance of personal revelation," March 22, 2010, blog post.

861 "Philosophies of men," May 6, 2010, blog post.

862 "Be still and know that I am God," June 2, 2010, blog post.

863 *Second Comforter*, 416.

864 *TPJS*, 355; *JSP, Journals* Vol. 3:220, the original states "as though we were destitute of bodies"; *WJS*, 341–342, 346, 352, 360; *WWJ*, 2:386.

865 "The Power of Words: 50 Words – Words that Lift, Inspire, Motivate, Elevate, and Transform Us," Aug. 24, 2009, video, https://www.youtube.

com/watch?v=iQCLroJ9wuM.

866 "Alma 13:10," June 11, 2010, blog post.

867 "3 Nephi 12:20," Oct. 11, 2010, blog post.

868 "Melchizedek," April 24, 2017, blog post.

869 "1 Nephi 13:36," July 1, 2010, blog post.

870 *Eighteen Verses*, 51.

871 "3 Nephi 11:39," Sept. 29, 2010, blog post.

872 "Our Divine Parents," March 25, 2018, 3, paper.

873 Ibid., 3n17.

874 Ibid., 3.

875 Strong's Concordance, H7307.

876 "JS Discourse, 17 May 1843–B, Ramus, IL, as reported by William Clayton," p. [18], J, CHL, accessed Aug. 23, 2018, http://www.josephsmithpapers.org/paper-summary/discourse-17-may-1843-b-as-reported-by-william-clayton/1, spelling corrected.

877 "2 Nephi 32:1–2," August 31, 2010, blog post. See also 2 Nephi 4:4.

878 "Our Divine Parents," March 25, 2018, 38, paper.

879 Ibid., 38n160.

880 Ibid., 38, emphasis his, 38n161.

881 Commentary added to Glossary Dec. 15, 2018.

882 Email to Scripture Committee, Dec. 16, 2018.

883 500th Year Reformation Talk Two, 17–18, Dallas, TX, Oct. 19, 2017.

884 *Preserving the Restoration*, 398.

885 "Christ's Sacrament," June 1, 2014, blog post.

886 "3 Nephi 18:6–7," Nov. 8, 2010, blog post.

887 "3 Nephi 18:3–4," Nov. 6, 2010, blog post.

888 "3 Nephi 18:5," Nov. 7, 2010, blog post.

889 *Preserving the Restoration*, 521.

890 "3 Nephi 18:1–2," Nov. 5, 2010, Blog post.

891 "3 Nephi 18:5," Nov. 7, 2010, blog post.

892 "3 Nephi 18:10," Nov. 9, 2010, blog post.

893 "3 Nephi 18:6–7," Nov. 8, 2010, blog post.

894 *Preserving the Restoration*, 486.

895 "3 Nephi 18:6–7," Nov. 8, 2010, blog post.

896 "3 Nephi 18:11," Nov. 10, 2010, blog post.

897 Remarks at the Joseph Smith Restoration Conference, June 24, 2018, Boise, Idaho, transcript, 12.

898 "3 Nephi 18:6–7," Nov. 8, 2010, blog post.

899 *The Second Comforter*, 265.

900 "3 Nephi 14:6," Oct. 27, 2010, blog post.

901 "Sacrifice," Dec. 12, 2011, blog post.

902 "Belief Becomes Knowledge," May 5, 2010, blog post.

903 500th Year Reformation Talk Two, 1, Dallas, TX, Oct. 19, 2017.

904 *40 Years in Mormonism Lecture 2*, "Faith," 20.

905 *The Second Comforter*, 185–187.

906 Ibid., 195.

907 *Strong's Concordance*, G40.

908 "But if" is a Hebraism for "unless." See Royal Skousen, *Analysis of Textual Variants of the Book of Mormon*, 2:1173–1174.

909 "3 Nephi 12:38–39," Oct. 15, 2010, blog post.

910 *Strong's Concordance*, H8004, G4532.

911 Instructions to Scripture Committee, May 31, 2018.

912 *WJS*, 246, 244, spelling in the original; *JSP, Journals* Vol. 3:85–86.

913 *TPJS*, 321, spelling in the original; *WJS*, 244, 246; *JSP, Journals* Vol. 3:85.

914 *WJS*, 302n4.

915 "3 Nephi 14:6," Oct. 27, 2010, blog post.

916 *WJS*, 202; *JSP, Journals* Vol. 3:17–18, Editorial Note.

917 *Passing the Heavenly Gift*, 151.

918 "No Man Will Save You," Aug. 22, 2011, blog post.

919 "3 Nephi 20:23," Sept. 19, 2010, blog post.

920 *Preserving the Restoration*, 302.

921 Ibid., 81n207.

922 "Cursed: Denied Priesthood," Q&A, Jan. 7, 2018, 20–21, transcript of talk.

923 "3 Nephi 12:20," Oct. 11, 2010, blog post.

924 "BFHG, Conclusion," Aug. 25,2012, blog post.

925 "BFHG, Part 5," Aug. 24, 2012, blog post.

926 "2 Nephi 31:8–9," Aug. 24, 2010, blog post.

927 "God's Many Works, Part 5," Aug. 17, 2012, blog post.

928 "BFHG, Part 5," Aug. 24, 2012, blog post.

929 "Last Week's Comments," May 19, 2012, blog post.

930 "Alma 13:11," June 12, 2010, blog post.

931 *T&C* 158:9 *Answer to Prayer for Covenant*.

932 *Preserving the Restoration*, 76.

933 Ibid., 12–13.

934 *A Man Without Doubt*, 179.

935 Email to Scripture Committee, Feb. 8, 2018.

936 *WJS*, 242; *JSP, Journals* Vol. 3:77n352; *TPJS*, 321.

937 *Preserving the Restoration*, 200–204.

938 "Book of Mormon as Covenant," talk given at the Book of Mormon Covenant Conference in Columbia, SC, on Jan. 13, 2019.

939 "Christ's Discourse on the Road to Emmaus," Fairview, UT, April 14, 2007, Q&A, 27–28, transcript.

940 *TPJS*, 274; *WJS*, 156, 158, 159; *WWJ*, 2:216.

941 *Preserving the Restoration*, 340–341.

942 *Eighteen Verses*, 135.

943 Ibid., 55.

944 Ibid., 129.

945 Ibid., 136.

946 Ibid., 136.

947 Ibid., 135.

948 Ibid., 139.

949 Ibid., 139.

950 Ibid., 129n77.

951 Ibid., 139.

952 Ibid., 135.

953 "Who can be a Seer?," Feb. 19, 2010, blog post.

954 *Eighteen Verses*, 325–326, emphasis his.

955 *Preserving the Restoration*, 209–210, "King Benjamin's Self-Reliance," Jan. 23, 2014, blog post.

956 "3 NE 13:26–32," Oct. 25, 2010, blog post.

957 *Preserving the Restoration*, 176.

958 *A Man Without Doubt*, 179.

959 *TPJS*, 310; *WJS*, 211, 212, 213, 215; *WWJ*, 2:241.

960 Royal Skousen, *Analysis of Textual Variants of the Book of Mormon*, 1:32.

961 *Eighteen Verses*, 343–344. See this reference for a description of the third and highest level of holiness in the temple.

962 Online Etymology Dictionary, https://www. etymonline.com/word/ shewbread#etymonline_v_23387; *Strong's Concordance*, H3899, H6440.

963 Margaret Barker, *The Hidden Tradition of the Kingdom of God*, 125–126.

964 "Things to Keep Us Awake," expanded paper of address given in St. George, UT, March 19, 2017, 21–22.

965 "Adultery," Dec. 16, 2018, blog post.

966 "3 Nephi 21:1," July 12, 2010, blog post.

967 500th Year Reformation Talk One, 9, Los Angeles, CA, Sept. 21, 2017.

968 "God's Mysteries," Nov. 14, 2016, blog post.

969 "Our Divine Parents," March 25, 2018, 15n77, paper.

970 Ibid., 16n82.

971 "God is no respecter of persons," April 27, 2010, blog post.

972 "Repentance," March 8, 2012, blog post.

973 *Strong's Concordance*, G266.

974 Hugh Nibley, *Approaching Zion*, 66–67.

975 *40 Years in Mormonism Lecture 8*, "A Broken Heart and Contrite Spirit," 12.

976 *Essays: Three Degrees*, "The Mission of Elijah Reconsidered," 86–87.

977 *Preserving the Restoration*, 492–493.

978 Ibid., 255.

979 *40 Years in Mormonism Lecture 7* "*Christ: The Prototype of the Saved Man*," 11–12.

980 "Keep the Covenant: Do the Work" Sept. 30, 2018, 15, transcript of talk.

981 "2 Nephi 31:14," Aug. 26, 2010, blog post.

982 Email to Scripture Committee, Feb. 23, 2018

983 *Preserving the Restoration*, 329.

984 Ibid., 330–331.

985 Ibid., 327.

986 Ibid., 340.

987 "The Holy Order," Oct. 29, 2017, 6, paper.

988 Ibid., 6–7; 7n18.

989 "3 Nephi 21:15–18," July 17, 2010, blog post.

990 Email to Scripture Committee, Jan. 31, 2018.

991 *Preserving the Restoration*, 304n796.

992 *TPJS*, 352–353; *WJS*, 346, 352, 359; *WWJ*, 2:385.

993 *TPJS*, 207–208.

994 "God's Many Works, *Part 5*," Aug. 17, 2012, blog post.

995 "2 Nephi 31:14," Aug. 26, 2010, blog post.

996 *WJS*, 203; *TPJS*, 301–302, the original source of this entry is the William Clayton Diary; *JSP, Journals* Vol. 3:18, 3:18n48.

997 "God's Many Works, Conclusion," Aug. 18, 2012, blog post.

998 Email to Scripture Committee, May 1, 2018.

999 "2 Nephi 32:7," Sept. 2, 2010, blog post.

1000 "Question on Priesthood/ Monarch," Feb. 24, 2012, blog post.

1001 "Ancient Gospel," March 25, 2015, blog post.

1002 "God's Mysteries," Nov. 14, 2016, blog post.

1003 "Follow-up Question," Jan. 3, 2012, blog post.

1004 "A Couple of Questions," Jan. 30, 2013, blog post.

1005 *The Second Comforter*, 48.

1006 Ibid., 49–50.

1007 Ibid., 120–121.

1008 "Keep the Covenant: Do the Work" Sept. 30, 2018, 2, transcript of talk

1009 "But if" is a Hebraism for "unless." See Royal Skousen, *Analysis of Textual Variants of the Book of Mormon*, 2:1173–1174.

1010 *Second Comforter*, 233.

1011 "The Doctrine of Christ," Sept. 11, 2016, transcript of talk, 18–19; Podcast 48: "Prophecy," Dec. 8, 2018, transcript, 10.

1012 "Repentance and Redemption," April 29, 2010, blog post.

1013 "Alma 13:12," June 12, 2010, blog post.

1014 Online Etymology Dictionary, https://www.etymonline.com/word/surety#etymonline_v_22408.

1015 "Christ is the Surety," Oct. 25, 2017, Instructions to scripture committee.

1016 Email to Scripture Committee, Nov. 10, 2017.

1017 T&C 158:57 *Answer to Prayer for Covenant*.

1018 *Preserving the Restoration*, 511–512.

1019 "This and That," Jan. 5, 2019, blog post.

1020 *Strong's Concordance*, G4864.

1021 "The Holy Order," Q&A, 15, Oct. 29, 2017, 7n21, paper.

1022 *Preserving the Restoration*, 20–21.

1023 *Beloved Enos*,166–167.

1024 *JSP, Journals* Vol. 2:140, December 1841–April 1843.

1025 *Preserving the Restoration*, 400, 400n1069.

1026 Ibid., 341n913.

1027 Ibid., 298n777.

1028 "Remembering the Covenant," 500th Anniversary of the Christian Reformation, video, Sept. 1, 2018.

1029 *Come, Let Us Adore Him*, 23.

1030 "Why a Temple?" April 29, 2016, blog post.

1031 *Passing the Heavenly Gift*, 53.

1032 *Beloved Enos*, 55.

1033 "The Holy Order," Q&A, 15, Oct. 29, 2017, transcript of recording.

1034 "Scripture, Prophecy and Covenant," March 27, 2017, 14, paper.

1035 "The Holy Order," Oct. 29, 2017, 4, paper.

1036 Ibid., 30.

1037 "Plural Marriage," March 22, 2015, Sandy UT, 34, paper.

1038 *Preserving the Restoration*, 99, 99n251.

1039 "Pursuing Happiness," July 5, 2015, blog post.

1040 "3 Nephi 18: 24–25," Nov. 15, 2010, blog post.

1041 "Interview By My Wife," Feb. 20, 2012, blog post.

1042 "Reply to Questions," Oct. 20, 2011, blog post.

1043 "2 Nephi 28: 24–25," Aug. 4, 2010, blog post.

1044 *Come, Let Us Adore Him*, 2–3.

1045 "1 Nephi 13:40–41," July 3, 2010, blog post.

1046 500th Year Reformation Talk Seven, "What is God up to today?" Boise, ID, Nov. 3, 2018, transcript of recording.

1047 "False Spirits," Jan. 19, 2012, blog post.

1048 "Today and Yesterday," July 21, 2014, blog post.

1049 *A Man Without Doubt*, 181.

1050 *Preserving the Restoration,* 173.

1051 500th Year Reformation Talk Two, 6–7, Dallas, TX, Oct. 19, 2017.

1052 *Preserving the Restoration*, 256, 258–259.

1053 Commentary added to Glossary Dec. 15, 2018.

1054 *Preserving the Restoration*, 1n24.

1055 TPJS, 170–171; WJS, 41–42.

1056 *Essays: Three Degrees*, 97.

1057 Emails to Scripture Committee, April 30, 2018, May 1, 2018.

1058 "2 Nephi 28:31," Aug. 7, 2010, blog post.

1059   "Nephi's Brother Jacob, Part 4,"
       March 14,2012, blog post.

1060   "The Whole Not the Parts," Dec.
       28, 2011, blog post.

1061   *Preserving the Restoration*, 341n913.

1062   *A Man Without Doubt*, 181.

1063   "1 Nephi 14:5," July 6, 2010, blog
       post comment.

1064   *Passing the Heavenly Gift*, 52.

1065   "All things bear testimony," March
       9, 2010, blog post.

1066   Email to Scripture Committee,
       Jan. 31, 2018.

1067   "The Power of Words: 50
       Words – Words that Lift,
       Inspire, Motivate, Elevate, and
       Transform Us," Aug. 24, 2009,
       video, https://www.youtube.
       com/watch?v=iQcLroJ9wuM.

1068   *TPJS*, 358; *WJS*, 347, 353; *WWJ*, 2:387;
       JSP, Journals Vol. 3:175.

1069   *TPJS*, 357; *WJS*, 342, 353, 360, 361.

1070   *Preserving the Restoration,* 162–163.

1071   "Our Divine Parents," March 25,
       2018, 1; 1n5, paper.

1072   *Eighteen Verses,* 126n71.

1073   D&C 130:8–11. Section 130 of the
       LDS Doctrine and Covenants first
       appeared as canon in the 1876
       edition prepared by Orson Pratt
       under the direction of Brigham
       Young. Its inclusion here is for
       reference. For original sources
       see *JSP, Journals* Vol. 2:323–326,
       (Dec. 1841–April 1843), 2 April
       1843. Willard Richards didn't
       accompany Joseph Smith on his
       four-day trip to Ramus, IL, and
       reconstructed the Joseph Smith
       Journal entry from the Journal of
       William Clayton. See *JSP, Journals*
       Vol. 2:403–405, Appendix 2, 1–4
       April 1843. *WJS*, 169, 267n4, 268n14.

1074   "2 Nephi 32:1–2," Aug. 31, 2010,
       blog post.

1075   "2 Nephi 32:4–5," Sept. 1, 2010,
       blog post.

1076   "Fullness of Priesthood," Jan. 2,
       2012, blog post.

1077   "LDS Temple Ordinances," May
       25, 2015, blog post.

1078   "Mosiah 3:2–4," May 24, 2012,
       blog post.

1079   "The Trick to Avoiding Apostasy,"
       June 22, 2012, blog post.

1080   "'This' and 'That' Part 3", Jan. 8,
       2019, blog post.

1081   "Our Divine Parents," March 25,
       2018, 34, paper.

1082   "'This' and 'That' Part 3", Jan. 8,
       2019, blog post.

1083   "Power in the Priesthood, Part 3,"
       May 22, 2012, blog post.

1084   *40 Years in Mormonism Lecture 5,*
       "Priesthood," 30.

1085   *Nephi's Isaiah*, 287–297. See *Nephi's*
       Isaiah, Ch. 18 for a more detailed
       discussion.

1086   "Communication from the Lord,"
       April 30, 2010, blog post.

1087   *Nephi's Isaiah*, 287–297.

1088   *Beloved Enos*, 41.

1089   "3 Nephi 18:17–18," Nov. 12, 2010,
       blog post.

1090   "Alma 13:17–18," June 15, 2010,
       blog post.

1091   *TPJS*, 150; *WJS*, 5; John 9:7–9.

1092   "3 Nephi 18:19–20," Nov. 13, 2010,
       blog post.

1093   *The Second Comforter*, 21.

1094   "The Mormon Whatever,"
       Daymon C. Smith, Aug. 1, 2015, 7,
       paper.

1095   Royal Skousen, *Analysis of Textual*
       Variants of the Book of Mormon,
       2:899.

1096   Hugh Nibley, *Teachings of the Book*
       of Mormon, Semester 1 (Provo, UT:
       Foundation for Ancient Research
       and Mormon Studies, 2004), 15.

1097   "Alma 13:11," June 12, 2010, blog
       post.

1098   "Alma 13:12," June 12, 2010, blog
       post.

1099   "Last Week's Comments," May 19,
       2012, blog post.

1100   D&C 130:10–11. Section 130 of the
       LDS Doctrine and Covenants first
       appeared as canon in the 1876
       edition prepared by Orson Pratt
       under the direction of Brigham
       Young. For the original source

from the Journal of William Clayton, see *JSP, Journals* Vol. 2:404, Appendix 2, 1–4 April 1843; *WJS*, 169, 171, 267n4.

1101 See *WJS*, 5; 17n1; JS, Discourse, Commerce, IL, between 26 June and 2 July 1839; in *Willard Richards Pocket Companion*, pp. 19–21; handwriting of Willard Richards; Willard Richards, Journals, CHL, *JSP*, https://www.josephsmithpapers.org/paper-summary/discourse-between-circa-26-june-and-circa-2-july-1839-as-reported-by-willard-richards/3.

1102 "White stone and a New Name," March 23, 2010, blog post.

1103 *Beloved Enos*, 66.

1104 "Zion Will Come," Moab, UT, April 10, 2016, 16–17.

1105 "3 Nephi 18:19–20," Nov. 13, 2010, blog post.

1106 *The Second Comforter*, 236.

1107 *Strong's Concordance*, H2451.

1108 *Preserving the Restoration*, 310.

1109 Ibid., 310.

1110 "Our Divine Parents," March 25, 2018, 6, paper.

1111 "Wo, wo, wo," March 6, 2010, blog post.

1112 "Nephi 28:15," July 30, 2010, blog post.

1113 *WJS*, 60, 82n1, 25n9; JS, Discourse, Nauvoo, IL, 5 Jan. 1841; in L. John Nuttall, journal, pp. 4–8; handwriting of L. John Nuttall; *L. John Nuttall, Papers,* BYU. "Account of Meeting and Discourse, 5 January 1841, as Reported by William Clayton," 5, *JSP*, https://www.josephsmithpapers.org/paper-summary/account-of-meeting-and-discourse- 5-january-1841-as-reported-by-william-clayton/2.

1114 *TPJS*, 101; *WJS*, 13, 25n9.

1115 *Preserving the Restoration*, 320–323.

1116 Ibid., 511.

1117 "Alma 13:30," June 21, 2010, blog post.

1118 *40 Years in Mormonism Lecture 8, "A Broken Heart and Contrite Spirit,"* 2.

1119 "1 Nephi 14: 15–16," July 12, 2010, blog post; *Preserving the Restoration*, 350.

1120 "Alma 13:23," June 17, 2010, blog post.

1121 Online Etymology Dictionary, https://www.etymonline.com/search?q=wrest.

1122 *Thayer's Greek-English Lexicon of the New Testament*, s.v. "στρεβλόω," No. 4761, 590.

1123 *TPJS*, 276; *WJS*, 234, 236.

1124 *40 Years in Mormonism Lecture 10, "Preserving the Restoration,"* 5.

1125 *A Man Without Doubt*, 183; *TPJS* 362; *WJS*, 363–365, 401n12; *WWJ* 2:388.

1126 "All or Nothing, 6," Nov. 6, 2016, blog post.

1127 Ibid.

1128 "Authority And Abuse," Sept. 21, 2016, Part 2, blog post.

1129 "Opening Remarks," Covenant of Christ Conference, Boise, Idaho, Sept. 3, 2017, 3.

1130 "Zion Will Come," April 10, 2016, 18, transcript of talk.

1131 "King Benjamin's Self Reliance," Jan. 23, 2014, blog post.

1132 "The Mission of Elijah Reconsidered," paper, Oct. 14, 2011, 12.

1133 Ibid., 16.

1134 "Things to Keep Us Awake," expanded paper of address given in St. George, UT, March 19, 2017, 7.

1135 Email to Scripture Committee, March 31, 2018.

1136 "3 Nephi 11: 27," Sept. 26, 2010, blog post.

1137 *Essays: Three Degrees*, "The Mission of Elijah Reconsidered," 131.

1138 "Restoration Scriptures," March 24, 2017, blog post.

1139 "All or Nothing, 7-Conclusion," Nov. 8, 2016, blog post.

CPSIA information can be obtained
at www.ICGtesting.com
Printed in the USA
LVHW091024011219
639059LV00001B/133/P